Nyakyusa-English-Swahili
and
English-Nyakyusa
Dictionary

Nyakyusa-English-Swahili and English-Nyakyusa Dictionary

compiled
by
Knut Felberg

Mkuki na Nyota Publishers

Mkuki na Nyota Publishers Limited,
6 Muhonda Street, Mission Quarter, Kariakoo;
P.O. Box 4246, Dar es Salaam, Tanzania.

ISBN 9976 973 32 2

Printed and bound by Creda Press,
Eliot Avenue, Eppindust II,
Cape Town, South Africa.

CONTENTS

ACKNOWLEDGEMENTS

The main group of dictionary workers has consisted of four people during the three years the work has lasted. Without them the dictionary would not have been what it is today.

Justin Mwakasege
Abysai Mwakipole
Elias Mwaisaka
Joseph Mwalituke

I would also like to express my thanks to the following people who also have put in many long hours correcting and improving this work. Ally Mlaghila Jumbe, Mary G. Mgaya, Benny Mwaipaja and Ambele Mwaipopo.
And I would especially like to thank Donald Joseph Mwaihoba and other people from the Mwaja area who supplied vast amounts of language material in form of traditional and modern stories and songs.
To mention all the other people in ubuNyakyusa who have given valuable input would be impossible; I can only express my thanks to all of you.
Mark Mattison and E. Kinyamasongo did their best to remove my many mistakes in the English and Swahili sections. Thanks to both of you.
And asante sana for all the support from the Linguistics Department at the Chuo Kikuu, TUKI, BAKITA and the people at the Ofisi ya Utamaduni in Mbeya. Without you this book would never have recieved the generous financial support we got from NORAD.

And finally, thanks to Tatjana who came up with the idea of writing this dictionary and who inspired me to go on when the heat of Ipinda was at its worst.

Ndaga fíijo

PREFACE

Approximately a thousand languages are spoken on the African continent today. Most of these are small languages spoken by maybe a few hundred or a few thousand people. Some of these languages are strong and some are weak. In real life this means that in a few generations many of the weak languages will disappear. There are however many people who are proud of their cultures and these people want their languages to survive. They see that the indigenous language is part of what makes the national culture strong. After all, what would a modern African country have to offer in terms of original culture if it had to be presented only in a colonial language. Tanzania is a leading actor in Africa with Swahili as the main language. But even in Tanzania there are still people who think that only foreign languages are good enough. Just think about it. How many so called developed nations use a foreign language in their schools and administration? There is only one reason why the language of a given people can not be used for higher education and that is lack of political will and lack of pride in the national culture. In a country with numerous languages it is of course impossible to use every language at every level of administration and education. Therefore it is important to view languages like Nyakyusa as they really are. They are building blocks of the national language, and they are the backbone of local culture in their respective areas. In this respect it is important to have these languages, their literature and cultural wisdom recorded both in book form and in other media. And it is important that this is done with as little political or religious bias as possible. To record a culture with the ulterior motive of changing it, is to destroy rather than to build up and preserve. It is my hope that this first edition of the Nyakyusa dictionary will become one of the building blocks for preserving Nyakyusa and Tanzanian culture.

K.F.
Oslo, Norway
November 1995

vii

ABBREVIATIONS

adj	adjective	Kye	Kyela dialect
adv	adverb	med	medical term
anat	anatomical term	n	noun
appl	applicative	num	numeral, number
Arab	Arabic	off	offensive, vulgar term
arch	archaic term	part	particle
aug	augmentative	pn	personal noun
bot	botanical term	prep	preposition
Brit	British English	pron	pronoun
conj	conjunction	pt	past tense
det	determiner	recip	reciprocal
dim	diminutive	Swa	Swahili
e.g.	for example	Tuk	Tukuyu dialect
Eng	English	UK	regional English
expr	expression, idiom	US	standard English
fig	figurative	vb	verb
Ger	German	vi	intransitive verb
interj	interjection	vt	transitive verb
iterr	interrogative	zool	zoological term

BIBLIOGRAPHY

Various translations of the Bible or parts thereof.
- *Baibulo Inongwa inunu*. Bible Society of Malawi, Blantyre. 1992
- *Ubwandilo kalata gwa Mose ugwakwanda*. United Bible Societies. 1982
- *Tesitamenti umpya*. Chama cha Biblia cha Tanzania, Dodoma. 1988
- *Inyimbo*. Bible Society of Tanzania, Dodoma. 1987
- *Ulwitikano Ulupya*. The Bible Society in East Africa, Nairobi. 1971

- *The White Fathers' Bemba - English Dictionary*. 1991. The society of the Missionary for Africa, Zambia
Doke, C.M., D.M. Malcolm, J.M.A. Sikakana, and B.W. Vilakazi. *English - Zulu and Zulu - English Dictionary. Combined edition*. 1990, Witwatersrand University Press, Johannesburg

Feeley, G., *The Friendly Modern Swahili - Modern English Dictionary*. MS-tryk, Denmark

Felberg, K., (Forthcoming). *Nyakyusa Handbook.*

Halemba, A., 1994. *Mambwe-English Dictionary*. Mission Press, Ndola, Zambia

Haukøy, J., 1978. *Tysk-Norsk*. Kunnskapsforlaget, Oslo

Johnson, F., and Madan. 1939. *Standard Swahili / English Dictionary*. Oxford

Johnson, F., and Madan. 1939. *A Standard English - Swahili Dictionary*. Oxford

Meyer, T., 1989. *Die Konde Ethnographische Aufzeichnungen (1891-1916) des Missionssuperintendenten Theodor Meyer von den Nyakyusa (Tanzania)*. Monographien zur Völkerkunde, Klaus Renner Verlag

Meyer, T., *Wa-Konde Maisha, mila na desturi za Wanyakyusa*. 1993 (Swahili translation). Motheco Publications, Mbeya, Tanzania

Sanderson, G.M., 1954. *A Dictionary of the Yao Language*. The Government Printer, Zomba, Nyasaland

Wilson, M., 1951. *Good Company.* Oxford

A TYPOLOGICAL LOOK AT THE NYAKYUSA LANGUAGE

Geographical location

Nyakyusa (called Ngonde in Malaŵi) is spoken by approximately one million people and stretches geographically from the North Rukuru river near Karonga in Malaŵi to Mbeya town in Tanzania. The majority of the speakers live in Tanzania.

Figure 1

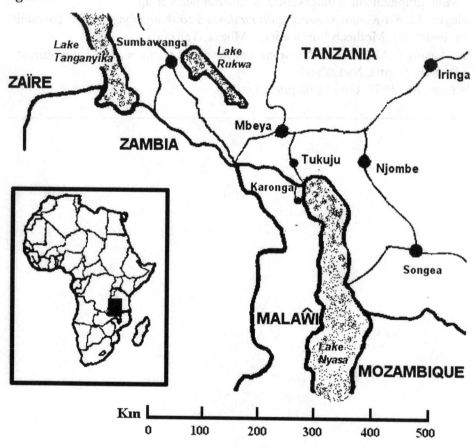

Nyakyusa is registered as M.31 in the list of Bantu languages. It is the only language in group M.30. Group M is put together more on a geographical than on a linguistic basis and one should not expect too many similarities within the group. Nyakyusa is one of the relatively few Bantu languages that doesn't make use of tones, but it also differs substantially from surrounding languages in terms of vocabulary. A monolingual speaker of Nyakyusa can not understand any other Bantu language.

The "tree-structure" for Nyakyusa in the Niger-Cordofanian family looks like this:

Niger-Cordofanian -> Niger-Congo -> Benue-Congo -> Bantoid -> M31 -> Nyakyusa

The other languages in group M are (Guthrie 1967):

	Group 10	Group 20	Group 30	Group 40	Group 50	Group 60
1	Pimbwe	Wanda	Nyakyusa	Taabwa	Biisa	Lenje
2	Rungwa	Mwanga		Bemba	Lala	Soli
3	Fipa	Nyiha			Swaka	Ila
4	Rungu	Malila			Lamba	Tonga
5	Mambwe	Safwa			Seba	
6		Iwa				
7		Tembo				

Based on newer research with comparative wordlists it seems that the languages which come closest to Nyakyusa are the languages along the Zambian border. More work is needed to make any more exact statements.

THE SOUNDS AND LETTERS

The Alphabet

A, B, (ND), E, F, G, H, I, Í, J, K, L, M, N, NG', O, P, S, T, U, Ú, W, Y

Nyakyusa has in older texts been written using a variety of symbols. Some of these have been changed here in order to modernize the writing. The ideal writing system would be to have one symbol for each sound. This has for several reasons not been done, tradition being one of them.

The language has seven vowels which appear both as long and short. Long vowels are written as a double vowel and are listed after the short sound.

Vowels: A, AA, E, EE, I, II, Í, ÍÍ, O, OO, U, UU, Ú, ÚÚ

With many words there is a problem telling whether there is a long or a short vowel. This could be caused by dialectal differences or by the fact that there could be a choice (or a third lenght).

There are 16 consonants including the letter D or ND which is an allophone of T or L in combination with a nasal. This led some early writers to introduce ND as a separate letter of the alphabet. ND is a very common sound combination, e.g. ndaga, so it is understandable that they wanted to include it. The glides W and Y are only used with a consonant (e.g. gwa, twa, lya, …)

Consonants: B, (ND), F, G, H, J, K, L, M, N, NG', P, S, T, W, Y

The sounds

With the exceptions noted below, the vowels are like in most other Bantu languages and like many European languages like Italian, Spanish or German. Long vowels (written double) are long varieties of the short with no change in sound quality. For many vowel sounds one should note that there are no equivalent sounds in English.

i	Like English I in the words *sit, hit, admit*	E.g.: Ípinda, ikikota, ilísilya
ii	Long I	E.g.: biika, hiija
í	Like Swahili, Italian or German I	E.g.: Ípinda, ilísíku
íí	Long Í	E.g.: ikííbo, ikíílilo
u	A sound between Ú and O	E.g.: umúndu
uu	Long U	E.g.: -puufú, suuja
ú	Like Swahili, Italian or German U	E.g.: umúndu
úú	Long Ú	E.g.: túúfya, akalúúlú
o	Similar to Swahili or Italian O	E.g.: ikikota
oo	Long O	E.g.: akoogo, boola
e	Similar to Swahili or Italian E	E.g.: enda
ee	Long E	E.g.: ee, eleesya

Consonants are with few exceptions like in English. P, T and K are lightly aspirated.

b	After nasal like B in English *symbol*	E.g.: akaambwe, ikambaaní
	Otherwise like in Spanish *saber*; IPA [β]	E.g.: abandu, ikibafu
g	After nasal like G in English *good*	E.g.: bangatuka
	Otherwise like Spanish G in *luego*, or	
	German G in *wagen*; IPA [γ]	E.g.: ndaga
l	A sound between L and R like in	
	many Bantu and Asian languages.	E.g.: ikipalo,
ng	Like in English *finger*	E.g.: ikipaanga, ubutengamojo
ng'	Like in English *thing*	E.g.: ing'osí, akakang'ang'a

Diphthongs

There is a phonemic difference between the sounds which are represented in writing as **nya** and **nía**. Some writers have earlier written this as a separate consonant represented with the symbol Ń.

Foreign sounds

Many Nyakyusa are bilingual or multilingual (Swahili or Cheŵa, and often also other Bantu languages. AbaNyakyusa with higher education also speak English). This has led to a change in how foreign sounds are perceived. In the dictionary there is no standard system; we have followed what our informants have suggested and have not written the foreign letters. This does not mean that they are not pronounced. Substitutions like the following are common:

F for V, S for Z, L for R, R for L and S for TH

In the case of English loan-words the Nyakyusa speaker will normally ignore the English vowels and substitute from the Nyakyusa vowel set. Codeswitching is very common among bilingual or multilingual speakers.

Comments to the letters used in the Nyakyusa alphabet.

The oldest spelling of Nyakyusa dates back to German missionary translations at the end of the 19th century. They wisely observed that there was a seven vowel system and chose to write our letters Í and Ú as Į and Ų. They also used a macron over the vowel to indicate length (e.g. Ā, Ē, Ō). They were, after all, missionaries trained in classical Latin. They also used the letter Ń for the sounds that we now write NY and NÍ. These are not necessarily better or worse than our choices, they are just different. Another sound with a variety of visual appearances is our NG'. Our choice is based on the current system in Swahili and Cheŵa. The preferred symbol would be ŋ, but considering that most people learn Swahili or Cheŵa in school we have chosen NG'. The choices are also based on the fact that the older symbols (and ŋ) are more rare both on type-writers and in the common fonts on computers. Also if one does not have the accent marks on the typewriter one can as a temporary solution do like most British writers have done; ignore the fact that there could possibly be letters / sounds which would not be properly represented by using the British alphabet.

Wordstress and Tone

The main stress is on the penultimate syllable. There are just a few exceptions to this rule. In modern Nyakyusa there is no tone with semantic or syntactic significance. There are however a few words with non-standard pronunciation with some speakers. In the dictionary, some words are marked with an apos-trophe to indicate a change from the normal or expected pronunciation. As with word stress, more research is needed.

NOUNS

Most Nyakyusa nouns are made up of a preprefix, a prefix and a stem. The noun is classified according to its prefix and this makes the basis for agreement with verbs, adjectives and various other word classes. Some nouns which lack the preprefix follow the general system of agreement and may have the preprefix in other forms than the base form listed in the dictionary.

Except for a regular system of singular and plural there is very little one can say with certainty about the various classes. Classes 1/2 tend to be used for human beings and class 14 nouns are usually non-countable nouns and abstracts. New words are often put in classes 9/10 and trees are often in classes 3/4. The following table shows the nominal prefixes for Nyakyusa.

(NC = noun class, N = nasal, Sg. = singular, Pl. = plural)

NC	*Sg.*	*Pl.*
1-2	umú	aba
3-4	umú	imí
5-6	ilí	ama
7-8	iki	ifí
9-10	iN	iN
11-10	ulu	iN
12-13	aka	utu
14-4	ubu	imí
15	uku	
16	pa	
17	ku	
18	mú	

Nominal prefixes and preprefixes

We have chosen to list the words with preprefixes if they are at all known to be used and without when they are seen as extremely rare or never used. 'Extremely rare' means that many people react to their usage. An example is the word **mmapa** meaning armpit. Most people would not accept a preprefix here. Or a singular form for that matter.

The plural form ba- of noun classes 1a/2

There is in addition to the regular classes a class-set listed as 1a/2. This set will normally have no prefix in singular and no preprefix in its plural form. Otherwise it is like classes 1/2.

Noun classes 1a/2 and 9/10

It seems that for a number of words there is a choice between noun classes 1a/2 and 9/10. This may originally be dialectal differences.

Locatives

ikipanga	village
pakipanga	at the village
kukipanga	near the village
nkipanga	in the village

ikyai   - mukyai   tea - in the tea
Mkulonda isukali nulukama mukyai?   Do you want sugar and milk in your tea?

ADJECTIVES

Very few adjectives correspond directly with an English adjective. Most often we must use a verbal or nominal expression to obtain the meaning of an English adjective. Many stative verbs can easily be turned into adjectives by adding the appropriate nominal prefix to the stem and changing the final vowel to -e.

VERBS

The following chart shows the building blocks of the verb:

Neg   negative prefix
TAM   tense, aspect or mood prefix
SA   subject agreement
OA   object agreement
Der   derivational suffixes
FP   final particle

Prefixes		Suffixes
Neg-TAM-SA-TAM-OA-	-Stem-	-Der-TAM-FP

Examples of conjugation:
Ukukwesa : to smoke

	PRESENT	RECENT PAST	FUTURE
une	ngukwesa	nakwesile	aangukwesa
ugwe	kukwesa	kwakwesile	akukwesa
jula	ikukwesa	akwesile	aikukwesa
uswe	tukukwesa	twakwesile	atukukwesa
umwe	mukukwesa	mwakwesile	amukukwesa
bala	bikukwesa	bakwesile	abikukwesa

Personal pronouns are not necessary with the verbs. When used, they are used for emphasis.

PRONOUNS

Personal Pronouns

I	une	we	uswe
you	ugwe	you (pl)	umwe
he/she	uju, ujo, jula, umwene	they	aba, abo, bala, abeene

For "it" see next section.

Third Person Pronouns/Determiners (he, she, it, they)

There is a four-way distinction.
aba   - they (being where you are)
abo   - they (being nearby)
bala   - they (being somewhere over there, at a distance)
abeene - they (not present, not seen, "in your head")

The following are the pronouns/determiners for the various noun classes (numbers indicate noun class):

1 (3. person sg.about a person) uju, ujo, jula, umwene
2 (3. person pl. about people) aba, abo, bala, abeene
3 ugu, ugo, gula, ugwene
4 igi, igyo, gila, igyene
5 ilí, ilyo, lila, ilyene
6 aga, ago, gala, ageene
7 iki, ikyo, kila, ikyene
8 ifí, ifyo, fíla, ifyene
9 iji, ijo, jila, ijeene
10 isi, isyo, síla, isyeene
11 ulu, ulo, lula, ulweene
12 aka, ako, kala, akeene
13 utu, uto, tula, utweene
14 ubu, ubo, bula, ubweene

The pronominal prefix (on the noun for agreement) is here shown together in contrast with the nominal prefix. The main difference being the nasal form in the nominal form which has a non-nasal form in the pronominal form. This is standard for most Bantu languages.

Noun class	Nominal Prefix	Pronominal Prefix
1	m ú	g u (j u, m ú, a)
2	b a	b a
3	m ú	g u
4	m í	g i
5	(1) í	l í
6	m a	g a
7	k i	k i
8	f í	f í
9	n	j i
1 0	n	s í
1 1	l u	l u
1 2	k a	k a
1 3	t u	t u
1 4	b u	b u
1 5	k u	k u

Possessive Pronouns

	Singular	**Plural**
1.person	-angu	-itu
2.person	-ako	-inu
3.person	-ake	-abo

NUMERALS

Cardinal	Ordinal	
1 kamo	first	-a kwanda
2 tubili	second	-a bubili
3 tutatu	third	-a butatu
4 tuna	fourth	-a buna
5 tuhano	fifth	-a buhano
6 ntandatu		
7 tuhano na tubili		
8 lwele		
9 tuhano na tuna		
10 kalongo		

Many speakers will exchange some or all of these for Swahili numbers.

AGREEMENT / CONCORD

abaana batali	- tall children
abaana bangu batali	- my tall children
abaana aba bangu batali	- these tall children of mine
abaana aba bangu batali balisíle	- these tall children of mine came

INGAMWANA

A married Nyakyusa woman is not allowed to use the name of the father-in-law or a word sounding like that name. Since most names or words that sound like them carry meanings, a married woman will then have to use other words as substitutes for the tabu ones. The choices made here vary, but it frequently involves coining new words. Thus nobody would be surprised to hear a woman using terms that noone else does. Some of these words inevitably enter the regular language, but will for a long time be known as ingamwana. However, while working on the dictionary we frequently came across words that created great discussion as to whether or not a word was ingamwana. In either case it turned out to be a good excuse for not knowing a word.

CHOICE OF DIALECT

Informants from several parts of the Nyakyusa linguistic area have been consulted. However, there has been a certain attempt to stick to the forms used in the Masoko and Ipinda areas. Speakers of Ngonde have not been consulted, but some of the written material used has come from the Ngonde area.

ETYMOLOGY

Etymological information has in some cases been added where known. Much more research is needed here and this will be followed up in the next edition.

GRAMMATICAL NOTATION

Even though the first Nyakyusa grammar was published nearly a hundred years ago, it is fair to say that the study of the language is still in its early stages. The grammatical notations adverb, preposition, pronoun etc. should therefore be seen as indicators of word class only. Often they are better indications of the word class of the translation than of the Nyakyusa word itself. Especially the terms adverb and pronoun are used in a very wide sense. Pronoun includes words that more correctly would be called determiners or particles. Adverbs include words that belong to a variety of groups. More research is needed here and this will be dealt with further in the Nyakyusa Handbook (forthcoming) and in subsequent editions of the dictionary.

SWAHILI WORDS

Some "Nyakyusa" entries are either pure Swahili or modified Swahili words, the reason being that the informants did not have a Nyakyusa word and that the Swahili word is commonly used, understood and thus felt to be a better entry than explaining the word in Nyakyusa. Naturally this will be a very subjective view and although several informants have agreed on each and every entry, there will always be better ways of expressing something. There is also the danger of entering only the words of the multilingual or the educated.

IMPROVEMENTS AND ADDITIONS TO THE DICTIONARY

We welcome all constructive critisism, all corrections and additional words for the next edition of the dictionary. Please send any suggestions you may have concerning the dictionary to

Knut Felberg/ Nyakyusa Dictionary
c/o Mkuki na Nyota
S.L.P. 4246
Dar-es-Salaam
Tanzania

or send e-mail to
felberg@telepost.no

The Nyakyusa Home Page
URL http://home.sol

Nyakyusa-English-Swahili

Aa

-a *part* The "-a of reference", connector, genitive etc. It connects one word or phrase with another, it is often translated with "of" or with another genitive expression.(gwa, bwa, gya, lya, twa etc) = -a

aba **1** *det* these = hawa **2** *pron* who = ambao **3** *pron* they (being where you are) = wao

aba bo aba they (people) are the ones = hawa ndio

abaangi *n, pron* others = wengine

abeene *pron* they (not present, not seen) = wao

abo *pron* they, those (people nearby) = wale, hao

-aabo *pron* their = -ao

abuka *vi (pt abwííke)* the moving in of a fiancée = kuolewa kwa msichana

-abuke *adj* free = huru

abula *vt (pt abwííle)* **1** marry a woman = oa **2** help = saidia

abula *vt (pt abwíle)* open, loosen, untie, banish, undo, disentangle = fungua

abulana *vt.rec (pt abuleene)* **1** help each other = saidiana **2** get married = oana /The 2. meaning is very "modern", old people may reject this definition

abulígwa *vi.pass (pt abulíígwe)* **1** be released (eg from jail) = funguliwa **2** be taken to one's husband (marriage) = pelekwa kwa mume

Afilíka *pn* Africa = Afrika

-a Afilíka *adj* African = -a Afrika

afúla *vi (pt aafwíle)* creep, crawl = tambaa

aga *det,pron* these = haya

aga *vt (pt agíle)* **1** meet, find = kuta; **Numwagíle pa Ípinda** I met him in Ipinda = Nimemkuta Ipinda; **2** diminish, decrease = pungua; **Kwagíle kumalííke** I am alone (ie. all my relatives are dead) = Niko peke yangu (m.y. ndugu zangu wote wamekufa)

agana *vt.recip (pt ageene)* **1** (indicates a planned get-together) meet, get together, assemble = kutana **2** contact = kutana

agania *vt (pt agenie)* **1** cause to meet, reconcile = kutanisha, patanisha **2** catch in the act (esp sex) = fumania **3** comprehend, understand = fahamu

aganíla *vt.appl (pt aganííle)* meet = kutana; **Twaganíle pa Ípinda** Let's meet in Ipinda = Tukutane Ipinda

agígwa *vi.pass (pt agíígwe)* be available = patikana

agikisya *vb (pt agikíísye)* add to = ongezea

agula *vt (pt agwííle)* found, invent = buni, anzisha, vumbua

aje *interj (Tuk)* interjection of surprise = alaa!

ajiila *vi (pt ajííle)* make a sound like that of approaching rain, or water about to boil in a pot = fanya sauti kama ya mvua ikaribiayo au maji yakaribiayo kuchemka chunguni

ajula *vi (pt ajwííle)* yawn = enda mwayo, piga mwayo

aka *det,pron* this, which = hiki

akababye *n (utu-, 12/13)* spot, dot, blemish = doa, waa

akabalilo *n (utu-, 12/13)* **1** time = muda, wakati

~ **aka** nowadays = siku hizi

~ **aka kíkwísa** future = wakati ujao

~ **kakutuusya** recess, break = pumziko

~ **kalibule?** what's the time? = saa ngapi?

~ **ka** during = wakati wa

~ **kakí** when = lini

Kulembuka kabalilo kakí nulubunju? When do you get up in the morning? = Huamka muda gani asu-buhi?

~ **akangi** another time = mara nyingine, muda mwingine

~ **kamo** sometimes = muda fulani

bo ~ **kakindílepo** after some time = baada ya muda/kitambo fulani

2 season, period = majira, kipindi

~ **ka fúla** rainy season = msimu wa mvua

2 season, period = majira, kipindi
~ ka fúla rainy season = msimu wa mvua
3 opportunity = nafasi, fursa, nafasi ya
kuweza kufanya jambo fulani
**Nhobwíke fííjo ukukaba akabalilo
aka…**
I am very happy to have this opportunity…
= Ninafurahi sana kupata nafasi kama
hii…
akabalilo koosa *adv* always, all the time =
muda wote
akabelele *n.zool (utu-, 12/13)* falcon, kite =
kipanga

The AKA- Prefix

Aka- is the prefix for nounclass 12. Aka- is
the Nyakyusa diminutive prefix, ie. it can add
the meaning of smallness to nouns. Some
words get a derogatory meaning with this
prefix. Similar to ki- in Swahili.

---

akabíní *n (utu-, 12/13)* destruction of
other people's property because of
jealousy (The basic idea being that if I
can't have something than neither
should you) = uharibifu wa mali ya
watu wengine kwa sababu ya wivu /
choyo
akabombo *n (utu-, 12/13)* **1** activity =
shuguli **2** *n.dim (> imbombo)* piece of
work = sehemu ya kazi
akaboneko *n (utu-, 12/13)* result = athari,
tukio, tokeo la jambo
a'kaabugogí *n (utu-, 12/13)* danger = hatari
akabúlúlúkisya *n (utu-, 12/13)* crumb, spill
over, left overs, remainder = sazo, baki
akabyondo *n.dim (utu-, 12/13)* dimple = kishimo kidogo (hasa kwenye shavu)
/ See **ilíbyondo**
akafínye *n (utu-, 12/13)* cell, the place
one is put when arrested = mahabusu
akafúla *n.dim (utu-, 12/13)* light rain
shower, drizzle = manyunyu
akafwalilo *n (utu-, 12/13)* style (dressing,
clothing) = mtindo wa kuvaa
akagindwa *n (utu-, 12/13)* material for

mats from palm trees = makuti ya
mnazi au mmea jamii yake
akaaja *n (utwaja, 12/13)* **1** homestead,
household = kaya **2** village, town, city =
kijiji, mji **3** place, area = mahali, eneo, sehemu
/The term covers any place of human habi-
tation from a single house or a home to a
big city. Another newer term for city is **un-
jíni** (> Swa mji)
akajabo *n (utu-, 12/13)* share = hisa
akajaja *n.slang.med (utu-, 12/13)* venereal disease = ugonjwa wa zinaa
akajiilo *n (utu-, 12/13)* **1** manner = jinsi **2**
state, condition, health = hali; **Umbíne ali
nakajiilo kakí?** How is the patient? =
Mgonjwa ana hali gani? **3** habit, behavior
= mazoea, desturi, mwenendo, tabia **4** type
= aina, mtindo **5** case = jinsi, namna
akajinja *n (utu-, 12/13)* curry = binzari,
bizari
akajobelo *n (utu-, 12/13)* dialect
(literally small language) = lahaja;
**Injobelo ja kiNyakyusa jili nutujo-
belo tulinga?** How many dialects are
there in Nyakyusa? = Lugha ya
Kinyakyusa ina lahaja ngapi?
akajugandete *n.bot (utu-, 12/13)* type
of plant for medicine = aina ya mmea
utumikao kama dawa
akakali *n.anat (utu-, 12/13)* bile =
nyongo
akakang'ang'a ka nyúma *n.anat (utu-,
12/13)* spine, backbone = uti wa
mgongo
akakínilo *n (utu-, 12/13)* style of playing,
playing formation = mbinu / namna ya
kucheza, uchezaji
akakínya *n.med (utu-, 12/13)* fever =
homa
akakooho *n.anat (utu-, 12/13)* protruding bone at elbow = mfupa uliojitokeza kwenye kiwiko cha mkono
akakololo *n (utu-, 12/13)* brook = kijito
aka kubalila *n (utwa kubalila)* abacus =
mashine ya kujumlishia

akakubilo *n (utu-, 12/13)* rhythm = mpigo (wa ngoma nk.)

akakyo *n (12)* happiness = furaha

akalaso *n (utu-, 12/13)* sharp pain, cramp, stabbing pain = kichomi

akalefaní *n.dim (utu-, 12/13)* teaspoon = kijiko kidogo

akalimí *n.anat (utu-, 12/13)* uvula = kimeo

akalukilo *n (utu-, 12/13)* weaving = namna au mtindo wa kusuka, ususi, ufumaji

akalúúlú *n (utu-, 12/13)* ululation, exultation = kigelegele

akalulungila *n (utu-, 12/13)* that which is at the topmost point = kitu ambacho huwa kwenye ncha ya juu kabisa

akalulunje *n.zool (utu-, 12/13; Kye)* francolin = aina ya ndege /Tuk: **imbesí**

akaamba *n.dim (utw-, 12/13; > ikyamba)* hill = kilima

akambakaasya *n (utu-, 12/13)* **1** a thing = kitu, jambo **2** *n.zool* insect = mdudu

akaambwe *n.zool (utuumbwe, 12/13)* jackal = bweha, mbweha

akamelelígwa *n (utu-, 12/13)* debt = deni

akamelelo *n (utu-, 12/13)* bud = chipukizi, jicho la ua

a'kaameme *n.anat (utu-, 12/13)* diaphragm = kiwambo, baina ya kifua na tumbo

akamenya *n (utu-, 12/13)* chop = kipande kilichokatwa, kinofu

akamogelo *n (utu-, 12/13)* dancing style = mtindo wa uchezaji

akamúlímúlí *n.zool (utu-, 12/13)* firefly, lightbug with greenish light = kimulimuli, kimetameta

akaana *n.off (utwaana-, 12/13)* very small child, newborn baby up to four months old = kitoto, katoto; **Akaana ka nkííkulu jula kíkulila fííjo.** That woman's baby is crying a lot = Katoto wa mwanamke yule analia sana

akaandu, akandu *n (utu-, 12/13)* thing, object, substance = kitu

akanjelenjele *n (utu-, 12/13)* type of song = aina ya wimbo

akanwa *n.anat (utu-, 12/13)* mouth = kinywa

akanyama *n.dim (utu-, 12/13, >inyama)* piece of meat = kipande cha nyama, kinofu

akanyasa *n (utu-, 12/13)* long decorated mat (for funerals) = mkeka mrefu uliopambwa (hutumika kwenye vilio)

akanyegesí *n.zool (utu-, 12/13)* small ant = sisimizi mdogo

akanyongo *n.anat (utu-, 12/13, > Swa)* bile = nyongo

akanyoselo *n (utu-, 12/13)* fork = uma

akanywanywa *n.med (utu-, 12/13)* small sore eg. inside the mouth or under the foot = vidonda vya ndani ya mdomo au chini ya nyayo

akapalapala *n (utu-, 12/13)* danger = hatari

akapaango *n (utu-, 12/13)* story, tale, anecdote = hadithi

akapaatu *n (utu-, 12/13)* twig, sliver = kijiti

akapegeso *n (utu-, 12/13)* small hole, cavity = tundu

akapeka *n (utu-, 12/13)* bracelet = bangili

akapelafúmbi *n (utu-, 12/13)* whirlwind = upepo mkali unaovuma na kuleta maafa; chamchela, kimbunga, tufani, dhoruba

akapelígwa *n (utu-, 12/13)* creature = kiumbe

akapembemílo *n.anat (utu-, 12/13)* Adam's apple = kongomeo

akapene akanywamú *n.med (12)* chicken pox = tetekuwanga

akapepo akanúnú *n (utu-, 12/13)* breeze = upepo mwanana

akapingafúla *n (utu-, 12/13)* rainbow = upinde wa mvua

akapolomondo *n (utu-, 12/13)* small piece of meat left on a plate = salio dogo la nyama chomboni

4

akapombo (Euphoria sp.) *n.bot (utu-, 12/13)*
1 type of tree, gumtree = aina ya mti,
mnyaa **2** the gum-like substance that
comes from it. The gum is used as glue =
utomvu hutomika kama gundi unaotoka
kwenye mti huo

akapopo *n.dim (utu-, 12/13)* small axe
= shoka dogo

akapote *n (utu-, 12/13)* a short narrative
poem which is performed as a song, typically heard in the local pubs, without in-
struments or dancing, type of folk song =
wimbo mfupi wa kusifia au malumbano

akapuula *n.zool (utu, 12/13)* falcon =
kipanga

akapungunyo *n (utu-, 12/13)* small
knot = kifundo kidogo

akapuupi *n.med (utu-, 12/13)* a very
painful abscess on a finger; = uvimbe
unaouma sana unaojitokeza kwenye
kidole
/An abscess elsewhere on the body is
usually referred to as **ilyuúlu**

akapúúto *n.anat (utu-, 12/13)* ankle =
nguyu

akasanda *n.med (12)* diphteria = aina
ya ugonjwa

akasebwe (Combretum sp.) *n.bot (utu-,
12/13)* type of tree = aina ya mti

akaseke *n (utu-, 12/13)* **1** pill = kidonge,
punje **2** *n.dim* small seed = mbegu ndogo

akasenyenda *n (utu-, 12/13)* earthquake = tetemeko la ardhi

akasetuka *n (utu-, 12/13)* vision = ono,
maono

a'kaasosí (Dracaena marginata) *n.bot
(utu-, 12/13)* type of tree (Madagascar
Dragon tree); used for medicine,
when branches are broken a lot of liquid comes out = aina ya mti ambao
vitawi vyake vikivunjwa hutoa maji
mengi, hutumika kwa dawa

akasúmo *n (utu-, 12/13)* tale, story =
ngano, hadithi

akasunía *n (utu-, 12/13)* type of small
fly = aina ya inzi mdogo

akaswebele *n.bot (utu-, 12/13)* type of
tree = aina ya mti /(Ochna sp.)

akaswende *n.med (utu-, 12/13)* syphilis
= kaswende

akasya *n.zool (utu-, 12/13)* type of
small antelope = aina ya swala
mdogo, paa

akasyesye *n (utu-, 12/13)* **1** small, often
round, lawn found in front of many
homesteads = kifungu cha nyasi laini
mbele ya nyumba **2** *n.dim* a piece of
bread, small bread = mkate mdogo

akasyonono *n.med (12)* gonorrhea =
kisonqno

akateefu akatibe short closely knit and
decorated mat = mkeka mfupi ulio-
sukwa kwa karibu uliko pambwa

akaato *n (utwaato, 12/13)* small boat,
dinghy = mtumbwi mdogo

akatonolelo *n (utu-, 12/13)* arrow =
mshale

akatundu *n (utu-, 12/13)* small basket =
kikapu kidogo

akatuusí *n (12)* urine = mkojo

-ake *pron* his, her(s), its = -ake

akeendelo *n (utw-, 12/13)* style of walking,
way of walking = mtindo wa kutembea

akeesí *n (utweesi, 12/13)* new moon
(arch down) = mwezi mchanga /
mwandamo

akíko *n (utwíko, 12/13)* teaspoon = kijiko kidogo

akíingililo *n (utwí-, 12/13)* **1** approach
= mjio **2** a kind of dance performed
by a group of dancers when entering
the arena at the traditional dances =
aina ya mchezo, mtindo uchezwao na
wachezangoma waingiapo jukwaani /
uwanjani **3** also used about a choir
when about to face the audience = pia
hutumika na waimbaji wakaribiapo
kuikabili hadhira (hadhara) yao

akiisí *n (utw-, 12/13)* brook = kijito

akisya *vt.caus (pt akíísye)* to light smth
for = washia; **Amwakíísye ingaambo
ummanyaní** He has lit his friend's

cigarette = Amemwashia rafiki yake sigara

akoogo *n (utoogo, 12/13)* undistinguishable sound heard from a distance (like the sound from a funeral procession) = kelele za kila aina zinazosikika zikiwa zenye mchanganyiko za furaha na za huzuni; **Akoogo kalinkujogoja ndimba inyumba jikupya**. Shouting was heard while the house burned down = Wakati nyumba inaungua kelele za huzuni zilisikika

ala *vt (pt aalíle)* **1** spread out (eg tablecloth, bedsheet, mat) = tandika (km kilago) **2** to put something in between/under smth to protect it from dirt = funika
ala paasí unkwela put the mat underneath = tandika mkeka chini
ala ulwalo lay a foundation = weka msingi

alama *vi (pt aleeme)* **1** settle at the bottom (form a sediment) = tulia chini; **ubunyalí bwaleeme paasí pamiisi** The dirt has settled at the bottom of the water = takataka zimetulia chini ya maji; **2** duck (bend down) = kwepa, kepa, epa

alamíla *vb (pt alamííle)* **1** brood, incubate, hatch = atamia **2** cover to protect = okoa kwa kulala juu ya

alangana *vi (pt alangeene)* worry = hangaika; **Kwalangana siliku ?** What are you worried about ? = Una shida gani ? / Unahangaika kwa nini?

alanganía *vt (pt alangeenie)* daze, confuse, puzzle = tatiza, pumbaza

alelesí *n (baalelesí, 1a/2, > Eng >Latin ad directus)* address = anwani

alisya *vt.caus (pt alíísye)* spread, roll out = tandika; **alisya unkwela** roll out the mat = tandika mkeka
/see **ala**

aluka *vi.stat (pt alwííke, >ala)* stand up, get up, set out = simama, inuka

alula *vt.rev (pt alwííle, > ala)* **1** roll up = tandua, anua **2** remove the thing on top = tandua **3** peel = menya

alulígwa *vi.pass* be rolled up (like a mat) = kunjwa

alumasí *n (ba-, 1a/2; > Swa)* diamond = almasi

amabiju *n.med (6)* rickets (legs bend inwards) = matege

amabuba (Chrysanthemum cinerariaefolium) *n.bot (6)* pyrethrum = pareto

amabwaní *n (6; > Swa)* glasses, spectacles = miwani
/See **amangalasí**

amafi *n (6)* excrement, feces, shit = mavi

amafíla *n.med (6)* pus = usaha

amaafíílú *n.bot (6)* grapes = zabibu
ubwalwa bwa maafíílú wine = divai

amafúkú *n (6)* **1** sweat, perspiration = jasho **2** heat = joto

amafúne *n (6)* **1** fatigue, strain = uchovu, mavune **2** depressed feelings = mawazo makali; **Ugoníle amafúne?** How are you feeling today? (after working hard yesterday) = Vipi hali ya mawazo makali uchovu

amafúta *n (6)* oil, fat, grease, diesel, fuel etc = mafuta

amagesyo *n (6)* exam, test = mtihani, jaribio

amaago *n (6)* the space between ones legs, between the knees etc. = nafasi iliyopo katikati ya miguu, magoti nk

amahala *n (6, for sg. usage see ilí-)* **1** intelligence, wisdom, knowledge = akili, ufahamu, busara, ujuzi, welevu, utambuzi **2** learning = elimu, hekima
-a mahala *adj* reasonable, rational, sensible = -enye maana, -enye akili, -tambuzi

amahono *n (6)* snore, snoring = koromo, mkoromo

amaaja *n (6)* rage, strong grief, wrath = hasira kwa ajili ya tendo zito lililomtokea mtu; **Umúndu uju afwíle**

amaaja. This man has died because of sorrow (for example because of the bad doings of a son). = Mtu huyu amekufa kwa ajili ya huzuni; **sopela amaaja** cause strong grief to sb by witchcraft = loga mtu apatwe na huzuni kubwa

amajolo *n (6)* evening = jioni

amaka *n (6)* **1** power, strength, force, violence = nguvu **2** ability = uwezo wa kufanya **3** authority = mamlaka **onyoka** ~ despair = kata tamaa, vunjika nguvu

papo ~ give power to, encourage = pa moyo, tia nguvu, weka nguvu, saidia

amakambo *n.bot (6)* **1** cannabis, hashish, marijuana **2** *slang*: grass, pot) = bangi

amakeketo *n.anat (6)* wrinkles on the neck (this is a sign of beauty) = michirizo ya shingoni

amakosí *n.anat (6)* neck (nape and throat) = shingo

amakululukila *n (6)* the wet spot on the cup (bottle, glass etc) after spilling its contents = mabaki ya kimiminiko kwenye chombo baada ya kuyamwaga

amalaka *n (6)* the ability to be quick at making decisions = kuwa na papara

amalembo *n (6)* writings = maandishi

amalesí (Eleusine corocana) *n.bot (6)* finger millet = ulezi

amalimbo *n.bot (6)* sap of a plant = utomvu

amanaati *n (6)* slingshot = manati

amandeletele *n.med (6)* venerial disease, herpes = ugonjwa wa ngozi wa vilengelenge

amanga *n (6)* witchcraft = wanga, ulozi

amangalasí *n (6; > Swa)* glasses, spectacles = miwani

amangamba *n.bot (6)* type of climbing beans = maharagwe yatambaayo

amaanja *n (6)* applause, clapping = makofi **koma amaanja** clap = piga makofi /Clapping is used in many instances of Nyakyusa life:

- used by women to show presence, to greet the father-in-law or to answer him
- instead of thanking with words upon recieving gifts at funerals women clap hands/

amanyago *n (6)* resin = utomvu wa miti

amapemba *n.bot (6)* **1** bulrush millet = uwele **2** sorghum = mtama

amapepo *n (6)* winter, cold/cool season (June - August in ubuNyakyusa) = majira ya baridi, kipupwe

amasapa *n (6)* cotton = pamba

amasendo *n.med (6)* syphilis = kaswende

amasesí *n.med (6)* (after shave) scabbies = upele unaotokea baado ya kunyoa

amasíka *n (6)* dregs or lees of local beer = machicha

amasimbi *n.bot (6)* cocoyam = maole, gimbi

amasulu *n (6)* whey = maji yatokanayo na maziwa mgando

amasúsú *n (6)* bird droppings = mavi ya ndege

amasyasya *n.med (6)* fungus on the toes = kuvu miguuni, nyungunyungu

amasyalílo *n (6)* left overs (food) = masao, mabaki

amasyu *n (6)* **1** news = habari **2** discussion = mjadala **3** *pl of ilíísyu* words = maneno

amata *n (6)* saliva, spit = mate

amatanga *n.anat (6)* buttocks = matako

amatego (Kye), **amatege** (Tuk) *n.med (6)* bow legs, rickets = matege

amatende *n.med (6)* elephantiasis = matende /**ilítende** also heard

amateesí *n (6)* vomit, puke = matapishi

amatíka *n (6)* waterpipe for smoking hashish = kiko cha maji kwa ajili ya kuvutia bangi

amatíngo *n (6)* **1** arrogance, pride, boasting, bragging, conceit, disregard, impudence, insolence = majivuno, kiburi, ufidhuli **2** contempt, disdain = dharau, bezo

Umúndu uju ali namatíngo This man is arrogant/conceited = Mtu huyu anajivuna

amatugalilo *n.anat (6)* buttocks, bum, behind = matako

amatuse *n.med (6)* mumps = matumbwi-tumbwi

amatuusí *n.anat (6)* urine = mkojo

amba *vt (pt ambíle)* Hold out a dish or hand(s) in order to receive smth, as when you are being served food = Kinga chombo au mikono ili upewe kitu

ambila *vb (pt ambííle)* ask for permission = omba ruhusa

ambilila *vt.appl (pt ambilííle)* 1 recieve, accept = pokea 2 entertain (guests) = pokea, kirimu

ambililana *vb (pt ambilileene)* take turns in doing smth (eg carrying loads) = pokezana

ambúka *vi (pt ambwííke)* cross over, sail across = vuka

ambukisya *vt.caus (pt ambukísye)* infect = ambukiza

ambula *vb (pt ambwíle)* 1 *vt* duplicate, copy = nakili 2 *vi.med* get infected by sb (especially with VD) = ambukizwa

ambulanía *vt (pt ambuleeníe)* 1 take sb by surprise = tokea ghafla bila kutara-jiwa, jia kwa hila 2 take sb's things without asking permission (not steal-ing) = chukua vitu vya watu bila ruhusa zao

ambulanígwe ítolo to be decieved or fooled = jia kwa hila

amiisi, amiisí *n (6)* water = maji

amítúúmbo *n (6)* boasting = majivuno

amúla *vt (pt amwííle)* answer, reply = jibu

ana *vi (pt aníle)* cackle = tetea (kuku)

anda *vt (pt andíle)* 1 begin, start = anza 2 repeat = rudia

andana *vi (pt andeene)* be early = wahi, jihimu

andilako *vb (pt andííleko)* to return back for smth (eg. that you may have forgotten) = rudi tena

andilamo *vb (pt andíílemo)* repeat = rudia

andisanía *vt (pt andiseeníe)* 1 have a return match/round = rudiana mi-chezo 2 reunite = rudiana

andisya *vt.caus (pt andíísye)* 1 repeat = rudia, fanya au sema tena 2 establish, found, launch = anzisha, weka

-andufú *adj* changeable = badilifu

anduka *vi (pt andwííke)* be changed, be altered = badilika

andula *vt (pt andwííle)* 1 change, alter, transform = badilisha, badili 2 con-vert = geuza

angala *vi (pt angeele)* 1 be well, feel fine = jisikia vizuri 2 converse, talk, chat, be in good company = ongea, ongea na wenzi; **Gwangeele?** How are you? = umeshindaje **Nangeele kanúnú** I feel fine = salama; **Ati-kwangala kanúnú na bakamu bake** He is not on good terms with his rela-tives Haongei vizuri na wenzake

angalila *vt.appl (pt angalííle)* 1 tease, make fun of, mock, bother, annoy = tania, dhihaki, sumbua 2 play with = chezea

angasya *vt.caus (pt angeesye)* 1 com-fort sb by visiting or passing time with them = liwaza mgonjwa au mfiwa 2 delay sb by forcing them to be sociable (keep talking to them when they want to leave) = chelewe-sha, kumpotezea mtu wakati wake

angila *vt (pt angííle)* catch (smth which is thrown or falling) = daka

angula *vt (pt angwííle)* skim, remove cream or froth = engua mafuta au povu

-aní *interr (la/2)* 1 who = nani; **Jo jwaní ujo?** Who is that? = Huyo ni nani? 2 whose = -a nani; **umwana gwaaní?** whose child? = mtoto wa nani?

anía *vt (pt aníísye)* ask (a question as oppos-ed to asking for smth or begging), inquire, consult = uliza

aníka *vt (pt aníike)* set out to dry or air = anika

anúla *vt.rev (pt anwíile, > aníka)* remove smth that was set out to dry = anua

apa *adv* **1** here, where = hapa; **kumbali kunyanja apa pali nunsanga** a sandy beach, lit. on the beach where there is sand = pwani iliyo na mchanga, ufukoni mwa bahari ambapo pana mchanga **2** *conj* because, since = kwa sababu, kwa kuwa; **Apa ísíle, alyemo**. Give him some food since he has come = Kwa kuwa amekuja mpe chakula ale

apa, ukwapa *vt (pt aapíle)* pick, pluck, harvest by plucking (tea leaves, tomatoes, pepper) = vuna kwa kuchuma

apakumanyílíla, pabumanyílilo *n (16)* school, place of study = shule, mahali pa kusomea

asama *vi (pt aseeme)* gape = achama

ase *interj* interjection of surprise = alaa!

asíma *vt (pt asííme)* borrow from = azima

asímisya *vt.caus (pt asímíísye)* lend to = azimisha

askofú *n (> Swa)* bishop = askofu

asya *vt.caus (pt asíísye, > aka)* light, ignite, turn on (light) = washa

aasya *vt.caus (pt aasísye, > aaga)* destroy, annihilate, burn, ravage, devastate = angamiza, maliza kabisa, teketeza

ata *vt (pt atíle)* start doing smth = anza kufanya kitu

aati *exp.arch* s/he said = alisema /Modern form: **aatíle**

Bb

baba *vb (pt babíle)* **1** *vi* hurt, be in pain = umia **2** *vt* (food) grill = banika

babígwa *vi.pass (pt babíígwe)* suffer = umwa, ona uchungu, umia

bafya *vt.caus (pt bafífye)* **1** cause pain = umiza **2** afflict = umiza

bagala *vt (pt bageele)* carry a load on the shoulder = beba mzigo begani

bagila *vt & vi (pt bagííle)* **1** be able, can, be possible, manage = weza **2** afford = weza, kuwa na uwezo **3** suit, fit, be useful = faa **4** deserve, be eligible = stahili **5** be favourable = pendeza **6** be worthy = kuwa na thamani
síkabagila it is impossible = -siowezekana

bagisanía *vt (pt bagiseeníe)* (about people) suit one another, be of use to each other = faana

bagula *vt (pt bagwííle)* kick = piga teke

bagwitu *interj* friends!, colleagues! = jamani!, wenzangu!

baaja *vt (pt baajíle)* kick = piga teke

bakusaje *interj* Said to sb who sneezed, gesundheit, bless you = pole

bala *pron* **1** they (people at a distance) = wao **2** those (people) = wale

bala *vb (pt balíle)* **1** *vt* count = hesabu **2** read = soma **3** *vi* shine (the sun) = angaza (jua)

baala *vt (pt baalíle)* **1** increase = ongezeka **2** thrive, prosper = ongezeka

balanía *vt (pt baleeníe)* **1** scatter, disperse, distribute, spread (around) = sambaza, tawanya **2** split = gawanya, tenganisha **3** broadcast = tawanya

balaníla *vi (pt balaníle)* be dispersed, be scattered = tawanyika, sambaa

baaluka *vi (pt baalwííke)* **1** bloom, blossom = chanua **2** expand = tanua, panua, enea; **Ikíísu kyako kinywamú? Ee, kibalwíke** Is your land big? Yes it is ("it stretches out") = Je, ardhi yako ni kubwa? Ndio, imepanuka

baalula *vt (pt baalwíile)* **1** open = fungua **2** unfold = kunjua **3** widen, expand, stretch, spread out, straighten = panua, tanua, tandaza, nyoosha

baamba *vi (pt baambíle)* **1** stand in line = panga msitari **2** slaughter cows for a funeral = chinja ng'ombe wakati wa matanga **3** start making a mat, the first steps of the making of a mat = anza kusuka mkeka **4** stretch a skin to fit a drum = wamba ngoma

bambika *vb (pt bambíike)* arrange (in line), match = panga (katika msitari), fananisha

bambula *vt (pt bambwíle)* peel, strip off = ambua (gome la mti nk)

bamo *pron* **1** others = wengine **2** some = baadhi

baanda *vt (pt baandíle)* **1** knead = kanda **2** *vt.med* To heal or soothe a wound in traditional medicine by pressing or massaging the body with hot water, compression with hot or cold water on a wound. Often local medicine is added to the water. = kanda (kwa maji ya moto au baridi) juu ya uvimbe au kidonda, mara nyingi maji hayo huchanganywa na dawa za miti shamba

banga *vt (pt bangíle)* redeem, save = komboa, okoa /Mostly religious

bangatuka *vi.med (pt bangatwíike)* walk with feet facing outward (common case with people whose feet /toes have been infested with jiggers) = tembea nyayo zikielekea pembeni (hasa kwa miguu iliyoshambuliwa na funza)

bangila *vt (pt baangíle)* exchange = badilisha

bapula *vt (pt bapwíile)* slap = zaba, zaba kofi

baasa *vi (pt baasíle)* converse = zungumza

baasya *vt.caus (pt beesye)* increase (in number) = ongeza

baata *vi (pt baatíle)* belch, burp = cheua, teuka, piga mbweu/ mbwewe

batama *vi (pt bateeme)* be silent, be quiet = nyamaza

-batamífu *adj* cool = nyamavu, tulivu

batamísya *vt.caus (pt batamíisye)* **1** silence sb, make quiet = nyamazisha **2** cool, soothe, appease = poza, tuliza **3** caress = bembeleza

baati *interj* **1** to call sb's attention: hey, hey you, look here = ewe, eti **2** to express disbelief: really, indeed = ati! eti!

batika *vt (pt batíike)* soothe, calm sb down = tuliza

baatika *vt (pt baatíke)* **1** arrange, sort, put in order, put in a row, classify, plan = panga **2** fix = tengeneza **3** decorate = remba

baatula *vb.rev (pt baatwíile, > baatika)* offload, unload = pakua

beleluka *vi (pt belelwíike)* **1** flutter, blow = pepea **2** fly = pepea, peperuka **3** be blown away = peperushwa

belenga *vt (pt belengíle; >Bemba 'check, verify, read')* **1** count, reckon = hesabu **2** read = soma; **Umenye ukubelengala?** Do you know how to count? Unajua kuhesabu?; **Ummenye ukubelengela kalata?** Do you know how to read? Unajua kusoma?

begala *vt (pt begeele)* carry a load on the shoulder = beba mzigo begani

beka *vb (pt bekíle)* give a present (money) during wedding or traditional dance = tuza

bendekela *vt (pt bendekelíile)* sneak = nyata

bendekelela *vt.appl (pt bendekelíle)* sneak up on = nyatia

beene *pron* themselves = wenyewe

benga *vt (pt bengíle)* hate, detest, dislike, loathe = onea, chukia

-bengí *adj* offensive, hateful = -a chukí

beseela *vi (pt beseelíle)* change color as

in the infestation of hookworm =
badilika rangi kama mgonjwa wa sa-
fura

beeta vi *(pt beetíle)* wander = tangatanga

betabeta vi *(pt betabeetíle)* loiter = tangatanga

beteka vt *(pt betíike; Tuk; Kye ->
batika)* calm down, soothe = tuliza

beetesya vt.caus *(pt beetíisye)* **1** go around
selling = tembeza bidhaa zinunuliwe **2**
cause someone to wander aimlessly =
hangaisha, zungusha mtu bila sababu

-bíbí adj **1** bad = -baya **2** ugly = -baya
kwa sura

bíbuka vi *(pt bíbwíike)* become ugly =
badilika sura kuwa mbaya

bíbusya vt.caus *(pt bíbwíisye)* deform =
chakaza, haribu

bifwa vi *(pt bifwífwe / bifífwe)* be ripe
(fruit) = iva, komaa, kukomaa kwa
zao; **amabifú gabifífwe** the bananas
are ripe = ndizi zimeiva

-bifwe adj ripe = -bivu

bíga vt *(pt bígíle)* throw down = bwaga,
tupa chini

biika vt *(pt biikíle)* **1** put, lay, place, set,
deposit = weka **2** store, set aside for
later use, reserve = tunza **3** calve =
zaa (ng'ombe)

biika amaka make an extra effort, do
one's utmost, exert = fanya juhudi,
jibidisha

bikilila vt.appl *(pt biikilíile)* stock,
hoard, conserve = tunza, hifadhi,
weka akiba

bilama vi *(pt bileeme)* bend = pinda

bilamika vb *(pt bilamíike)* bend = inamika

-bilamufú adj bent, curved = -liopinda,
-liopindika

-bili num.adj two = -wili

bilikila vt *(pt bilikíile)* call = ita

bilingana vi *(pt bilingeene)* cloud over,
become cloudy = jaa mawingu
kumwanya kubilingeene the sky is
cloudy = anga imejaa mawingu

bílítula vt *(pt bílítwíile)* spark = toa cheche

biluka vt *(pt bilwíke)* nauseate = tia
kichefuchefu, chefua; **Ubwalwa
bukuumbiluka kummilo** Beer nause-
ates me = Pombe huniletea kichefuchefu, hunichefua

bína vi *(pt biníle)* fall sick, become sick
= ugua, kuwa mgonjwa

bíínda vt *(pt bíindíle)* **1** squeeze out =
kamua **2** pinch = minya

-bíne adj sick = -gonjwa; **unkííkulu
mmbíne** the woman is sick = mwanamke anaumwa; **ing'ombe mbíne**
the cow is sick = ng'ombe anaumwa

bíndikila vt *(pt bíndikíile)* press on,
suppress = gandamiza, kandamiza

bingilila vt *(pt bingilíile)* intend = kusudia

-bíní adj evil, malicious = -ovu

bíníka vt *(pt biníike)* spoil, ruin, destroy
= haribu

bínisya vt.caus *(pt bíníisye)* make sb
sick = fanya mtu augue

-bisi / -bisí adj raw, unripe = bichi

biisya vt.caus *(pt biisísye; >ukubiika)*
1 helping a cow to give birth = saidia
ng'ombe kuzaa, zalisha ng'ombe
2 get profit = pata faida, zalisha

bítila vt *(pt bítíile)* close (buttons) =
funga vifungo

bítula vi.rev *(pt bítwíile; > ukubítila)*
unbutton = fungua vifungo

bo adv,conj **1** when = vilevile kama kiambilishi awali cha kitenzi -po- **2** like, as =
kama; **bo lululo** likewise = vilevile; **bo
akaali** before (a person) = kabla ya;
Alondíle ubunnyafyale bo ubwa gwíse
He wanted a chiefdom like that of his father = Alitaka ufalme kama alivyo baba
yake; **bo ísíle** when he came = alipofika

bo prep after = baada ya

bo adv,conj **1** when = vilevile kama
kiambilishi awali cha kitenzi -po-
2 like, as, such = kama; **bo lululo**
likewise = vilevile; **bo akaali** before
(a person) = kabla ya; **Alondíle ubunnyafyale bo ubwa gwíse** He wanted a

chiefdom like that of his father = Alitaka ufalme kama alivyo baba yake

bo bunobuno *adv* like this, like that = kama hivi, kama hivyo

bobota *vi (pt bobwííte)* snore = koroma

bobukaali *prep* before (time)= kabla ya

-bofú *adj* 1 rotten = mbovu 2 damaged, out of order = -lioharibika

bogoja *vi (pt bogwííje)* talk or sing in a deep voice = ongea au imba kwa sauti nzito

bola *vi (pt bolíle)* rot, go bad, decay = oza

boola *vt (pt boolíle)* 1 cut (with a sharp blade) = kata 2 slaughter = chinja

bomba *vb (pt bombíle)* 1 work = fanya kazi 2 do = fanya

bombela *vt (pt bombííle)* 1 use, employ = tumia 2 serve, work for = tumikia 3 treat = tendea

-bombí *adj* active, industrious, vigorous, efficient = -tendaji

bona *vt (pt bwene)* see = ona

boneka *vi.stative (pt bonííke)* 1 become visible, appear, be seen, emerge, seem = onekana, tokea 2 rise = jitokeza 3 happen, occur = tukia

boneka pabwelu become known, come out in the open, become exposed = fichuka

bonela *vt (pt bonííle)* 1 belittle = onea 2 persecute = umiza, tesa, dhulumu 3 oppress = onea, kandamiza, tawala bila haki

bonela ikisa *(> bona)* 1 feel pity for = onea huruma 2 feel for = hisi, onea

bonesya *vt.caus (pt boníísye)* show, reveal, display, depict = onyesha, funua

bopa *vi (pt bopíle)* 1 run = kimbia 2 escape, flee = toroka

boope *pron* they also = na wao

bopela *vb.appl (pt bopííle)* run to, seek refuge = fukuzia, kimbilia

bopesya *vt.caus (pt bopíísye)* 1 speed up, quicken, accellerate, hasten = kimbiza 2 chase = fukuza, kimbiza 3 drive fast = endesha kwa mwendo mkali

bosya *vt.caus (pt bosíísye, > bola)* cause smth to rot = ozesha

bota *vt (pt botíle)* be calm, still, settled = tulia

botoka *vb (pt botokíle)* be in abundance, be blessed, be prosperous = neemeka, jaa tele

botosya *vt.caus (pt botwíísye)* fertilize = weka mbolea, rutubisha

-a bubili *num.ord* second = -a pili

bububo *adv* 1 like that, as it is = hivyo hivyo 2 in that manner = vivyo hivyo

-bubufú *color.adj* gray = -a kijivu

bugala *vi (pt bugeele)* (about infants) become big enough to be carried around (approx one month old) = (watoto wachanga) pata umri na umbo la kuwa wezesha kubebwa na mama zao waendapo kwenye shughuli mbalimbali

buganda *n.bot (ba-, 1a/2)* type of banana = aina ya ndizi itwayo uganda

-bugujufú *adj* broken = -liovunjika **indeko imbugujufú** a broken pot = chungu kilichovunjika

bugujuka *vi (pt bugujwííke)* erode (about items like pots) = bomoka, mong'onyoka, momonyoka

bugujula *vt (pt bugujwííle)* 1 break, wreck = vunja 2 make smth brake into pieces, esp. food or firewood = vunjavunja, katakata hadi vipande vidogovidogo sana

-a buhano *num.ord* fifth = -a tano

búja *vt (pt bújíle)* 1 return (as in go back to somewhere) = rudi 2 be absent (as in not coming when expected to come) = shindwa kuhudhuria, tokuwapo 3 remain (as in stay where you are rather than leaving) = baki, kaa; **búja lululu** come back soon = rudi haraka

bujana *vb (pt bujeene)* reunite (Used about married couples who divorced, but have started living together again) = rudiana tena hasa kwenye ndoa

bújanila *vt (pt bújaniíle)* **1** reunite (Used about married couples who divorced, but have started living together again) = rudiana tena hasa kwenye ndoa **2** move closer (like to make room for another person to sit) = sogeleana karibu (ili kupata nafasi ya kukaa mtu mwingine)

bujila *vt.appl (pt bujiíle)* repeat = rudia

bujilako *vi (pt bujiíleko)* come back, go back, return = rudi

bujilamo *vb (pt bujiílemo)* repeat = rudia

buuka *vi (pt buukíle)* go = enda
  buuka kakeete visit = tembelea
  buuka nkyení advance = jongea
  buuka kalambalale go to bed = nenda kalale

buukila *vt.appl (pt buukíle)* go for, go because of (indicating being forced to) = endea; **Kubuukila kunongwa ja baana** You are going because of the children = Unaenda kwa sababu ya watoto

búkúka *vi (pt búkwíke)* flare = lipuka, waka

bukye *adv* all night long = usiku kucha

buula *vt (pt buulíle)* **1** tell = ambia **2** report = arifu, toa habari

bule *interr* **1** how = je **2** how much = kiasi gani, bei gani

bulebule *adv* how = vipi

búlíka *vt (pt búlíke)* box, hit with the fist = piga kwa ngumi

buulila *vt (pt buulííle)* tattle on, denounce = chongea

buuluka *vi (pt buulwíke)* fade = pauka

-buulufú *adj* **1** faded, pale = -liopauka **2** dirty = chafu

búlúla *vt (bulwíile)* knock down fruit or leaves indiscriminately = pura

-bululu *color.adj* blue = buluu

-búlúlúfú *adj* loose (in single units rather than stuck together) = -sioshikamana
  ihela mbúlúlúfú coin = sarafu
  unsanga umbúlúlúfú loose sand = mchanga usioshikamana

búlúlúka *vi.stat (pt búlúlwíke)* be scattered = tawanyika

búlúlúsya *vt.caus (pt búlúlwísye)* disperse, scatter = tawanya

búlúnga *vt (pt búlwíinge / búlúngíle)* roll up = viringa

búlúngana *vi (pt búlúngeene)* become round = kuwa mviringo; **Ikipapa kya búlúngeene papo bakakikomíle** The dried skin rolled up ("became round") because it was not stretched. = Ngozi imejiviriga kwa vile haikuwambwa / haikufungwa

-búlúnge *adj* round, circular = -a mviringo

-buluunge *adj* tasty = iliyo kolea

búlúngika *vi (pt búlúngíike)* be round, spherical = kuwa duara

buulusya *vt.caus (pt buulwísye)* cause fading = pausha

búlútúka *vi (pt búlútwíike)* collapse, breakdown = bomoka

búlútúla *vt (pt búlútwíle)* shell corn/maize = pukuchua mahindi

bumba *vt (pt bumbíle)* **1** mold, knead clay with hands = finyanga **2** create = umba **3** to come to the aid of one party in a fight = changia

bumbula, limbula *vt (pt bumbwíle)* **1** get, have = ambua, pata **2** gather honey = rina **3** Cause bees to fly from their places so that they sting sb = chokoza nyuki manyigu ili yaume watu

bumbulila *vt.appl (pt bumbuliíle)* profit from = ambulia

bumbuluka *vi (pt bumbulwíike)* get well, get healed = pona, takasika kwa ugonjwa

bumbulusya *vt.caus (pt bumbulwísye)* heal = takasa, ponyesha

-a buna *num.ord* fourth = -a nne

buna *vi (pt buníle)* grunt, mutter, grumble = guna

búna *vi (pt búníle)* **1** (about color) become darker = kolea (kuhusu rangi tu) **2** roar = nguruma

búnda *vi (pt búndíle)* be moist = kuwa na unyevunyevu

-bundafú *adj* wet = -enye unyevu, unyevunyevu

-búndifú *adj* damp = -enye unyevu

bundisya *vt.caus (pt bundíísye)* wet, water = lowanisha, lowesha, tia unyevunyevu
/Kyangonde: bundasya

-búne *adj* (color) very bright, intense, the opposite of faded = kolevu (kuhusu rangi tu)

bungaana *vi (pt bungeene)* **1** be assembled = kusanyika **2** be gathered = kusanyika, kuwa pamoja; **Abaandu babungeene palukomano pakipanga** People are gathered for a meeting in the village = Watu wamekusanyika kwenye mkutano kijijini

bungaanía *vt.caus (pt bungeníe)* gather, assemble, collect, accumulate = kusanya

bungaanía imbalilo add (in math) = jumlisha hesabu

-bungu *color.adj* **1** copper color = rangi ya shaba **2** light brown = kahawia

búngúlúka *vi.stative (pt búngúlwíke)* toss and turn, roll from side to side = gaagaa

búngúlúsya *vt.caus (pt búngúlwísye)* roll, rotate = viringisha

buno *adv* **1** this way, thus, so = hivi, namna hii; **Abombíle buno** He did it like this = Amefanya hivi; **2** accordingly = kama ilivyo, jinsi ilivyo

bunobuno *adj*
-a bunobuno ordinary = -a kawaida

bunobuno *adv* **1** just like this, just this way = hivi hivi, vivi hivi **2** in vain = bure; **Abombíle bunobuno 1** He did it just like this = Amefanya hivi hivi **2** He did it in vain = Amefanya bure

búsanía *vi (pt búseeníe)* go to a place and come back the same day = nenda rudi bila kupitisha siku

búsya *vt.caus (pt búsíísye, > buja)* **1** return, bring back = rudisha **2** reply, answer, = jibu, toa jawabu

búúta *vt (pt búútíle)* **1** cut = kata **2** slaughter = chinja
~ **ingolomilo** slaughter = chinja
~ **untu** behead, decapitate = kata kichwa
~ **kukyení** circumcise = tahiri

bútama *vi (pt buteeme)* fall face down = anguka kifudifudi/ kifulifuli

buutanía *vb (pt buutenie)* cut into pieces = katakata

buutaníabuutanía *vt (pt buutenie-buutenie)* cut into pieces, chop = kata vipande vipande, katakata

-a butatu *num.ord* third = -a tatu

-a butungulu *adj* untrue = -a uwongo, -a uongo

bwabwata *vb (pt bwabwatíle)* blab, talk nonsense = onyea maneno yasiyo ya maana (ya kijinga)

-bwafú *adj* habitually dirty = -enye tabia ya uchafu

bwaka *vi (pt bwakíle)* **1** (animals) give birth to several offspring, farrow = zaa vitoto vingi kwa mara moja (km. mbwa) **2** whelp = kuzaa kwa mbwa

-bwapufú *adj* **1** negligent, lazy = -zembe, -vivu **2** dirty = chafu

-bwasí, -a bwasí *adj* **1** open = -wazi **2** blank = -wazi, tupe

bwasya *vt.caus (pt bwasíísye)* unintentionally cause a hunted animal to flee = sababisha mnyama mwindwa kukimbia bila kukusudia

bwíla *adv* always = kila mara, kila wakati

bwíla na bwíla forever = milele, daima

bwila *vt (pt bwilíle)* throw or put smth into the mouth (eg. nuts, snuff, pieces of food) = bwia, bwakia

bwílabwíla *adv* **1** daily, every day = kila siku **2** often = mara zote, mara nyingi

-a bwílabwíla *adj* **1** daily = mara kwa mara **2** durable = -a kudumu **3** ordinary, common = -a kawaida

bwílabwíla *adv* eternity = milele, daima /Also **bwíla na bwíla**

bwima *adv* while standing = -a kusimama, akiwa amesimama

byala *vt (pt byalíle / byeele)* plant, sow = panda (mbegu)

byooka *vt (pt byookíle)* throw up, vomit, puke = tapika

byula *vb (pt byulíle)* poke an eye = chokoa jicho

byúsya *vt.caus (pt byúsísye)* **1** swing (eg. arms while marching) = rusha kitu hewani, ning'inia **2** thrust a stick while dancing traditional dances = rusha fimbo hewani unapocheza ngoma

Ee

ee *adv* yes = ndiyo

ega *vt (pt eegíle)* **1** marry a woman = oa **2** take, get, acquire = pata, chukua **3** adopt (a concept) = kubali kitu / wazo kwa matumizi

egama *vi (pt egeeme)* lean = egemea, inama, kuwa katika hali ya kulalia

egamíla *vt (pt egamííle)* **1** lean upon = egemea **2** prop, support = tegemeza **3** depend upon = tegemea

egana *vb (pt egeene)* **1** match, resemble = lingana, chukuana **2** suit each other = faana

egeka *vt (pt egííke)* lean smth against / prop sth up against a wall or a tree = simamisha ukutani, egesha kitu kwenye ukuta

egekesya *vt.caus (pt egekíísye, > egeka)* prop up, stake up (as in putting a supporting rod under a banana plant that is falling) = simikia nguzo kitu ilikisianguke

egela *vt (pt egííle)* **1** adopt (concept) = kubali kitu / wazo kwa matumizi **2** imitate, copy = iga, nakili **3** pay off mortgage = lipia kitu kilichowekwa rehani **4** exchange = badilisha **5** pick up ('buy back') something you have pawned = gomboa

egesya *vt (pt egíísye)* marry off a child = oza

egígwa *vt (pt egígwe)* be married to a man = olewa

ehemwa *adv* yes = ndiyo

ela *vi (pt elíle)* **1** clear up (the sky) = takata (anga) **2** (crops) yield = toa mazao, zaa matunda

ele *interj* here you are (when giving sb smth) = mtoaji anasema chukua

-eleefú *adj* broad = pana

eleela *vi (pt eleelíle)* float = elea

eleluka *vi (pt elelwíke)* come to the surface = ibuka

15

elelusya *vt.caus (pt elelwísye)* make smth float = fanya ielee

eleesya *vt (pt eelesisye)* make more space for sb, widen = tanua, panua nafasi

-eelú *adj* 1 *color.adj* white, clear, silver colored, shiny, shining = -eupe, rangi ingbayo, rangi ya fedha 2 innocent = -siye na makosa 3 clean = safi

eluka *vi (elwíke)* become clean, become white = kuwa safi, kuwa -eupe

elukaga *ingamwana: isaga* welcome = karibu

-eluke *adj* free = huru

elusígwa *vb (pt elusíigwe)* become clean = takasika

elusya *vt.caus (pt eelwísye)* 1 clean, purify, clear = safisha 2 rinse = suza, suuza

-embeelí *adj* loafing = -zururaji

embeela *vi (pt embeelíle)* wander, roam = zunguka, tangatanga; **Umúndu uju mwembeeli** This man never stays at home, he keeps moving around = Mtu huyu mtembezi, hakaikai mahali pamoja; **Ameenye injobele nyingi paapo embeelíle mfíisu fíngi bo íkumanyísya** He knows many languages because he has gone to many countries as a teacher = Anafahamu lugha nyingi kwa kuwa ametembelea nchi nyingi akiwa mwalimu

embeesya *vt.caus (pt embesíisye; > embeela)* 1 take or show around = tembeza 2 go around selling = zungusha

eena *adv* 1 yes = ndiyo 2 thank you = asante 3 used as final answer to **ndaga** in greetings = hutumika kama asante baada ya salamu

enda *vi (pt endíle)* 1 walk, move around = enda, tembea 2 (female animals) to mate, breed = pandwa na dume

endekesya *vt.caus (pt endekísye)* (male animals) mate, breed = panda jike; **Ingambakú jili pakwendekesya** The

bull is mating the cow. = Fahali anampanda ng'ombe jike.

endelela *vi (pt endelíile)* continue, progress, go on, keep on, keep up, proceed, carry on = endelea

endeelela *vi (pt endeelíle)* hurry up = fanya haraka

endenda *vb (endendíle)* 1 *vi* wander or go around looking for smth, with a purpose = zungukazunguka, tembeatembea, tangatanga 2 *vt* bewitch sb = roga

endesya *vt.caus (pt endíisye, > enda)* drive = endesha

-eene *adj* 1 only = tu 2 oneself = mwenyewe, pekee 3 alone = peke yake

enelela *vt (pt enelíile)* 1 take charge of = simamia 2 take care of = tunza, linda, chunga

eneesya *vt.caus (pt eneesísye)* 1 inspect, examine, search, look at, browse = chunguza, angalia 2 visit sb = tembelea

-engo *adj* swift, sharp, cunning = -epesi kufanya jambo

enguka *vi (pt engwííke)* melt = yeyuka

epa *vt (pt epíle)* dodge = epa

epuka *vt (pt epwíke)* avoid, evade = epuka

epulila *vt (pt epulíle)* to clear an area (esp. of plants or grass) = safisha eneo au njia

epusya *vt.caus (pt epwísye)* avoid, shun = epusha

esya *vt (pt esísye)* make smth pass under, over or through smth = pitisha chini ya, juu ya au kwenye

16

Ff

falaganía *vt (pt falageenie)* mix, combine = changanya

fesa *n (-, 9/10, > Swa)* silver = fedha

fifa *vt.arch (New word: fisa)* hide = ficha

fifílwa *vi (pt fifilwe)* be weakened, be faded (about material, color) = fifia

fíífya *vt (pt fififye)* think about revenge, hurt sb = fikiria kulipiza kisasi

fíga *vb (pt figíle)* 1 (**fíga ingafi**) paddle, row = piga kasia 2 stir (food) = koroga (k.m. mboga chunguni)

figísa *vt (pt figíise)* 1 efface = futa, ondoa kabisa 2 rub (continuously with the hand/palm), crumble with the hands = sugua mikono, fikicha

fíguka *vi.med (pt figwíike)* be dislocated = teguka

figula *vt (pt figwíle)* 1 *vt.med* dislocate = tegua 2 pull out, withdraw = chomoa, chokoa 3 remove the support of smth (eg. the stone at the wheel of a truck) = chomoa /toa kiegemo (mf. kutoa jiwe kwenye tairi la gari)

fíijo *adv* 1 very, much, a lot = sana 2 immensely = sana 3 entirely, thoroughly, utterly = kabisa

fíka *vi (pt fikíle)* arrive, reach = fika, wasili

fíkapo *vb (pt fikílepo)* 1 show up, report at a place = ripoti 2 eat or drink a little (used when urging sb to eat at least a little bit) = kula/kunywa kidogo

fíkí *interr* 1 which things = vitu gani 2 why = kwa nini 3 what = nini

fíkila *vt.appl (pt fikíile)* arrive at, reach (destination) = fikia

-fíkilígwa *adj* accessible = -fikiwa, fikika

fíkisya *vt.caus (pt fikíisye)* 1 bring smth to its destination, deliver = peleka kitu / habari mpaka mwisho, fikisha 2 fulfill a promise = timiza ahadi

fíkuti it has to = inapaswa

filífíndika *vi (pt filifíndiike)* creep, crawl = tambaa

fímbilisya *vt (pt fimbilísye)* 1 persuade, enforce = shawishi 2 oblige, compel = lazimisha

fína *vt (pt finíle)* dance, play = cheza

fínda *vt (pt findíle)* 1 hold back the truth = ficha ukweli 2 hide, conceal = ficha

fínga *vt (pt fingíle)* 1 promise, engage = ahidi, ahadi 2 swear (to the truth) = apa

fíngana *vt (pt fingeene)* bet money on smth = pingana, wekeana masharti ya (maalipo ya pesa)
/The deal is sealed by the parties hooking their little fingers together

fíninga *vt (pt finingíile)* wrap = viringisha

fíningila *vt (pt finíngile)* 1 cover food with banana leaves so that the heat does not escape (even when cooking in a pot with a lid) = funika chakula kwa majani ya mgomba mvuke usitoke 2 *vt.appl* to wrap smth in, wrap with = funikia

fínyanila *vb (pt finyaniile)* be squeezed together = banana

-fínye *adj* narrow = embamba
   injila fínye narrow path = njia nyembamba

fípa *vt (fipíle)* 1 sip = kunywa kidogo kidogo 2 absorb = fyonza 3 suck = nyonya, fyonza 4 kiss = busu

fípuka *vi (pt fipwíke)* become thin and wasted, emaciate = konda

físa *vt (pt fisíle)* 1 hide, conceal = ficha 2 disguise = ficha, zuia 3 cover = funika

fúba *vt (pt fúbile)* 1 make something dirty = chafua 2 get losses, especially when children die or wives divorce = kukosa watoto au kuachwa katika ndoa 3 cook food improperly (so that it seems like it is still raw) = pika chakula kibichi

fúbika *vt (pt fúbiike)* soak = lowesha, loweka

-**fúbifú** *color.adj* ocher, light brown, pink = kahawia, hudhurungi

fúfanía *vt (pt fúfeeníe)* **1** interrupt = dakiza, katiza **2** cause a complication, mess up = vuruga

-**fúúfú** *adj* ripe = bivu

fúfúlila *vt (pt fúfúlíle)* **1** endure, tolerate = vumilia **2** seek information, investigate, find out = tafutia habari, pelelezea **3** interfere = jitumbukiza

-**fufulwisi, -fúfúlwisí** *color.adj* grey, ash-colored, brown = -a rangi ya kijivu, kahawia

fufya *vt (pt fufífye)* **1** preserve food by cooking it so that it does not go bad = chemsha chakula ili kisiharibike **2** place livestock with sb (eg. a friend) to keep them for you. The offspring are divided among you. = Mpa mtu mifugo ili aitunze kwa niaba yako. Mazao hugawanywa baina yao. /This is often done because of fear of jealousy (and thus witchcraft) like if you have many cows **3** (chickens) not brood properly = atamia mayai vibaya kiasi kwamba mayai mengine hayaanguliwi vizuri

fufye *n.zool* type of chameleon = aina ya kinyonga

fúga *vt (pt fúgíle)* **1** keep livestock, rear, tame = fuga mifugo, tiisha **2** mix soil with water, flour with water = kandakanda **Bajeetíle fíÍjo ukwaga afúgíle íbole** They were very surprised to see that he had tamed (that he kept) a leopard = Walishangaa sana kukuta amemfuga chui

fúgama *vi (pt fúgeeme)* kneel = piga magoti

fúganía *vt (pt fugeníe)* knead, mix up so as to distort shape = changanyachanganya

-**fugutifú** *adj* lukewarm = vuguvugu

fúgúta *vi (pt fúgwíte)* thresh grain/corn by hands or legs = pura nafaka

fugutila *vi (pt fugutíile)* become lukewarm = pata uvuguvugu

fúúja *vt (pt fúújíle)* despise, scorn, mock = dharau

-**fújúfú** *adj* inferior = -a chini, hafifu, duni

-**fújúke** *adj* loss of respect, status or wealth, decadent = -a kupungua thamani

fújúla *vb (pt fujwííle)* **1** humiliate = nyanyasa **2** dishonor, lose respect = fuja, aibisha **3** look down upon = dharau

fúúka *vi (pt fúúkíle)* **1** emit smoke = fuka (moshi); **fúúka ilyosí** emit smoke = fuka moshi; **2** expire (change taste, about, beer, medicine etc.) = haribika kwa sababu ya kukaa muda mrefu; **ubwalwa bufúúkíle** the beer is flat = pombe imepungua nguvu; **3** go crazy = pungukiwa akili **4** tell sb what is on your mind, release your feelings = kumwambia mtu mawazo yako, toa hisia zako

-**fukifu** *adj* lukewarm = vuguvugu

fúúkisya *vt.caus (pt fúúkísye)* **1** burn incense = fukiza, washa uvumba **2** cause smoke to bother sb = fukiza moshi **3** make proposal for marriage for sb else, to be a go-between /mediator = fanya ushenga

fúkwa *vi (pt fúkílwe)* be full beyond capacity, have indigestion, feel bloated = vimbiwa

fúla *vt (pt fúlíle)* castrate = hasi

fúúla *vt (pt fúúlíle)* **1** undress, take off = vua (nguo) **2** strip = toa nguo **3** open knots = fungua vifundo

fúlala *vi (pt fúleele)* be hurt, be injured = umia

fúlasya *vt.caus (pt fúlesye)* hurt, wound, injure, afflict = umiza, tesa, dhuru

-**fule** *adj* castrated = -liohasiwa

fúlila *vi (pt fúlíile)* to change color as a river which changes color because of material coming down during the rainy season = chafuka kama mto ufanyavyo unapopokea uchafu wakati wa mvua

ulwisí lufúlííle the river is muddy = mto umechafuka

fúúlila *vi (pt fúúlííle)* undress for sb = vulia

fúúlo *n.zool (ba-, 1a/2)* heron = korongo /There are two (or three) different species to this name, one dark blackish, one white, one grey (not accepted by all informants)

fúlúmbanía *vt (pt fúlúmbenie)* mix with dirt, cloud up, stir up = chafua, tibua

fúlúmbanía amiisi muddy up water = tibua maji

fulumbuka *vb (pt fulumbwíike)* startle, (be startled, jump & run) = kurupuka

fúlútúla *vt (pt fúlútwíle)* 1 defecate, shit = kunya mavi 2 *vb.slang* mass-produce children, give birth every year = kuzaa watoto mfululizo

fúma *vb (pt fúmíle)* 1 *vi* come from, be from = toka, tokea 2 *vt (> Swa)* embroider = fuma kwa uzi, tarizi

fúmba *vt (pt fúmbíle)* 1 to fill the cheeks with food or fluid like some animals do = tunza kitu mdomoni 2 enclose (in the mouth) = fumba

fúmbata *vt (pt fúmbete)* 1 close (eg mouth) = fumba 2 enclose smth in your hand (or hands) = fumbata kitu mkononi mwako

fúmbatila *vt (pt fúmbatíile)* embrace, hug = kumbatia, fumbata

-fumbi *color.adj* grey, greyish color = rangi ya kijivu

fúmbúla *vt (pt fumbwíle)* solve, reveal = fumbua, tatua tatizo

fúmbwa *vi (pt fúmbílwe)* 1 need, require = hitaji, dai, omba 2 want, desire = taka, tamani

fúmúka *vi (pt fúmwike)* be famous = kuwa maarufu

-fúmúke *adj* famous = mashuhuri

fúmúsya *vt.caus (pt fúmwísye)* 1 declare, proclaim, announce, advertise = tangaza 2 publish, announce, broadcast = tangaza, chapisha, tangaza redioni 3 extend = eneza

fúmúsya amasyu *expr* make a speech,

preach = tangaza maneno, hutubu

fúnda *vt & vi (pt fúndíle)* 1 correct, punish = rekebisha, adhibu 2 rear a child = lea mtoto 3 advise = shauri 4 afflict = tesa, umiza 5 teach sb a lesson (punish, correct) = toa adabu 6 go bad, get spoiled = oza, haribika 7 ferment = chacha, oza

fúndika *vt (fúndíike)* 1 plug = ziba 2 prepare smth in such a way that it quickly gets ripe, store for riping = ficha ili viive haraka, vundika

fúndúla *vt (pt fúndwíle)* open, undo (knot, button), untie = fungua kifundo

fúngamila, fúngamíla *vt (pt fúngamíile)* put pressure on = kamia

fúnja *vt (pt fúnjíle)* 1 harvest, reap = vuna 2 change money = badilisha, vunja

funjúla *vt (pt fúnjwíile)* break = vunja

fuuta *vb (pt fuutíle)* pant, breathe heavily (usually about animals) = pumua kwa nguvu pengine tokana na kuvimbiwa

-fwa, ukufwa *vi (pt fwíle)* die = kufa

-fwa maso *adj* blind

fwala *vt (pt fwele)* 1 wear, dress, clothe = vaa 2 receive a salary = pata mshahara

fwana *vi (pt fwene)* 1 be enough, suffice = tosha 2 be satisfied, be content = ridhika, shiba 3 resemble = fanana 4 fit, suit, be useful = faa 5 compromise come to terms with, be in agreement, be on good terms, get along well= patana, ridhiana, sikilizana, elewana

fwanía *vt (pt fwenie)* 1 match, make smth be of the same quantity, balance = linganisha, sawazisha 2 reconcile = patanisha

fwaníkisya *vt.caus (pt fwaníkisye)* compare, relate = linganisha, fananisha, toa kama mfano

-fwene *adj* 1 alike = sawa sawa, -a kufanana, -a kushabihiana 2 sufficient = -a kutosha, -a kufaa

fwika *vt (pt fwikíle)* 1 dress, clothe = valisha 2 pay sb a salary = lipa mshahara

fwila *n (ba-, 1a/2)* an old course of a river = mahali ulipopita mto

fwila *vt.appl (pt fwilíile)* die for = fia

fwililígwa *vi.appl.pass (pt fwililíigwe, > -fwa)* to be bereaved = fiwa

fwima *vt (pt fwimíle)* hunt, chase = winda

-fwimí *adj* hunting = windaji
  imbwa ifwimí hunting dog

fwota *vt (pt fwotíle)* devour = gugumia

fyata *vt (pt fyatíle)* fasten, tighten = funga barabara, funga kwa kukaza sana (kamba)

fyatúla *vt (pt fyatwíle)* activate, set off, release a spring = fyatua
  fyatúla amapamba make bricks = fyatua matofali

-fyele *adj* prolific = -a kuzaa sana, -zazi sana

fyelile *n.zool (ba-, 1a/2)* type of eagle = aina ya tai

fyelúka *vi (pt fyelwíke)* give birth = zaa

fyengenyúka *vi (pt fyengenywíke)* be sprained, be wrenched = pepetuka, popotoa

fyengenyúla *vt (pt fyengenywíle)* sprain, twist = pepetua

fyika *vt (pt fyikíle)* insert, place between = pachika

fyo *pron (8)* which = ambavyo

fyogoka *vi (pt fyogwíke)* be sprained = teguka

fyogola *vt (pt fyogwíle)* sprain = tegua

fyongolomya *n.bot (ba-, 1a/2)* pigweed = mchicha pori

fyuka *vt & vi (pt fyukíle)* climb, ascend = panda, paa

fyula *vt (pt fyulíle)* remove, pull out; Indicates something which is covered and then removed or taken out eg. fly from a glass, sb stuck in mud, piece of meat from a curry dish = toa, chomoa, opoa

fyulila *vt.appl (pt fyulilíle)* pull out for sb = chomolea, opolea
  fyulila amaso gaze = ona

fyúnda *vt (pt fyundíle)* pinch = finya

fyusya *vt.caus (pt fyusísye)* raise, hoist = pandisha, inua
  fyusya ikiboko kyako kumwanya raise your hand = inua mkono wako

-fyusí *adj* clean = safi

fyutula *vt (pt fyutwíle)* pull out, snatch away, withdraw, remove, release smth which is stuck = chomoa / Indicates smth which is partly seen, but it is stuck and then removed from whatever it is stuck to eg. cap from a pen, thorn from a finger, key from a keyhole

Gg

-gaafú *adj* Basic meaning is loss in
weight or reduction in size (people,
animals) **1** skinny, thin, emaciated =
-liokonda **2** physically weak = dhaifu

gaga *vi (pt gagíle)* ferment = chacha

gajaabi *n (ba-, 1/2)* guava = pera
/Also **gwajaabi**

gajagaja *vi (pt gajagajíle)* **1** be worried,
fret = hangaika **2** be extra careful,
give respect = jali sana; **Bikungaja-
gaja ngati mwana nnini** They handle
him carefully as if he was a small
child = Wanamjali sana kama mtoto
mdogo

gajula *vt (pt gajwíile)* open the mouth =
fungua mdomo

gala *pron* those = yale

gaala *vi (pt gaalíle)* get drunk = lewa

galabuka *vi (pt galabwíke)* be changed
= geuka

galabula *vt (pt galabwíile)* turn, turn
around = geuza

-galagala *adj* **1** unruly, impudent = -tundu,
fidhuli **2** headstrong, determined = -tundu
3 charming, sb creative = changamfu
/Can carry both positive and negative
meaning

galama *vi (pt galeeme)* lie on the back
= lala chali

-galamú *adj* flat = tambarare

-gaale *adj* intoxicated, drunk = -liolewa

gaalisya *vt.caus* intoxicate = lewesha
/also **gaasya**

gamba *vb (pt gambíle)* speak = sema

gana *vt (pt ganíle)* love, like, enjoy =
penda; **nguganíle** I love you = naku-
penda

ganana *vi.recip (pt ganene)* **1** be friends
= kuwa marafiki **2** love each other =
pendana **3** (polite term) make love =
fanya mapenzi

ganda *vi (pt gandíle)* emaciate, become

lean = konda

gangaluka *vb (pt gangalwíike)* get well
= pona

gangula *vt (pt gangwíle)* treat medically, cure = ganga, tibu, ponya

gasama *vi (pt gaseeme)* open mouth in
suprise = fungua mdomo kwa
mshangao

-gaasí *adj* couragous, daring, brave =
jasiri

undosí ungaasí fíijo advanced level
witch = mchawi kuzidi mno

gasuka *vi (pt gaswíke)* be astonished, be
surprised = shangaa

gasula *vt (pt gaswíle)* amaze, surprise,
astonish = shangaza

gasusya *vt.caus (pt gaswísye)* astonish
= ajabisha, shangaza, stajabisha

gaasya *vt.caus (pt gaasísye; > gaala)*
1 intoxicate = lewesha **2** (when milk-
ing) make the cow produce more milk
(eg. by bringing a calf) = toa maziwa
zaidi

-a kugaasya *adj* alcoholic = -enye
pombe; **Ikahabwa jitíkugaasya** Coffee is not an alcoholic drink = Kahawa sio kinywaji cha kulevya; **Ubwalwa kyo kinwegwa kya kugaasya iki
kiganíígwe fíijo mwa Kyela** 'Ubwalwa' is a popular alcoholic drink in
Kyela = 'Ubwalwa' ni kinywaji cha
kulevya kinachopendwa Kyela

gela *vt (pt gelíle)* **1** try, undertake, test
= jaribu **2** examine, measure = pima
3 dare, venture = thubutu **4** taste =
onja **5** tempt = jaribu

gelapo *expr* expression telling somebody to try or to dare to do something:
just try, go for it, I dare you, try me =
jaribisha

geleka *vt (pt gelíike)* thatch = ezeka
nyumba

gelela *vb (pt gelíle)* **1** guess = kisia **2**
vt.appl try with, try for etc = jaribia **3**
wait for = ngojelea, subiria

gesya *vt.caus (pt gesísye)* **1** test, try =

jaribu 2 examine = tahini, pima

geesya *vt.caus (pt geesísye)* transfer = hamisha

gíla *vi (pt gílíle)* visit a place or a friend frequently = zuru mara kwa mara

gíndika *vt (pt gindíike)* glorify, praise = weka, ongezea, heshimu

gíndikisya *vb (pt gindikisye)* 1 press = kandamiza 2 emphasize = sisitiza

go *pron* which = ambayo

goga *vt (pt gogíle)* 1 kill, murder, execute = ua 2 slaughter = chinja 3 break = vunja

-gogí *adj* cruel = -katili

gogwa *vi (pt gogílwe)* 1 dream = ota (ndoto) 2 predict = tabiri

-golofú *adj* 1 straight = nyofu 2 honest, sincere = -a kweli, aminifu 3 correct = sahihi 4 fair = zuri, -eupe, safi 5 direct = -lionyoka, nyofu

goloka *vi (pt golwíke)* 1 be straight = nyoka 2 go straight on = enda moja kwa moja 3 (figurative) be straight forward, be honest (practical, steadfast, effective) = sema /tenda kweli bila haya wala kuonea, kuwa mkweli

---

Ugoníle !

This common greeting has its base in the verb **ukugona** "to sleep". A literal translation is "Have you slept? /You have slept."

-goloke *adj* straight = nyoofu

-gololo *adv* smoothly = kwa ulaini, bila shida

golosya *vt.caus (pt golwísye)* 1 straighten, stretch, extend = nyoosha 2 correct = sahihisha 3 advise = shauri, elekeza 4 inspire, lead = ongoza

gomoka *vi (pt gomwíke)* 1 return, come back = rudi 2 reprove = jirudi

gomokela *vb (pt gomokííle)* repeat = rudia

gomola *vt (pt gomwíle)* 1 return, bring

back = rudisha 2 redirect sb who has gone astray or is going the wrong way (person or animal) = ongoa 3 hinder, obstruct, prevent, restrain = pinga, zuia

gomolela *vt (pt gomolííle)* 1 return smth to sb = rudishia 2 check = zuia

gomolela kunyúma hinder sb or holding sb back (eg in development, work, studies) = rudisha maendeleo yake nyuma

gomosanía *vi (pt gomoseníe)* go on a journey and return on the same day = nenda safari na kurudi siku hiyohiyo

gomosya *vt.caus (pt gomwísye)* 1 restore = rudisha 2 send back, bring back, render = rudisha

gona *vi (pt goníle)* 1 sleep = lala 2 live, stay = ishi

gona utulo be asleep, sleep = lala
gwagonile? did you stay for the night? = ulilala?
Ugonílepo utolo? Have you had a nap? = Umelala usingizi

gonana *vb (pt goneene)* make love = jamiana, pendana

gonda *vt (pt gondíle)* catch fish by pressing hands against mud and small stones in the river banks and beds. Done during the night or when the river is muddy = vua / kamata samaki kwa mikono kwenye matope au kwenye mawe madogo katika kingo za mto

-gone *adj* old, of the past = -zee, -a zamani

unkangale unngona a very old person = mzee sana

goonja *vt (pt gonjíle)* 1 bend = pinda, kunja 2 warn (as to a misbehaving child) = onya

gúba *vi (pt gúbíle)* sulk = nuna

gúbatila *vt (pt gúbatííle)* embrace, hug = kumbatia

gúúla *vi (pt gúúlííle)* wait = ngoja

gúúlila *vt.appl (pt gúúlííle)* wait for, expect =

ngojea, subiri

gúúlilila *vt (pt gúúlilíle)* wait for sb =
ngojelea

guluka *vi (pt gulwííke)* wake up suddenly =
amka ghafla

gulusya *vt.caus (pt gulwíísye)* wake sb
by force = amsha mtu kwa nguvu,
shitua

gúlútú *n.bot (ba-, 1a/2)* type of banana,
originally from Zambia, small, must
be boiled, used for making beer (mbe-
ge) = aina ya ndizi

gúlútúka *vi (pt gúlútwíke)* be startled
and run = shituka na kimbia

gúlútúla *vt (pt gulutwííle)* startle = shitua, stua

-gumba *adj* barren, sterile = tasa,
gumba

Ukugúna - To Curse

A parent can curse a (grown) child for
bad actions. These can be for example
not visiting the parents or not sending
money to them and thus ignoring those
who have brought him/her up. The
curse can be performed by the mother
exposing her private parts to the bad
son or daughter. The bad offspring is
then expected to go crazy.

---

gúmbe *n (ba-, 1a/2)* **1** *n.zool* baboon =
nyani **2** *n.slang* person who lives
alone = mtu akaaye pekee, anayeji-
tenga na wenzie

gúna *vt (pt gúníle)* condemn, curse,
damn = laani

gúndama *vi (pt gundeeme)* **1** stoop,
droop = inama **2** incline = telemka

gúndamika *vt (pt gundamííke)* bend
over, bend down = inamisha

gúúsa *vt (pt gúúsíle)* rub, scrub, polish
= sugua

gúta *vt (pt gútíle)* **1** push = sukuma
2 poke = kumba, sukuma

-gwa *vi (pt gwíle)* fall, stumble, tumble
= anguka

gwajaabi *n.bot (ba-, 1/2)* guava = pera
/Also **gajaabi**

-gwala *adj* cool, calm = -tulivu, -lio-
tulia

gwali kuugu *expr* where were you =
ulikuwa wapi

gwandege *interj* Used to warn sb to be
extra careful, beware, be on guard,
take care = tahadhari, jihadhari

gwangeele *greeting* how are you =
umeshindaje

gwaasya *vt.caus (pt gwaasísye)* cause to
be like, equalize, level off, synchronize = sawazisha

gwatwaku *expr.arch* Where are you going? = Unaenda wapi?
/Modern phrase: **kutwaku**

gwe kanya *interj* Used to get the attention of sb of similar status or age =
Neno la kumvuta mwenzio akusiki-
lize

gwegweesa *pron* any, anyone = yeyote

gwila *vt (pt gwilííle, > -gwa)* fall into/
on/onto = angukia

gwilila *vt (pt gwilííle)* **1** beg pardon =
omba msamaha **2** tumble into = angukia **3** fall down on sb or smth = angukia mtu au kitu
~ **mbwíte** **1** attack = shambulia **2** invade = vamia
gwila ulupi beg pardon = omba
msamaha

gwisya *vt.caus (pt gwisísye, > -gwa)*
1 overturn = pindua **2** throw down,
bring to ruin, overthrow, let down,
disappoint = angusha

gwisya ítelení derail = angusha gari-
moshi

Hh

haaba *vi (pt haabíle)* be quick, early =
wahi; **uhabíle** you are early = umewahi; **ukahabako** you are early = huja-
chelewa, umewahi

haha *vt (pt hahíle)* 1 persuade = shawishi 2 propose (marriage) = omba
uchumba 3 court a woman = tongoza

-haají *adv* abusive, negative = tukana

haala *vt (pt haalíle)* fear = ogopa

halísya *vi.med (pt halíisya)* have diarrhea = hara, harisha

hamúka *vi (pt hamwíke)* talk nonsense
= payuka, ropoka

-hangajifú *adj* 1 unconcerned = -siojali
2 lazy, idle = -vivu

hangajika *vi (pt hangajíike)* fret, be
worried = hangaika

-hano *num* five = tano

heeha *vi (pt heehíle)* 1 whisper =
nong'ona 2 slander, gossip = teta

hehelana *vb.recip (pt heheleene)* whisper to each other = nong'onezana,
teteana

helúla *vt (pt helwíle)* abuse, insult =
tukana

hema *vi (pt hemíle)* breathe heavily,
pant = hema, tweta, pumua

hena *vt (pt heníle)* renounce, reject =
kataa, dharau

henula *vb (pt henwíile)* despise = dharau

-heesya *adj* foreign, strange, irregular =
-geni

hiija *vt (pt hiijíle)* steal, rob = iba

himma, mma *adv* An expression of dis-
agreement, no, not, not so = hapana

hinja *vt (pt hinjíle)* slaughter = chinja

-hobofú *adj* 1 happy = -enye furaha 2
free = -huru 3 loose = -legevu, -lio
legea 4 forgiving = -samehevu

hoboka *vi (hobwíke)* 1 be happy, be
glad = furahi 2 cheer = furahia

3 celebrate = sherekea

hobokela *vt (pt hobokíile)* forgive, pardon, = samehe, toa msamaha
uhobokelege excuse me = unisamehe

hobola *vt (pt hobwíle)* 1 free sb, loosen
= fanya nafuu (mtu, ng'ombe), legeza
2 relax = pumzisha

hobosya *vb (pt hobwíisye)* be enjoyable,
be delightful, amuse = furahisha

homba *vt (pt hombíle)* pay, disburse,
recompense = lipa

hona *vi* snore = koroma usingizini
hona amahono snore = koroma

honga *vb (pt hongíle; > Swa)* bribe =
honga, toa mlungula

honyoka *vi (pt honywíle)* be slackened
= legea

honyola *vt (pt honywíile)* 1 slacken,
loosen = legeza 2 relax = pumzika;
honyola amaka make sb lose energy
after being disappointed by hearing
bad news = tengua nguvu (k.m. kwa
taarifa ya majonzi)

hotí *interj* Word used instead of knock-
ing on the door in Bantu culture =
hodi

húhúla *vb (pt huhwíile / húhúlíle)* jeer
at = zomea

huluhuja *n.zool (ba-, 1a/2)* type of
chicken without feathers on the neck
= kuku asiye na manyoya shingoni

24

Ii

If you can not find a word under **í - / íí-** try under **ilí-** and vice versa

íba *vt (pt iibíle)* steal = iba

ibakúlí *n (-, 9/10; >Arab)* bowl = bakuli

ibalutí *n (-, 9/10)* gunpowder = baruti

ibamía (Abelmoschus esculentus) *n.bot (-, 9/10)* okra, lady's finger = bamia, binda

íbila *vi (pt íbííle)* sink = zama

íbililamo *vi (pt íbilílemo)* hide oneself in = jifiche ndani ya

ibílínganía *n.bot (-, 9/10; > Persian)* egg-plant, aubergine (UK) = biringani, biringanya, biringiani

íbisya *vt.caus (pt íbiísye)* **1** drown, immerse sb/sth = zamisha **2** dip = zamisha, chovya

ibofesí *n (-, 9/10; > Eng)* office = ofisi

íbona *vi (pt íbweene)* boast = jiona, jivuna

ibujisanía *vi (pt ibujiseenie)* go and return again = nenda na rudi

íbuka *vi (pt íbwííke)* spring up, emerge = ibuka

  ulwísí lwíbwíke a stream has sprung up = chemchemi imetokea

ibúkya *n (-, 9/10)* butchery = mahali pa kuuzia nyama

ibulausí *n (-, 9/10; > Eng)* blouse = blauzi

íbuna *vi (pt íbuníle)* be perplexed, be depressed = fadhaika

íbúnesya *vi (pt íbunesíísye)* grumble, complain, growl = nung'unika

íbwa *vt (pt íbíbwe)* forget = sahau

idígílíí *n (-, 9/10)* degree = shahada

ielía *n (-, 9/10)* (radio) antenna = eria, chuma kitokezacho juu ya redio ili kuongeza usikivu wa matangazo

ifí *pron (8)* which = ambavyo

ifí *pron* these = hivi

ifífítusyungutíle *n (8)* environment,

surrounding = vinavyotuzunguka, mazingira

ifílimbí *n (-, 9/10)* whistle = filimbi

ifílombe *n.bot (8)* corn /maize (UK) on the field or the final produce = mahindi

ifímba *n.med (-, 9/10)* **1** type of disease with pain in hipjoints (mostly older people. Commonly caused through witchcraft) = Aina ya ugonjwa wenye kuleta maumivu kwenye viungo (hasa kwa watu wazee. Mara nyingi husababishwa na uchawi) **2** type of disease whereby a person feels pain in the bones = ugonjwa wa mifupa

ifíndu *n (8)* food = chakula

ifínga *n (8)* a bitter drink like vinegar = kinywaji kichungu kama siki

ifíngila *n.med* type of medicine = aina ya dawa ya kienyeji

ifíngwa *n (8)* **1** pile of rocks = fungu la mawe **2** pile of shit = fungu la mavi

ifítwalo *n (8)* cargo = shehena

ifúbú *n.zool (-, 9/10)* hippopotamus = kiboko

ífufuma *n.zool (-, 9/10)* type of owl = aina ya bundi

ifújo, ifúújo *n (10)* **1** confusion = fujo **2** scorn, contempt = dharau

ifúko *n.zool (-, 9/10)* mole = fuko

ifúla *n (9)* rain = mvua

ifúlúbili *n.zool (-, 9/10)* type of small black bird = aina ya ndege, mdogo mweusi akaaye kando ya maji (hasa hasa bwawani)

ifulupu *n (-, 9/10)* envelope = bahasha

ifumbaalo *n.anat (-, 9/10)* calf (of leg) = sehemu ya nyuma ya mguu chini ya goti, juu ya kisigino

ífúna *vi (pt iifúníle)* boast = jisifu

ifúngila *n.med (-, 9/10)* medicine made of fat from a python = dawa iliyotengenezwa kwa mafuta ya chatu

ifungo *n.zool (ba-, 1a/2)* civet cat = fungo

ífúngú *prep* under something (eg. bed,

table) = uvungu, chini ya, hasa chini
ya kitanda au meza

ifwa *n (9)* mourning, funeral = msiba,
kílio, matanga

ifwagilo *n (-, 9/10)* work = kazi
utwa fwagilo How is work (greeting)
= Habari za kazi

ifwefwe *n (-, 9/10)* bamboo straw for
drinking ikimpumu/kipumu (type of
beer) = mkenge, mrija wa mwanzi wa
kufyonzea pombe (ikimpumu)

ifwingili *n.zool (-, 9/10)* maggot = funza

ifya *part (8)* of = ya

ifyakulya *n* food = chakula

ifyakumela *n* something which grows,
plants = mimea, uoto, vitu vyenye
kuota

ifyuma *n (8)* wealth, valuables = mali

-ifyusí *adj* clean all the time, smart
looking, fashionable = tanashati,
-enye ulimbwende
/Opposite bwafú, bwapufú

ígala *vt (pt ígeele)* close, shut (eg.
door), lock, bolt = funga (mlango)

igalila *vt.appl (pt igalíile)* fasten, tie,
lock etc. with, in etc = fungia (ndani)

ígana *vt (pt íganíle)* **1** prefer = pendelea
2 like, love = penda; **íganapo** choose
(among these) = chagua; **Níganíle
ikyai** but **Nunganíle umúndu**

íganía *vi (pt ígeníe)* imitate, act (theater
etc.) = igiza

igongo *n (-, 9/10)* illicit liquor = gongo

ígubogubo *n (imí-)* cast off skin = ngozi
iliyochubuliwa

íguka *vi.stat (pt ígwííke)* be opened =
funguka

ígula *vt (pt ígwíle)* **1** open, unlock, undo
= fungua **2** reveal = onyesha wazi,
fumbua **3** disclose = weka wazi, fungua

ígwila *vi (pt ígwilíile)* arrive from a
long journey only to find your hosts
not present = fika toka safari ya mbali
na kukuta wenyeji wako hawapo

ihalale *n.bot (-, 9/10)* **1** banana, generic

term for banana = ndizi **2** type of banana, fat = bokoboko

iheka *n (-, 9/10; > Eng)* acre = ekari

ihela *n (-, 9/10, > Germ. Heller)*
money, cash = pesa, fedha

ihelení *n (ba-, 1a/2)* earring = hereni

ija, ja *part (ijia)* "of" ("genitive"), with
= -a
ikyai ja lukama tea with milk = chai
ya maziwa
ija lukama it (eg. tea) with milk = ya
maziwa

íjaja *vb (pt íjajíle)* complain = lalamika

íjanda *vi (pt íjandíle)* repeat, start
things anew = anza mambo upya, jita-
yarishe

íjeekela *vi (pt íjeekíile)* be in privacy,
be in seclusion = kaa faragha

íjelusya *vi (pt íjelwísye)* purify oneself
= jitakasa

íjepusya *vt (pt íjepwíísye)* avoid =
jitenga, jizuie

íjimika *vi (pt íjimíike)* behave = kuwa
na mwenendo mzuri

íjimilisya *vb (pt íjimilíísye)* urinate, pee
= enda haja ndogo, kojoa

ijogobele *n.zool (-, 9/10)* type of bird =
aina ya ndege

ijogolofía *n (-, 9/10)* geography =
jiografia

íjolo *adv* old times, the past, long ago =
zamani, kale

-a íjolo *adj* ancient = -a zamani

ijometeli *n (-, 9/10)* geometry = jiome-
tria

ijomola *vb (pt íjomwííle)* somersault =
pinduka

íjuula *vi (pt íjuulíle)* struggle, work
hard = fanya juhudi, jitahidi

íjúmbata *vi (pt íjúmbeete)* be hunched
up, cross ones arms = jikunyata

íjumilisya *vt.caus (pt íjumilíísye)* make
an effort = jitahidi

íka *vi (pt íkíle)* **1** descend, climb down
= shuka **2** drop, fall (eg. tears, sweat)
= teremka, dondoka (machozi, jasho)

ikaabatí *n (-, 9/10, > Eng)* cupboard = kabati

ikaabíkí *n.bot (-, 9/10)* cabbage = kabeji, kabichi

ikabuundu *n (-, 9/10)* shorts = kaptula

ikahabwa *n (-, 9/10, < Arab.)* coffee = kahawa

ikalata *n (-, 9/10)* 1 letter, card = barua 2 book = kitabu

ikalenda *n (-, 9/10; Latin)* calendar = kalenda

ikalotí *n.bot (-, 9/10)* carrot = karoti

ikambaaní *n.bot (-, 9/10)* type of banana = aina ya ndizi, kisukari

íkasya *vb (pt íkasísye)* 1 bear, tolerate = vumilia 2 try one's best = jikaza

ikataní *n (-, 9/10)* sisal fibre = katani

íkemo *adj* 1 sacrificial = -a sadaka 2 sacred, holy, pious saintly = -takatifu

iki *pron* which = ambacho

ikibabiilisí *n (ifí-, 7/8)* sympathy, mercy, pity = huruma

ikibafu *n (ifí-, 7/8)* 1 direction = uelekeo 2 side = upande

ikibaga *n (ifí-, 7/8)* 1 byre, stable (for cows) = nyumba ya mifugo 2 shed = banda 3 hip roof house, house, hut (for people) = nyumba mgongo wa tembo

ikibalali *n (ifí-, 7/8)* the half (cut lengthwise) = nusu (kwa kugawanya kwa marefu)

ikibaanja *n (ifí-, 7/8)* field, plot of ground = kiwanja

　ikibaanja kya ndege airport = kiwanja cha ndege

ikibebe *n.med (ifí-, 7/8)* ringworm = punye, bato

ikibeja *n.anat (ifí-, 7/8)* shoulder = bega

ikibili *n (ifí-, 7/8)* Tuesday = Jumanne

ikiíbo *n (ifí-, 7/8)* the most typical basket seen in ubuNyakyusa, it is square and ideally colored black by soot (from hanging over the stove) = namna ya kikapu kidogo

ikiboko *n.anat (ama-, 7/6)* hand = mkono

ikibonesyo *n (ifí-, 7/8)* brand = alama

ikiboota *n (ifí-, 7/8)* type of song, along with dancing, but no use of instrument = aina ya wimbo unaoimbwa na kucheza bila kupiga vyombo

ikibugutila *n (ifí-, 7/8)* 1 heap, pile, bundle = lundo 2 group of people = kusanyika la watu

ikibuule *n.med (ifí-, 7/8)* eczema = ugonjwa wa ngozi kama upele mbaya sana

ikibúlí *n.anat (ifí-, 7/8)* fist = konde, ngumi

ikibumba *n (ifí-, 7/8)* 1 red soil = udongo mwekundu 2 hard dried soil = udongo mkavu mgumu

ikibumbígwa *n (ifí-, 7/8)* creature = kiumbe

ikibúndya *n (ifí-, 7/8)* 1 club (for hitting) = rungu, kirungu 2 smth short and fat = kitu ambacho ni kinene lakini kifupi
/Also **ikibúndyabúndya**

ikibuungú *n.metal (ifí-, 7/8)* copper = shaba

ikibúsú *n (ifí-, 7/8)* latrine, toilet = choo

ikiíbwa *n (ifí-, 7/8)* forgetfulness = usahaulifu

ikidakí *n* German (eg. language) = kijerumani

ikifígo *n (ifí-, 7/8)* 1 address = anwani 2 doorway (where a door can be put) = mlango, sehemu ya kuingilia ndani ya nyumba

ikifíla *n.off (ifí-, 7/8)* cunt = kuma

ikifúba *n.med (ifí-, 7/8)* pregnancy = mimba

PREGNANCY AND DEATH
If a pregnant Nyakyusa woman dies, the child is taken out and buried in a separate grave

---

ikifufumbwa *n (ifi-, 7/8; Kye)* bird's nest = kiota

ikifuge *n (ifi-, 7/8)* type of dish, crushed sweet potato and beans = mchanyato wa viazi vitamu na maharagwe uliopondwapondwa

ikifuja *n (ifi-, 7/8)* arable land, uncultivated but fertile land = shamba lenye rutuba ambalo halijalimwa

ikifúlalo *n.med (ifi-,7/8)* wound = jeraha

ikifúlú *n (ifi-, 7/8)* type of large calabash = aina ya kibuyu kikubwa

ikifúmbwa *n (ifi-, 7/8; Tuk)* bird's nest = kiota

/Kye: **ikifufumbwa**

ikifúmo *n (ifi-, 7/8)* nature = asili

ikifúndikililo *n (ifi-, 7/8)* **1** knot = kifundo, fundo **2** cork = kizibo

ikifundikilo *n (ifi-, 7/8)* lid = mfuniko (aina ya magunzi, kimti, majani yaliyo sokotwa) eg **ikifundikilo kya lupaale** lid of … = kifuniko cha kibuyu

ikifúndiko *n (ifi-, 7/8)* **1** lid, cover = mfuniko **2** cork, bung = kizibo

ikifúndo *n (ifi-, 7/8)* knot = fundo

ikifunga *n (ifi-, 7/8)* underskirt = vazi la kike la kuvaa kiunoni ndani ya gauni / mavazi ya nje

ikifúngo *n (ifi-, 7/8)* bond = kifungo

ikifúngúla *n (ifi-, 7/8)* A small banana bunch. Withered banana plant that has brought little fruit. That fruit is called **ifúpúla** = Mkungu wa ndizi mdogo. Mgomba ulionyauka na uliozaa mkungu mdogo. Mkungu huo itwa ifúpúla

ikifúpa *n (ifi- 7/8)* bone = mfupa

/Also **ulufúpa**, **umfúpa**

ikifwambilo *n (ifi-, 7/8)* opening in a fishtrap, The opening in the fishtrap that allows the fish to enter but not to go back out= fumiko wa mgono wenye shimo la kuingilia samaki

ikifwaní *n (ifi-, 7/8)* **1** picture = picha **2** statue, figure = sanamu, umbo

3 carving = kinyago **4** image = taswira

ikifwaníkisyo *n (ifi-, 7/8)* example = mfano

íkífya *vt.caus (pt íkífifye)* do your best, try your best = jikaza

ikigala *n.bot (ifi-, 7/8)* water lily = aina ya mmea uotao majini

ikíígalilo *n (ifi-, 7/8)* lock = komeo

ikigamba *n (ifi-, 7/8)* patch = kiraka

ikigane *n (ifi-, 7/8)* darling, boyfriend, girlfriend, lover = mpenzi, kipenzi

ikigela *n (ifi-, 7/8)* The metal connecting the spear and the stick = chuma kiunganisha mkuki na mti

ikigelelo *n (ifi-, 7/8)* criterion = kigezo

ikigeletí *n (ifi-, 7/8)* chariot = gari la farasi

/Also **igeletí**

ikigemo *n (ifi-, 7/8)* **1** kiln = tanuri **2** The area of the church where the priest performs during the sermon, pulpit, altar = mahali pa kufanyia ibada, mimbari, madhabahu, altare

ikigemo kya kwíkemekesyapo *n (ifi-, 7/8)* place where sacrifice is offered, this could be in a church or at the **ilísyeto** = mahali pa hutolea kafara

ikíígí *n (ifi-, 7/8)* **1** a small door on the fish trap = kimlango kati ya mihimili unapo tegwa mgono **2** stick to block the door of the house from the inside

ikigili *n (ifi-, 7/8)* madness = kichaa, wazimu

ikigíma *n (ifi-, 7/8)* cliff = genge

ikigogo *n (ifi-, 7/8)* yoke = nira

ikigubo *n (ifi-, 7/8)* hide, skin, leather = ngozi

ikigugu *n.bot (ifigugu, 7/8)* napier grass, elephant grass = bingobingo

ikíígulilo *n (ifiígulilo, 7/8)* opener = kitu kitumikacho kufungulia, kifungulio

ikigulu *n (ifi-, 7/8)* thunder = ngurumo

ikigúne *n (ifi-, 7/8)* curse = laana

ikigwaja *n (7)* plague = tauni

ikigwata *n.med (ifi-, 7/8)* type of infant's abnormality characterized by growling sounds = hali ya mtoto mchanga kutoa mikoromo mara kwa mara

ikihaano *n (ifi-, 7/8)* Friday = Ijumaa

ikihombígwa *n (ifi-, 7/8)* fine = faini, adhabu ya kulipwa

ikijabo *n (ifi-, 7/8)* 1 part, fraction, piece, share = sehemu, sehemu ya chakula au mali, hisa 2 allocation = mgawo, fungu, kifungu 3 talent, gift = kipawa, kipaji; **ikijabo kya kíísu** area = eneo la ardhi; **Ajabilígwe ikijabo ikya buhiji** He is a talented thief = Ana kipawa cha wizi

ikijinja (Musa spp) *n.bot (ifi-, 7/8)* banana plant = mgomba

ikijínulilo kya kuntu *n (ifi-, 7/8)* pillow = mto wa kulalia

ikijolo *n (ifi-, 7/8)* the day before yesterday = juzi

ikiika *n (ifi-, 7/8)* miracle, marvel, wonder = maajabu, kioja

ikikahula *n (ifi-, 7/8)* pliers = koleo

ikikalangilo *n (ifi-, 7/8)* frying pan = kikaango

ikikali *n.slang (ifi-, 7/8)* expensive things esp. clothing, fish (fish is more expensive than meat) = vitu vya gharama

ikikanda *n (ifi-, 7/8)* skin = ngozi

ikikando *n (ifi-, 7/8)* dough = mkando, kinyunga

ikikangato *n.anat (ifi-, 7/8)* heel = kisigino

ikikanísyo *n (ifi-, 7/8)* check = kizuizi, kizuio

ikikapu *n (ifi-, 7/8; >Swa)* basket = kikapu
/See **ikitundu**

ikikaasa *n (ifi-, 7/8)* roe = mayai ya samaki

ikikasíngilo *n (ifi-, 7/8)* frying pan, pan for dry frying = chombo cha kukaangia k.m. bisi, karanga

ikikato *n (ifi-, 7/8)* footprint = wayo

ikikele *n (ifi-, 7/8)* tip of the penis = kichwa cha mboo

ikikeno *n.anat (ifi-, 7/8)* gums = ufizi

ikikeetelo *n (ifi-, 7/8)* mirror = kioo (cha kujitazamia)

ikikíngí *n (ifi-, 7/8)* 1 peg = mambo 2 peg for tethering an animal = kigingi

ikiko *n (ifi-, 7/8)* the dirt which is rubbed off the body when one perspires= nongo, taka za mwili

ikííko *n (ifi-, 7/8, > Swa)* pipe, something used for smoking = kiko

ikikohekano *n (ifi-, 7/8)* cross = msalaba

ikikoho *n.anat (ifi-, 7/8)* tip of the elbow = ncha ya kiko

ikikole *n (ifi-, 7/8)* Money given to the fiancée so she can inform her parents of her engagement. The money is kept by the girl and she will use it for smth useful like plates or clothes = pesa za utambulisho kwa uchumba, kishika uchumba

ikikolelanyale *n (ifi-, 7/8)* lamp holder (candle) = chombo cha kuwekea mshumaa

ikikolelo *n (ifi-, 7/8)* 1 tongs = koleo 2 handle = mpini 3 hinge = bawaba 4 rudder = usukani

ikikolo *n (ifi-, 7/8)* 1 tribe, nationality = kabila, utaifa 2 family, kin, kindred = jamaa, ukoo 3 birth = uzao 4 type = aina 5 quality = ubora 6 shape = namna, sura 7 stem, tree trunk = shina
~ **kya sítíma** fleet = kundi la meli aina moja
~ **kya mpíkí** stem, stock = shina

ikikombe *n (ifi-, 7/8)* cup = kikombe

ikikome *n (ifi-, 7/8; Tuk)* uncultivated plot = eneo lisilolimwa muda mrefu

ikikongotí *n (ifi-, 7/8)* 1 pillar = nguzo 2 stump (of a tree), stalk, stem = shina, kisiki 3 origin = asili

ikikope *n (ifi-, 7/8)* hem = pindo au ukingo

wa nguo

ikikopo *n (ifí-, 7/8)* **1** can = kikopo
2 jug = jagi
/**ijagi** is commonly heard

ikikosa *n (ifí-, 7/8)* spear (with a flat
metal tip) = mkuki uliobapa mwis-
honi
/ Same as **ingwego**

ikikose *n (ifí-, 7/8)* bundle, bunch =
shada (flowers), kichala (fruits),
chana, chane, kole (bananas)

ikikosí *n.anat (ifí-, 7/8)* back of neck =
upande wa nyuma wa shingo

ikikota *n (ifí-, 7/8)* chair = kiti

ikikuba *n (ifí-, 7/8)* **1** copper, brass =
shaba, shaba nyeupe **2** anklet, bracelet
(made of copper/brass) = bangili
/Base meaning: a reddish metal. The
secondary meaning comes from the
most common usage

ikikubililo *n (ifí-, 7/8)* smth used for
blowing fire, fan, bellows = kitu cha
kupulizia moto

ikikubilo *n (ifí-, 7/8)* drumstick = kidu-
ndio cha ngoma

ikikufí *n (ifí-, 7/8)* a handful = ujazo wa
kiganja, konzi

ikikuga *n (ifí-, 7/8)* remains of burnt
shoots which have been dug out =
mabaki ya vishungi vilivyo chomwa
na kulimwa

ikikúlú *n.anat (ifí-, 7/8)* hip = nyonga,
kiweo

ikikungilwa *n (ifí-, 7/8)* a talent, a natural endowment = kipaji, kipawa

ikikuupe *n (ifí-, 7/8)* diaper = nguo za
kumwisha mtoto

ikikupikililo *n (ifí-, 7/8)* cover, lid,
mask = mfuniko, kifuniko

ikikútúlo *n (ifí-, 7/8)* a cloth made from
sacks = vazi la gunia

ikikwaakwa *n (ifí-, 7/8)* sickle with
teeth = mundu wenye meno kwa ajili
ya kuvunia nafaka

ikikwama *n (ifí-, 7/8)* wallet = pochi,
mkoba mdogo, mfuko

ikikyetí *n (ifí-, 7/8; > Swa)* certificate =
cheti

ikilabú *n (ifí-, 7/8)* **1** bar, pub = kilabu
cha pombe **2** club = kilabu

ikilaambo *n (ifí-, 7/8)* **1** mineral, salt,
soda = magadi **2** the area (pond,
river) where this soda is found = mahali (bwawa, mto) magadi
yanapopatikana

ikilamú *n (ifí-, 7/8)* **1** image = taswira
2 picture = picha **3** statue = sanamu
4 symbol of worship, totem = sanamu
ya ibada

ikilaso, akalaso *n.med (*ifí-, 7/8)* sharp
pain, cramp, stabbing pain = kichomi

ikilasilo *n (ifí-, 7/8)* **1** any tool used for
stabbing = kitu cha kuchomea mf.
Mkuki **2** implement for piercing = ki-
faa cha kuchomea

ikilato *n (ifí-, 7/8)* shoe = kiatu

ikilebe *n.dim (ifí-, 7/8)* small piece of
(metal) tin = kipande cha debe

ikilefú *n.anat (ifí-, 7/8)* chin = kidevu

ikilega *n.anat (ifí-, 7/8)* jaw = taya

ikilema *n.med (ifí-, 7/8)* physical disability, deformity, blemish, defect of
the body = ulemavu, kilema

ikilembeko *n.med (ifí-, 7/8)* type of local medicine = aina ya dawa ya
kienyeji

ikilembelo *n (ifí-, 7/8)* Monday = Jumatatu

ikilepa *n (ifí-, 7/8)* net (for fishing) =
wavu (wa kuvulia samaki)

-íkilí *adj* faithful = -aminifu, -enye
imani

íkilila *vb (pt íkilíile)* **1** head southwards, face southwards = elekea
upande kusini **2** to move back up /
down if you have slid off the mat
while sleeping = kusogea kwa chini
unapokuwa umezidi kwenda juu
wakati wa kulala

ikíílilo *n (ifí-, 7/8)* right hand = mkono
wa kulia

ikilimígwa *ingamwana: ikyaalo* farm,
field = shamba

ikilimilo *n (ifí-, 7/8)* **1** Name of one specific constellation seen in September - October = jina la jamii ya nyota **2** ingamwana word for ikyaka = handle = mpini

ikilimo *n (ifí-, 7/8)* agriculture = kilimo

ikilingo *n (ifí-, 7/8)* form of inheritance whereby only one person is entitled to inheritance = urithi wa mtu mmoja tu

Ikilisímasí *n (ifí-, 7/8)* Christmas, X-mas = Krismasi

ikilo *n (ifí-, 7/8)* night = usiku

ikiloboko *n (ifí-, 7/8)* river crossing, ferry, ford = kivuko

ikilombe *n.bot (ifí-, 7/8)* one single cob of corn /maize = mhindi /you have **ifílombe** in the field, a single cob is **ikilombe**, and the final product is **ifílombe**

ikiloonda *n.med (*ifí-, 7/8) **1** wound = jeraha **2** sore = kidonda **3** ulcer = jipu

ikilugu *n (ifí-, 7/8)* enmity, aggression = uadui

ikilumyana *n (ifí-, 7/8)* young boys' village = mji wa vijana wasiooa

ikiluundi *n.anat (ama-, 7/6)* leg = mguu

ikilundiko *n (ifí-, 7/8)* heap = rundo, fungo

ikilundilo *n (ifí-, 7/8)* **1** a group of people, crowd = mkusanyiko wa watu wengi, kikundi **2** troop = jeshi **3** multitude, gathering = mkusanyiko **4** party = jamii, chama **5** flock, herd = kundi (la wanyama) ~ **kya nsanga** pile of sand = lundo la mchanga

ikilundo *n (ifí-, 7/8)* garment = vazi (hasa refu)

ikilúngú *n.zool (ifí-, 7/8)* porcupine = nungu, nungunungu

ikiluungo *n (ifí-, 7/8)* limb = sehemu ya mwili

ikilwilo *n (ifí-, 7/8)* weapon = silaha

ikímama *n (ifí-, 7/8)* left hand = mkono wa kushoto

ikimanyílo *n (ifí-, 7/8)* **1** sign, mark, signal, signpost = alama, kibao, ishara **2** token, badge, peculiarity= alama, ishara **3** lesson, subject, topic = funzo, somo **4** evidence = ushahidi **5** seal = muhuri ~ **kya fínyamaana** zoology = zoolojia

ikimbímbí *n (ifí-, 7/8)* cone shaped drum = tumba

ikimbumila *n (ifí-, 7/8)* A table which is inside. If it is outside it is called **ikitalati** = meza ya ndani

ikimbúsú *n (ifí-, 7/8)* latrine, toilet = choo /Variation of **ikibúsú**

ikimeele *n (ifí-, 7/8)* type of song, use of calabash and dancing = aina ya wimbo unaocheziwa kutumia vibuyu

ikimeenya *n (ifí-, 7/8)* piece = kipande

ikimetelo *n (ifí-, 7/8)* scissors = mkasi

ikimogo *n (ifí-, 7/8)* dance = mchezo wa ngoma

ikimpumu, ikipumu *n (ifí-, 7/8)* type of millet beer. It is drunk with a bamboo straw called **ifwefwe** = Aina ya pombe ya ulezi inywewayo kwa kufyonza kwa mkenge

ikimweku *n (ifí-, 7/8)* flash = metameta

ikimwemweta *n (ifí-, 7/8)* mirror = kioo

ikina *n (ifí-, 7/8)* Thursday = Alhamisi

ikíína *n (ifí-, 7/8)* **1** well, waterhole, waterpit = kisima **2** hole, pit = shimo **3** cavity = tundu, shimo **4** burrow = shimo la wanyama **5** ravine = korongo

ikinaganíko *n (ifí-, 7/8)* defect = upungufu

ikinanaasí *n.bot (ifí, 7/8)* pineapple = nanasi

ikinangisyo *n (ifí-, 7/8)* **1** brand = alama **2** show = maonyesho

ikindimbwíili *n (ifí-, 7/8)* puddle = dimbwi, bwawa

ikindíngo *n.zool (ifí-, 7/8)* hyena = fisi

ikinena *n.anat (ifí-, 7/8)* groin, crotch = kinena

ikingelesí *n (ifí-, 7/8)* English (language) = kiingereza

iking'oko *n.anat (ifí-, 7/8)* fist = ngumi

ikingotí *n (ifí-, 7/8)* whip (esp from

hippo skin) = kiboko, mjeledi

ikiníe *n.anat (ifi-, 7/8)* liver = ini

ikiníelo *n (ifi-, 7/8)* **1** *n.off* asshole = mkundu **2** *n.anat* anus = mkundu, mwaranda

ikinúúnú *n.med (ifi-, 7/8)* muteness, dumbness = ububu, hali ya kutokuzungumza; **ugwa kinúúnú** a mute = bubu

ikinwegwa *n (ifi-, 7/8)* drink = kinywaji

ikinwelo *n (ifi-, 7/8)* smth used to drink with = kitu cha kunywea k.m. bakuli, kikombe n.k.

ikinyamaana *n (ifi-, 7/8)* animal = mnyama

ikinyambi *n (ifi-, 7/8)* **1** small bag, purse = mfuko mdogo **2** pocket = mfuko

ikinyanyasí *n (ifi-, 7/8)* nausea, disgust = kinyaa, karaha

ikinyonyo *n (ifi-, 7/8)* longing, craving, desire = tamaa

ikinyonywo *n (ifi-, 7/8)* longing, lust = tamaa

ikinyoselo *n (ifi-, 7/8)* fork = uma

ikipagasa *n (ifi-, 7/8)* hanging chicken coop = kichanja cha kuku kinacho-ning'inia

ikipahu *n (ifi-, 7/8)* indifference, apathy = utepetevu, bila upole, bila wema, bila imani
/Also **ikipaho**

ikipake *n (ifi-, 7/8)* **1** gourd used to store oil (often castor oil) = aina ya kibuyu (mara nyingi cha duara) cha kutunzia mafuta ya mbarika au mibu-ni **2** *n.zool* duck = batamaji

ikipala *n (ifi-, 7/8)* something which is difficult to get = kitu kigumu kupatikana

ikipaala *n (ifi-, 7/8)* baldness = upara

ikipalo *n (ifi-, 7/8)* floor = sakafu

ikipambaga *n.anat (ifi-, 7/8)* chest, bosom = kifua
kuja nikipambaga to cough = kohoa

ikipambo *n (ifi-, 7/8)* a banana bunch-let, banana cluster = chane

ikipande *n (ifi-, 7/8)* **1** bill = karatasi ya

malipo **2** card (hospital card, work card) = kadi (kadi ya hospitali, kadi ya kazi) **3** piece = kipande

ikipaanga *n (ifi-, 7/8)* village, town = kijiji; **aba kipaanga** villagers = wa-nakijiji

ikipapa *n (ifi-, 7/8)* **1** hide, skin of an animal, leather = ngozi **2** *n.slang* lean, tasteless meat = nyama isiyo-nona

ikipata *n (ifi-, 7/8)* **1** gate = lango **2** button = kifunguo

ikipatala *n (ifi-, 7/8)* hospital, clinic = hospitali

ikipatala ikinandi dispensary = zahanati

ikipaatu *n (ifi-, 7/8)* **1** piece of bark = gamba **2** splinter = kibanzi

ikipeegwa *n (ifi-, 7/8)* cap = kofia

ikipela *n (ifi-, 7/8)* cause = sababu, asili

ikipelígwa *n (ifi-, 7/8)* creature = kiumbe

ikipembelo *n (ifi-, 7/8)* hearth = meko

ikipepele *n (ifi-, 7/8)* honey comb = sega

ikipeepe *n (ifi-, 7/8)* diaper = vitambaa

ikipepo *n (ifi, 7/8)* shade = kivuli

ikipeto *n (ifi-, 7/8)* **1** bag (with contents) = kipeto **2** piece of cloth of mat = kipande cha nguo au mkeka

ikipíkí *n (ifi-, 7/8)* **1** trunk, log = gogo **2** stump, wooden bar = kisiki, ubao, mambo **3** *n.slang* medicine = dawa

ikipiko *n (ifi-, 7/8)* wing = ubawa

ikipímba *n (ifi-, 7/8)* **1** the half (divided across) = nusu (kwa kugawanya kwa mapana) **2** *n.bot* type of tree used to produce a powder which is mixed with oil as a body lotion = aina ya mti unatoa poda ichanganywayo na mafu-ta kwa ajili ya kupaka mwilini **3** type of red root used as a die and cosmetic (Bought in the old days from the Ma-hasi from Usangu) = aina ya mzizi

ikipimbilo *n (ifi-, 7/8)* **1** carriage = cho-mbo cha kubeba **2** stretcher = mache-la, kitu cha kubebea wagonjwa

ikipimilo *n (ifi-, 7/8)* **1** measure = kipimio

2 gauge = kigezo

ikipimilo ikibúlúnge circumference = mzingo

ikipimilo kya lufuku thermometer = pimajoto

ikipímo *n (ifí-, 7/8)* measure, rate = kipimo, kiwango

ikipiindo *n (ifí-, 7/8)* trap = mtego

ikipindupindu *n.med (*ifí-, 7/8) cholera = kipindupindu

ikipogojo *n (ifí-, 7/8)* shelf = rafu

ikipolopolo *n (ifí-, 7/8)* gun = bunduki

ikipome *n (ifí-, 7/8)* crushed peanuts = karanga zilizopondwapondwa, hutumika kuunga kwenye chakula kama vile mboga, viazi, ndizi n.k.

ikipondo *n (ifí-, 7/8)* trough (for feeding livestock) = hori

ikipotelo *n (ifí-, 7/8)* **1** steering wheel = usukani **2** rudder = usukani

ikipululilo *n (ifí-, 7/8)* (tool) plane = randa

ikipúmú *n (ifí-, 7/8)* local beer made from fingermillet = pombe ya ulezi, kipumu

ikipúngúnyo *n (ifí-, 7/8)* (trees) knot, nodule = fundo

ikipuusí *n.dish (ifí-, 7/8)* boiled banana mixed with peanuts = ndizi za kupikwa zilizochanganywa na karanga

ikipúúto *n.anat (ifí-, 7/8)* the protruding bones of the ankle or elbow = kifundo cha mguuni na mikononi cha mfupa uliojitokeza

ikisa *n (ifí-, 7/8)* **1** sympathy, mercy, pity= huruma **2** grief, sadness = huzuni **3** courtesy = adabu
gwa kisa merciful = -enye rehema

ikisaguka *n.bot (ifí-, 7/8)* type of parasitic plant = aina ya mmea unaoota juu ya mwingine

ikisaka *n (ifí-, 7/8)* parcel, packet = mzigo, kifurushi

ikisaame *n (ifí-, 7/8)* deserted place, abandoned village = mahame

ikisanjulilo *n (ifí-, 7/8)* comb = chanuo

ikisaasaa *n (ifí-, 7/8)* bunch of paddy / wheat etc. = suke

ikisegeselo *n (ifí-, 7/8)* sieve (for flour) = chekecho

ikisene *n.med (ifí-, 7/8)* hydrocele, swelling of scrotum = busha

ikiseenga *n (ifí-, 7/8)* colostrum (first milk) = maziwa ya mwanzo

ikisengeela *n (ifí-, 7/8)* **1** any small bush in a rather open space = kichaka kidogo katika sehemu iliyo wazi **2** *n.bot* type of strong grass = aina ya nyasi ngumu

ikiseseketo *n (ifí-, 7/8)* large basket = aina ya kikapu kikubwa

ikisíba *n (ifí-, 7/8)* **1** pond, pool, a body of water smaller than a lake = bwawa **2** the deep part of a body of water = kina cha maji **3** dam = bwawa

ikisíge *n (amaso, 7/6)* eye = jicho
-fwa maso blind = pofu

ikisíku *n (ifí-, 7/8)* rainy season, long rains = masika

ikisínga *n* **1** log = gogo **2** stump = kisiki

ikisingo *n (ifí-, 7/8)* type of medicine used to protect against thieves = aina ya dawa ambao kutumika dhidhi ya wezi

ikisípa *n (ifí-, 7/8)* fishing line = mshipi

ikisípa *n (ifí-, 7/8)* a non-twined fishing line = mshipi

ikisítu *n (ifí- 7/8, Tuk; Kye -> ilítengele)* forest, wood = msitu, mwitu

ikisondela *n (ifí-, 7/8)* type of basket = aina ya kikapu

ikisondelo *n (ifí-, 7/8)* funnel = mpare

ikisonge *n (ifí-, 7/8)* **1** conical shaped roof = msonge, paa la ghala au nyumba la mviringo **2** tower = mnara /For tower see Ubwandilo 11.4

ikisotolelo *n (ifí-, 7/8)* **1** any tool used for piercing / boring = kitu chochote cha kutobolea **2** drill = kekee

ikíísu *n (ifí-, 7/8)* **1** country, nation = nchi **2** land, earth, ground = udongo, ardhi

ikisugujila *n (ifi-, 7/8)* a bush which stands alone = kichaka kinachojitegemea

ikisujilo *n (ifi-, 7/8)* strainer, filter = chujio

ikisuujwa *n (ifi-, 7/8)* porridge made from tender maize = uji wa mahindi mateke

ikisulu *n (ifi-, 7/8)* a sewing machine = cherehani

ikisyanju *n (ifi-, 7/8)* small bush, shrub, thicket = kichaka

ikiswígo *n (ifi-, 7/8)* amazement, wonder, miracle = mshangao, maajabu, kioja

ikisyesye *n (ifi-, 7/8)* bread, loaf = mkate

ikitabu *n (ifi-, 7/8)* **1** *n.med* stammering, stuttering = kigugumizi **2** *n (< Swa < Arab)* book = kitabu

ikitajataja *n (ifi-, 7/8)* thunder = ngurumo

ikitala *n (ifi-, 7/8)* bed = kitanda

ikitalati *n (ifi-, 7/8)* An outdoors table. If it is inside it is called **ikimbumila** = kichanja, kichaga. /Used for drying coffee berries, parethrum flower etc.

ikitambaala *n (ifi-, 7/8)* cloth, rag = kitambaa

ikitambaala kya kusugusulila towel = taulu

ikitambaala kya mmaboko handkerchief = leso

ikitambaala kya kuntu headcloth, turban = kitambaa cha kichwa

ikitambaala kya kilonda bandage = utambaa

ikitana *n (ifi-, 7/8)* a bamboo cup = kikombe cha mwanzi

ikitanda *n (ifi-, 7/8)* poison = sumu

ikitangalala *n (ifi-, 7/8)* The dwelling of a chief (the house(s) and the surrounding property), palace = makazi ya mfalme, mtawala

ikitapwa *n.derog.dim (ifi-, 7/8, >ilítapwa)* **1** a small piece of timber = ubao mdogo **2** a small left over piece of timber = ubao mdogo uliosalia

ikitaasya *n.med (ifi-, 7/8)* cattle disease (from inbreeding) = ugonjwa wa

ng'ombe unaotokana na wao kuzaliana wao kwa wao

ikitatu *n (ifi-, 7/8)* Wednesday = Jumatano

ikitele *n (ifi-, 7/8)* **1** brooding nest = mahali pa kutagia mayai **2** the place in birds where there is ova = sehemu ndani ya mwili wa ndege ambayo huifadhi mayai

ikitembe *n (ifi-, 7/8)* hut, cottage, booth = kibanda

ikitende *n.anat (ifi-, 7/8)* heel = kisigino

ikitendeko *n (ifi-, 7/8)* thing = kitu

ikitengusí *n (ifi-, 7/8)* astonishment = mshangao

ikitílí *n (ifi-, 7/8)* hat, cap = kofia

ikitílu *n (ifi-, 7/8)* lawn = nyasi zilizostawishwa na kutunzwa /Also **akatílu**

ikitíma *n (ifi-, 7/8)* emotion = mchomo wa moyo

ikitondolelo *n (ifi-, 7/8)* any tool for harvesting corn = kifaa chochote cha kuvunia mazao ya nafaka

ikituuba *n (ifi-, 7/8)* granary, store room = ghala

ikitubulo *n (ifi-, 7/8)* a drilled hole = shimo lililopekechwa

ikitugu *n.bot (ifi-, 7/8)* yam = kiazi kikuu

ikituli *n (ifi-, 7/8)* **1** mortar = kinu **2** mill = mashine ya kusaga / kukoboa, kinu

ikitúlí *n (ifi-, 7/8)* **1** piece (of meat) = kipande cha nyama **2** lump of food = tonge

ikitulutulu *n (ifi-, 7/8)* **1** dynamite = baruti **2** copper sulphate $CuSo_4$ used to cure sores, a disease which prevailed before the 1960'es = dawa iliyotumika kutibu vidonda ndugu mruturutu

ikitúmbwike *n (ifi-, 7/8)* type of Nyakyusa dance with drums = ngoma ya asili ya wanyakyusa

ikitundu *n (ifi-, 7/8)* small basket of plaited leafstrips or grass with two handles = kikapu kilichosukwa kwa makuti au ukindu

ikitungulu *n.bot (ifi-, 7/8)* onion = kitunguu

ikitungulu saumu *n.bot* garlic = kitunguu saumu

ikitúsú *n (ifi-, 7/8)* bizzarre doings = majisifu

ikitwa *n (ifi-, 7/8)* teat discharge from pregnant mammals about to give birth = maji meupe kama maziwa yatokayo kwenye maziwa ya mnyama au mwanamke akaribiaye kuzaa

ikitwalo *n (ifi-, 7/8)* **1** baggage, luggage = mzigo **2** load, bundle = mzigo

ikitwanga *n.dim (ifi-, 7/8; > indwanga)* hatchet = kishoka

ikokoto *n (10; > Swa)* gravel = kokoto /Also **isangalabwe**

íkola *vi.refl (pt íkolíle)* get caught, be stuck, get stuck= kamatwa, naswa, kwama

íkolaanía *vi (pt íkoleníe)* be engaged in various businesses at a time = shughulika na mambo mengi kwa wakati mmoja

íkúnda *vi.reflex (pt íkúndíle)* come near = jivuta, jisogeza

íkuta *vi (pt íkwíte)* be full, be satisfied (from eating) = shiba

íkutisya *vt.caus (pt íkutísye)* satisfy = shibisha

ikwaja *n (-, 9/10; > Eng)* choir = kwaya

ikyabupe *n (ifya-, 7/8)* gift (normally an offering to a god), present = sadaka, zawadi

ikyaí *n (9, < Persian)* tea = chai

ikyaka *n (ifyaka, 7/8)* **1** handle = mpini; **Ikyaka kya ikumbulu** hoe handle = mpini wa jembe **2** holiday = sikukuu

ikyakufyukisya *n (ifya-, 7/8)* hoist = kitu cha kupandisha

ikyala *n.anat (ifyala, 7/8)* finger- or toenail = kucha

ikyalíkí *n (ify-, 7/8, >Eng)* church = kanisa

ikyaalo *n (ify-, 7/8)* farm, field, cultivated land = shamba

ikyaama *n (ifi-, 7/8, < Swa)* cooperative, political party = chama

ikyamafí *n.off (ifyamafí, 7/8)* anus, asshole = mkundu, msamba

ikyamba *n (ify-, 7/8)* mountain = mlima

ikyambilo *n (ify-, 7/8)* container for receiving smth (eg milk) = kitu cha kukingia (k.m. maziwa)

ikyambuko *n.arch.ingamwana (ify-, 7/8)* river crossing, ford = kivuko /new term -> **ikiloboko**

ikyana *n (ifyana, 7/8)* **1** pipe (smoking) = kiko **2** *n.off* small child = kitoto

ikyandalula *n (ifyandalula, 7/8)* mosquito net = chandarua

ikyandilo *n (ify-, 7/8)* a start (salary) = kianzio

ikyanja *n.anat (ifi-, 7/8)* palm of the hand = kiganja, kitanga cha mkono

ikyela *n (ify-, 7/8)* metal = chuma

íkyela *vb (pt íkyelíle)* consent = ridhia, kubali

íkyeela *vi (pt líkyelíle)* be very pleased with = pendezwa

ikyelo *n (ify-, 7/8)* small fishnet = wavu mdogo

ikyembete *n (ify-, 7/8)* plough's share = ulimi wa plau

ikyengenyúma *n.med (ifye-, 7/8)* a hunchback = kibiongo, kibyongo

ikyení *n.anat (ifyení, 7/8)* forehead = paji, paji la uso

ikyeo *n (ifyeo, 7/8)* **1** designation = cheo **2** rank = cheo, daraja

ikyima *n.anat (ifyima, 7/8)* thigh = paja

ikyimilo *n (ifyimilo, 7/8)* **1** stand, something used to stand on = kitu kinachotumika kusimama, kusimamia, ngazi **2** bicycle stand/support = kisimamio cha baisikeli

ikyimo *n (ifyimo, 7/8)* place where livestock rest after returning from grazing before they are driven into the sleeping sheds = mahali pa kupu-mzikia mifugo iliyotoka malishoni kabla ya kuingizwa kwenye banda la kulala

35

ikyindi *n (ify-, 7/8)* stiff poridge = ugali

ikyinja *n (ifi-, 7/8)* year = mwaka

ikyogelo *n (ify-, 7/8)* bathroom = bafu

ikyokela *n (ify-, 7/8)* body odor = harufu ya mwili

ikyokelo *n (ify-, 7/8)* **1** grill for roasting = kichomeo, jiko la kuchomea **2** the grid between the food and the source of heat on a grill = chombo cha fito za chuma cha kuokea nyama, waya wa kuchomea

ikyoko *n (ifyoko, 7/8; > Eng, > Greek khalix)* chalk = chaki

ikyokolelo *n (ifyokolelo, 7/8)* utensil for carrying fire = kitu cha kuchukulia / kubeba moto

ikyole *n.off (-, 9/10)* cunt = kuma

ikyoloko *n.bot (-, 9/10)* **1** (Vigna aureue) green gram (tiny peas) = choroko za kijani **2** (Vigna mungo) black gram = choroko nyeusi

ikyombo *n (ify-, 7/8)* **1** vessel = chombo **2** thing = kitu

ikyubi *n (ify-, 7/8)* **1** type of basket = type of basket **2** a cattle horn used by to suck out blood (bleeding) or pus = pembe wa ng'ombe ambaye hutumiwa kufyonza damu au usaha kutoka sehemu iliyovimba au inayouma

ikyububu *n (ifyububu, 7/8)* the petal of a banana flower. It is often used as a cup for medicine = sehemu ya ua la mgomba ambalo wenyeji hutumia kama kombe la kunywea dawa

ikyuga *n (ify-, 7/8)* hoof = kwato

ikyugiila *n (ifyugiila, 7/8)* joke = mzaha

ikyula *n.zool (ify-, 7/8)* frog = chura

ikyulu *n.zool (ifyulu, 7/8)* **1** ant hill, termite mound = kichuguu **2** (Tuk) non flying termite = mchwa

ikyuma *n (ifi-, 7/8)* **1** property, goods, possession = mali **2** riches, treasure = utajiri, hazina

ikyúmba *n (ify-, 7/8)* room, chamber = chumba

ikyumbi *n (ify-, 7/8)* **1** pretence = kiji-

fanya = unatania **2** type of physical deformity = shindano (mwili); **ikyumbi iki** that's a joke, you're kidding, oh come on

ikyumilwa *n (ify, 7/8)* thirst = kiuu

ikyúsí *n (ify-, 7/8)* pestle = mchi

íla, ukwíla *vi (pt lílíle, bwalílíle)* **1** set (of the sun) = chwa **2** be dusk/sunset = chwa, kuchwa

ilaba *n (-, 9/10)* tennis shoes = viatu vya raba

ílaba *vb (pt ílabíle)* paint or decorate oneself = jipamba kwa kujichorachora

ílabanía *vb (pt ílabeníe)* paint or decorate oneself = jipamba kwa kujichorachora

ílaga *vb (pt ílagíle)* **1** do for the last time = fanya kwa mara ya mwisho **2** slang die = aga dunia; **Unkasí ílagíle ndubunju** His wife died this morning = Mkewe amefariki leo asubuhi

ilaamí *n (-, 9/10)* tar = lami

ílaamwa *vi (pt íleemwe)* **1** disregard = dharau **2** doubt = ona shaka

ilaamya *n (-, 9/10)* asphalt, tar = lami

ilangí *n (-, 9/10)* color = rangi

ilefaní *n (-, 9/10, >Ger. der Löffel)* spoon = kijiko

ilembuka *n (-, 9/10)* special market day = gulio

ilíbabu ilísimya *n (ama-, 5/6)* poorly burning firewood = ukuni usiowaka vizuri

ilíbagaja *n.anat (ama-, 5/6)* lung = pafu

ilíbala *n (ama-, 5/6)* kick = teke

ilíbale *n.bot (ama-, 5/6)* palm = ngazi, mchikichi

ilíbaalika *n (ama-, 5/6)* temporary partition or wall cover woven from reeds used in traditional houses = kuta za nyumba za Kinyakyusa zinazotengenezwa kwa kusuka matete au mizanzi

ilíbangala *n (ama-, 5/6)* bell = kengele

ilíbangalala *n (ama-, 5/6)* **1** (Ensete

ventricosum) *n.bot* type of tree = aina
ya mti (wild forest banana) = mgomba mwitu **2** *n* Viral disease in rice,
known as transitory yellowing. Symptoms leaves turn yellowish, later turn-
ing to bright yellow or even orange =
ugonjwa usababishwao na virusi
kwenye mpunga, majani huwa ya
njano, baadaye huwa njano kolevu na
hata kuwa mekundu meupe

ilíbaasa *n (ama-, 5/6)* **1** pleasant conversation = mazungumzo mazuri, ya-
kupendeza **2** the concept of sitting together and talking (like in the pub),
conversation = maongezi

ilíbeju *n (ama-, 5/6)* stems and leaves of
sweet potato = malandi, matembele

ilíbeele *n.anat (ama-, 5/6)* **1** breast (of
person) = ziwa (la mtu) **2** nipple, teat
= chuchu

ilíbeengwe *n.anat (ama-, 5/6)* spleen =
bandama

ilíbese *n.med (ama-, 5/6)* type of children's disease with swelling of pan-
creas; This swelling is often one of
the symptoms of chronic malaria in
children = ugonjwa usababishwao na
uvimbe wa bandama (hasa watoto)

ilíbifú *n (ama-, 5/6)* ripe banana = ndizi
mbivu

ilíbílíka *n (ama-, 5/6; >Swa)* kettle, teapot,
jug, reservoir, cistern, tank = birika

ilíbingu *n (ama-, 5/6)* cloud = wingu

ilíbítabwe *n (ama-, 5/6)* button = kishi-
kizo, kifungo

ilíbokosí *n (ama-, 5/6, >Eng)* box = sanduku

ilíboole *n.zool (ama-, 5/6)* leopard = chui

ilíbooma *n (ama-, 5/6)* **1** fort = ngome
2 enclosure, stockade = boma

ilíbomú *n (ama-, 5/6; >Eng)* bomb = bomu

ilíbondo *n.anat (ama-, 5/6)* shinbone =
kongoro

ilíboti *n (ama-, 5/6, > Eng)* boat = boti

ilíbuba *n (ama-, 5/6)* **1** (usually pl **amabuba**) rice stalks that remain in the
field after harvesting rice = vikonyo

vya mpunga vibakiavyo shambani
baada ya mavuno **2** State of rice and
finger millet field after harvesting in
which only stalks remain = hali ya
shamba la mpunga /ngano baada ya
kuvunwa

ilíbubusi *n.zool (ama-, 5/6)* type of insect = aina ya mdudu

ilíbulubusí *n.zool (ama-, 5/6)* type of
insect = aina ya mdudu

ilíbungila *n (ama-, 5/6)* dung hill, a
heap of earth and grass = kifusi

ilíbwe *n (ama-, 5/6)* stone = jiwe

ilíbwe lya fúla *n* hail = jiwe la mvua

ilíbyondo *n (ama-, 5/6)* **1** dent = kibonyeo, kishimo **2** *n.anat* dimple = kishimo, kifinyo kidogo hasa kwenye
shavu au kidevu

ilífíga *n (ama-, 5/6)* cooking stone =
figa, jifya

ilífílífílí *n.zool (ama-, 5/6)* caterpillar,
larva = kiwavi

ilífíningo *n (ama-, 5/6)* leaf for wrap-
ping = jani litumikalo kuzuia mvuke
usitoke upikapo

ilífúfú *n.food (ama-, 5/6)* ripe banana
which has been cooked = ndizi mbivu
iliyopikwa

ilífúfúma *n.zool (ama-, 5/6)* large owl =
bundi mkubwa

ilífugo *(Kye),* **ilífúbo** *(Tuk), n (ama-,
5/6)* sb with "green fingers" and/or
prosperous in terms of getting more
and more animals = kuwa na baraka
katika kazi za uzalishaji hasa mazao
ya kilimo na mfugo

ilífúúmbi *n (ama-, 5/6)* egg = yai

ilífúngú *n (ama-, 5/6)* empty space under
smth (eg. a bed or a table) = chini ya ki-
tanda/meza, uvunguni **Afísíle umuunyu
kwífúngú lya kitala kyake** She hid salt
underneath her bed = Alificha chumvi
uvunguni mwa kitanda chake

ilífúsí *n.anat (ama-, 5/6)* pubic hair = mavuzi

ilífwililo *n (imí-, 5/4)* dead part of seed
in a plant = sehemu ya mbegu iliya-

kufa kwenye mmea, kapi

ilífúndo *n.anat (ama-, 5/6)* knee = goti

ilígagana *n.med (ama-, 5/6)* crack on the heel = mpasuko kwenye wayo, kenya

ilígalasí *n (ama-, 5/6; > Eng)* glass (for drinking) = bilauri ya kioo

ilígali *n (ama-, 5/6)* car, vehicle with wheels = gari

ilígege *n.zool (ama-, 5/6)* type of fish, tilapia = perege

ilígengelemya *n (ama-, 5/6)* cliff, rock = genge, mwamba

i'lígobe *n.bot (ama-, 5/6)* type of plant = aina ya mmea

ilígolole *n (ama-, 5/6)* **1** sheet worn across one shoulder by elderly men = mgolole **2** bed sheet = shuka (ya kulalia)

ilígúlúmbilo *n (ama-, 5/6)* a livestock route to and from grazing = njia ya mifugo kwenda na kutoka malishoni

ilígúlútúmú *n (ama-, 5/6)* tire = gurudumu

ilígúnila *n (ama-, 5/6)* sack = gunia

ilíhahama *n.anat (6)* lung = pafu

ilíhandakí *n (ama-, 5/6)* ditch = handaki

ilíheelú *n (ama-, 5/6, Normally pl.)* insult, insulting/ abusive language, abuse = tusi

ilíjabú *n.bot (ama-, 5/6)* cassava = mhogo

ilíjando *n (ama-, 5/6)* exercise = mazoezi

ilíjefwa *n (ama-, 5/6; Tuk; Kye ilíjegwa)* wave = wimbi

ilíjenje *n.zool (ama-, 5/6)* cockroach = mende

ilíjesí *n (ama-, 5/6; > Swa)* army, military = jeshi

ilíjibijibi *n (ama-, 5/6)* watery substance, gel = ute, kitu chenye majimaji kama ute

ilíjiga *n (ama-, 5/6; Kye)* wave = wimbi

ilíjíko *n (ama-, 5/6; > Swa)* kitchen, fireplace = jiko, meko

ilíjoja *n (ama-, 5/6)* feather = manyoya

ilíjongolo *n.zool (ama-, 5/6)* millipede = jongoo

ilíjugunju *n.med (ama-, 5/6)* blister = lengelenge

ilíjulu *n (ama-, 5/6)* area above a room where one can store items, loft-room = dari

ilíjúnila *n (ama-, 5/6)* sack = gunia

ilíjúsí *n.zool (imí-, 5/4; Tuk; Kye akambwe)* **1** jackal, fox = mbweha, bweha **2** type of wild cat = aina ya paka /Possible variety **injusí**

ílika *vb (pt ílikíle)* squeeze = kamua

ilíkakafúla *n.zool (ama-, 5/6)* beetle = kifukusi

ilíkakala *n (ama-, 5/6)* **1** scale (of fish) = gamba **2** eggshell = kaka la yai

ilíkalang'asila *n (ama-, 5/6)* shell = konokono

ilíkandi *n (ama-, 5/6)* **1** peel of fruit = ganda **2** bark, rind = gome la mti

ilíkanga *n.zool (ama-, 5/6)* guinea fowl = kanga

ilíkangaga *n.bot (ama-, 5/6)* papyrus = mafunjo

ilíkang'ang'a *n (ama-, 5/6)* shell (snail, egg) = konokono, kaka (yai)

ilíkato *n (ama-, 5/6)* footprint = unyayo

ilíkemo *n (ama-, 5/6)* **1** contribution = zaka, sadaka **2** offering, sacrifice = sadaka

ilíkiba *n (ama-, 5/6)* "mourning belt" ie. piece of cloth given to in-law at funeral of in-law's husband/wife to confirm future relationship. = kitu kinachotolewa kudumisha udugu kilioni /Traditionally a bark-cloth belt, nowadays a kanga

ílikila *vt (pt ílikííle)* **1** fall onto = angukia **2** press hard = gandamiza

ilíkíla *n.med (ama-, 5/6)* atavism; Part of anus that grows which indicates bad luck to offspring. Traditional doctors cure it by cutting it off with a razorblade = Sehemu ya mkundu ambayo ikiota inaleta madhara kwa watoto

ilíkina *n (ama-, 5/6)* machine = mashine

ilíkiino *n.anat (ama-, 5/6)* calf (of leg) = sehemu ya nyuma ya mguu chini ya goti, juu ya kisigino

ilíkobokobo *n.bot (ama-, 5/6)* papyrus = mafunjo

ilíkofí *n (ama-, 5/6)* a slap by the palm of the hand = kofi, kibao

ilíkoga *n (ama-, 5/6)* river valley = bonde la mto

ilíkoko *n.med (ama-, 5/6)* scar = kovu

ilíkooko *n.bot (ama-, 5/6, > Nahuatl cachuati)* cocoa = kokoa, mkakao

ilíkole *n.anat (ama-, 5/6)* tendon = msuli mgumu, mshipa

ilíkolokoto *n.zool (ama-, 5/6)* butterfly = kipepeo

ilíkolokotwa *n.zool (ama-, 5/6)* **1** butterfly = kipepeo **2** moth = nondo

ilíkoloso *n.bot (ama, 5/6)* cashew nut = korosho

ilíkoolwa *n (ama-,5/6; Tuk;Kye -> itone)* (empty) shell of a snail = konokono

ilíkomamanga (Punica granatum) *n.bot (ama-, 5/6; > Swa)* (fruit) pomegranate = komamanga (ma-)

ilíkomang'ombe *n (ama-, 5/6)* **1** whip from a horse's or cow's tail (used at traditional dances) = kipande cha mkia wa ng'ombe au farasi na manyoya yake **2** type of insect = aina ya mdudu

ilíkombe *n.anat (ama-, 5/6)* point at the shoulderblade = sehemu ya juu ya mfupa wa bega

ilíkombelo *n (ama-, 5/6)* sling = kombeo, teo, kumbwewe

ilíkoonda *n.zool (ama-, 5/6)* wasp = nyigu

ilíkongolo *n (ama-, 5/6)* **1** *n.anat* the lower part of the animal's leg, ie between the hoof and knee = sehemu ya chini ya mnyama baini ya kwato na goti **2** *n.dish* bananas cooked with a shinbone/ shank = ndizi zilizopikwa na kwato **3** *n.slang* old woman = mwanamke mzee

ilíkosa *n (ama-, 5/6)* bracelet, bangle = bangili

ilíkosa lya mmalundi anklet = bangili ya mguu

ilíkosí *n.anat (ama-, 5/6)* nape, the back of the neck = sehemu ya nyuma ya shingo

ilíkosomolelo *n (ama-, 5/6)* phlegm = kohozi

ilíkotí *n (ama-, 5/6; > Eng)* coat = koti

ilíkufí *n.med (ama-, 5/6)* a blister on the palm of the hand caused by working with a hoe, axe or similar tool = lengelenge mkononi

ilíkúfúlí *n (ama-, 5/6)* padlock = kufuli

ilíkuju *n.bot (ama-, 5/6)* fig (fruit) = tini, tunda la mkuyu

ilíkuka *n (ama-, 5/6)* burnt mound of soil for planting sth on = kiunga cha udongo kilichochomwa shambani kwa ajili ya kupanda vitu

ilíkúkújilo *n (imí-, 5/4)* dead part of seed in a plant = sehemu ya mbegu iliyakufa kwenye mmea, kapi

ilíkumbulu *n (ama-, 5/6)* hoe = jembe

ilíkumbulu ilya maso *n* eye hoe = jembe lenye tundu la mviringo

ilíkúnda *n (ama-, 5/6)* **1** Homestead which is hidden by trees from the main road. The trees give shade and the homestead is therefore cool. Such a home is typical for elderly people. = Makazi yaliyozungukwa na miti / migomba mingi. Hali hii huyafanya makazi yawe na hali ya hewa iliyapoa. Makazi haya hupendelewa sana na wazee **2** bay, gulf = ghuba

ilíkungulu *n.zool (ama-, 5/6)* crow, raven = kunguru

ilíkúng'undo *n (ama-, 5/6)* strainer = chujio, kung'uto

ilíkungwe *n (ama-, 5/6)* (corn) ear, cob = gunzi

ilíkwelelo *n (ama-, 5/6)* **1** shoulderstrap for pants = ukanda wa begani wa suruali **2** ladder = ngazi

ilílaka *n (ama-, 5/6)* haste = papara

39

ilílalangí *n.bot (ama-, 5/6)* lemon = limau

ilílaluusyo *n (ama-, 5/6)* question = swali

ilílasí *n.bot (ama-, 5/6)* bamboo = mwanzi

ilílata *n (ama-, 5/6)* **1** corrugated iron sheet = bati **2** tin = bati
Umúndu uju ílata He is not easy to convince = Asiyeshawishika kirahisi

ilílatikilo *n (ama-, 5/6)* building pole, purlin = ufito

ilílebe *n (ama-, 5/6)* measure: one can of smth (approx. 18 l) = debe

ilílelema *n.arch.anat (ama-, 5/6, new term ilíbagaja)* lung = pafu

ilílesí *n.slang:ubwalwa (5)* type of local beer = aina ya pombe

ilíliígwa *ingamwana:ilísosí* tear = chozi

ilílínga *n (ama-, 5/6)* wall or partition inside a house = ukuta ndani ya nyumba

ililisya *vb (pt ililisísye)* growl, grumble, complain = kusemasema kwa huzuni /kulia, nung'unika

ilílobi *n (ama-, 5/6)* stain = doa, waa

ilílogota *n (ama-, 5/6)* sack = gunia

ilíloonda *n.med (ama-, 5/6)* persistent or spreading ulcer / wound = donda ndugu

ilílonge *n (ama-, 5/6)* flute = filimbi

ilílopa *n.anat (5)* blood = damu

ilíluuka *n (ama-, 5/6)* shop = duka

ilílunduko *n (ama-, 5/6)* afternoon = alasiri; **mwílunduko** in the afternoon = alasiri

ilímaage *n.aug (imímaage, 5/4)* a big knife, a special knife, dagger = jisu

ilímato *n (ama-, 5/6)* outside wall = ukuta

ilímoma *n (ama-, 5/6)* lump of earth, clod = bonge la udongo lililokauka

ilindu *n.aug (imí-, 5/4)* **1** giant = jitu **2** *n.zool* a big insect = dudu mkubwa **3** any particle in an unwanted place, dirt, filth = kitu chochote kilichotua mahali pasipo pake

ilíndúndú *n.zool (imí-, 5/4)* type of ant

= aina ya siafu

íliinga *interr* how much/many? (price) = kiasi gani

ílinganía *vi (pt ílingeníe)* decide, judge for oneself = kata shauri, jiamulia, jishauri

ilíng'eng'esí *n.zool (ama-, 5/6)* cicada = mdudukama mbung'o mkubwa atoaye mlio mkali wakati wa kiangazi

ilíng'olong'ondo *n (ama-, 5/6)* xylophone = marimba, chondo

ilíng'oma *n (ama-, 5/6)* traditional dance, song with drums and dance, use of calabash as instrument = ngoma ya ling'oma /Many think that it originated in Malawi

ilíngotí *n.med (ama-, 5/6)* dandruff, scurf in the hair = mba

ilíno *n.anat (amíno, 5/6)* tooth = jino

ilínoge *n.med (ama-, 5/6)* nose bleeding = mnoga, mhina

ilínombo *n.zool (ama-, 5/6)* vulture = tumbusi

ilínona *n (ama-, 5/6)* stain = doa, waa

ilínyagisí *n.zool (ama-, 5/6)* type of animal, a large rat-like animal reputed for storing large quantities of food in its hole (also kapenga) = mnyama kama panya mkubwa

ilínyama *n.anat (ama-, 5/6)* placenta, afterbirth = kondo la nyuma

ilínyegesí *n.zool (ama-, 5/6)* black ant = sisimizi, nyenyere

ilínyele (Anona senegalensis) *n.bot (ama-, 5/6)* (fruit and tree) custard apple = mtopetope

ilínyeta *n (ama-, 5/6)* metal ring used as ornament around the waist. Used by men and women in traditional Nyakyusa attire. Fell out of use in the early part of the 20th century = namna ya pete kubwa za chuma zilizovaliwa kama mapambo kiunoni na wanyakyusa

ilínyíkí *n.med (ama-, 5/6)* epilepsy = kifafa

ilínyombo *n.zool (ama-, 5/6)* vulture = tumbuzi

ilípalakata *n (ama-, 5/6)* dry leaf = jani kavu

ilípalalila *n.zool (ama-, 5/6)* locust = nzige

ilípalapaata *n (ama-, 5/6)* dry leaf = jani kavu

ilípalasila *n.zool (ama-, 5/6)* centipede = tandu

ilípamandila *n.zool (ama-, 5/6)* locust = nzige

ilípamba *n (ama-, 5/6)* brick = tofali

ilípango *n (ama-, 5/6)* native stringed instrument, kind of guitar = zeze, gitaa la kienyeji

ilípasa *n.fam (ama-, 5/6)* twin = pacha

ilípaasí *n.zool (ama-, 5/6)* locust = nzige

ilípatama *n.zool (ama-, 5/6)* cheetah = duma

ilípenenga *n (ama-, 5/6)* type of Nyakyusa dance with drums = Ngoma ya lipenenga

ilípepala *n (ama-, 5/6; > Eng)* **1** paper = karatasi **2** *n.slang* cash, dough = hela

ilípepo *n (ama-, 5/6)* genie = jini

ilíípi *n.anat (ama-, 5/6)* slap = kofi

ilíípí lya kunyúma slap with the backside of the open hand = kofi la nyuma

ilípiko, ikipiko *n (ama-, 5/6)* wing = bawa

ilípíípa *n (ama-, 5/6)* barrel, cask = pipa

ilíposo *n (ama-, 5/6)* fine for act of adultery = faini ilipwayo kwa kosa la ugoni

ilíposyo *n (ama-, 5/6)* ration, share = malipo baada ya kufanya kazi

ilípuba *n.zool (ama-, 5/6)* hartebeest = kongoni

ilípúkú *n (ama-, 5/6)* type of big mat made from banana leaves = aina ya mkeka mkubwa, jamvi /Also **umpúkú**

ilípuula *n.zool (ama-, 5/6)* eagle = tai

ilípúlúmúsí *n.zool (ama-, 5/6)* bat = popo

ilípumba *n (ama-, 5/6)* grave, tomb = kaburi

ilípútilo *n.anat (ama-, 5/6)* bladder = kibofu

ilípúútilo *n.anat (ama-, 5/6)* bladder = kibofu cha mkojo

ilípyana *n (5)* **1** sympathy, mercy, pity = neema, rehema **2** grace = huruma, rehema

ilísabíbu *n.bot (ama-, 5/6)* cashew apple, the red fleshy fruit-stalk that the nut hangs from = tunda la mkorosho / see **ilíkoloso**

ilísapa *n (ama-, 5/6)* rag = tambara /See **amasapa** for cotton

ilísaasa *n (ama-, 5/6)* wawe = wimbi ya maji

ilísasí *n (ama-, 5/6, >Arab)* bullet = risasi

ilísasí *n.zool (ama-, 5/6)* tse-tse fly = mbung'o, ndorobo

ilíseeke *n (ama-, 5/6)* **1** vegetable = mboga za majani **2** "The side dish", ie. everything that goes with the rice / ugali/bananas in a meal. This could be: vegetables, meat, beans or fish. In Bantu custom the carbohydrates constitute the main dish, not the protein. = kitoweo

ilíseekwa *n.zool (ama-, 5/6)* **1** duck = bata **2** goose = bata bukini

ilíseengo *n (ama-, 5/6)* sickle, chopper = nyengo, mundu

ilísíku *n (ama-, 5/6)* day (24 hours) = siku

ilísílika *n (ama-, 5/6)* corporation = shirika ~ **lya ndege** airline = shirika la ndege

ilísílísílí *n.med (5)* epilepsy = kifafa

ilísilya *n (ama-, 5/6)* beyond / on the other side of (a body of water), abroad = ng'ambo

ilísilya ilí this side of the river = ng'ambo hii

ilisilya lila that side of the river = ng'ambo ile

ilísiimbí *n (ama-, 5/6)* cocoyam = jimbi

ilísimula *n.zool (ama-, 5/6)* type of eagle = aina ya tai

ilísísí *n (ama-, 5/6)* soot = sizi

ílísongo *n (ama-, 5/6)* a wave = wimbi

ilísosí *n.anat (ama-, 5/6)* tear = chozi

ilísoso *n.anat (ama-, 5/6)* temple = nafasi wazi bila nywele kwenye paji

41

ilíísú *n (5)* grass = nyasi

ilíísu *n (5)* weed = majani, manyasi

ilísuba *n (ama-, 5/6)* **1** sun = jua **2** clock = saa

ilíswebele *n.zool (ama-, 5/6)* white termite in the flying stage = kumbikumbi, ngumbi

ilíswile *n (ama-, 5/6)* lump of food preground in the mouth to be fed to a child = chakula kilichota funwa apewacho mtoto

ilísyabala *n.bot (ama-, 5/6)* peanut (UK groundnut) = karanga

ilísyenga *n (ama-, 5/6)* a round house or hut, a circular enclosure or shed = msonge

ilísyeto *n (ama-, 5/6)* **1** Holy place, shrine where people pray and offer sacrifice to their ancestors/ forfathers. This is usually the actual burial place of the chiefs, ancestors or forfathers. There is normally a section of natural forest around the ísyeto. Some **ama-syeto** are / were so important as cult centers that the people of the area claim to belong to the ilísyeto rather than being under a chief (malafyale) = Patakatifu ambapo watu huomba na kutoa sadaka kwa mababu zao. Mahali hapo ni makaburi ya watemi, na mababu. Huachwa msitu wa asili kukua kulizunguka eneo hilo. **2** cemetery, burial ground = makaburi, maziara

ilíísyu *n (amasyu, 5/6)* **1** word = neno **2** sound = sauti **3** voice = sauti **4** sentence = sentensi **5** remark = neno, maoni

ilítabulo *n (ama-, 5/6; > Eng)* towel = taulo

ilítafula *n (ama-, 5/6)* gill = tamvua

ilítafúnilo *n (ama-, 5/6)* what remains after something is chewed = kinachobaki baada ya kitu kutafunwa

ilítaago *n (ama-, 5/6)* **1** garbage dump = mahali taka hutupwa na kuteketezwa **2** hell = jehenamu

ilítalabusí *n (ama-, 5/6; >Brit. 'trousers')*

pants = suruali

/Also: **isulubalí**

ilítambo *n (ama-, 5/6)* step, pace = hatua

ilítaambo *n (ama-, 5/6)* stride = hatua

ilítaanga *n.anat (ama-, 5/6)* buttock = tako

ilítango *n.bot (ama-, 5/6)* cucumber = tango

ilítapa *n (ama-, 5/6)* porridge, gruel = uji

ilítapwa *n (ama-, 5/6)* plank, board = ubao

ilítebe *n (ama-, 5/6)* run off water (after rains) = maji yatititikayo (baada ya mvua)

ilítekenya *n.zool (ama-, 5/6)* jigger = funza
/also **indekenya**

ilítembe *n (ama-, 5/6)* shed = banda

ilítende lya moto *n (ama-, 5/6)* furnace = tanuri

ilítenene *n (ama-, 5/6)* beehive = mzinga wa nyuki

ilítengele *n (ama-, 5/6; Kye)* **1** forest = msitu **2** wilderness, bush = mwitu, pori

ilítítí *n (ama-, 5/6; usually pl.)* eye discharge = tongo, tongotongo

ilítíka *n (ama-, 5/6)* waterpipe for tobacco = aina ya kiko

ilítookí *n.bot (ama-, 5/6)* **1** type of banana (Long, for cooking or roasting. Prepared while green.) = aina ya ndizi **2** *n.med (ama-, 5/6)* type of disease that kills children. Cure: Traditional doctors make the parents (not the child) take medicine = Ugonjwa unaoua watoto

ilítondobya *n (ama-, 5/6)* drop of water = tone

ilítone *n.zool (ama-, 5/6)* snail = konokono

ilítonyela *n (ama-, 5/6; Tuk)* drop = tone (la maji, mvua)
/Kye: **ilítondobya**

ilítúbwí *n (ama-, 5/6)* pool, puddle, pond, bog, swamp = dimbwi, bwawa
~ **pamwanya pakyamba** crater lake = bwawa juu ya mlima

ilítugalilo *n.anat.ingamwana (ama-, 5/6)*

buttock = tako

ilítuulo *n (ama, 5/6)* window = dirisha

ilítúlúndú *n.med (ama-, 5/6)* blister = lengelenge

ilítumbi *n (5, Tuk)* pride = kujiona, majivuno

ilítúmbú *n.anat (ama-, 5/6)* navel = kitovu
  ilítúmbú lya lusípulilo buoy = boya

ilítúnda *n.bot (ama-, 5/6; < Swa)* fruit = tunda
  /see **uluseke**

ilítundubili *n.anat (ama-, 5/6, Tuk)* **1** rumen = tumbo la mnyama, acheuaye (la kwanza) **2** entrails, intestines = utumbu, matumbu

ilítupa *n (ama-, 5/6)* dead fish = samaki wafu

ilíyabe *n.bot (ama-, 5/6)* (Ficus spp) type of fig tree = aina ya mkuyu

íluka *vi (pt ílwíke)* frown = kunja uso, kunja ndita, badilika uso kwa hasira, chuki au wivu

íluumbu *n.fam (aba-, 5/6)* sibling of opposite sex = ndugu wa kike kama aitwavyo na nduguye wa kiume na ndivyo huyo wa kiume aitwavyo na nduguye wa kike
  /Also **ulíluumbu**

ilyabi *n (ama-, 5/6)* cloth made from bark, worn by women = nguo ya ndani iliyokuwa ikivaliwa na wanawake zamani; gome la aina fulani ya mti lililo pondwapondwa kwa ajili ya kuvaliwa na wanawake

ilyafúlí *n (ama-, 5/6)* umbrella = mwavuli

ilyambafú *n.med (amambafu, 5/6)* swollen lymph gland = mtoki

ilyambepa *n* misfortune, an excuse, bad luck = bahati mbaya

ilyaní *n (amaaní, 5/6)* leaf = jani

ilyebe *n.zool (ameebe, 5/6)* kite = mwewe

ilyojo *n (5)* anger = hasira

ilyokelo *n (ify-, 7/8)* roasting / baking instrument, or area for roasting / baking, grill = chombo au mahali pa kuokea, jiko la kuchomea

ilyosí *n (5)* smoke = moshi

ilyububu *n (amububu, 5/6)* bark of banana plant = ganda la mgomba

ilyulilo *n (amuulilo, 5/6)* market = soko

ilyuulu *n.med (amuulu, 5/6)* **1** boil = jipu **2** abscess = jipu

ilyundu *n (5)* thatching grass = fefe, nyasi za kuezekea nyumba

ilyúngú *n.bot (amúngú, 5/6)* pumpkin = mboga

ilyungulu *n.zool (amungulu, 5/6)* type of ant, brown, safari ant = siafu

ima *vi (pt imíle)* **1** stand, stand up, arise = simama **2** stop = simama

íma *vt (pt ímíle)* deprive, not give = nyima, hini

imba *vt (pt imbíle)* **1** sing, chant = imba **2** read = soma

imbabala *n.zool (-, 9/10)* type of antilope or gazelle, bushbuck = mbawala
  ~ **inandi** gazelle = paa

imbabu *n (10)* firewood, wood = kuni

imbagi *n.anat (-, 9/10)* gap between the front teeth = mwanya (kwenye meno)

imbago *n.zool (-, 9/10)* otter = fisi maji

imbagukano *n (-, 9/10)* road split = njia panda

imbako *n (imbako, 9/10)* **1** cave = pango **2** When sb is buried without a coffin a room is dug into the side of the grave for the body so that the earth will not fall directly on him/her = shimo dogo linaloongezwa kwenye kaburi ili kumficha maiti huko ili labda udongo usimfikie mara moja

imbaalo *n (-, 9/10)* surname = jina la ukoo

imbalaga *n.dish (-, 9/10)* peeled and cooked banana (in a sort of stew, mixed with meat or fish) = ndizi mtori, ndizi zilizopikwa mchanganyiko

imbalilo *n (-, 9/10)* account, number, sum, calculation, figure (arithmetic) = hesabu

imbamandila *n.zool (-, 9/10)* locust = nzige

imbamba *n.med (10)* Type of local medicine that prevents heart palpitation, a condition brought about by anger. Imbamba will cure amaaja = Aina ya dawa ya kienyeji inayozuia mapigo ya moyo ugonjwa utokanao na hasira (mf mzazi akiudhiwa na mtoto); **Abíníle amaaja tunnwesye imbamba** He is grief stricken, let's make him drink 'imbamba'= Ameugua kwa sababu ya simanzi tumnyeshwe 'imbamba' / Kazongwa na huzuni tumnywesha dawa ya 'mbamba'

imbanda *n (-, 9/10)* **1** beam, post, pillar, pole, column, flag pole = boriti, nguzo **2** pole (eg. for electricity) = mlingoti, mwongoti **3** supporting pole (construction) = mlingoti, mwongoti

imbange (Cajanus cajan) *n.bot (-, 9/10)* pigeon pea = mbaazi

imbaní *n.zool (-, 9/10)* flea = kiroboto

imbapa *n (-, 9/10)* skin = ngozi

imbaapo *n.anat (-, 9/10, < paapo)* uterus = kizazi

imbasa *n.zool (-, 9/10, < -pasa)* type of fish in lake Nyasa = aina fulani ya samaki ipapatikanao katika ziwa Nyasa

imbaasa *n.zool (-, 9/10)* cow with white spot on the forehead = ng'ombe mwenye baka jeupe utosini

imbasaana *n (-, 9/10)* **1** The split in branches of a tree = mgawanyiko wa matawi ya mti **2** road split where two branches meet = makutano ya barabara, njia panda

imbaasí *n.zool (-, 9/10)* grasshopper = panzi

imbataata *n.bot (-, 9/10; >Taino batata)* sweet potato = kiazi kitamu

imbaatiko *n (-, 9/10)* **1** culture = utamaduni **2** law = sheria

imbeba *n.zool (-, 9/10)* rat, mouse = panya

imbega *n.zool (-, 9/10; < -pega)* colobus monkey = aina ya kima mwenye manyoya meusi marefu na meupe mabegani; mbega

imbege *n (-, 9/10)* banana beer (from the gulutu banana) = pombe ya ndizi

imbeegwa *n (-, 9/10)* first name = jina la kwanza, jina la kupewa

imbejú *n (-, 9/10; < -peju)* seed = mbegu

imbele *n.med (9)* **1** scabies = upele **2** eczema = ugonjwa wa ngozi kama upele

imbelebeeswa *n.zool (-, 9/10)* swallow = mbayuwayu

imbelele *n.zool (-, 9/10)* type of fish in lake Nyasa/Malawi, herring family = aina ya samaki, nungu

imbembenúka *n (10)* parade = gwaride, mkusanyiko

imbene *n.zool (-, 9/10; < -pene)* goat = mbuzi

imbenga *n (-, 9/10)* **1** *n.med* drilling wound = kidonda cha kupekecha **2** hole on bamboo suger cane = tundu ndani ya kwenye mwanzi au muwa

imbenú *n (-, 9/10)* eaves = upenu

imbepo *n (-, 9/10; < -pepo)* **1** wind = upepo; **imbepo inúnú** breeze = upepo mwanana; **2** air = hewa **3** spirit = roho; **imbepo inyalí** demon = pepo mchafu; **4** a mental disturbance = ukichaa

umúndu uju ali nimbepo he is crazy
imbepo sya bandu
Abiníle kunongwa ja mbepo sya bandu bo antukíle ugwíse. He got sick (because of 'imbepo sya bandu') after having abused his father = Anaumwa kwa sababu ya maneno ya watu baada ya kumtukana babaye

---

Imbepo sya bandu
When somebody commits an offence in the community there may be a meeting of elders to deal with the case. The crime may be breaking social rules (eg. offensive behavior, a son who has beaten his mother etc.). There will be no open physical or verbal action taken against the offender, but he will become sick, die or suffer loss in one way or another.

---

imbesí *n.zool (-, 9/10; Tuk)* francolin =

aina ya ndege mdogo jamii ya kanga
/Kye: **akalulunje**

imbeta *n.zool (-, 9/10)* type of bird,
guelea family = aina ya ndege, jamii
ya guelea

imbíbí *n.relig (-, 9/10)* sin = dhambi

imbiifwa *n (-, 9/10)* **1** segment, internode,
plant cutting = pingili; **imbiifwa ja
múúba** a segment of sugar cane = pingili
ya muwa; **2** the lower or upper part of an
arm or a leg = sehemu ya juu au chini ya
mguu au mkono

imbiifwa ja kiboko *n.anat* wrist = kifundo cha mkono

imbígíta *n (-, 9/10)* charm = hirizi, talasimu

imbíkípíkí *n (-, 9/10)* tail = mkia
/Also **umpíkípíkí**

imbila (Sorghum vulgare) *n.bot (-, 9/10; < -
pila)* millet, sorghum = mtama

imbilila *vb* sing for, sing continuously
= imbia, imba kwa mfululizo

imbílípílí *n.bot (-, 9/10; < -pílípíli)*
pepper = pilipili

imbína *n.med (-, 9/10; Tuk)* disease, illness = ugonjwa, ndwele
/Kye **ububíne**

imbindipindi *n.zool (-, 9/10)* type of
green snake, (green garden snake or
green mamba) = aina ya nyoka wa kijani au koboko wa kijani

imbinga *n (-, 9/10)* type of local
medicine = aina ya dawa ya kienyeji

imbingo *n (-, 9/10)* gyve, chain,
shackle, handcuffs = pingu

imbingú *n (-, 9/10)* handcuffs, gyve,
chain = pingu

imbiiso *n (-, 9/10)* adze = tezo

imbogo *n.zool (-, 9/10; < -pogo)* buffalo
= nyati, mbogo

imbogoso *n.zool (-, 9/10)* cow with
horns pointing downwards = ng'ombe
mwenye pembe ziangaliazo chini

imbolo *n.off (-, 9/10)* cock, dick, prick
= mboo

imbombo *n (-, 9/10)* **1** work, affair,
business, job, labor, occupation, func-

tion, undertaking = kazi, shughuli
2 duty = wajibu **3** action = kitendo

imbondanía *n.med (-, 9/10)* local
medicine in powder form for curing
various diseases = dawa ya kienyeji ya
kutibu magonjwa mbalimbali

imbondelo *n (-, 9/10)* hammer = nyundo

imbongolo *n (-, 9/10)* spear with flat
metal tip = aina ya mkuki

imboní *n.anat (-, 9/10)* eye pupil =
mboni ya jicho

imboopo *n (-, 9/10)* small axe (for decoration) = shoka dogo (hutumika kwa
mapambo)

imbosyo *n.med (9; < -posya)* A medicine
which causes other medicines to rot =
Dawa inayoozesha dawa nyingine

imboosyo *n (-, 9/10, Tuk)* joke = mzaha,
utani

imboto *n (-, 9/10)* plentifulness of everything, but esp of food, fertility = tele,
neema ya vitu hasa chakula

imbotola *n (-, 9/10)* trap net (for fish) =
mgono, mtego wa samaki

imbuufú *n.zool (-, 9/10)* type of fish,
catfish = aina ya samaki aitwaye ki-
toga

imbuuga *n.zool (-, 9/10)* type of bird = ndege
jamii ya korongo mwenye ushungi
/maybe crowned crane

imbúgújo *n (-, 9/10)* waterfall, cascade
= maanguko / maporomko ya maji

imbuje *n (-, 9/10)* bulb, root shaped like
onion = mzizi (kama kitunguu)

imbúkúla *n.zool (-, 9/10)* honey badger
= nyegere

imbulangete *n (-, 9/10; > Eng)* blanket
= blanketi
/Orig. Nya: **ingokoma**

imbuli *n (-, 9/10)* fist = ngumi

imbúúlí *n.zool (-, 9/10)* hornless cattle
= ng'ombe asiye na pembe

imbúlo *n.anat (-, 9/10; < púlo)* nose = pua

imbulu *n.zool (-, 9/10)* monitor lizard =
kenge

imbulukutu *n.anat (-, 9/10)* ear = sikio

imbúlúlúfú *n (-, 9/10)* coin = sarafu

imbúlúlúkisya *n (10)* that which is added at the top of a container, left overs, remainders, remaining grains = mabaki, masalio, punye zinazosalia

imbumba *n (-, 9/10; > Chewa)* **1** (group of) children = (mkusanyiko wa) watoto **2** family = familia

imbumbuhilí *n.zool (-, 9/10)* type of bird, small pigeon = aina ya ndege

imbúnda *n.zool (-, 9/10)* donkey = punda

imbunganíe *n (-, 9/10)* sum = jumla, jumlisho

imbungapunga *n (-, 9/10)* pollen = mbelewele

imbungo *n (9)* **1** *n.med* contagious disease (especially VD) = ugonjwa hasa wa zinaa **2** catarrh = mafua **3** *n.anat* nasal mucus, snot = kamasi

imbungo ja kwambula VD = ugonjwa wa zinaa

imbungu ja makete leprosy = ukoma

imbútútú *n.zool (-, 9/10)* ground horn-bill = vumatiti, mumbi

imbwa *n.zool (-, 9/10)* dog = mbwa

imbwagalala *n (-, 9/10)* ankle bell = njuga

imbwele *n.zool (-, 9/10)* **1** fly = inzi **2** mosquito = mbu

imbwele inandi *n.zool (10)* gnat = mdudu mdogo kama mbu

imbwíbwí *n (-, 9/10)* bubble = povu

imbwíga *n.bot (-, 9/10)* ginger = tangawizi

imbyabyatila *n.zool (-, 9/10)* type of bird = aina ya ndege

imbyu *n (-, 9/10)* belch = mbweu

imeesa *n (-, 9/10; > Swa >Port. mesa)* table = meza
/Nya: **ilítalati**

-ímí *adj* stingy, miserly = -nyimi, ny-imivu, enye tabia ya kunyima

imika *vt (pt imííke)* **1** erect = simika **2** honor, respect = heshimu **3** bring to a halt = simamisha **4** set up = weka, simamisha, sitawisha **5** brake = piga breki

imika imbombo force sb out of a job = simamisha kazi

imíkululukila *n (4)* drainage traces remaining in container after emptying it = mabaki ya maji baada ya kujichuja / mabaki ya maji kwenye chombo baada ya kumwaga

imila *vt (pt imííle)* preside, stand over, sponsor, be on behalf = simamia

imíla *n.anat (4)* intestine, bowels = matumbo

imilila *vt (pt imilííle)* administer, supervise, control, manage, take care of = simamia

imílola *n.bot (4)* type of mangrove trees = aina ya miti iotao majini

imíndu *n (4)* filth = uchafu

imínyeenya *n (4)* **1** *n.med* somnambulism, sleepwalking = kusema na kutembea usingizini **2** *n.med* delirium = mapayo, weweseko **3** illusion = kitu kisichokuwapo kama ndoto

imípulilo *n (4)* straw (eg of rice after threshing) = kapi

imisya *vt.caus (pt imíísye)* erect = simika

imísyuka *n (4)* ancestors = mizimu

ímuka *vi (pt imwíke) (Tuk, Kye -> milwa)* drown = kufa maji

imwamúnyíla, *n.bot (-, 9/10; Tuk)* type of banana (red/yellow and thick, typically found in the Itete area) = ndizi nene za rangi nyekundu

imwaana *n (ibaana, 1a/2)* the young of an animal or bird = mtoto wa mnyama au ndege

ína, ukwína *vi (pt iníle)* get soiled, be dirty = chafuka, badilika rangi kuwa nyeusi kwa uchafu

ínama *vi (pt íneme)* stoop, bend, crouch, bow, droop = inama, pinda chini

ínamika *vt (pt inamííke)* (cause to) bend, bow = inamisha

ínamisya *vt (pt inamísye)* bend down, direct smth downwards = inamisha

inaulí *n (-, 9/10; >Swa)* (eg. bus) fare = nauli

indafú *n (-, 9/10)* drooling, saliva = udelele, udenda

indaafú *n.zool (-, 9/10)* type of grasshopper, katydid = senene

indala *n (-, 9/10)* sandal, slipper = ndala, malapa

indalama *n (-, 9/10; >Arab dirham)* money = fedha

indalíngo *n (-, 9/10)* longish gourd for milk = kibuyu kirefu kwa ajili ya maziwa

indama *n.zool (-, 9/10)* **1** cow which has not yet conceived = ng'ombe jike **2** heifer = mtamba

indamba *n (-, 9/10)* small, usually round building used to store unprocessed foodstuffs = ghala

indamwa *n.med (-, 9/10)* illness, sickness = ugonjwa, ndwele

indamyo *n (10)* torture = mateso

indefú *n (10)* beard, mustache = ndevu /For sg. usage see **ululefú**

indege *n (-, 9/10)* airplane = ndege

indeka *n.bot (9)* young green grass = nyasi changa

indekenya *n.zool (-, 9/10)* jigger = funza /also **ilítekenya**

indeko *n (-, 9/10; < -teko)* pot = chungu

indekuleku *n.zool (-, 9/10)* type of bird, swift = aina ya ndege

indelema *n (-, 9/10)* **1** plate, dish = sahani **2** basin = bakuli

indemba *n.zool (-, 9/10)* hen = kuku jike

indembeela *n (-, 9/10; Tuk)* flag, banner = bendera /Kye: **ibendela**

indende *n (-, 9/10)* banana corm = sehemu ya chini ya shina la mgamba

indengo *n (-, 9/10)* fishnet support (pole) = kitu cha kushikilia wavu wa samaki

indení *n.zool (-, 9/10)* cricket = chenene, nyenze, nyenje

indepa *n.med (-, 9/10)* glandular swelling = tezi

indesí *n.med (-, 9/10)* **1** glandular swelling = tezi **2** *n.zool* type of bird = aina ya ndege

indeto *n (10)* murmur, secret information = mnong'ono

indiifú *n.bot (-, 9/10)* type of banana = aina ya ndizi

indílolo *n.bot (-, 9/10)* olive = zeituni

indilu *n.bot (-, 9/10)* couch grass = aina ya nyasi

indíngala *n (-, 9/10)* **1** drum = ngoma **2** folk dance = ngoma

indoba *n.zool (-, 9/10)* type of bird, black, waterbird= aina ya ndege

indobo *n (-, 9/10)* **1** bucket, pail = ndoo **2** vessel = chombo

indofanía (Solanum tuberosum) *n.bot (-, 9/10)* potato, Irish potato = kiazi

indofú *n (9)* cultivated land, ploughed field = sesa

indogolo *n (-, 9/10)* free, gratis = bure, dezo

indola (Ficus thonningii) *n.bot (-, 9/10)* type of parasite tree which when cut gives white liquid like milk, type of fig tree = aina ya mti /sometimes sacred

indope *n (10)* **1** dung, manure = samadi **2** excrement = kinyesi, kitokanacho na wanyama /sg usage see **ulutope**

indubi *n.med (10; < -tubi)* smallpox = ndui

indúgútú *n.zool (-, 9/10)* type of bird, like the white browed coucal = gude, shundi dudumizi, tipitipi

induku *n (-, 9/10)* miss (a target) = ukosefu wa shabaha

indukwe *n.zool (-, 9/10)* type of ant, large and black ant, it bites = aina ya siafu mkubwa na mweusi anayeuma / Also **ulutukwe**

indululukila *n (-, 9/10)* ash dust = vumbi la guri

indúmba *n (-, 9/10)* amulet = ndumba, talasimu

indúmbúla *n (-, 9/10)* **1** heart = moyo **2** bosom = kifua
~ **akajiilo** character = tabia

~ **iji jikusoka** conscience = ufahamu

indumí *n (-, 9/10; < -tumi)* **1** message, errand = ujumbe **2** news = habari, taarifa

indumilakosa *n.zool (-, 9/10)* **1** aina ya nyoka = type of snake **2** blind worm = ndumakuwili

indundu *n (-, 9/10)* spoon made from banana leaf = kijiko kilichotengenezwa kwa kipande cha jani la mgomba

indundulí *n.med (-, 9/10)* swelling on body after a blow = uvimbe mwilini baada ya kipigo

indungwa *n (-, 9/10)* dew = umande

indúsú *n (-, 9/10; < -lúsú)* gun, rifle = bunduki

indúsú innandi pistol = bastola

indútú *n.anat.off (-, 9/10)* vagina, cunt = kuma

indwanga *n (-, 9/10)* axe = shoka

indyalí *n.bot (-, 9/10)* green banana = ndizi mshale

indyokolílo *n.zool (-, 9/10)* type of small bird with a small black crown, sparrow = aina ya ndege mdogo, shore kishungi, shorewanda /Same as **mwantyoko**

inenga *vb (pt inengíle)* **1** brag = jisifu, jidai **2** have selfconfidence = fanya kitu kwa uhakikaa japo si kweli au kutotaka unguswe na mtu

ingafí *n (-, 9/10)* **1** paddle = kasia, kafi **2** *n.anat* anus = mkundu

ingaaja *n (-, 9/10)* **1** banana plantation = shamba la migomba **2** seeds of a certain lily like flower which are put inside of the calabash to produce sound = mbegu za mti wa maua ambazo huwekwa kwenye chombo ili kutoa mlio

ingala *n (-, 9/10)* snow, ice = theluji

ingaala *n (9)* drunkenness = ulevi

ingalaba *n (-, 9/10)* **1** boat, dug-out canoe = mtumbwi **2** *n.relig* Noah's ark = safina

ingalabuka *n (-, 9/10)* charcoal = mkaa

ingalalisí *n (-, 9/10)* **1** anger, rage = hasira **2** hate, hatred, aversion = chuki

ingalamú *n.zool (-, 9/10)* lion = simba

ingambaku *n.zool (-, 9/10)* ox, bull = ng'ombe dume

ingambili *n.zool (-, 9/10)* monkey (generic) = kima, tumbili ngedere, nyani, kima, mbega, sokwe n.k.
  ikikolo kya ngambili monkey family = jamii ya nyani

ingaambo *n.bot (9)* tobacco, cigarette = sigara, tumbaku

ingamí *n (-, 9/10)* rust = kutu

ingamila *n.zool (-, 9/10)* camel = ngamia

ingamú *n (-, 9/10; < kamú)* name = jina

ingamwana *n.cult (-, 9/10)* name or word sounding like the name of the father-in-law that the wife is not allowed to use = Jina la baba mkwe (ambalo mkwe halitaji)

ingangabwíte *n (-, 9/10)* trumpet, horn = tarumbeta, parapanda /MW 1959 A kudu horn used for blowing

ingangasyungu *n.anat (-, 9/10)* gizzard = firigisi

ingangata *n (-, 9/10)* a strong person or animal, indication of great strength = mtu mwenye nguvu /Original meaning was a large animal, possibly a buffalo or a rhino, some people say it was an animal bigger than a buffalo

inganí *n (-, 9/10; Kye)* disobedience, obstinacy = hali ya kutotii, utoru wa utii, ukaidi /Tuk: **ubusísí**

inganú (Triticum spp) *n.bot (-, 9/10)* wheat = ngano

ingata *n (-, 9/10)* anything used by women to put between the head and that which they are carrying on their head, a head pad = kata

ingata (ja ífúndo) *n.anat (-, 9/10)* kneecap = pia ya goti, kilegesambwa

ingaata *n (-, 9/10)* a dish of maize and beans cooked together = kande

ingaati *n (-, 9/10; Tuk)* dish of maize mixed with beans = kande

ingego *n.bot (-, 9/10)* type of banana, big = mkongo wa tembo, mkono wa tembo

ingeeke (Bracken) *n.bot (-, 9/10)* type of tree, fern = aina ya mti

ingeleketa *n.med (-, 9/10)* bilharzia = kichocho

ingeelwa *n.zool (-, 9/10)* type of fish = aina ya samaki

ingelwa *n (-, 9/10)* Ash made from dried banana peels which is used in preparing (tobacco) snuff = Jivu la maganda ya ndizi lichanganywalo na ugoro

ingende *n (-, 9/10)* a lost tooth = pengo la jino

ingenge *n.zool (-, 9/10)* cane rat = ndezi

ingeníuka *n.med (-, 9/10)* ulcerous cracks or sores on the feet under the toes = mpasuko au kidongo chini ya kidole

ingenyuka *n.med (-, 9/10)* painful crack which appears under the toes = mpasuko wenye maumivu makali utokeao chini ya vidole; nyungunyungu

ingeesa *n.zool (-, 9/10)* type of ant, small = aina ya siafu, mdogo

ingese *n (-, 9/10)* **1** cut = mkato **2** *n.med* wound (from a cut) = kidonda cha kukatwa; **ingese indali** deep cut; **ingese ja íkumbulu** a hoe cut = mkato wa jembe hasa wakati wa kulima

-íngí *adj* much, many = -ingi, tele

ingiga *n (-, 9/10)* **1** crown = taji **2** piece of cloth tied around the head, ribbon = kitambaa kifungwacho kichwani, kilemba

íngila *vt (pt íingíle)* **1** enter = ingia **2** inherit = rithi

íngilapo *vb (pt ingíílepo)* succeed = badili, rithi

ingili *n.zool (-, 9/10)* warthog = ngiri

ingíli *n (-, 9/10; < -kíli)* walking stick, staff, crutch, stick, cane = mkongojo, fimbo

íngilila *vi (pt ingilíile)* intrude = ingilia, jipenyeza, vamia, ingilia kati

ingímbuko *n (-, 9/10)* anger, ill temper, wrath = hasira

ingímú *n (-, 9/10)* anchor = nanga

ingíísí *n (-, 9/10; < -kísí)* darkness, gloom = giza; **Ali mungíísí** He doesn't know = Hajui litu

íngisya *vt.caus (pt íingísye)* **1** admit = ruhusu, kubali **2** insert = weka, tia, ingiza **3** set = weka

ingíta *n.zool (-, 9/10)* fatling = mnyama kama ng'ombe, kondoo au mbuzi aliyene-nepeshwa kwa ajili ya kuchinjwa

ingííto *n (-, 9/10)* riddle, mockery = sema kwa mafumbo, kebehi

ingobyo *n (-, 9/10)* moss = nyasi ndogo nyororo

ingoka *n (-, 9/10)* bunch of grass for lighting purposes, blazing torch = mwenge

ingokola *n (-, 9/10)* line woven on a mat = mstari unaosukwa kwenye mikeka

ingokoma *n (-, 9/10)* blanket = blanketi

ingolele *n (-, 9/10)* sound = sauti

ing'olí behind the hill = nyuma ya mlima

ingolo *n.zool (-, 9/10)* louse = chawa

ingoolo *n (-, 9/10)* scream = mwito wa sauti ya juu, kilio

ingolokoko *n.zool (-, 9/10)* hen = koo la kuku, tembe

ingolokolo *n.zool (-, 9/10)* type of fish, with a spiny back = ngogo, aina ya samaki mwenye mwiba mgongoni

ingolombe *n.zool (-, 9/10)* heifer = mtamba

ingolomílo *n.anat (-, 9/10)* **1** throat = koo **2** gullet, larynx = koromeo

ingolwa *n (-, 9/10)* tooth decay = uozo wa meno

ingolya *n (-, 9/10)* **1** glue = gundi **2** *n.bot* type of tree giving out a substance that is used as glue = aina ya mti unaotoa utomvu mweupe utumikao kama gundi

ingombe *n (-, 9/10; -kombe)* snail shell = ganda la konokono

ing'ombe *n.zool (-, 9/10)* cow, cattle = ng'ombe

ing'ombe isulula striped cow = ng'ombe mwenye milia

ingonga *n (-, 9/10)* '8-shaped' gourd for containing milk = kibuyu chenye umbo la nambari 8 kinacho tundika kutunza maziwa

ingongobe *n.zool (-, 9/10)* rooster = jogoo

ingongola *n (-, 9/10)* return a favor done at a local dance = huduma atoayo mtu kwa mwenzie aliyekirimu wakati wa mchezo wa awali wa ngoma

ingong'ondelo *n.zool (-, 9/10)* **1** wood-pecker = kigong'ota **2** instrument made of cattle horn for softening bark (to be used for clothing) **(ilyabi)** = ki-faa cha kulainishia gomba la mti

ingono *n.anat (-, 9/10)* nape, the nape of the neck = kisogo

ing'osí *n.zool (-, 9/10)* sheep = kondoo

ing'osi imbikí *n.zool* ewe = kondoo jike

ing'osi imbongo *n.zool* ram = kondoo dume

ingosyo *n (-, 9/10)* **1** birthmark = alama ya mwili mtu azaliwayo nayo **2** any resem-blance of an offspring to its parent

ingosyola *n.zool (-, 9/10)* type of fish, type of mudfish = aina ya samaki, mfano wa kambare

ingooto *n.med (-, 9/10)* Disease charac-terized by emaciation with no other symptoms. It is caused by people's ignorance of taboos or by bad spirits in the family. The family will hold a meeting to solve the problem. = Ku-konda mwili kunakotokana na uvun-jaji wa miiko

ingubi *n.zool (-, 9/10)* cricket =.nyenje

ingubo *n (-, 9/10; < -kubo)* cloth or skin used to carry children on the back = mbeleko

ingubwa *n (-, 9/10; < -kubwa)* a hockey-like type of children's game, a stick is hit with a stick, not commonly seen anymore = namna fulani ya mchezo uliochezwa na watoto un-yakyusa zamani

ingufí *n (-, 9/10)* applause, clapping of hands = makofi

inguku *n.zool* chicken, fowl, poultry = kuku

ingúleke *n.zool (-, 9/10)* green pigeon = njiwa wa kijani, niuga

ingulilo *n (-, 9/10; < kulio)* **1** agegroup = rika **2** type of thicket = aina ya kichaka

ingulu *n (-, 9/10)* shield = ngao

ingulube *n.zool (-, 9/10)* pig = nguruwe

ingulube imbongo *n.zool (-, 9/10)* boar = dume la nguruwe

ingúlúpa *n.zool (-, 9/10)* tick = kupe

ingulyo *n (10)* water rapids = maji yaendayo kasi

inguma *n.anat (-, 9/10)* vagina = kuma

ingumba *n.zool (-, 9/10)* freshwater cat-fish, barbel = kambare

inguna *n (-, 9/10)* curse = laana

ingúúmbe *n (-, 9/10)* large pot, pitcher = mtungi mkubwa, chungu kikubwa

ingunde *n.zool (-, 9/10)* (a domesticated bird) pigeon, dove = njiwa, hua **/ingungubija** is a similar, but wild bird

ingunga *n.zool (-, 9/10)* **1** conger, a large scaleless eel = mkunga **2** Type of very small fly which occurs in smoke or cloudlike swarms near / on lake Nyasa / Malawi. Eaten by the lo-cal people. Given this name because of the belief that such flies are emitted from the mouth of a conger during certain months of the year. = aina ya inzi wadogo ambao huliwa ziwani Nyasa

ingungubija *n.zool (-, 9/10)* (wild bird) pigeon, dove = hua, njiwa manga

/**ingunde** is a similar, but domesticated bird

ingungulu *n.zool (-, 9/10; Tuk)* crow = kunguru
/Kye: **ilíkungulu**

ingúngúní *n.zool (-, 9/10)* bedbug = kunguni

ingúpí *n (-, 9/10)* a portion of stiff porridge = tonge, kipino cha ugali

inguuti (Maesa lanceolata or Brachystegia spiciformis) *n.bot (-, 9/10)* type of tree (black seeds with red top housed in a 10-15 cm pod) = aina ya mti

ingúto *n (-, 9/10)* angle = pembe, kona

ingúúto *n (10)* cry = kilio

ingwabo *n (-, 9/10)* small wooden hoe = jembe dogo la mti

ingwale *n.zool (-, 9/10)* partridge, red-necked spur fowl = kwale

ingwamba *n (-, 9/10)* **1** Mourning belt worn by women at funerals. This is normally a kanga which is folded up three or four times and tied around the waist = Nguo ifungwayo kiunoni na wanawake wakati wa msiba **2** portion of marriage fund given to mother as her right = sehemu ya mahari anayopewa mama kama sehemu yake ya mali

ingwasí *n.zool (-, 9/10)* type of bird of prey, eagle = tai

ingwata *n.zool (-, 9/10)* calf (young cow) = ndama

ingweego *n (-, 9/10; < -kwego)* spear with flat metal tip = mkuki

ingwehe *n.zool (-, 9/10)* crab = kaa

ingweta *n (9)* type of drum = ngoma ambayo ilikuwa inachezwa na wazee. ngoma ilitengenezwa na ngozi ya kenge

ingwíína *n.zool (-, 9/10)* crocodile = mamba

ingwítwa *n.zool (-, 9/10)* owl = bundi

iníela *vi (pt inielíle)* to dirty oneself, "to shit in one's pants" = jinyea

iníngu *n.zool (-, 9/10)* type of fish, like herring = ningu

iníongo *n (-, 9/10)* water current (especially a circular one) = mazunguko ya maji

ínisya *vt.caus (pt iníísye)* dirty, soil, make a mess of = chafua, chakaza

injala *n (9)* hunger, famine = njaa

injasí *n (-, 9/10)* **1** lightning = radi **2** thunder = ngurumo **3** thunderclap = mpasuko wa radi

injefweela *n (-, 9/10)* wave = wimbi

injegele *n.bot (-, 9/10)* pea = njegere

injila *n (-, 9/10)* **1** road, street, path = njia, barabara **2** journey = safari **3** means = namna ya, uwezekano

injiinga *n (-, 9/10)* bicycle = baisikeli

injisí *n (-, 9/10)* ankle bells (worn at traditional dancing) = njuga

injobelo *n (-, 9/10)* **1** language = lugha **2** intonation, accent = matamshi fulani ya maneno
/Also **injobele**

injoka *n.zool (-, 9/10)* snake, adder, serpent = nyoka

injoka ja munda *n.med.zool* helminth = mnyoo wa tumboni

injosí *n (-, 9/10)* dream, vision = njozi, ndoto, maono

injugu *n (-, 9/10)* hard peanuts, type of nuts that must be boiled before they can be eaten = njugumawe

injuki *n.zool (-, 9/10)* bee = nyuki

injuní *n.zool (-, 9/10)* bird = ndege

ínogona *vb (pt inogwííne)* **1** think, consider, reflect, calculate, imagine = fikiri, fikiria, dhani, wazi, wazia **2** decide = amua **3** deduce = fasiri maana **4** resolve = nuia

ínogonela *vt (pt inogonííle)* **1** think of, intend, resolve = fikiria, nuia **2** aim = lenga, wazia **3** suspect = dhania, tuhumu
~ **fííjo** deliberate = kusudia

inongwa *n (-, 9/10)* **1** news, information = habari **2** case (criminal or civil), lawsuit, crime = kesi, kadhia, tendo la kuvunja sheria **3** affair, matter, circumstance = jambo, neno **4** purpose, reason = madhumuni, sababu **5** debt =

deni

~ **ja** concerning = kuhusu

inswi *n (-, 9/10, Tuk)* fish = samaki
/Kye **iswi**

-ínufú *adj* raised = -enye mwinuko,
iliyo inuka

ínuka *vi (pt ínwííke)* raise up = inuka, amka

ínula *vt (pt inwííle)* lift, hoist, raise, jack up,
boost, elevate = nyanyua, inua

ínulila *vt.appl (pt inulííle)* support with
= inulia na

inya *interj* exclamation drawing attention of equal; hello = aisee, mwenzangu

inyagano *n (-, 9/10)* estuary = makutano ya mito au maingilio ya mito ziwani

inyale *n (-, 9/10)* lamp, lantern = taa ya
mafuta, kandili

inyale inandi candle = mshumaa

inyama *n (9)* **1** meat, flesh = nyama
2 live game = mnyama

inyambi *n (-, 9/10)* pocket, wallet =
pochi, mkoba mdogo, mfuko

inyanga *n.med (-, 9/10)* eye cataract =
mtoto wa jicho

inyangalo *n (-, 9/10)* **1** discussion =
maongezi, mazumgumzo **2** dialogue,
conversation = mazungumzo **3** planned conversation, like between the in-
laws that goes on with the feasting =
maongezi yaliyoandaliwa kati ya mtu
na wakweze ambayo huandamana na
makulajio, maakuli

inyangenyange *n.zool (-, 9/10)* egret,
cattle egret = yangeyange

inyango *n (-, 9/10)* aim, target = lengo,
shabaha

Uju aka ni nyango This man is a bad
shot = Huyu hana shabaha

inyanja *n (-, 9/10)* sea, ocean = bahari

inyege *n (-, 9/10)* erotic stimulation = nyege

inyelesi *n.zool (-, 9/10)* **1** aina ya nyoka
= type of snake **2** blind worm = ndumakuwili

inyemba *n.bot* **1** castor oil seeds = mbarika **2** oil = mafuta

inyíbuko *n (-, 9/10)* a spring = chemchemi

Inyimbo *pn* Psalms (Bible) = Nyimbo,
Zaburi
/Kyangonde: Masalimo

inyibisyo *n (-, 9/10)* whirlpool, current
= mzunguko ya maji usababishwao na
shimo chini ya mto

inyiki *n.med (-, 9/10)* epilepsy = kifafa

inyínogono *n (10)* **1** decision = uamuzi **2** disposition = tabia, elekeo, nafsi **3** opinion =
oni, maoni, mawazo **4** purpose = kusudi **5**
calculation = fikira **6** thought, idea, mind =
fikra, wazo **7** fantasy = mawazo

ínyombo *n.zool (-, 9/10)* vulture = tumbusi

inyongelapo *n (-, 9/10)* addition, sup-
plement, increment = nyongeza

inyongesya *n (-, 9/10)* addition, supple-
ment, increment = nyongeza

inyongo *n.anat (-, 9/10)* bile = nyongo

inyoselo *n (-, 9/10)* fork = uma

inyúma *n.anat (-, 9/10)* back = mgongo

inyúmba *n (-, 9/10)* house, building =
nyumba

inyumbu *n.zool (-, 9/10; >Swa)* wildebeest, gnu = nyumbu

inyundo *n (-, 9/10)* hammer = nyundo

inyusulilo *n (-, 9/10)* small ripped off
piece = kimenya

ípa, ukwípa *vt (pt ípíle)* **1** uproot =
ng'oa **2** pluck = chuma

ípaka *vt (pt ípakííle)* board, get on
board, get aboard a plane, ship, bus =
panda chomboni

ípaka *vi.reflex (pt ípakíle)* paint oneself, put on makeup, decorate oneself
= paka mafuta

ipaleto (Chrysanthemum cinerariaefolium) *n.bot (-, 9/10; > Swa)*
pyrethrum = pareto

ipamba (Gosypium spp) *n.bot (-, 9/10)*
cotton = pamba

ipampú *n (-,9/10; > Eng)* pump = pampu

ipasaka *n.relig (-, 9/10)* Easter = pasaka

ipaatisí *n (-, 9/10)* long woolen cloth which is wound on the legs by policemen as stockings = kitambaa kirefu cha sufu kinachozungushwa miguuni kama stockingi (aghalabu huvaliwa na askari), patisi

ípela *vb (pt ípelíle)* pretend = jifanye

ipelekete *n (-, 9/10)* a small drum used at traditional dances = ngoma ndogo itumikayo katika ngoma ya wenyeji

ipila *n (imí-, 9/4)* rubber = mpira

ípila *vb (pt ípíile)* weed = palilia

ípilika *vi (pt ípilíike)* **1** feel = -jisikia, hisi; **Kwípilika bulebule** How do you feel = Unajisikiaje; **2** detect, sense = vumbua

Ípinda *pn* Ipinda (village in Kyela district) = Ipinda, kijiji katika wilaya ya Kyela

ípingula *vi (pt ípingwíle)* (animals) be in heat, have desire to mate = pata joto /Also **neena**

ípingula *vi (pt ípingwíile)* get in heat = pata joto kwa mnyama hasa jike

ipoola *n (-, 9/10; > Eng)* powder = poda, unga

iposolo *n (-, 9/10)* spade = sepetu

ípúkúlanía *vi (pt ípúkúleníe)* do = fanya, shugulika

ípuula *vi (pt lípuulíle)* go from place to place looking for money or a bride = hangaika kutafuta mali au mchumba

ípúúta *vi (pt ípúútile)* **1** pray = sali **2** worship = abudu

ísa, ukwísa *vi (pt ísíle)* come = kuja

ísabula *vb (pt ísabwíile)* to eat the best part of a meal (eg. the good meat, the dessert) = kula sehemu nzuri ya mlo / chakula

ísaga! *interj* welcome!, come in! = karibu!, njoo!

ÍSAGA

This very common term carries a general meaning of invitation. This covers English expressions like: come closer, come here, come in, come along

---

isahaní *n (-, 9/10; > Swa)* plate = sahani

isaka *n (-, 9/10)* girl's house = nyumba ya msichana

isala *n (-, 9/10)* hour, watch, clock = saa **isala sya lubunju** morning hours = masaa ya asubuhi

isalala *n (-, 9/10)* spring of water = chemchemi

ísalila *vb (pt ísalíile)* choose (for oneself) = jichagulia, chagua

isaalú *n.zool (-, 9/10)* fowl with naturally ruffled feathers = kuku mwenye manyoya yaliosimama, mangisi, kidimu, nungu

isamú *n (-, 9/10; >Swa)* turn = zamu /Nya: **ulusoolo**

isangalabwe *n (10; pl of ulusangalabwe)* gravel = changarawe

isangulanandala *n.zool (-, 9/10)* type of bird = aina ya ndege

isanja *n (-, 9/10)* skirt made from leaves or grass = nguo inayovalisha kiunoni iliyotengenezwa kwa nyasi au majani

isanya *n (-, 9/10)* morning time between sunrise and midday = saa za asubuhi

ísasa *n (-, 9/10)* temporary hut = kibanda cha muda

isefulilo *n (-, 9/10)* pot, saucepan = sufuria

iseke *n.slang (10)* testicles, balls = mapumbu, kordani

isekema *n.med (-, 9/10)* fever = homa

iseko *n (-, 9/10)* laughter = kicheko

isementí *n (-, 9/10, Eng)* cement = saruji

isengo *n (-, 9/10)* sickle = mundu

isenjebele *n.zool (-, 9/10)* zebra = punda milia

isenjele *n (-, 9/10)* type of large basket made from reed or bamboo = aina ya kikapu kikubwa kilichosukwa kwa matete au mianzi

isenyenge *n (-, 9/10; > Swa)* barbed wire = seng'enge

isí *pron* these = hizi

isí *pron* who, which, that = amba-

isiba *n (-, 9/10)* charm, amulet = hirizi, talasimu

ísíbila *vi (pt ísíbííle)* acquaint, get used to, accustom = zoea

ísíbiṣígwa *vi.pass* acquaint = zoewa

ísíbisya *vt.caus (pt ísíbíísye)* **1** tame = zoeza **2** practice, train, accustom = zoeza **3** adapt = rekebisha

ísígila *vb (pt ísígííle)* protect oneself = jikinge

isígíta *n (-, 9/10)* charm = hirizi, talasimu

isilibili *n (-, 9/10)* type of bird = aina ya ndege

isílíkali *n (-, 9/10; < Swa)* government = serikali

isilisili *n.med (-, 9/10)* epilepsy = kifafa

isilya *n.bot (-, 9/10)* type of banana = aina ya ndizi

isímbilo *n (-, 9/10)* pen, pencil, writing implement = kalamu

isímbo *n (-, 9/10)* **1** sign = alama **2** tattoo = chale

isíndano *n (-, 9/10)* needle = sindano

isíndilila *n (-, 9/10)* brassiere, bra = sidiria

isípu *n (-, 9/10)* zipper = zipu

isísala *n (-, 9/10; >Eng)* scissors = mkasi /See **ikimetelo**

isofú *n (-, 9/10)* **1** *n.zool* elephant = tembo, ndovu **2** the inner room of a typical Nyakyusa house = chumba cha ndani

isogosela *n.zool (-, 9/10)* weaver (bird) = aina ya ndege

isolo *n (-, 9/10)* bao (type of game) = bao

isombyo *n.zool (ba-, 1a/2; Kye)* sunbird = chozi /Tuk **nsombyo**

ísomola *vi (pt ísomwííle)* dive (into water, head first) = chupa majini, piga mbizi

isonelo *n (-, 9/10)* needle = sindano

isoní *n (10)* **1** shame, disgrace = aibu **2** shyness = haya, soni

isongo *n (-, 9/10)* **1** tax, fee = kodi, ada **2** customs = kodi ya forodha, ushuru **3** rent = kodi ya nyumba, pango **4** tribute = kodi ya mchango, mapato

isopelo *n (-, 9/10; > Eng. spell)* letter (alphabet) = herufi ya alfabeti

  isopelo sya njobelo alphabet = alfabeti

isopo *n (-, 9/10, > Eng)* soap = sabuni

ísosya *vb (pt ísosísye)* submit = jiondoe

isota *n* **1** *n.zool (-, 9/10)* python = chatu **2** *n (imi-, 9/4)* snake which is believed to dwell inside the stomach of a witch which enables him/her to harm men and cattle = mnyoo uliomo tumboni mwa mchawi kwa ajili ya kuchawia / kurogea watu wengine

istonkení *n (-, 9/10; > Eng. stockings)* sock (esp. long) = soksi ndefu

isúkalí *n (-, 9/10)* sugar = sukari

isúkúúlú *n (-, 9/10; > Eng)* **1** school, academy = shule **2** education = elimu **Súkúúlú nnki iji mukumanyíla?** What kind of education do you have? = Ni elimu ya aina gani uliyonayo?

ísula *vi (pt íswííle)* be / become full, swell = jaa, vimba

isúlo *n (-, 9/10)* point, tip = ncha

isúlúa *n.med (-, 9/10)* measles = surua

isúlúbalí *n (-, 9/10)* pants = suruali

isulula *n.zool (-, 9/10)* any animal with stripes (cow, goat, sheep etc) = mnyama mwenye milia

isundo *n.zool (-, 9/10)* leech = ruba

isuunga *n (-, 9/10)* joke = utani

ísúnyata *vi (pt ísúnyeete)* brood, ponder = fikiria, shika tama

isúpa *n (-, 9/10)* bottle = chupa

ísusya *vt (pt iswíísye)* fill, fill up = jaza; **ísusya ilítenkí** fill up the tank = jaza tangi

iswela *n.zool (-, 9/10)* antelope = swala

iswi *n.zool (-, 9/10, Kye)* fish = samaki

iswílílí *n.zool (ba-, 1a/2)* speckeled mousebird = aina ya ndege

iswímbílí, akaswímbílí *n.off (-, 9/10)* penis, cock, dick = dhakari, zubu

ísya *vt (pt ísísye; > ukwísya)* unload = pakua

isyagí *n (9; < Swa)* butter = siagi

isyala *n (-, 9/10)* large pot = mtungi mkubwa

isyasúkúúlú *adj* academic = -a masomo

ísyona *vb (pt ísyoníle)* express distaste by making a sucking sound between the teeth = sonya, fyonya

ítabanía *vb.reflex (pt ítabeeníe)* slip, slid = teleza, jikwaa

itala *n (-, 9/10)* lamp = taa

italaka *n (-, 9/10, > Swa)* divorce = talaka

ítelení *n (ama-, 5/6)* train = gari moshi

ítetesya *vi (pt ítetesíísye)* walk slowly = enda polepole

ítika *vt (pt ítííke)* 1 answer, reply = itika, jibu 2 agree, consent, accept, admit, approve = kubali, ruhusu 3 let = ruhusu 4 believe, trust = amini 5 confess = kiri, tubu

ítikana *vt.recip (pt ítikeene)* 1 promise each other, agree = ahidiana, kubaliana 2 compromise = patana, sikilizana, ridhiana 3 bargain = patana bei, afikiana bei

ítikila *vt (pt ítikííle)* 1 answer = itikia, jibu 2 approve, appreciate = kubalia

ítikisya *vt.caus (pt ítikísye)* allow = ruhusu

ítoga *vt (pt ítogíle)* mount a horse or a donkey = panda juu ya farasi / punda/ ng'ombe

ítolo, -a ~ *adj* 1 vain = bure 2 gratis, free (of charge) = bure

ítolo *adv* 1 only, simply, merely = tu 2 in vain, vainly = bure 3 empty = wazi, bila kitu 4 bare = tupu 5 idly = vivihivi
  fwanía ~ make equal = sawazisha
  kafwene ~ complete = tosha
  mwene ~ he alone = peke yake

ítúfya *vi (pt ítúfíífye)* boast, brag = jisifu, jivuna

ítugala *vb (pt ítugeele)* 1 dwell = ishi mahali 2 sit down = kaa chini

ítúlika *vi (pt ítúlííke)* hang oneself = jinyonga kwa kamba

ítúlúfú *n (-, 9/10)* trump or ace in cards = turufu

ítúmba *vi (pt ítúmbíle)* boast = jisifu, jiona, ringa

ítúpíka *vi (pt ítúpííke)* throw oneself into, meddle, get into trouble = jiingiza matatizoni

itwíga *n.zool (-, 9/10)* giraffe = twiga

ítwika *vt (pt ítwikíle)* lift a load to the head = jitwishe mzigo kichwani, twika

iwílaja *n (-, 9/10; > Swa)* district = wilaya

Jj

-ja, ukuja *vb (pt jíle)* be, become = kuwa

ukuja múndu gwa ... to begin to, to become = anza...

-ja ni, ukuja ni *vb* have = kuwa na

jaba *vt (pt jabíle)* **1** divide = gawa, gawanya **2** distribute = sambaza **3** dish up = pakua **4** classify = ainisha

jabana *vt.recip (pt jabene)* divide among each other, share = gawia

jabanía *vt (pt jabeeníe)* distribute, divide = gawanya

jaganika *vb (pt jaganíike)* get tired = choka

jagúla *vt (pt jagwíle)* chew loudly = tafuna kwa sauti

-jako *vi (pt jíileko)* exist = kuwa, ishi

jalalu *n.zool (ba-, 1a/2)* type of snake, thin, long, striped snake (longitudinal stripes) = aina ya nyoka mrefu mwembamba mwenye milia kuelekea mkiani

jangala *vi (pt jangele, jagalele; Tuk; Kye jagalala)* be amazed = shangaa

-janja *adj* clever, tricky = -janja

janjika *vt (pt janjíke)* defraud = danganya

-japo *vi (pt jíilepo)* **1** be around, be present = kuwapo **2** exist = kuwa, ishi

jaata *vi (pt jaatíle)* walk, carouse, travel, wander = tembea

jaatila *vt (pt jaatíile)* visit = tembelea

jeela *vi (pt jelíle)* be abundant, be plentiful = jaa, jaa tele, patikana kwa wingi

jenga *vt (pt jengíle)* build, construct = jenga

jenjeluka *vi (pt jenjelwíike)* dawn = pambazuka

jeeta *vb (pt jeetíle)* be surprised = shangaa

jíganika *vt (pt jiganíike)* swear = apa

jigisya *vt.caus (pt jigíisye)* shake, wave smth = tikisa

jila *pron (9)* that = ile

-jinja *color.adj* yellow = -njano

jo *pron* **1** whom = ndiye **2** it (is) = ni; **Bakaalimmenye ukuti jo ju Knut** They did not know that [he was] it was Knut = Hawakujua kwamba alikuwa Knut

joba *vt (pt jobíle)* **1** speak, say, talk, chat, express, mention, name, remark = sema, tamka, taja **2** propose = toa shauri, pendekeza

jobana *vi (pt jobeene)* converse = zungumza, semezana

jobesanía *vb (pt jobeseníe)* argue, discuss, dispute = bishana, zungumza

joofúka *vi (pt jofwíke)* press in = bonyea

jogoja *vb (pt jogwíije)* make an undistinguishable sound like that made by a crowd at a distance = fanya sauti isiyotambulika kama ile ifanywayo na kundi la watu lililo mbali

jojobala *vi (pt jojobele)* be hunched up = jikunyata

jokesya *vt.caus (pt jokísye)* make sb escape to another place = toroshea

joola *vt (pt joolíle)* gather (in piles) = zoa

joonga *vi (pt jongíle)* run away, escape, flee, disappear, vanish = toroka, potea

jongeela *vt & vi (pt jongelíle)* disappear = toweka, potea

-jonjolo *adj* calm, quiet = tuli, kimya

joope *conj* **1** and she, and he= naye **2** and it [noun in class 9] = nayo

josya *vt.caus (pt josísye)* **1** elope (with a girl) = torosha (mwanamke) **2** lose = poteza

juuba *n.fam (aba-, la/2)* mother = mama

juuba senga *n.fam.arch* paternal aunt = shangazi

/the current word is **unnyasenga**

júbika *vt (pt júbíike)* dip, soak = loweka, weka majini

júfúla *vt (pt júfwíle)* slit, lance = tumbua

juganía *vt (pt jugeníe)* **1** shake, stir =

tingisha **2** agitate = sukasuka, suka

juganíka *vi (pt juganíike)* **1** tremble =
tingishika **2** shake, wobble = tingishika

jugila *vi (pt jugíile)* be shaky, be un-
steady = tikisika

juujo *pron* **1** she, he, him, her = yeye **2** -self
= -enyewe

jula *pron* that (person) = yule

juulajuula *vi (pt juulajuulíle)* be inse-
cure, be worried, be uncertain about
how to act = kuwa na wasiwasi

júmba *vi (pt jumbíle)* (river) swell =
kujaa kwa mto

júmbika *vt (pt júmbíike)* glorify, praise
= tukuza

jumo **1** *pron* someone, a certain one =
fulani **2** *num* one = mmoja

junganíka *vi (pt juganíike)* tremble,
shake, wobble = tingishika

jusila *vt (pt jusíile)* make a wife pregnant
while she is still breastfeeding another
child = fanya mke apate mimba wakati
bado ana mtoto mwingine mchanga

júsúmala *vi (pt júsúmele)* squat = chu-
chumaa

juusya *vt.caus (pt juusísye)* **1** persecute,
torture = tesa **2** disturb = sumbua **3**
annoy, trouble, tease = sumbua, onea,
chokoza

jwaní *interr (1;> -aní)* whose = -a nani

jwega *vi (pt jwegíle)* shout, scream,
shriek, make a noise, be noisy = piga
kilele

~ **unjwego** make a noise = piga
kelele

jwegele *n.zool (ba-, 1a/2)* type of bird,
rufous mannikin, = aina ya ndege

jweleluka *vi (pt jwelelwíke)* float = elea

jwelufu *adj* gentle, meek = pole

jwelúka *vi (pt jwelwíke)* fade, be faded
= pauka

jwelúla *vt (pt jwelwíle)* degrade = dhili,
dhalilisha

jwíba *vi (pt jwibíile)* sink = zama

jwíbisya *vt.caus* sink = zamisha

Kk

-ka- *neg.pref* verbal past tense negative
prefix: not = si-, ha-...-ja-, ha-...-ku-

ka *interj* Expression of surprise: look! =
tazama! (mshangao)

kaba *vi (pt kabíle)* **1** gain, get, obtain,
acquire, procure, achieve, earn, gain
profit = pata, pata faida **2** benefit =
faidika **3** own = miliki **4** govern,
reign = tawala **5** win = shinda; **kaba
kangi** recover = pata tena; **kaba
ilípyana** prosper, turn out well = pata
neema

kaba ikifúba become pregnant = pata
mimba

-kabi *adj* rich = tajiri

kabíbí *adv* badly, wrongly = vibaya

kaabila *vi (pt kaabíile)* **1** be late = chelewa **2** linger, delay = chelewa, kawia
3 be slow = kuwa polepole katika kutenda

kabili *adv* twice = mara mbili

kaabisya *vt.caus (pt kaabíisye)* delay =
chelewesha

kaabuno *interj* behold, really = kumbe

kaabuno *conj* that is why = kwa vile,
ndiyo maana

-kafú *adj* **1** hard, difficult, tough, stiff, callous = -gumu **2** whole, entire = -zima
3 solid, firm, sound = imara **4** (about people) not sick, well, healthy = hai, zima,
-enya afya

-kafúkafú *adj* solid, callous = yabisi

kaafya *vt (pt kaafífye)* mock, joke with
= fanyia mzaha

kaga *vt (pt kagíle)* **1** expel, chase, exile
= fukuza, ondosha kwa lazima **2** dismiss, divorce = ondosha, taliki
3 when a hen stops moving with it's
chicks = kitendo afanyacho tembe cha
kufukuza vifaranga wake

kagisya *vt.caus (pt kagíisye)* pursue,
chase = fukuzia

kajamba *n.zool (ba-, 1/2)* tortoise = kobe

Kajolo *pn* name of a spesific planet or star, possibly the planet Venus = jina la nyota au sayari fulani, labda Zuhura

kajula *vt (pt kajwííle; Tuk, Kye ajula)* open mouth with force (as when about to administer liquid drug to animals) = fungua kinywa kwa nguvu

kaka *vi (pt kakíle)* be hardened, be dry, curdle, coagulate = shikamana, ka-uka, ganda

kakajúla *vt (pt kakajwííle)* **1** gnash with teeth = saga kwa meno **2** claw = shika kwa kucha
/Also: **kakasula**

kakamala *vi (pt kakameele)* become tough, be callous = kuwa -gumu, imara

kakasula *vt (pt kakaswííle)* **1** gnash with teeth = saga kwa meno **2** claw = shika kwa kucha
/Also: **kakajúla**

kakí *interr (12, >-ki)* what type of = aina gani

kakí *n.zool (ba-, 1a/2)* baboon = nyani

kalala *vi (pt kaleele)* **1** be angry = chukia **2** be annoyed = udhika

-kalale *adj* angry = -enye hasira

kalalila *vt (pt kalalíle)* hate, loathe = chukia

kalalisya *vt.caus (pt kalalíísye; Kye)* **1** enrage, agitate, make angry, provoke = kasirisha, chukiza **2** harass, offend, annoy, disgust = udhi, kosea, kirihi
/Tuk: **kalasya**

kalanga *vt (pt kalangíle; > Swa)* fry = kaanga
/Nyakyusa: **kasínga**

kalasya *vt.caus (pt kaleesye; Tuk)* **1** enrage, agitate, make angry, provoke = kasirisha, chukiza **2** harass, offend, disgust, annoy = udhi
/Kye: **kalalisya**

kalata *n (ba-, 1a/2)* **1** letter, card = barua **2** book = kitabu

/also **ikalata**

-kali *adj* **1** hot (spicy), spicy, wild, bitter = kali **2** strict, angry, severe = kali **3** sour = -chungu

kalinga *interr* how often = mara ngapi

kalípa *vi (pt kalíípe)* be fermented, go sour = chachuka

kalíísa *n.zool (ba-, 1a/2)* scorpion = nge
/Also **kalíísya**

kalongo, mulongo *num* ten = kumi

kalongo na kamo *num* eleven = kumi na moja

kalulu *n.zool (ba-, 1a/2)* rabbit, hare = sungura

kaluma *n.bot (ba-, 1a/2)* type of banana, short, sweet, green, yellow (dwarf cavendish) = aina ya ndizi

kama *vt (pt kamíle)* **1** milk = kamua maziwa **2** squeeze = kamua, minya **3** filter liquor = kamua pombe

kamandana *vt (pt kamandene)* **1** be hardened fast, be stuck together = gandamana **2** be hunched up = jikunyata

kamandana ni be connected with = kuwa pamoja

kamandanígwa *vi (pt kamandanígwe)* be pressured, be stressed by work = banwa na shuguli

kambatula *vt (pt kambatwíle)* grip, get hold of with force = kamata, shika kwa nguvu

kamo *num* Used in general counting: one = moja
kamo - tubili - tutatu - tuna - tuhano one -two - three - four - five = moja - mbili - tatu - nne - tano

kamo ítolo 1 only one, just one = moja tu **2** once = mara moja

kamo kamo *adj* each = moja moja

kamo kene, kamokene *adj* once = mara moja

kamo ntuna quarter = robo moja, moja ya nne

kamúla *vt (pt kamwíle)* squeeze out = kama, kamua

kamútú *n.zool (ba-, 1a/2)* wild dog, African hunting dog = mbwa mwitu

kaana *vt (pt kaaníle)* **1** refuse, object, deny = kataa **2** renounce, reject, disown, disapprove = kana, kataa, tokubali **3** neglect = puuza

kanankubi *n.zool (ba-, 1a/2)* type of bird, black fisheater = aina ya ndege

kanda *vt (pt kandíle)* plaster = kandika

kangala *n* type of beer = aina ya pombe (mahindi na ulezi)

kangala *vi (pt kangeele)* become old and worn = zeeka

-kangale *adj* old = -zee

kangi *adv,conj* **1** again = tena **2** then = halafu **3** also, more, further, moreover = pia, tena, vilevile, zaidi, na tena **na kangi** and again = na tena, mara nyingi tena

kang'ula *vt (pt kang'wíle)* remove a stopper or plug, uncork = zibua, funua kizibo

-kaaníka *adj* obstinate, stubborn = kaidi, bisha

kaaníka *vi (pt kaaníke)* dispute, disagree, disapprove, oppose, refuse = bisha, tokubali, pinga, kataa

kanikana *vb (pt kaníkene)* argue = bishana

kaanila *vt (pt kaaníile)* refuse, refuse a request = katalia

kaanísya *vt.caus (pt kaanísye)* **1** forbid, ban = kataza **2** prevent, hinder, oppose, bar = zuia **3** rebuke = kataza

kanja *vt (pt kanjíle)* slap = piga kofi

kankuulu *n.zool (ba-, 1a/2)* type of bird, type of dove = aina ya ndege /Similar to **injiwa**

kankuulu *n.slang (ba-, 1a/2)* a drifter, sb who does not stay in one place = asiye na makao maalum (anaye hamahama)

kanúnú *adv* **1** well, right = vizuri **2** properly, thoroughly = kwa kufaa **3** all right = sawa

kanya *vt (pt kanyíle)* tread on = kanyaga

kanyama *n.bot (-, 9/10)* type of banana = aina ya ndizi

kanyanga *vt (pt kanyangíle)* trample, tread = kanyaga

kanyangakanyanga *vb.redup* trample again and again = kanyagakanyaga

kanyisya *vb (pt kanyíísye)* overpack, stuff = shindilia

kaasa *vt (pt kaasíle)* scratch = paruza

kasegano *n.zool (ba-,1a/2)* type of chicken with short legs = malindi

kasínga *vt (pt kasíngíle)* fry = kaanga

kasúkú *n.zool (ba-,1a/2)* parrot = kasuku

kaasula *vt (pt kaaswíle; Tuk)* scratch = paruza /Kye **palasula**

kasweswe *n.zool (ba-,1a/2)* **1** kingfisher = aina ya ndege **2** wagtail = aina ya ndege

kasya *vt.caus (pt kasísye)* **1** encourage = -pa mtu moyo **2** fasten, tighten, strain = kaza

-katafú *adj* **1** weary = -liochoka **2** weak, faint, decrepit = dhaifu **3** (about clothes) worn = --chakavu

katala *vi (pt kateele)* **1** become tired = choka **2** exhaust = choka

-katale *adj* weary = chovu

katapila *n (ba-, 1a/2)* bulldozer = katapila

katasya *vt.caus (pt kateesye)* **1** tire sb, exhaust = chosha **2** annoy, bother, bore, displease = sumbua, chukiza **3** bully, harass, trouble = onea, chokoza **4** tease = chokoza, tania

katíka *vt (pt katíke)* **1** put smth on the stove/fire, put on to cook = injika **2** place between, insert = pachika

kayamba *n* rattle (of dry grain) shaken inside a flat case of reeds = aina ya vyombo vya muziki

kekanía *vt (pt kekeníe)* cut into slices = katakata

-keke *adj* **1** young = changa **2** childish = -toto

kelenganía *vt (pt kelengeníe)* **1** look at

= angaza macho **2** look around =
angaza macho huko na huko

keelwa *vb* plenty, be plentyful = -ingi,
kuwa -ngi

kema *vi (pt kemíle)* bark = bweka

kemela *vt.appl (pt kemííle)* **1** reproach,
reprove, rebuke, reprimand, scold =
gombeza, karipia, kataza, kemea
2 bark at = bwekea

keng'enda *vt (pt keng'endíle)* level off
= sawazisha

-keenja *adj* not married, celibate = kapera

kenya *vi (pt kenyíle)* feel shy, be
ashamed = ona aibu

keenya *vt (pt keenyíle)* insult = tukana
(matusi)

kenyúla kukanwa *vt (pt kenywíle)* grin
= kenua

kenyúla amiino grin foolishly =
tabasamu kipumbavu

kenyúlila *vt (pt kenyúlíile)* oversalt food =
zidisha chumvi kwenye chakula

kesa *vt (pt kesíle)* **1** sow and cover rice / finger millet randomly with a hoe = panda
mazao kama mpunga au ulezi kwa
kumwaga **2** sow seeds by hoeing = panda
mbegu kwa kwifukia kwa jembe

-kesefu *color.adj* red = -ekundu

keseela *vi (pt keselíle)* become reddish
= kuwa -ekundu, pata rangi nyekundu

keeta *interj* but why, so, tell me = mbona
Keeta Tanya akíísa But why hasn't
Tanya come = Mbona Tanya hajaja

keeta *vt (pt keetíle)* **1** look, watch, gaze,
see = tazama **2** visit sb who is sick =
tembelea mgonjwa

keetela *vb (pt keetííle)* **1** watch, peep
(Like when you are cheating on an
exam by looking at your neighbor's
paper) = angalia, chungulia **2** go to
the river/lake to check on your fish
trap = enda mtoni kuliko na mtego wa
samaki

ketelela *vt (pt ketelííle)* **1** take care of,
attend = ngojea, kuwa chini ya uan-
galizi **2** supervise, watch = chunga,

angalia, simamia

ketesya *vt.caus (pt ketíísye)* make sb look at
smth, direct smth to = tazamisha

ketuka *vb* be split, be cracked (eg. skin)
= pasuka

-kí *interr.suffix (No preprefix is used)*
1 (connective ~) why = kwa nini;
bíísíle baakí why have they come =
kwa nini wamekuja **2** *vb* ~ what,
which = nini; **kuulisyakí** What are
you selling = Unauza nini; **ng'ombe
nkí** which cow = ng'ombe gani

kíba *vi (pt kíbíle)* **1** be quiet, be silent,
shut up = nyamaza **2** dare, be courageous, be brave = thubutu, pata ushujaa **3** be firm = kuwa thabiti **4** stop
crying = nyamaza, acha kulia **5** tolerate = vumilia **6** remark with astonishment = toa neno la mshangao

kífí *n (ba-, 1a/2)* chief = chifu

-kífú *adj* brave, daring, courageous,
bold = enye thubutu, jasiri

kifúkí *adv* **1** near, approximately, about,
close = karibu **2** almost = nusura
3 soon = upesi

kifúkí fííjo *adv* nearly = karibu kabisa,
nusura

kifúkí na *prep* **1** near to = karibu na
2 about = karibu na

-kigane *adj* favorite = kipenzi

kigili, -a ~ *adj* mad, demented = kichaa

-kigíma *adj* steep = -iliyoinuka

kííko *n.zool* cobra = aina ya nyoka na
sumu kali sana, swila

kikolo kimo kyene same kind = aina moja

kikisya *vt.caus (pt kikísye)* increase =
zidishia, ongezea zaidi

kilaabo *adv* **1** tomorrow = kesho **2** the
next day, the following day **ukulinda
kilaabo** the day after tomorrow =
kesho kutwa

kílanía *vt (pt kileeníe)* **1** break tribal
customs or taboo, go against = vunja
miiko, kiuka **2** jump over, step over =
kiuka, pita juu ya mtu au kitu

60

kílanía ulwítikano break a promise = vunja ahadi

kílanía ikimíla break a custom, go against a custom = enda kinyume cha mila

-kííliilo *adj* right (side) = kulia

kílula *vb (pt kílulíle)* anger sb = chukiza

-kiimama *adj* left (side) = kushoto

kimbila *vi (pt kimbíle)* 1 go mad = kuwa kichaa 2 run around without purpose = kimbia bila mwelekeo

kímbuka *vi (pt kímbwíke)* be angry, be vexed = kasirika

kína *vt (pt kíníle)* 1 play = cheza 2 boil = chemka

kína isimbi play cards about money = weka dau (weka fungu la fedha au kitu chochote katika mchezo wa kamari. Kitu kilichowekwa huchkuliwa na aliyeshinda

kinda *vt (pt kindíle)* 1 pass, go by, elapse, overtake = pita, fikia toka nyuma kama gari 2 go forward = tangulia, pita mbele 3 surpass, exceed = zidi, pita 4 appeal = kata rufaa

kinda amaka overpower = zidi nguvu

kinda kumaka rush = pita kwa mabavu

kindana *vb (pt kindanile)* differ = tofautisha

kindanía *vt (pt kindeenie)* distinguish, differentiate = tofautisha

kindapo *conj* 1 beyond (measure) = kuzidi kipimo 2 than = kuliko, zaidi ya

-kindíle *adj* past = -liopita, -a zamani

kindilila *vi (pt kindilíle)* 1 be to much = zidi 2 expand = tanua, zidisha, panua

-kindililí *adj* 1 dire = -liozidi 2 ahead of others = mbele ya wengine; **Ali abakindíle amahala abanine boosa mwídalasa lyake** Ali was the best student in his class = Ali aliwapita wenzie darasani

kínga *vt (pt kíngíle)* cover, conceal, disguise = funika

kingamo *adv* perhaps = labda

kíngí *adv* often = mara nyingi

kíngíma *vb (pt kíngííme)* shiver = tetemeka

kínguka *vi (pt kíngwííke)* be uncovered, be exposed, be open = funuka

kíngula *vt (pt kíngwíle)* uncover, expose, reveal = funua

kínila *vt (pt kinííle)* 1 mock = chezea, tania 2 bully = chokoza 3 *vt.appl* play with = chezea

kínisya *vt.caus (pt kíníísye)* wiggle, make smth play, shake, put into play = chezesha

kínya *vt (pt kinyíle)* hit, knock = gonga

kinyana *vb (pt kinyeene)* knock into, collide, bump into each other = gongana, kunja

/Also **tikana**

-kínyufú *adj* disappointed = -liokirihika

kínyula *vb (pt kínywíle)* disappoint = vunja ari

kipajapaja *n (ba-, 1a/2)* sb who gossips, discloses secrets, babbles nonsense = mpayukaji

kipanjamakolo *n.zool (-, 9/10)* type of bird = aina ya ndege

kipimba *n.bot (imí-, 3/4)* type of plant = mmea inaweza kusababisha kuzaliwa mapema kwa mtoto

kiisanía *vt (pt kiisenie)* pass by = pitiliza

Kisíba *pn* The crater lake on the western side of the road at Masoko, 20 km south of Tukuyu on the Matema road. = Jina la ziwa karibu na Masoko

kisíta *prep* without = bila, bila ya

kíísya *n.fam (ba-, 1a/2)* When a mother gives birth to twins they are called **mbasa** and **sinde**. The first child born after the twins is called **syoola** and the second one born after the twins is called **kíísya**. (All of these can be proper names) = Baada ya kulwa na doto anakuja syoola, na baada ya syoola anakuja kíísya

kiisya *vt.caus (pt kiisísye)* 1 allow = ruhusu 2 pass smth through = pitisha 3 exaggerate, zidisha = zidisha, piga chuku, kuza

kiita *vt (pt kiitíle)* mock, slander = tania, fanyia kejeli

kítíka *vb (pt kítííke)* stick smth into the
ground = kita

kituumbi *n.zool (ba-, 1/2)* puff adder =
kifutu

ko *pron* where = ambako, ndiko; **Kuno
ko kuno afwilííle** This is where he
died = Huku ndiko alikofia; **Ko kuno
aliko Fanta** This is where Fanta is =
Huku ndiko Fanta yuko

-kobefú *adj* weak = dhaifu

kobeka *vt (pt kobiike)* hang = tundika

kofuka vi *(pt kofwííke)* wither = nyauka

kokoosa 1 *pron* anything = yoyote
2 *adv* anywhere = popote, kokote

kokuti *conj* **1** that means = ina maana
2 because = kwa sababu

kola *vt (pt kolíle)* **1** capture, hold, arrest,
catch, seize, hold, grasp, grip = shika, kamata **2** stick, cling = nata, ambata **3** snare
= nasa, kamata **4** memorize = shika kwa
kichwa

kolana *vt.recip (pt kolene)* contact, hold
each other = shikana, gusana

kolania *vt (pt koleeníe)* carry out two or
more tasks at a time = shughulika na shughuli mbili au zaidi kwa wakati mmoja

kolekela *vt (pt kolekíle)* establish =
imarisha

kolela *vt (pt kolííle)* hold for sb =
shikia, shika kutumia kitu fulani

kolela vi *(pt kolííle)* catch fire = waka moto

kolela umoto be lit, burning = waka

koolela *vt (pt koolíle)* **1** call, talk about
= ita **2** name = -pa jina, taja, ita jina
3 bid (invite) = alika **4** call (phone) =
piga simu

koolela *vb (pt koolíle)* shout, (like to get
sb's attention) = ita kwa sauti

kolelela *vt (pt kolelíle)* grip = shika
sana, ng'ang'ania

kooleligwa *vb.pass (pt kooleligwe)* be
called = itwa

kolesya umoto *vt.caus* ignite = washa moto

kolika *(amata) vt (pt kolíke)* drip saliva
in the corners of mouth = vuja mate
ktk kingo za midomo

kologa *vt (pt kolwíge)* stir = koroga

kologanía *vt (pt kologeníe)* stir, stir up,
upset = koroga

kolola *vt (pt kolwíle)* draw lines, put stripes =
chora michirizi, mistari; chiriza

-kololaníe *adj* striped = -enye michirizi

kololoka *vi (pt kololwíke)* slacken =
kuwa -tepetevu, legea

koloma *vb (pt kolomíle)* groan = lia

koma *vb (pt komíle)* **1** beat, hit, jab, strike =
piga **2** bang, knock = gonga, twanga **3**
conquer, subdue = shinda **4** get ripe = iva,
komaa **5** (in war) attack = piga, shambulia
6 become dirty, stained, lose color, fade =
chakaa

koma amaanja applaud, clap hands = piga makofi

koma isímu make a phonecall = piga
simu

koma íbala kick = piga teke

koma indúsú shoot = piga bunduki, piga
risasi

koma ingufí clap hands = piga makofi

koma ipasí iron = piga pasi

koma nulukoba whip = chapa kwa
mjeledi, piga kiboko

komakipíkí *n.zool (ba-, 1a/2)* lizard
(generic) = mjusi

komana *vi.recip (pt komeene)* fight =
pigana

komaana *vi (pt komeene)* hold a meeting,
assemble, be crowded = kusanyika

komaanía *vt (pt komeeníe)* bring together = weka pamoja, unganisha

-kome *adj* **1** dirty, worn out = -chafu
2 tough, rough (due to old age),
experienced = -zee

komela *vt (pt komííle)* shoot, fire = piga
(kwa manati au bunduki)

komela pakikohekano crucify = suli-
bisha

komeelesya *vt.caus (pt komeelísye)*

62

command = amuru

-komú *adj* **1** clever, cunning, shrewd = janja, -erevu **2** wily = -erevu, -janja **3** subtle = -janja

-ja nkomú *vi* **1** get clever, wise up = janjaruka **2** be clever = kuwa mjanja

komwa *vi (pt komwíle)* sob = lia kwa kwikwi

koonga *vt (pt koongíle)* **1** obey = tii **2** pursue, follow, succeed = fukuzia, fuata, fuatia **3** adopt (concept) = fuatisha, fuata (wazo)

kongana *vb (pt kongeene)* go or come one after another = fuatana, fuata

konganaga *vb (pt kongeene)* follow each other = fuatana

kongela *vb (pt kongeele)* follow = fuata

koongesya *vt.caus (pt kongesísye)* **1** copy = nakili **2** trace = fuatisha

kong'onda *vb (pt kong'ondíle)* **1** knock, bang = gonga **2** knock on door, say hodi = bisha hodi **3** soften bark by beating = gongagonga gamba la mti

kong'osola *vb (pt kong'oswíile)* peck = donoa

-konyofú *adj* stupid, dumb, ignorant, silly, dull, foolish = mjinga, pumbavu

konyoka *vi (pt konywíike)* be broken = vunjika

konyola *vt (pt konywíile)* **1** break = vunja **2** wreck = vunja, haribu, angamiza

kopa *vt (pt kopíle)* borrow = azima

koopa *vb (pt koopíle)* gesticulate = onyesha maana kwa kutumia mikono

koosa *adv* **1** all of it = kila kitu **2** on both sides (ends) = sehemu zote

kosomola *vi (pt kosomwíle)* cough = kohoa

kosya *vt.caus (pt kosísye)* **1** look alike, resemble = fanana, landa **2** set on fire, fire, ignite, burn, light = washa

kotoka *vi (pt kotwíke)* stop working and go home from work (after working time) = acha na ondoka kazini

kootoka *vi (pt kootwíke)* lose weight, slim, get thin = konda

ku *locative* **1** Describes relative location, at, around = mahali, eneo, kwenye inaelezea **2** Describes direction to, at, toward = mpaka

Nsumwíke ku sokoní I'm going to the market = Naenda sokoni

Nsumwíke ku Tukuju I'm going to Tukuyu = Naenda Tukuyu

kuba *vt (pt kubíle)* **1** beat a drum = piga ngoma **2** ring (a bell) = piga (kengele) **3** play (an instrument) = piga chombo cha muziki

kuba ingufí applaud, clap hands = piga makofi

kuba umpunga take husks out of rice by winnowing = pepeta, koboa

kubilila *vb (pt kubilíle)* flap, fan, blow (fire) = pepea (moto)

kubilwa *vb (pt kubíilwe)* suffer, be tortured = teseka

kububo *adv* at last = mwishowe, hatimaye, mwishoni kabisa

kubujongelo *n (17)* west = magharibi

kubulongelo *n (17)* place of judgement = mahali kwa kuhukumia, mahali pa hukumu

kubumalikisyo *adv* at last = hatimaye, mwishoye

kubunandi *adv* seldom = mara chache

kubupímba *adv* in short, briefly = kwa kifupi, kwa ufupi

kubusookelo *n (17)* east = mashariki

kubususulilo *n (17)* at/on the top = kileleni, nchani

kúbwasya *vt.caus (pt kúbwasísye)* throw smth into water = tupa majini

kubwíngí *adv* generally, plenty, in abundance = kwa wingi, kwa ujumla, kwa kawaida

kufya *vt (pt kufífye)* cause trouble = tesa

kuugu *interr* where = wapi

kuuja *vi (pt kuujíle)* hurry up, hasten = harakisha, fanya haraka

kuujisya *vt.caus (pt kuujísye)* **1** hurry, hasten = harakisha **2** accelerate = ongeza, zidisha

kúúka *vb (pt kúúkíle)* **1** hop = kunga **2** walk with a limp = chechemea, enda chopi

kukaaja *n (17)* at home = nyumbani

-a kukatasya *adj* tiresome = -a kuchosha

kukíílilo *adv* on the right side = kulia

kukíímama *adv* on the left side = ku-shoto

-a kukindilila *adj* **1** tremendous, enor-mous = -a kuzidi **2** sth larger, greater beyond comparison = kubwa zaidi kuzidi kiasi

kúúkú *n.zool (ba-, 1a/2)* ring necked dove = njiwa pori mkubwa

kukuko *adv* just there = hukuhuko

kukuti *adv* every = kila

kukyení *n (17)* private parts, genitals = sehemu za siri

kula *adv* there, over there, yonder = kule

kula *vi (pt kulíle)* **1** grow, develop, be-come full-grown = kua **2** escalate = ongezeka

kuula *vt (pt kuulíle)* pull out teeth = ng'oa meno

kúla *vb (pt kúlíle)* **1** (wind) blow, roar = vuma (upepo) **2** drift, be blown away by the wind = chukuliwa na upepo **3** be blown/taken away by speeding water / waves = chukuliwa na maji / mawimbi **Imbwa jikúlíle nulwisí** the dog has been blown / taken downstream = Mbwa ame-zolewa / chukuliwa na mkondo wa maji /Also **húla** *(pt húlíle)*

kulabuuka *n (17)* in the early morning = mapema asubuhi

kulakula *adv* over there = kulekule

-kuulu *adj* old = -a zamani, -kuukuu

kúlúfanía *vt (pt kúlúfeníe)* throng, crowd up, compact = songa, songa-songa

kuluulu *n* north = kaskazini

kuluka *vi (pt kulwíke)* drain, ebb = ku-pwa, pungua maji

kúlúma *vi (pt kúlwíme)* thunder = nguruma

-kulumba *adj* **1** big, great = -kuu **2** older,

elder = -kubwa

kuulupa *vi (pt kuulwípe)* become old and worn = chakaa

kulusako *adv* accidentally, by chance, by luck = kwa bahati tu

kumalundi *n (17)* bedroom = chumba cha kulala

kumapumba *n (17)* cemetery = mak-aburini

kumba *vt (pt kumbíle)* dig = chimba

kumbali / pambali *adv* aside, on the side of, beside = kando, upande

kumbali *n (17)* the side, shore = pwani

kumbalilo ja *conj* because (of) = kwa sababu, kutokana na

kúmbatana *vi (pt kúmbateene)* embrace = kumbatiana, kumbatia

kúmbatila *vt (pt kumbatíile)* embrace = kumbatia

kumbuka *vt (pt kumbwíke)* **1** remem-ber, recollect, recognize = kumbuka, tambua **2** consider = fikiri

kumbusya *vt.caus (pt kumbwísye)* re-mind = kumbusha

kummalikisyo *adv* at last, finally, in the end = hatimaye, mwishoni, mwisho

kumwanya *adv* high up, above = juu

kumwanya ku *prep* above, over, on = juu ya

kumyabo *adv* their home = kwao

kumyinú *adv* your (pl) home = kwenu

kumyitu *adv* our home = kwetu

kumwanya *n (17)* heaven = mbinguni

kúnda *vi (pt kúndíle)* **1** become less hot (esp in the evenings) = pungua nguvu ya jua (hasa jioni) **2** (sun) become hidden by clouds = (jua) zibwa na mawingu

kúúnda *vt (pt kúúndíle)* **1** drink = kun-ywa **2** wake sb up during the night = amsha mtu usiku

-kundwe *adj* beloved = -pendwa, -a ku-pendeka

kunga *vt (pt kungíle)* tie = funga

kúnga *vb (pt kúngíle)* pour out, pour into = mimina

kungisanía *vt (pt kungisenie)* tie in pairs = funga vitu au wanyama ktk jozi

kungujuka *vi (pt kungujwíke)* falter = pepesuka

kúngúlúka *vt (pt kúngúlwíke)* foretell, prophecy, forecast, interpret dreams = tabiri

kúng'únda *vt (pt kúng'úndíle)* **1** shake off = kung'uta **2** *slang* beat sb up = piga mtu, kung'uta

kuno *adv* **1** here = hapa, huku **2** where, where there is = palipo na, ambapo kuna, ambako; **Ko kuno afwilíle** This is where he died = Huku ndiko alikufia

kuno na kuno here and there, this side and that side = huku na huko

kuno na kula here and there, this side and that side = huku na kule

kunokuno *adv* just this side = hukuhuku

kunongwa ja *conj* because, because of, on account of = kwa sababu

kúnwa *vi (pt kúnílwe)* be in great need of something = hitaji sana, kuwa mhitaji

kúúnya *vt (pt kúúnyíle)* pull up, push = vuta

kunyanja *n (17)* beach = pwani, ufuko

kunyúma *adv* backward = nyuma ya, mgongoni

kunyúma *prep* behind, afterwards = nyuma, baadaye

kúpama *vi (pt kupeeme)* lie on the stomach = lala kifudifudi

kúpikila *vt (pt kúpikíle)* **1** cover = funika **2** close (book) = funika, funga (kitabu)

kúpúka *vi (pt kúpwíike)* capsize, overturn = pinduka

kúúpúka *vi (pt kúúpwíike)* be uprooted = ng'oka

kúpúla *vt (pt kúpwíle)* **1** gulp = piga funda moja kubwa
2 pour out (of a container) = mwaga

kúúpúla *vt (pt kúúpwíle)* uproot = ng'oa

kúpúsya *vt.caus (pt kúpúsísye)* overturn

= pindua

kuputula *vb (pt kuputwíile)* uncover, open = funua, fungua

kuusi / kuusi ku *prep* beneath, underneath, at the bottom of, under = chini, chini ya

kuusí *n.anat (17)* genitals = sehemu za siri

kususulilo *n (17)* at the tip/top/end/summit = nchani, mwishoni, kileleni

-kuswígisya, -a *adj* fabulous = -a kushangaza, -a ajabu

kusya *vt.caus (pt kusísye)* **1** make grow, raise, enlarge = kuza **2** bring up = lea **3** exaggerate = piga chuku, ongeza sifa mno, kuza **4** grow = stawisha

kuusya *vt.caus (pt kuusísye)* pour, pour out/ into = mwaga, mimina

kusyanaloolí sya *conj* because of, on account of = kwa sababu

kúúta *vi (pt kúútíle)* **1** shout, scream, cry for help = piga kelele ili kupata msaada **2** cry, weep, groan, wail = lia, angua kilio

-a kutílisya *adj* fearful = -a kuogofya, -a kutisha

kutwaku *interr* where are you going? = unakwenda wapi?

gwatwangaku where were you going? = ulikuwa unakwenda wapi?

-kwa *vb (pt kwíle)* pay dowry = toa mahari

kwaba *vt & vi (pt kwabíle)* **1** drag, pull, draw = vuta **2** hoist = nyanyua

kwaba ingafí row a boat = piga kasia

kwaba umuují breathe, inhale = vuta pumzi

kwanda/-a kwanda *num.ord* first = -a kwanza

kweela *vt.app (pt kweelíle)* to pay dowry, pay the father-in-law cows for the wife = kutoa mahari kwa ajili ya mke

kweela *vt (pt kweelíle)* **1** climb, ascend, rise, go up to = panda, endea, kwea **2** pass an exam = faulu mtihani **3** pass = pita, faulu **4** board = panda chomboni

kwema *vt (pt kwemíle)* **1** clean oneself after defecating (used about small children) = sogona, kokona, sosona **2** crawl (like a lame person or like a very small child), move using buttocks, crawl = tambaa, sota

kwesa *vt (pt kwesíle)* smoke = vuta

kwesya *vt (pt kwesísye)* boost, enhance = pitisha, faulisha, pandisha, inua

kwígíma *n (17)* on the mountain side = kando ya mlima

kwíjala *n (17)* in the valley = bondeni

kwilanila *vi (pt kwilaníle)* be adequate, be enough = tosheleza

kwínya *vi (pt kwínyíle)* **1** wither, waste away, shrink = sinyaa, kunyata **2** wrinkle = sinyaa **3** frown = kunya uso

kwísilya *adv, prep* **1** the other part /side of a body of water, across, overseas = ng'ambo, toka upande huu mpaka upande wa pili **2** abroad = ng'ambo

kwítongo *n (17)* south = kusini

kya *part (7)* of = cha

-kya, ukukya *vi (pt kííle)* **1** cease raining = acha kunyesha **2** dawn, be daylight = pambazuka, cha/kucha

-kyaji *adj* **1** better, rather = afadhali **2** preferable = heri

kyala *n (ba-, 1a/2)* god = mungu

kyalalika *vb (pt kyalalíike)* move fast = enda mbio (k.m. samaki juu ya maji au baisikeli barabarani)

kyamení *n (aba-, 1/2, Eng)* chairman = mwenyekiti

kyanyúma *adv* from behind = kutoka nyuma

kyeela *vt (pt kyelíile)* please = pendeza

LI

-la *det* (jula, kala, bala…) that, those = yule, wale…

laba *vb (pt labíle)* **1** *vi* be tormented, afflicted, suffer = teseka, sumbuka, taabika, umia **2** *vt* paint, whitewash a wall = paka ukuta choka, paka rangi

labasya *vt.caus (pt labasisye)* pretend = jifanya, kujitia hamnazo, kumbe zipo

labaasya *vb (pt labeesye)* talk unintelligibly = zungumza mambo juuujuu

labila *vb (pt labííle)* go following a certain direction, go in a certain direction = elekea (sehemu fulani)

laabila *vi (pt laabííle)* **1** get up early = jidamka, jihimu asubuhi **2** be early = wahi

labisya *vt (pt labíísye)* direct = elekeza

-lafu *adj* (people, animals) skinny, thin = -liokonda

laga *vt & vi (pt lagile)* bid farewell = aga; **Nundagíle pa Ípinda** I bade him farewell in Ipinda = Nimemwaga Ipinda

lagila *vt (pt lagíile)* **1** enforce, order, instruct, direct, command, appoint = agiza **2** dictate = toa imla **3** rule = tawala, amuru

lagilila *vt.appl (pt lagilíle)* order for = agizia

lagisya *vt.caus (pt lagíísye)* **1** order for = agizia **2** command = amuru

lagukisya *vt (pt lagukísye)* guess = bahatisha, kisi

lagula *vt (pt lagwíle)* guess, foretell, divine = agua, bahatisha, piga ramli, tabiri, baskivi

lala *vi (pt lalíle)* **1** get thin, lose weight = konda **2** wither = nyauka

lalamuka *vi (pt lalamwííke)* wither = nyauka

lalamúka *vi (pt lalamwíke)* worry = shituka (moyo), hangaika

lalata *vi.med (pt laleete)* become paralytic = pooza

laluusya *vt.caus (pt laluusísye, lalwíísye)* **1** ask (a question), enquire, inquire, question = uliza **2** ask for, request, beg = omba **3** spy = peleleza **4** apologize = omba radhi

laamba *vt (pt laambíle)* apologize = omba radhi

lambalala *vi (pt lambalele)* sleep, lie down = lala

lambalika *vt.caus (pt lambalíke)* put to bed, make sb lie down = laza

lambika *vt (pt lambíike)* oppress = kandamiza

laambika *vt (pt laambíike)* subdue = tawala, tiisha

lambilisya *vt.caus (pt lambilíisye)* persuade = shawishi

lambiisya *vt.caus (pt lambíisye)* persuade, coax = bembeleza mno, sihi

lamúla *vb (pt lamwíile)* **1** stop a fight = amua **2** judge, arbitrate, solve = amua

lamúlanía *vt (pt lamúlenie)* stop a fight between people, settle things between warring factions = amua ugomvi, suluhisha

lamúsya *vt (pt lamwíisye) ingamwana* greet = salimia

langala *vi (pt langeele)* glisten, glitter, shine = mulika, angaza

-langalí *color.adj* scarlet, bright red = -ekundu, enye kung'aa; **unselekesye umwílangalí** scarlet robe = vazi ng'aavu

langasya *vt.caus (pt langeesye)* make smth shine = angaza

lapa *vi (pt lapíle)* swear, vow = apa

lapisya *vt (pt lapíisye)* damn = apiza

lasa *vt (pt lasíle)* stab, pierce (with spear or knife), jab, sting = choma (mkuki)

laasuka *vb (pt laaswíike)* be torn = chanika

laata *vt & vi (pt laatíle)* **1** shout = piga kelele **2** speak loudly = paza sauti

laata ubusobí confess = ungama, kiri kosa

latuka *vi (pt latwíke)* be cut, be ripped, be torn, be broken, break down = katika, raruka, tatuka

latula *vt (pt latwíle)* rip, shred, cut = kata, pasua, chana

le *adv* now = sasa

leeba *vt (pt leebíle)* steal = iba

lefúka *vi (pt lefwíke)* stretch, be stretched = tanuka

legana *vb (pt legeene)* be different, differ = hitilafiana

leganía *vt (pt legenie)* **1** differentiate, distinguish, discriminate = tofautisha, pambanua **2** confuse = changanya **3** dodge sb, avoid sb = kwepa mtu usionane

leganika *vb (pt leganíike)* evade, avoid, dodge sb, = epuka, jifichefiche, kutoonekane

legela *vi (pt legeele)* slacken = legea

lejaníla *vt (pt lejaníile)* **1** betray each other = semeleana, chongeana **2** blame each other = laumiana

leejela *vt (pt leejíile)* betray = semelea, shitakia, chongea

leka *vt (pt lekíle)* **1** stop doing smth, abolish, leave, desert, forsake, neglect, quit, cease, stop, abandon, omit = acha, acha kufanya jambo fulani, telekeza **2** excuse = samehe **3** release = achia, achilia **4** let = ruhusu

lekana *vi* get separated = achana

lekela *vb (pt lekíile)* **1** to leave smth for sb else. eg to leave food for sb who has not yet arrived or for sb who is a slow eater = achia, rithisha **2** bequeath, convey (something) from one generation to the next

lekeelela *vt (pt lekeelelíle)* leave behind, forget = acha, sahau nyuma

lekesya *vt.caus (pt lekíisye)* **1** release = achilia, toa **2** dismiss = achisha, achilia

-lekígwa *vb.pass* abandoned, left = achwa

lelema *vt (pt lelíime)* shake, make vibrate = tikisa

lelo *conj* but = lakini

-lema *adj* stupid, dumb, foolish = mpumbavu

lemala *vi (pt lemele)* be crippled, be disabled = lemaa

lemba *vb (pt lembíle)* draw, decorate = chora

lembe *n.zool (ba,1/2)* type of wild cat = aina ya paka wa porini

lembuka *vi (pt lembwíke)* awake, wake up, get up = amka

lembusya *vt.caus (pt lembwísye)* wake sb up = amsha

lemúka *vi (pt lemwíke)* sober, clear up = kupungua ulevi, pata fahamu

lendemuka *vi (pt lendemwííke)* 1 crack = pata ufa 2 (of heart) palpitate = pwita, tutuma

leenga *vt (pt leengíle)* saw = pasua kwa msumeno

lengeteka *(amasosi) vi (pt lengetíike)* to have tears in your eyes, be near crying = jaa machozi machoni, lengalenga; **amaso gíkundengeteka** his eyes are full of tears = machozi yake yanam-lengalenga

leesya *vt (pt leesísye)* peel (potatoes) = menya

-lí *vb* be = kuwa
   alíko, he is there = yupo

-libe *interr* which? = -ipi?

-libe *pron*
   undibe somebody = mtu fulani
   bulibe some type of = aina fulani
   akalibe something = kitu fulani

-libule *interr* what kind = aina gani, ikoje

liga *vt (pt ligíle)* make a mistake, err, offend against, do wrong to = kosea

lígíta *vt (pt ligíte)* intentionally make smth fall down = angusha

liigwa *vi (pt liigílwe)* lose = kosa, pata hasara

-liku *interr* which? = nani? kitu gani?
   unkííkulu aliku which woman = mwanamke yupi

lubafú luliku which direction = pande ipi, upande upi

lila *vb (pt lilíle)* 1 cry, weep = lia 2 sound = toa sauti 3 mourn = lia, huzunika, kaa matanga

liila *vb (pt liilíle)* swindle = danganya

lilaníka *vi (pt lilaníike)* complain = lalamika, nung'unika

lili bule 1 what's the time = saa ngapi 2 how is it = likoje

lilalila *n.bot (ba-, 1a/2)* type of grass with thorns = aina ya mmea wenye miba

lilila *vt.appl (pt lilíile)* cry for, lament for = lilia

lilili *adv* this very one = hili hili, hii hii **mwísíku lilili** on this very day = siku hii hii ya leo

lilino *adv* 1 now, at this time = sasa 2 today = leo

lilino ulu *adv* now = sasa

-lilisí *adj* persistent, clinging to, clutching, eg. strong mother feeling = ng'ang'anizi

lima *vt (pt limíle)* farm (cultivate, hoe, till, dig) = lima

limbula *vt (pt limbwíile)* gather honey = rina asali

linda *vi (pt lindíle)* 1 remain = baki 2 be absent = shinda, kutokuwako 3 stay = kaa

lindilila *vt (pt lindilíle)* 1 defend, protect, guard, shield = linda 2 wait = ngoja 3 keep watch= linda 4 take care (of), watch = angalia, tunza 5 cherish = penda

-lindilili *adj* cautious = -enye hadhari, tahadhali

línga *vt (pt língíle)* peep through = chungulia

liinga *conj* 1 if, perhaps, when, whether = kama, endapo, iwapo, ikiwa 2 that, in order that = kwamba 3 whether = endapo, iwapo

lingaanía *vt (pt lingeeníe)* 1 analyze = chambua, elezea 2 narrate = simulia

3 explain, describe, instruct, educate, define , express, elaborate = elimisha, elekeza, elezea, eleza, fafanua

lingisanía *vt (pt lingisenie)* explain = elezea, elekeza

língulila *vt & vi (pt língulíle)* peep = chungulía

lípuka *vi (pt lípwíike)* erupt = lipuka

lípula *vt (pt lípwíile)* detonate = lipua

lisya *vt.caus (pt lisísye)* make sb cry = liza

liisya *vt.caus (pt liisísye)* feed = lisha

litaasi *adv* early = zamani, baadaye

loba *vt (pt lobíle)* fish = vua samaki

loboka *vt (pt lobwíike)* cross over water, ford, wade = vuka

lobosya *vt.caus (pt lobwísye)* ferry across = vusha

-lofú *adj* greedy = lafi

loga *vt (pt logíle)* bewitch, put a spell on, enchant, cast a spell = roga, loga, wanga, pendeza mno

loganía *vt (pt logenie)* spoil, destroy = haribu

logwa *vb* copulate, make love = fanya mapenzi, zini

lokoka *vb (pt lokwíike)* **1** *vb.relig* be saved = okoka **2** be converted = mche mungu, ongoka

loolí *conj* **1** but, however = lakini **2** except = ila

londa *vt (pt londíle)* **1** want, wish, desire = taka **2** look for, find = tafuta **3** need = hitaji **4** enquire = uliza, ulizia, chunguza

londa ubwegí propose (marriage) = hitaji kuoa

londeesya *vt (pt londesíisye)* **1** look for = tafuta kwa makini, chunguza **2** follow = fuata **3** follow up behind = fuatilia

londeesya ububíne *vb.med* diagnose = tafuta ugonjwa na chanzo chake, chunguza ugonjwa

-londo *adj* poor, destitute = fukara, fakiri

londoka *vb (pt londwíke)* become/be poor, be bankrupt = kuwa fukara, kuwa maskini

-londoke *adj* bankrupt, impoverished, poor = fukara, maskini

londosya *vb.caus (pt londwíisye)* impoverish, bankrupt sb, make sb poor = fanya mtu kuwa maskini

loonga *vt (pt loongíle)* **1** judge = hukumu **2** convict = tia hatiani **3** to do justice = shauri kesi

loongana *vt & vi (pt loongeene)* **1** settle things before the elders = suluhisha **2** counsel = shauri, shauriana

longela *vt.appl (pt longíile)* **1** dispose of = hukumia **2** give judgement on (for, at etc.) = hukumia

longígwa *vi.pass (pt longíigwe)* be accused = hukumiwa

loongola *vt & vi (pt loongwíle)* lead, go ahead = ongoza, tangulia

longosanía *vt (pt longosenie)* accompany = ongozana

longosya *vt.caus (pt longwísye)* **1** lead, govern, guide, administer = ongoza, shika usukani, elekeza njia, tawala **2** make sb go before you = tanguliza

loosa *adv* absolute, entirely, absolutely, utterly, completely = hasa, kabisa

lota *vi (pt lotíle)* in the process of glowing = kukolea kwa moto; **akoto aka kalotile** glowing embers = moto unaowaka

lubukilwa *vb (pt lubukíilwe)* do for the first time, eat the first fruits of a new crop, enjoy for the first time = limbuka, limbua

luka *vt (pt lukíle)* **1** braid hair, plait hair = suka **2** knit, weave = fuma **3** splice, twine = fuma, suka, sokota

luukí *n.bot (baaluukí, 1a/2)* orange = chungwa

lulalula *adv* likewise = vilevile

lulala *vi (pt luleele)* be still = lulia tuli

lulasya *vt.caus (pt luleesye)* bewilder, dazzle, stun = pumbaza

luulo *adv* accordingly, in that manner = jinsi ilivyo, jinsi hiyo, namna hiyo, hivyo hivyo

lulikila *vb (pt lulikíle)* aim at = lenga

lululu *adv* **1** right now, at once, this very minute = sasa hivi **2** in a moment, soon = bado kidogo
-a lululu *adj* current = -a sasa, -a karibu

lulungila *vi (pt lulungíile)* be or stay at the highest point of smth = kuwa kileleni

lulungisya *vt.caus (pt lulungíisye)* fill up a container = weka/jaza mpaka kileleni
lulungisya mpaka pamwanya (common in measuring grains in containers) fill up the container to the best of its capacity = jaza chombo nafaka mpaka uwezo wake wa juu kabisa

lúlútila *vt (pt lulutíile)* **1** ululate = piga vigelegele, piga kigelegele, shangilia **2** exult, rejoice = shangilia

luma *vt (pt lumíle)* **1** bite = uma **2** sting = ng'ata
jíkubaluma injala they are hungry (lit: hunger is biting them) = wana njaa

lumba (caprimulgus spp) *n.zool (ba-, 1a/2)* nightjar, type of bird = mraruasanda, mpasuasanda

lumba *vt (pt lumbíle)* to sing/read a poem about someones (usually bad) deeds without mentioning them directly = imba / soma shairi kuhusu matendo mabaya ya mtu bila kuyataja waziwazi

lumbilila *vt (pt lumbilíile)* preach = hubiri

lúmbúka *vi (pt lumbwíike)* be stretched, expand = tanuka

lúmbúla *vt (pt lúmbwíle)* stretch = tanua

lumbuusya *vt.caus (pt lumbusísye)* humiliate = simanga

lumo maybe, sometimes = huenda, pengine

lúndanía *vt (pt lúndenie)* separate = tenga

lundika *vt (pt lundíike)* **1** pile up = rundika **2** accumulate = kusanya

lundukila *vt (pt lundukíle)* raise an uproar against = shambulia kwa maneno

lundula *vt (pt lundwíile)* **1** to take the cows out for grazing = kupeleka ng'ombe malishoni **2** divide = gawanya

lúndúma *vi (pt lúndwíme)* thunder = unguruma, toa muungurumo, toa ngurumo, toa sauti kubwa kama ngurumo

lúndúmúla *vt (pt lúndúmwíle)* draw, pull, drag = vuta

lunga *vt (pt lungíle)* **1** join, connect = unga **2** season food = unga chakula

lunganía *vt (pt lungenie)* join = unganisha, unga

lungi *adv* contrarily = kinyume

lungisanía *vt (pt lungisenie)* put together, connect, arrange, fix = unganisha

lungula *vb (pt lungwíile)* dissolve = yeyusha

-a lupasyo *adj* anxious = -a hangaiko

lúúsa *vt (pt lúúsíle)* stretch, pull, drag = vuta

-a lusaalo *adj* happy = -a furaha

lusanía *vt (pt lusenie)* cause anxiety = hangaisha

lúúsanía *vb (pt lúúsenie)* pull out and scatter items = tawanya vitu bila mpango

lusanje *n.zool (ba-, 1a/2)* type of monkey, small monkey (rhesus monkey) = ngedere, tumbili
/Same as **nkekwa**

lúúsúka *vi (pt lúúswíike)* **1** be prolonged, be stretched = refuka, vuta mguu tokana na uzito au maumivu **2** *vi.slang* become broke = ishiwa

-a lutúfyo *adj* glorious = -tukufu

-lwa *vi (pt lwíle)* **1** fight = pigana **2** quarrel = gombana

lwana *vi.recip (pt lwene)* quarrel = gombana

lwanía *vb (pt lwenie)* **1** confront = tofautiana, farakana, pinga **2** cause to quarrel = gombanisha

lwasya *vt.caus (pt lwesye)* **1** nurse the sick = uguza **2** care for = uguza

lwele *num* eight = nane

lwele ikingi ntanda *num* seven = saba

lwele kimo *num* nine = tisa

lwembe *n (ba-, 1a/2)* **1** *n.arch* an important medicine man , (originally a person from historical traditions, at the turn of the century this was an established political office, the first Lwembe was buried at Lubaga, Kinga priests still come to sacrifice there) = Mganga mkuu wa kienyeji, mtu wa mwanzoni kabisa katika historia toka Ukinga. Lwembe alizikwa Lubaga, bado Wakinga wanaafudu pale **2** *n.slang* elder brother = kaka mkubwa

-lya *vt (pt lííle)* eat = kula

lyolyoosa *pron* any, anything = lolote, yoyote

-a lyojo *adj* easily angered = epesi kukasirika

lyope *adv* also the (noun in class 5) = nalo

Mm

Mafíningo *pn* name of a certain star or planet = jina la nyota au sayari fulani

-maganyí *adj* skillful, capable, brave, courageous = tundu, hodari

-maganyífú *adj* artistic = -a sanaa

-a mahala *adj* wise = -a hekima, -a akili

-maka, -a ~ *adj* able = -enye uwezo

makosí ga nyoko / mwísukulugo / guso *off* literally: "your mother's, grandpa's , father's neck" = shingo ya mama/babu/baba yako

mala *vt (pt malíle)* finish = maliza
Akwísa kumala ndilí imbombo jako? When will you finish your work? = Utamaliza lini kazi yako?

malangalanga *n (ba-, 1a/2)* beautiful girl = msichana mrembo, kisura

malika *vi.stat* be finished, perish = malizika

malikila *vb (pt malikíile)* end up, culminate = ishia

malikígwa *vb (pt malikígwe)* run out of = poteza

-malikilwe *adj* bankrupt = -aliye filisika

maliisya *vt.caus (pt maliisísye)* **1** accomplish, complete, finish, conclude, decide, exhaust = maliza, amua **2** eliminate = ua, ondoa, toa, futa, ondosha

mama *n.fam (ba-, 1a/2; > Swa)* mother = mama
/This word is more and more replacing the Nyakyusa **juuba** (my mother). Also commonly heard is mama gwako (your (sg.) mother) instead of **unyoko** which today carries a somewhat offensive meaning like in Swahili.

-manga *adj* corpulent, fat = -nene

manguka *vb* be / become corpulent, be / become fat = nenepa

manya *vt (pt meenye)* **1** know, understand, grasp = fahamu, jua, elewa **2** recognize, identify, detect = tambu, gundua

71

manyana *vi (pt manyeene)* **1** make love, copulate (polite expression) = jamiana, pendana **2** be acquainted, be friends = elewana, kuwa marafiki

manyanía *vt (pt manyeníe)* reconcile, make people become friends = patanisha, fanya watu wawe marafiki

-manyí *adj* cunning = mwerevu, -juaji, juzi

manyígwa *vb.pass (pt manyíigwe)* famous, known = julikana, kuwa maarufu

manyíla *vb (pt manyíile)* **1** to be educated = elimika **2** learn, study = jifunza

manyísya *vt.caus (pt manyísye)* teach, educate, instruct, train = fundisha

mata *vb (pt matíle)* **1** plug, stop up, fill in (crack) = ziba (ufa) **2** plaster = siriba, kandika

matila *vb (pt matíile)* plug, stop up, fill in (crack) = ziba (ufa), piga lipu

matisya *vt.caus (pt matíisye)* fasten to, attach = bandika, ambatisha, natisha

matula *vb (pt matwíile)* demolish a mud wall = bomoa udongo uliokandikwa kwenye ukuta

mbala *adv* scarce = adimu

Mbamba *pn* name for old "deity" = jina ya zamani kwa "mungu" mmoja

mbasa *n (ba-, 1a/2)* the first-born of twins (the second is called **sinde/ sindika**) = kurwa

mbelíle please = tafadhali

mbepa *used in the phrase:* **lya mbepa** it doesn't matter, never mind = haidhuru

mbibimbibi *adv* fast, quickly = haraka, kwa haraka, haraka haraka, upesiupesi

mbimbibi *adv* as soon as = haraka, upesi

-mbindipindi *color.adj* green = kijani

mbolambola *adv* gradually, slowly = taratibu, polepole

mbumalikilo *adv* at the end of, ultimately = mwishoni mwa, mwishowe

mbunandi *adv* **1** in small quantities = kidogo **2** in short = kwa kifupi

mbupepe *adv* easily = kwa urahisi

mbusapala *adv* at last = mwishowe, hatimaye, mwishoni kabisa

mbwananoli *adv* actually = kwa kweli

mela *vi (pt melíle)* **1** grow, sprout = ota **2** claim = dai

melela *vb (pt melíile)* **1** prosecute = dai, shitaki **2** *vt.appl* = claim for = daia

melelígwa *vi (pt melelíigwe)* owe, be in debt = daiwa

memena *vb (pt memeníle)* grind with teeth, nibble, gnaw = tafuna, guguna, tikita, ng'ong'ona

mendamenda *n (ba-, 1a/2)* sb who does petty business = mchuuzi anayetembeza bidhaa

mendamenda *vt (pt mendamendíle)* to do petty business by going around selling things = fanya biashara kwa kutembeatembea

menya *vt (pt menyíle)* **1** break, split = kata, mega **2** chop = katakata

menyanía *vb (pt menyeeníe)* chop = katakata

mesya *vt.caus (pt mesíisye, > mela)* make smth grow = otesha

meta *vt (pt metíle)* cut (esp hair) = nyoa (nywele)

meeta *vi (pt meetíle)* bleat, cry like a goat = lia kama mbuzi

mfundiko *num* five = tano

mfundiko fyoosa *num* ten = kumi

míla *vt (pt mílíle)* **1** swallow = meza **2** devour = meza

mílwa *vi (pt mílílwe; Kye)* drown = kufa maji; zama kwenye maji

míímwa *vt (pt mímimwe)* **1** crave, long for (smth you can't get)= tamani **2** envy = husudu

míísa *vt (pt míísíle)* sprinkle, spray = nyunyiza

mma, himma *adv* no = hapana

mmaapa *n.anat (18)* armpit = kwapa

mmajolo *adv* yesterday = jana

-mmalikisyo *adj* last = -a mwisho

mmwanya *prep* up in = juu
 Injuní jili mmwanya múmpíkí The bird is up in the tree = Ndege yuko juu mtini

-mmwanyamwanya *adj* on the surface = juujuu

mo *locative* Describes location inside of smth, at = mo, ndani ya

-mo *num* one = moja; **umúndu jumo** one man = mtu mmoja

moga *vt & vi (pt mogíle)* **1** dance, play = cheza, cheza ngoma **2** celebrate = sherehekea

mogela *vt (pt mogíile)* **1** be proud of = jivunia **2** *vt.appl* dance with = cheza na **3** *vt.appl* dance for = chezea mtu (cheza kwa ajili ya mtu)

-mogí *adj* proud = -enye fahari, -a madaha

mookí *prep* in where = wapi

momúmo *interj* all right, OK, precisely, right, correct = sawa, sawasawa

-a momúmo *adj* normal = -a kawaida

momuno that is ok, that is the way = ndivyo hivyo

mosa *pron* all (places), everywhere = pote

mosamosa *pron* everywhere = kila mahali, popote

mpaka *conj* until, unless = hadi, hata

mpaka *prep* up to = hadi, hata

mu *part* Describes location inside of smth, in = katika, mo, ndani ya, kwenye

múla *prep,adv* in there = mle, humo

múlamúla *adv* in there = mlemle

múlika *vi (pt múliíke)* **1** glow = mulika **2** shine = angaza

múlikamúlika *vi (pt múliíkemúliíke)* gleam, shine, sparkle = mulikamulika, meremeta, toa cheche

mulongo *num* ten = kumi

mumbafu *adv* on the side (of) = mbavuni, kwenye mbavu

mumbali *adv* aside, on the side = kando

múúmo *adv* **1** complete = kamili **2** exactly = halisi **3** as = kama; **múúmo abulíígwe** as she was told = kama alivyoambiwa; **4** perhaps, maybe = labda, pengine **5** accordingly, thus, in that way, in that same way = jinsi ilivyo, vivyo, vivyo hivyo, hivyo **6** in there = humohumo

mumumo *adv* in there = humo

múúnda *n (18)* inside the stomach = tumboni

múnda *vb (pt múndíle)* step on or trample with the heel (as in a football match) = kanyaga kwa kutumia kisigino; **Umpila gula gukanogíle, paapo bamúndanaga fííijo** That game was not good bwecause of the rough play = Mpira ule haukupendeza kwa sababu ya rafu nyingi

múno *adv* in here, in it = humu

munomuno *adv* just in here = humuhumu

musanya *adv* in the morning = asubuhi, mapema

mwa *prep* Indicates location in an enclosed area; in, inside of, at = -mo

-mwa *vt (pt mwíile)* shave = nyoa

mwa- *prefix* Most male last names start with these three letters. They are added to the name of the mother Mwakyusa "the son of Kyusa = bin Kyusa

mwakatílolo *n.zool (ba-, 1a/2)* type of bird = aina ya ndege

mwakikali *n.bot (ba-, 1a/2)* type of plant, small plant used for medicine = aina ya mmea, mmea mdogo utumikao kwa dawa /see **pupwa**

mwakilumbwa *n.zool (ba-, 1a/2)* fish eagle = koho, tai mvuvi

mwakinyomo *color.adj* dark blue = buluu nzito, buluu kolevu

mwalalo *n.zool (ba-, 1a/2)* type of bird, small = aina ya ndege mdogo

mwalo *adv* carelessly = ovyo

-a mwalo *adj* **1** absurd = -ovyo **2** boisterous

= -a fujo, makelele **3** naughty = -tundu **4** vulgar = chafu

mwalomwalo *adv* **1** all over = ovyo ovyo **2** clumsily = ovyo ovyo, shaghalabaghala

-a mwalomwalo *adj* zigzag = -ovyoovyo, shaghalabaghala

mwalukama *n.zool (ba-, 1a/2)* type of ant = aina ya sisimizi

mwamnyíla, *n.bot (-, 9/10; Kye)* type of banana (red/yellow and thick, typically found in the Itete area) = ndizi nene za rangi nyekundu

mwansomo *n (ba-, 1a/2)* diving, the act of diving into water = kitendo cha kuchupa majini, kupiga mbizi

mwantyoko *n.zool (ba-, 1a/2)* type of small bird with a small black crown, sparrow = aina ya ndege mdogo, shore kishungi, shorewanda / Same as **indyokolílo**

mwasíbalo *n.zool (ba-, 1a/2)* dragonfly = kereng'ende

-mwasúngo *color.adj* really black, very black = -eusi sana, eusi tii

mweka *vi (pt mwekíle)* glow = mulika

mwekúka *vi (pt mwekwíke)* light up, illuminate, shine on = mulika

mwela *vi (pt mwelíle)* shine, radiate = angaza, nururisha

mwela *vt.appl (pt mwelíile; > -mwa)* shave with = nyolea

mwembe *n (bamwembe, 1a/2)* **1** mango tree = mwembe **2** mango (fruit) = embe

mwemweka *vi (pt mwemweeke)* glitter = ng'ara, metameta, mulika

mwemwesya *vi (pt mwemwesísye)* **1** grin = cheka kipumbavu **2** take piece of glowing fire and move it around as if one is looking for smth = mulikamulika

-mwíko *adj* taboo, forbidden = mwiko, haramu

mwílunduko *adv* in the afternoon = alasiri

mwimba *n.zool (ba-, 1a/2)* anteater = mhanga

myalísya *vb (pt myalísye)* stick out tongue in contempt = ng'ong'a

myanda *vt (pt myandíle)* lick = lamba

myasya *vt (pt myasísye)* smear, spread on = paka

myatula *vt (pt myatwíle)* take off, detach, remove = bandua

myeka *vb (pt myekíle)* be silent, be quiet, become quiet, calm down, get calm = nyamaza, tulia

myemyemye *adv* quietly, silently = kimyakimya

myesya *vt.caus (pt myesísye)* silence sb = nyamazisha

myogoka *vi (pt myogwíke, myonywíke)* limp = chechemea

myogonyoka *vi (pt myogonywíke)* collapse, fall apart = bomoka

myonyoka *vi (pt myogwíke, myonywíke)* limp = chechemea

Nn

n-, na, ni, nu *conj,prep* and, with, by = na
/Normally written together with the following noun

-na, tuna *num* four = -nne

nafímo nothing = hakuna kitu, hamna kitu

naganía *vt (pt nageníe)* decrease, lessen, reduce = punguza

naganíka *vt (pt naganííke)* decrease, grow less = pungua, pungua idadi

nagwe with him/her = pamoja naye

najumo *pron* nobody = hakuna mtu

nakalinga *adv* **1** immediately = mara moja **2** suddenly, at once abruptly = ghafla, haraka

nakamo *adv* **1** nothing = tupu, hamna kitu, hakuna **2** zero, nought = sifuri **3** empty = tupu **4** it is impossible = haiwezekani, siowezekana **5** never = hakuna, kamwe

nakaníní *adv* not at all = hata kidogo

nakúmo *adv* anywhere, nowhere = popote; **Ndikubuka nakúmo** I'm not going anywhere = siendi popote

naala *vb (pt naalíle)* to auction, to sell = piga mnada

nalamba please = tafadhali

nalilino *adv* **1** even now = hata sasa **2** even today = hata leo

nalinga *conj* although, though, even if = ingawa

naloolí *adv* **1** really, indeed, actually, truly = kweli **2** certainly, OK, sure, exactly = hakika
-a naloolí *adj* **1** perfect = kamili, zima, sahihi, kabisa, hasa **2** real, true = kweli **3** certain, exact = halisi, bila shaka, hakika, -a hakika

namanga *conj* because, since = kwa sababu, kwa kuwa

namúmo *adv* anywhere, nowhere = popote; **Ndikubuka namúmo** I'm not

going anywhere = siendi popote

-nandi *adj* **1** small, little = -dogo **2** few, scarce = chache, haba

nangisya *vt.caus (pt nangíisye)* **1** show, demonstrate, display, depict = onyesha **2** point = onyesha, nyoshea kidole **3** direct = elekeza, ongoza **4** denote, designate = onyesha **5** mean = maanisha **6** determine = amua **7** identify = tambua

naaní *interr* with whom? = pamoja na nani?

naniíne/niíne *adv* **1** and I = nami **2** even I = hata mimi **3** with me = pamoja nami

nanúmwe *adv* with you (pl) = pamoja nanyi

nanúngwe/núngwe *adv* with you (sg) = pamoja na wewe

nanúswe/núswe *adv* with us = pamoja na sisi

naapa *adv* whereas, while = wakati ambapo

napalima *adv* even though = hata kama

naapalinga *adv* however, even if = hata iwapo, hata kama

napamo *adv* anywhere, nowhere = popote; **Ndikubuka napamo** I'm not going anywhere = siendi popote

napaapo *conj* although, though, even if = ingawa

nasiku *adv* never = kamwe

ndaga *interj* **1** thank you = asante **2** used as general greeting = salamu **3** used as answer to general greeting = jibu la salamu **4** hello, how are you etc. = jambo **5** sorry = pole **6** I agree = nakubali **7** condolence, receive my sympathy (at funerals etc.) = pole **8** congratulations = hongera

ndi *vb (> li)* I am = mimi ni, niko

ndiíla *n (ba-, 1a/2)* smth feared = kitu kinachoogopesha

ndilí *interr* when = lini

ndimba *interj,conj* expression of surprise: but, what, really = kumbe, lakini
/Also **ngimba**

ndiisí *expr* I don't know = sielewi, sijui, sifahamu

ndiisí *adv* maybe = labda, pengine

Ndolombwíke *pn* name of a pre-missionary-time "deity" = jina la "mungu" mmoja

nduko *interj* let's go = twende

ndúngú sya mwísukulugo! *off* your grandpa's balls = pumbu za babu yako

ndupu *adv* only = tupu
Kutwala ji nyama ndupu. Utwa-munda tulikuugu? You have only brought the meat. Where are the guts? = Umeleta nyama tupu. Je matumbo / vitu vya ndani viko wapi?

ndútú ja nyoko! *interj.off* your mother's cunt = kuma mayo

ndyimo *adv* the time when livestock come back from grazing (between 3.30 - 4.00 pm) = muda mifugo irudipo kutoka malishoni (kati ya saa 9.30 - 10.00 jioni)

nega *vb (pt negíle)* draw liquid, take up liquid a little at the time ie. in a small cup or vessel = chota maji

neena *vi (pt neeníle)* (animals) be in heat = pata joto
/Also **ípingula**

ng'alafula *vb (pt ng'alafwíle)* tear = rarua

-ngalalifú *adj* cross, angry = -enye hasira

-a ngalalisí *adj* hateful = -a kuchukia

ngali- *vb.prefix* I would have = ninge-

ngaali *expr* I'm still (not yet) … = ni-ngali (bado)
Ngaali ndiko I'm still alive = ningali hai

ngani *adv* 1 early = mapema 2 before = kabla

ngaaníla *adv* before = kabla, mapema

ngati *adv* as, like = kama
~ **ng'ombe** *adj* bovine = kama ng'ombe

ng'aatula *vb (pt ng'atwííle)* stare = ko-doa macho

ng'aatúlila *vt.appl (pt ng'aatúlíle)* stare at = kazia, kodolea

ng'aatúlila amaso stare at = kazia macho, kodolea macho

ngenenge *n (ba-, 1a/2)* 1 (Diospyros whyteana) *n.bot* type of tree whose leaves and roots are used to brush teeth. It makes the mouth and lips reddish, but the teeth become very clean. = aina ya mti jamii ya mpweke ambao majani na mizizi yake hutu-miwa kusugulia meno, midomo huwa myekundu na meno meupe; mdaa 2 mask = uso wa bandia

-ngi *adv* 1 other, another = -ingine 2 *pron* which = ipi, ambacho

ngimba *interj* 1 of surprise: but, what, really = kumbe 2 used to introduce / indicate a question = je

ng'oba *vt.arch (pt ng'oobíle)* dip your finger and lick = kwangua kwa kidole na kulamba
/New word: **ng'ola**

ng'oko *n.zool (ba-, 1a/2)* any large wasp or hornet = nyigu mkubwa, dondola

ng'ola *vb (pt ng'olíle)* scrape remains of food in container with finger or spoon = kwan-gua kwa kidole na kulamba

-Ngonde *n.ethn* The people in northern Malawi who speak the same language as the Nyakyusa = Watu wa Malawi ambao wanasema lugha ile ile kama Wanyakyusa

ng'ong'a *n.zool (ba-, 1a/2)* hornbill = hondohondo

ng'ong'ola *vb (pt ng'ong'wíle)* grimace = zomea kwa vitendo kama vidole, kichwa, dharau

nguma ja nyoko *off* your mother's cunt = kuma mayo

ng'wala *vt (pt ng'walíle)* scratch with claws = parua

ng'walafúla *vt (pt ng'walafwíle)* scratch with claws = parua

ng'wenya *vt (pt ng'wenyíle)* gnaw, nibble at = ng'wenya, guguna

-nía *vi (pt nííle)* shit, excrete = kunya

níalú *n.zool (ba-, 1a/2)* cat = paka

níalú *n.bot (-, 9/10)* very common fast-

spreading weed, the fern-like leaves
fold up when touched = kufa uwongo

níembetelela *vb (pt níembeteelíle)*
1 wrap = viringisha 2 conceal news or
information = ficha habari

níembula *vb (pt niembwíile)* disentangle = fungua, tatua

níenga *vt (pt niengíle)* 1 roll, wrap
around = viringisha, nienga 2 coil =
kunja kwa viringisha

níine, naníine 1 also I, even I = na
mimi, hata mimi 2 please give me =
naomba

nínga *vt (pt níngíle)* give = -pa

níngana *vi (pt níngeene)* be opposite
one another = tazamana, kabiliana

-níní *adj* small, little = -dogo

níola *vt.off (pt níolíle)* fuck, make love
= tomba

níonga *vt (pt níongíle)* strangle = nyonga
/Original meaning to strangle. Modern meaning to hang sb or any other
type of capital punishment

-níongafú *adj* twisted, crooked =
-liopinda

níongala *vi (pt níongeele)* be (become)
bent, be curved, be twisted, be
crooked = pinda, pindika

níongasya *vt.caus (pt níongeesye)*
1 bend, incline = pindisha, inamisha
2 divert = geuza upande

níongoka *vi (pt níongwíike)* reach puberty, attain manhood = balehe

níongotola *vt (pt níongotwíile)* spin,
strangle, twist= nyonga, popotoa

-njaní *color.adj* green = kijani

njítí *n.med (ba-, 1a/2; > Swa)* a prema-
turely born child = njiti

-njwejwe *color.adj* light, weak, faded
(eg. light green as opposed to green or
dark green) = rangi isiyokolea

-njwelúfú *color.adj* faint, faded = rangi
ya kufifia

nkati *prep* inside, in, within = ndani,
kati ya; **nkati ka** circa, approximately

= karibu na, kati ya; **nkati mú** into,
inside of, aboard = ndani ya, nkati mu

nkekwa *n.zool (ba-, 1a/2)* type of monkey, small (rhesus monkey) = ngedere, tumbili
/Same as **lusanje**

nkina *adv* on Thursday = siku ya alhamisi

nko *interj* give me = hebu nipe, nipe, lete

nkyení *adv,prep* 1 ahead, in front of,
forward = mbele 2 before = kabla ya

-a nkyinja *adj* annual = -a mwaka

nndapapapa *adv* during this time =
katika muda fulani kama huu, nyakati
hizihizi

nng'aa *n.zool (banng'aa, 1a/2)* bush
baby = komba

nnoono *adv* 1 so much = kupita kiasi,
mno 2 extremely = kupita kiasi, mno
3 exceedingly = mno; **Ali na matingo
nnoono na apa bankomíle** He is exceedingly arrogant so he has deserved
the beating = Ana kiburi mno mpaka
amestahili kupigwa

noga *vi (pt nogíle)* be satisfying, be
pleasing, be tasty = noga, kuwa na
ladha nzuri

-noge *adj* 1 delicious = -enye kunoga,
-enye ladha nzuri, tamu 2 wealthy =
-enye mali

nogela *vt.appl (pt nogíile)* 1 benefit from =
faidikia 2 become rich = tajirika

nogelesya *vb (pt nogelesísye)* taste = onja

nongí, nongí ndibe *pron* somebody =
mtu fulani

nosya *vt.caus (pt nosísye)* adorn, decorate, garnish, deck = pamba, remba,
ng'arisha

nseesye *n.zool (ba-, 1a/2)* type of small
brown animal, feeds on chickens and
birds = aina ya mnyama

nsombyo *n.zool (ba-, 1a/2; Tuk)* sunbird = chozi
/Kye **isombyo**

ntandatu *num* six = sita

-a ntengo *adj* expensive = ghali

-ntiga *adj* sole, only = moja tu
  -eene -ntiga the only one (eg no
  brothers or sisters) = pekee (mf. bila
  kaka au dada); **Jo mwana jumo jwe-
  ene ntiga gwa Fanta** He is the only
  son of Fanta = Ni mwana pekee wa
  Fanta

ntíítí *n.zool (ba-, 1a/2)* type of bird =
  aina ya ndege

ntukwe *n.zool (ba-, 1a/2)* type of black
  ant, large and ant = aina ya siafu
  mweusi wanaouma
  /Also **indukwe**

-nuguna *adj*
  -nuguna (animal)(mnyama)
  -nnuguna *adj* (person) (mtu)
  younger than sb = aliye mdogo kuliko
  wengine

númwe with you (pl) = nanyi, pamoja
  nanyi

numwísyugu even today= hata leo

núnga *vi (pt núngíle)* stink, smell = nuka

núngwe *adv* with you (sg) = nawe,
  pamoja nawe

-núnú *adj* This is a generic positive adjective **1** good = zuri **2** beautiful,
  pretty, nice, elegant = -zuri **3** pleasant
  = zuri, enye kupendeza **4** sound =
  zuri, -zima

núsya *vt.caus (pt núsísye)* smell = nusa

núswe/nanúswe *adv* with us = nasi,
  pamoja nasi

-nwa *vt (pt nwíle)* drink = kunywa

nwela *vt & vi (pt nwelíle)* drink water
  immediately after eating = kunywa
  maji baada ya mlo

nwela *vt.appl* drink with = nywea

nwesya *vt.caus (pt nwesísye)* **1** give a
  drink of water, irrigate = nywesha
  2 *slang* make sb drink, buy beer for sb
  = nunulia pombe

-nyaafú *adj* **1** tasty, sweet = -tamu **2** delicious = -enye ladha nzuri, -tamu

nyaafúla *vt (pt nyafwííle)* tear, tear up =
  chana

nyafúlanía *vt (pt nyafúleenie)* mangle,
  tear up, shred = chana, chanachana,
  rarua

nyaga *vt (pt nyagíle)* **1** reduce sb/sm to
  nothing = fanya mtu / kitu kiishe ki-
  maadili, kiumbo au kiakili **2** to steal
  crops through witchcraft = kuiba
  mazao kiuchawi

-nyagalufú *adj* (of food) appetizing,
  good = (chakula) tamu; **Nalyaga
  ikyindi ni kisambula, ngulonda
  ikyai ija kwínyagalusya** = Nilikuwa
  nikila ugali na kisamvu, nataka chai
  ya kujichangamsha kwayo

nyagaluka *vi (pt nyagalwííke)* (after illness) get well, get better = pona

nyaganya *vb (pt nyageenye)* drizzle =
  nyunya

nyagula *vi (pt nyagwííle)* to finish off
  the funeral ceremony = maliza
  matanga

nyaka *vt (pt nyakíle)* snatch, grab =
  nyakua, pokonya

nyala *vi (pt nyalíle)* **1** get dirty = chafuka **2** be bad = kuwa mbaya **3** get
  thin = konda

-nyalí *adj* **1** dirty, filthy, insanitary, foul,
  nasty = chafu, -a kuchukiza **2** profane =
  -sio takatifu
  umúndu unnyalí a dirty person = mtu
  mchafu

nyamba *vt (pt nyambíle)* throw, spread,
  separate = ondoa kitu (kwa kupan-
  gusa kwa mkono), tenga, tupa

nyambanía *vt (pt nyambenie)* scatter,
  disperse = tawanya, tapanya

nyasya *vt.caus (pt nyasísye)* **1** defile,
  make smth dirty = chafua **2** blunder =
  kosesha, kosa **3** disgrace = aibisha

nyaasya *vt (pt nyaasíísye)* burn, roast =
  unguza, banika

nyaata *vi (pt nyaatíle)* get fat = nona,
  nenepa

-nyaate *adj* (animals) fat, well fed =
  nono, -nene

nyaatúka *vi (pt nyaatwíke)* creep up on

= nyemelea

nyegela *vi (pt nyegííle)* itch = washa

nyegeesya *vt.caus (pt nyegesíísye)* tickle = tekenya

nyeela *vb (pt nyeelíle)* **1** jump, leap = ruka **2** bounce = ruka kama mpira

nyelanyela *vi (pt nyelanyelíile)* jump again and again, jump with joy = rukaruka

nyenyemúsya *vt.caus (pt nyenyemwísye)* excite = shitua

nyeesya *vt.caus (pt nyeesíísye)* make sb throw, toss = rusha

nyíga *vt (pt nyígíle)* style of weaving, knit very closely = suka kwa kubananisha sana

nyínyíla *vi (pt nyínyílíle)* squint = fumba macho kidogo

nyííta *vi (pt nyíítíle)* buzz = vuma kama nyuki

nyofya *vt.caus (pt nyofíífye)* allure, arouse longings = tamanisha

nyoko *off* your mother = nyoko

nyololoka *vi (pt nyololwííke)* **1** be soft = lainika **2** get wet from rain = tota, lowana na mvua

nyomo *adv* suddenly = ghafla

nyomoka *vi (pt nyomwííke)* **1** be surprised, be amazed = shituka **2** be roused = shituka

nyomosígwa *vi.pass (pt nyomosígwe)* be surprised = shitushwa

nyomosya *vt.caus (pt nyomwíísye)* frighten, horrify, scare, amaze, surprise = ogofya, shitusha, shangaza

nyopa *vi (pt nyopíle)* be soaked / drenched = lowa, lowana

nyonyofya *vt (pt nyonyofífye)* attract, be seductive, be alluring, rouse desires / passions = vutia, tamanisha

-nyonywa *adj* eager = -enye kutamani

nyonywa *vt (pt nyonyílwe)* long for, desire, covet = tamani

nyopesya *vt.caus (pt nyopíísye)* soak something = lowanisha kitu

nyosola *vt (pt nyoswííle)* peck = donoa

nyotoka *vi (pt nyotwííke)* jump off, dash off = chupa

nyúkúla *vt (pt nyúkwííle)* **1** pull up, pull out = ng'oa **2** harvest by uprooting (carrots, cassava) = ng'oa

nyúlúlúka *vi (pt nyúlúlwííke)* stand on tiptoe = chuchumia

-nyúma *adj* back, behind = -a nyuma, nyuma

nyúngúla *vt (pt nyúngwííle)* pull out = ng'oa

nyúngúla inywílí pull out hair = ng'oa nywele

nyúnyútúka *vb.med (pt nyúnyútwííke)* tiptoe, limp = chechemea

-nywamú *adj* big, large, fat = kubwa, nene

nywamúsya *vt.caus (pt nywamwíísye)* enlarge = kuza

-nywamúpo *adj* bigger than = kubwa kuliko

Oo

obela *vt (pt obelíle)* scorn, show contempt for = dharau, zomea

obeela *vt (pt obeelíle)* rumble, hum, buzz, rustle eg of wind, approaching rain, thunder or song sung at a distance = sikika, kuvuma kwa wimbo

oga *vb (pt ogíle)* bathe = oga

-oga *adj* afraid, cowardly, yellow = -a kuogopa, -oga

ogeela *vb (pt ogeelíle)* swim = ogelea

-ogeelefú *adj* healthy = -enye afya

oogo *interj,adv* OK = sawa

ohela *vt (pt ohelíle)* sneer, jeer = zomea

okya *vt (pt okíkye)* cook something on open fire, grill, roast = oka, choma

oko *interj* 1 give it to me = nipe 2 let's start = haya tuanze 3 that's that, Right, OK = haya! 4 call of attention = hebu

okola (umoto) *vb (pt okwííle)* fetch fire from a neighbor = paa moto kwa jirani

-olo *adj* lazy, idle = -vivu

oloba *vb (pt olwíbe)* get wet, be drenched, be soaked = tota, lowana (udongo)

olobeka *vt (pt olobííke)* soak = lowanisha, loweka

oloka *vb (pt olwííke)* increase in number of population, be prolific = zaa sana, ongezeka idadi
/*imper*: **golokege** (sg), **molokege** (pl)

-olokí *adj* prolific = -zazi, -enye kuzaa sana

-ololo *adj* 1 gentle, polite = pole 2 generous = karimu
/Opposite of **-kali**

ombolela *vb (pt ombolííle)* in mixing substances, put more than necessary of one substance = zidisha kimojawapo katika kuchanganya vitu, zidisha kipimo
ombolela umúnyú put more salt in food = zidisha chumvi ktk chakula

ombolela amiisi put more water in cooking = zidisha maji kwenye changu
ombolela ubufú - put more flower in making porridge = zidisha unga wakati wa kupika uji / ugali

omoka *vb (pt omwííke)* become void = hama, ng'oka

omola *vt (pt omwíle)* 1 demolish = bomoa 2 annul, cancel, delete = futa
omola ilangí discolor = ondoa rangi

omolela *vb (pt omolííle)* to sing together, join in singing = itikia katika wimbo

ona *vt (pt oníle)* spill (liquid) = mwaga

ona amiisi piss, urinate = kujoa

onanga *vt (pt onangíle)* 1 destroy, damage, ruin, devastate, spoil, demolish, harm = haribu, bomoa 2 contaminate, blur, dirty, mark = chafua, tia uchafu, tia doa 3 blunder = kosa; ~ **imbatiko** derange = pangua

-onange *adj* bad = mbaya

onangika *vi (pt onangííke)* 1 become spoiled, go bad = haribika, oza 2 become confused = changanyika 3 become disordered = vurugika 4 perish = potea

-onangike *adj* bad = mbaya

oneka *vi (pt oníike)* 1 gush = mwagika 2 be spilled, scattered = mwagika

onelela *vb (pt onelíle)* irrigate, water (eg. plants) = mwagilia

onga *vb (pt ongíle)* suck = nyonya

ongaana *vi (pt ongeene)* 1 to be together = kuwa pamoja, changanyika 2 be mixed = changanyika

onganía *vt (pt ongeníe)* 1 mix, combine, blend = changanya 2 sum up = jumlisha

ongela *vt (pt ongíile)* 1 increase, fill up, add, enhance, escalate, lengthen = ongeza 2 accelerate = ongeza mwendo 3 elongate = refusha, ongeza urefu 4 multiply = zidisha 5 add (in math) = ongeza, jumlisha 6 enlarge = kuza 7 breed = zaliana

ongela umoto *slang* accelerate = zidisha mbio, ongeza mwendo

ongelako *vt (pt ongíileko)* extend = ongezea, endeleza

ongelapo *vt (pt ongíilepo)* Basically the same as ongela with the addition of "a little, a little more" **1** add / increase a little = ongezea kidogo **2** continue a little = endelea kidogo **3** keep on = endelea

onyoka *vb (pt onywíike)* **1** fall = anguka **2** weaken, slacken = dhoofika, vunjika nguvu, legea **3** despair = kata tamaa
onyoka amaka be disappointed = toridhishwa

onyola *vt (pt onywíile)* pull down = vuta
onyola imípiki fell trees = angusha miti,
onyola inyúmba demolish houses = angusha nyumba

-onywa *adj* **1** weak, faint, feeble, slack = dhaifu, legevu **2** delicate = ororo **3** incompetent = sioweza

-ope *adv* even = hata

-oosa *adj* all, the whole, total = -ote, jumla

osígwa *vi.pass (pt osígwe)* **1** be baptized = batizwa **2** be bathed = ogeshwa

osya *vt.caus (pt osísye)* **1** wash = osha **2** baptize = batiza

ota *vb (pt otíle)* sit by the fire = ota moto

otela *vb (pt otelíile)* **1** get warm in the sun, sit by the fire, bask in the sun = otea jua, ota moto **2** guess = kisia

Pp

pa *locative* location at a not enclosed area; at,on = -ni

-pa, ukupa *vt (pt peele)* give = kupa, kutoa

pabubuko *n (16)* destination = mwisho wa safari
/Also **mbubuko, kububuko**

pabufíko *n (16)* destination = mwisho wa safari, sehemu uendako
/**mbufíko, kubufíko**

pabugono *n (16)* bedroom, sleeping place = chumba cha kulala, mahali pa kulala

pabulambalalo *n (16)* place for sleeping (i.e. a mat or a mattress, bed) = mahali pa kulala

pabusokelo *n (16)* exit = mahali pa kutokea

pabutasí *adv* formerly = zamani

pabwendo *n (16)* path = kijia, njia

pabwíkemekesyo *n (16)* **1** altar, place of sacrifice = madhabahu **2** sacred place = mahali patakatifu

pabwipútilo *n (16)* a place for worship (temple mosque church) = mahali pa kusalia (hekalu, mskiti, kanisa)

-pafú *adj* greedy = lafi

pagata *vb (pt pageete)* to put smth in the lap = pakata

paguka *vi (pt pagwíike)* collapse, fall apart = bomoka **Ulwígí lupagwíke** The door is jammed / broken = Mlango umeharibika / umebomoka

paaguka *vi (pt paagwíike)* **1** branch off = fanya panda **2** go another way at a crossroad or path = pita njia nyingine, nenda njia nyingine, njia panda

pagula *vt (pt pagwíile)* **1** force open (eg a door) = fungua mlango kwa nguvu **2** dismantle, tear down = haribu, bomoa

paagula *vb (pt paagwíile)* divert, separate = peleka upande

pajapaja *vb (pt pajapajíile)* talk nonsense =

bwata, payuka

paka *vt (pt pakíle)* **1** paint = paka rangi
2 apply medicine (rub, smear) = paka
dawa

pakaaja *n (16)* at home = nyumbani

pakana *vi (pt pakeene)* form a boundary with, border = pakana, fanya
mpaka na

pakanía *vi (pt pakeenie)* roam = zunguka huko na huko

pakati *adv* middle = katikati

pakati *prep* between = kati

pakati *n (16)* center = katikati

pakati na pakati *prep* between = katikati

pakati na pakati pa *prep* between, in
the middle of = katikati ya, kati ya

pakati pa *prep* between, among = baina
ya, kati ya

pakíjolo *adv* the day before yesterday = juzi

pakila *vt (pt pakíile)* load, load onto,
put into = pakia

pakina *n (16)* on Thursday = Alhamisi

paakípo *adj* **1** preferable = heri **2** better
= afadhali

pakisya *vb (pt pakíisye)* give sb a ride =
beba mtu (gari, baisikeli)

paakisya *vt.caus (pt paakíisye)* **1** pity =
hurumia **2** fear for, be afraid of, regret
= sikitikia, hofia, jutia

pala *adv* there = pale

-pala *adj* difficult, hard = -gumu

pala *vt (pt palíle)* scrape scales off =
paa magamba

    pala iswi scrape fish scales = paa
samaki

paala *vt (pt paalíle)* **1** praise = sifu **2** invite = alika, karibisha kwenye shuguli

palaganía *vt (pt palagenie)* destroy =
haribu, vuruga

palaganíka *vi (pt palaganíike)* **1** be in
disorder, break down = haribika,
bomoka **2** be exited, be agitated =
taharuki

-palamaní *adj* near, neighboring =

pakana, jirani

palamanía *vt (pt palamenie)* bring
things close to each other = weka vitu
kuwa karibu

palamana *vb (pt palameene)* be close to
each other = karibiana

palamasya *vt.caus (pt palameesye)*
1 touch = gusa **2** grope = papasa

-palapala *adj* **1** difficult = -gumu **2** occult = -a siri (uchawi)

palapala *adv* at the same place, right
there, just there = sehemu ile ile,
palepale

palasa *vt (pt paleese)* **1** scatter, disperse
= tawanya **2** scrape / search / paw the
ground = chakura

palatula *vt (pt palatwíile)* scrape,
scratch = paruza

paalema *conj* although = ingawa

pali there is = iliyo na, pana

palubunju *adv* the day after tomorrow
= mtondo, mtondogoo, keshokutwa

palumú *n (16)* the dry and hot season, July -
November, "summer" = kiangazi

pamanda *vt (pt pamandíle)* slap, pat = piga

pamba *n.zool (ba, 1a/2)* type of ant,
brown ant that lives in trees = mdudu
jamii ya sisimizi, rangi yake kahawia
na hupenda kukaa juu ya miti

pambali *adv* aside = kando, pembeni

pambali pa *prep* beside, on the side of
= pembeni mwa

pambikana *vi (pt pambikeene)* compete
= shindana

pamo 1 *conj* or = au **2** *adv* perhaps,
maybe = labda, pengine **3** *prep* at one
(place) = mahali pamoja

pamo ... pamo either ... or = ama ... ama

pamopeene *adv* **1** together (with),
along = pamoja na **2** at one go = kwa
mpigo, mara moja **3** also = pia

pamúsi *adv* in the afternoon (12 am.- 4
pm.) = alasiri

pamúsi *adv* **1** daylight = mchana **2**
midday, noon = mchana

pamwanya *prep* above, over, up, on top of = juu, juu ya

pamwanya pa *conj* **1** besides = tena, zaidi (ya) **2** upon = juu ya

pamwanya pa *prep* **1** against = dhidi ya **2** on top of, on = juu ya

panandi *adv* a little = kidogo

panandi itolo just a little = kidogo tu

panandipanandi *adv* slowly, little by little = polepole

panduka *vi (pt pandwíike)* burst = pasuka

pandula *vt (pt pandwíile)* dissect = pasua, tumbua

panga *vt (pt pangíle)* **1** tell (a story, tale), narrate, relate = simulia, toa habari **2** plan = panga, ratibu **3** talk, converse = zungumza

pangajeje (Helianthus annuus) *n.bot (ba-, 1a/2)* sunflower = alizeti

pangalatula *vt (pt pangalatwíile)* dismantle, tear down, break down = bomoa /Distroy by taking one and one part out

pangila *vb (pt pangíile)* **1** explain to sb = elezea **2** tell a story, narrate = simulia

pangisya *vt.caus (pt pangíisye)* (about houses) rent out = pangisha, kodisha

panguka *vi (pt pangwíike)* collapse, fall apart = bomoka

pangula *vt (pt pangwíile)* dismantle, demolish = bomoa

panja *prep* outside = nje

panja *vt (pt panjíle)* **1** split open, make a cut in = pasua **2** hatch = angua vifaranga; **panja ubufyele** take care of the mother after delivery = hudumia mama mzazi

panongwa ja *conj* because of = kwa sababu ya

panyúma *adv* **1** later, afterwards, after (in time) = baada ya, baadaye **2** on the back, behind = mgongoni, nyuma **3** then = kisha, halafu

panyúma pa on the back of = mgongoni mwa

panyúma pa *prep* behind = nyuma ya

paapa *vi (pt paapíle)* **1** give birth, bear, breed, yield (crops), produce = zaa, zaliana, zalisha, zaa matunda **2** carry = beba **3** curdle, coagulate = ganda

papapa *adv* just here = hapahapa

papapo *adv* just there = hapohapo

papatana *vb (pt papateene)* be squeezed together = banana

-papate *adj* broad = pana

-papí *adj* fertile = -zazi

paapígwa *vi (pt paapíigwe)* be born = zaliwa

papilila *vt* defend, shield = kinga, linda, funika

papipi *adv* near = karibu

paapo *adv* **1** just there = pale pale **2** enough = -tosha

paapo *conj* because = kwa sababu

pasa *vt (pt pasíle)* bear twins = zaa mapacha **pasa ulupaso** make a fence = jenga uzio, wigo

paasí / paasí pa *adv,prep* below, under, down, beneath, at the bottom of, on the floor = chini, chini ya

-a paasí *adj* **1** low = -a chini **2** basic = -a msingi, -a mwanzo

paasí *n (16)* bottom, ground = chini, ardhi **paasí pa melí** deck (on ship) = sitaha **paasí pa nyúmba** floor = sakafu

pasíma *adv* **1** differently = isivyo, tofauti, kwa jinsi nyingine **2** apart = mbali ya

pasíma *adj* other = -ingine

pasímapasíma *adj* different, various = mbalimbali, tofauti

pasula *vt (pt paswíile)* **1** operate = pasua **2** split = pasua

paasya *vt (pt paasísye)* **1** worry, fear, be anxious = hofu, hofia, kuwa na hangaiko **2** doubt = kuwa na shaka **3** care = jali

pasyele panandi 1 presently = bado kidogo **2** a little while = kitambo kidogo

83

patalí *adv* far = mbali

patanía *vt (pt patenie)* mediate, conciliate, reconcile, make peace = suluhisha

patilila *vb (pt patilíile)* prune = pogolea

paatula *vt (pt paatwíile)* peel = menya

peefya *vt (pt peefífye)* tempt, persuade = shawishi

pegesa *vb (pt pegíise)* 1 make a hole, drill, bore into = pekecha tundu 2 make fire with a stick = pekecha moto

pegesela *vt.appl (pt pegesíile)* make a hole for smth or sb = pekechea

peegwa *vi (pt peegígwe)* be given somthing = pewa

peha *vi (pt pekíle)* stink = nuka

pela *vt (pt pelíle)* 1 make = tengeneza 2 create = umba 3 *(Kye)* (penis) be erect = dinda, disa
/Tukuyu see **pila**
pela ubunúnú attract = vutia
pela ingíísí kumaso dazzle = tia kiwi ya macho
pela ulunyenyesi dim = tia giza, fifisha

peela *vi (pt peelíle)* have diarrhea = harisha

pelelesya *vt.caus (pt peleliísye)* Base meaning: be curious about, secretly examine 1 spy, investigate, enquire = peleleza, chunguza 2 detect, discover = vumbua, gundua

pelemba *vt (pt pelembíle)* twist, twine = sokota

pelemesya *vb (pt pelemíisye)* make sb become crazy = fanya mtu kuwa pungwani

peelígwa *vi.pass* be given, receive = pewa

pelúlanía *vb (pt pelúlenie)* pry, snoop, search around = pekua

pembela *vi (pt pembíile)* to keep a fire going by adding firewood = chochea, koka moto

pembele *n.zool (ba-, 1a/2)* rhinoceros = kifaru

pembenúka *vi (pt pembenwíike)* 1 be drilled (military training) = fanya ma-

funzo ya kijeshi 2 walk around = tembea huko na huko

pemeesya *vt.caus (pt pemekíisye)* curse = laani

penga *vi (pt pengíle)* blow the nose = penga

peenyeka *vi (pt peenyiíke)* molt, to lose feathers or hair = nyonyoka

pepa *vt (pt pepíle; > Bemba)* 1 smoke = vuta (sigara) 2 drink = kunywa

-pepe *adj* 1 light (not heavy), quick, swift = -epesi 2 easy, simple = rahisi 3 cheap = bei rahisi

pepetula *vt (pt pepetwíle)* wrench, twist, strain, distort = popotoa, pepetua

pepufu *adj* gentle, meek = pole

pepuka *vt (pt pepwíike)* diminish, decrease = pungua, punguka

pepula *vt (pt pepwíile)* lessen, reduce, lighten = punguza

pepusya *vt.caus (pt pepwísye)* diminish, lessen, reduce (weight), deduct = punguza

peesya *vt.caus (pt peesísye)* miss = kosa

peeta *vt (pt peetíle)* 1 sift grain = pembua 2 winnow = pepeta

petaníka *vi (pt petaníike)* shake with the wind = tikisika kwa upepo

petúsanía *vt (pt petúsenie)* turn back and forth = pinduapindua

petúsya *vt.caus (pt petwisye)* overturn, capsize, overthrow = pindua

pigula *vt (pt pigwíle)* 1 incite, stimulate = chochea 2 change opinion = badilisha usemi, pindua wazo

piija *vt (pt pijíle)* cook, boil = pika, chemsha
piija ubwalwa brew beer = pika pombe

piika *vi (pt piikíle)* boycott, refuse = susa, kana

pila *vi (pt pilíle; Tuk)* (about penis) be erect = dinda, disa
/Kye: see **pela**

pilika *vt (pt pilíike)* 1 hear = sikia

2 comprehend, sense, understand =
fahamu **3** be obedient, obey = tii, sikia

pilikisanía *vb (pt pilikisenie)* **1** compromise, negotiate = patana **2** conspire = patana kutenda jambo

pilikisanía untengo bargain = kubaliana bei, patana bei

pilikisya *vt.caus (pt pilikíisye)* listen =
sikiliza

pílula *vb (pt pílwíile)* appeal = kata rufaa

pima *vt (pt pimíle)* weigh, measure,
test, examine = pima

pimba *vt (pt pimbíle)* carry, lift = beba

-pímba *adj* short = fupi

pimbila *vt.appl* carry with, carry for =
bebea

pímbusya *vt.caus (pt pímbwísye)*
shorten, abbreviate = fupisha

pimila *vt.appl (pt pimíile)* measure with
= pimia

pimilamo *vb (pt pimíilemo)* estimate,
guess = kadiria, tabiri, kisi

-pina *adj* lone, alone, solitary, destitute
= -kiwa, -pweke, -peke

pínda *vt (pt píndíle; > Swa)* **1** bend,
fold, sew a hem = kunja, pinda, pinda
nguo **2** wrap = kunja (nguo)

pindana *vi (pt pindeene)* wrinkle = kunjana

píindanía *vt (pt píindenie)* **1** fold, bend,
wrap up, tuck = kunja **2** wind = ku-
nja, funga

pinduka *vi (pt pindwíike)* **1** repent =
tubu **2** be reformed, be converted =
ongoka

pindula *vt (pt pindwíile)* **1** convert =
badilisha dini **2** turn aside = geuza,
badili
~ **injobele** translate = tafsiri

pinga *vt (pt pingíle)* obstruct, oppose =
pinga, kabili

piinga *vb (pt piingíle)* to rain after a
long dry season = nyesha mvua baada
ya kiangazi

pingama *vi (pt pingeeme)* be changed, be
altered, be transformed = geuka, elekea

piingika *vt (pt piingíike)* set or put
across = kingamisha, weka kwa
kukingama

pingikila *vt (pt pingikíile)* pawn = weka
rahani /rehani

píinía *vi (pt píinile)* blink = konyeza

pínya *vt (pt pínyíle)* **1** tie, bind, fasten =
funga **2** detain, imprison = funga jela,
tia gerezani **3** fix = funga

pínyanía *vb (pt pínyenie)* splice, tie to-
gether= fungasha

-pínyígwa *adj* be imprisoned, be tied =
fungwa

píipa *vt (pt píipíle)* defecate = kunya

pípí *prep* near = karibu na

-a pípí *adj* current = -a kisasa

píita *vt (pt píitíle)* **1** bewitch = loga
2 strangle = songa koo, nyonga

pítaasí *adv* afterwards, later = baadaye

po *conj,adv* **1** so, then = basi, hivyo,
kisha **2** when = wakati wa, -po-

po lelo then = kisha

po papo *conj* **1** so = basi, hivyo basi
2 then, and then = halafu, kwa hiyo
3 that will do, that's all, that is
enough = inatosha, basi **4** well =
vizuri, hivyo basi **5** it doesn't matter,
never mind = haidhuru **6** merely = tu

pohola *vb (pt pohwíile)* beat with heavy
strokes with a big stick = piga kwa
nguvu

popapo lelo and then = kisha, halafu

poka *vt (pt pokíle)* base meaning: take
by force **1** plunder, rob = nyang'anya,
pata kwa nguvu **2** capture, seize,
snatch = shika, poka, kamata, twaa
3 *fig* save, rescue, redeem = okoa,
komboa

pokela *vb (pt pokíile)* relieve = pokea
zamu

pooki *interr* where = wapi

polelo /po lelo (Short form of **po apa
lelo**) therefore = kwa hiyo

pombolela *vb (pt pomboliíle)* put too
much water, dilute = zidisha maji

pona *vb (pt poníle)* **1** give birth, deliver = jifungua mtoto **2** be saved = pona, kuwa nafuu **3** recover, get well, get better = pona **4** escape = okoka

poonda *vt (pt poondíle)* **1** forge = fua chuma **2** hammer = piga nyundo, ponda

pondanía *vt (pt pondeníe)* crush = pondaponda, pigapiga

pondwa *vt (pt pondílwe)* **1** fail = shindwa, kutopata, kosa **2** miss, lose = kosa

ponesya *vt.caus.med* **1** cure, heal, make well = ponyesha **2** rescue, save = okoa

ponía *vt (pt poníísye)* **1** greet, salute = salimu, amkia **2** visit, call on = tembelea

-pongo *adj* a male (animal) = mnyama dume

  ingulube imbongo boar = nguruwe dume **akapene akapongo** young male goat = mbuzi dume mdogo

pope, na pope, na papo *prep* despite = halafu, hata hivyo

pope *adv* **1** again = tena **2** even if, even though = hata kama, ingawa, hata hivyo

popoosa *adv* anywhere = popote

popotola *vt (pt popotwíile)* **1** strain = nyonga **2** strangle = nyonga

posaposa *adv* everywhere, wherever = kotekote

posola *vt (pt poswíile)* make payments for one's act of adultery = lipa ugoni

poosya *vt (pt poosísye)* **1** kid, joke, ridicule = tania, fanya mzaha **2** cool = poza, poozesha

pota *vb (pt potíle)* **1** steer, twist, twine, drive = endesha, sokota (kamba) **2** *vb.med* have stomach cramps = sokotwa na tumbo

potanía *vb (pt poteníe)* twist, coil = pindapinda, zungusha, sokota

puba *vb (pt pubíle)* accustom, be aquainted, experience = zoea

-puufú *adj* **1** blind = -pofu **2** ignorant = -jinga

pufúka *vb (pt pufwíike)* burst, split

open, explode = pasuka

pufúla *vb (pt pufwíile)* **1** tear, split open = pasua **2** beat (violently) = piga

pufya *vt (pt pufíífye)* whistle = piga mruzi

puufya *vt (pt puufífye)* make warm = pasha moto

púgúsa *vt (pt pugwíise)* (cook by) stirring continously = (pika kwa) kukorogakoroga

  púgúsa ubuují make porridge = koroga uji

púgúta *vt (pt pugwíite)* shake off, shake out = kung'uta

pujuka *vi (pt pujwíike)* be bruised = chubuka

pujula *vt (pt pujwíile)* **1** bruise (skin) = chubua **2** rub off color = kwangua rangi

pukifya, pyukifya *vt.caus (pt pukíífye)* warm up for sb = pashia

puula *vt (pt puulíle)* **1** thresh = pura (nafaka) **2** have diarrhea = harisha

pulula *vt (pt pulwíile)* **1** scrape = paruza **2** shave = nyoa **3** plane (timber) = randa

púlúlúka *vi (pt púlúlwíike)* fly = ruka kwa kutumia mabawa

púlúlúsya *vt.caus (pt púlúlwísye)* launch in the air, make fly = rusha angani

pulunganía *vt (pt pulungeeníe)* traverse, go around the country = zunguka, tembelea sehemu kubwa ya nchi

pumbwa *vi (pt pumbílwe)* search for = tafuta (mbwa anatafuta windo kwa kunusa)

púnana *vb (pt púneene)* gamble = cheza kamari

punga *vb (pt pungíle)* gargle = sukutua (mdomoni)

pungiila *vi (pt pungííle)* wander, rove around = tangatanga

púngúsya *vt.caus (pt púngwíísye)* reduce = punguza

pupa *vt (pt pupíle)* **1** steal, plunder = iba (kila kitu) **2** *slang* make bankrupt = filisi

puupala *vi (pt puupele)* be blinded by a strong light = pata kiwi cha macho kutokana na mwanga mkali

puupasya *vt.caus (pt puupesye)* cause blindness by a glare = tia kiwi cha macho

pupila *vt (pt pupííle)* plunder = filisi, ibia

pupuluka *vi (pt pupulwííke)* stagger, totter, falter = pepesuka

puupu *n.bot* type of tree, the roots are used together with the roots of **mwakikali** for medicine. The roots are mixed and left to rot. It will then attract snakes. = Aina ya mti, ambao huchanganywa na mizizi ya **mwakikali** kwa ajili ya dawa, mizizi hiyo ikiachwa na kuoza huwavutia nyoka baadaye

pupuutika *vb (pt pupuutííke)* stagger = pepesuka

pupwa *vi (pt pupílwe)* get fresh air = punga upepo

puusanía *vt (pt pusenie)* harrow = lainisha shamba

pusí *n.zool (ba-, 1a/2)* cat = paka

puusya *vt.caus (pt pusísye)* subdue, conquer = tiisha

púúsya *vt.caus (pt púúsísye)* put smth in sb's mouth, feed sb = lisha

púúta *vt (pt púútíle)* **1** blow (with mouth) = puliza **2** blow (the fire)= puliza moto **3** blow out / spray water from the mouth while praying to the ancestors = puliza maji toka mdomoni wakati wa kuwaomba mababu

pútúka *vb (pt pútwííke)* bend down = bong'oa, furama

-pya *adj* new = -pya

pya *adv* completely = kabisa

-pya *vi (pt pííle)* be burnt, be scalded = ungua

pyagila *vt (pt pyagííle)* sweep, brush = fagia

pyagisya, pyagiisya *vt.caus (pt pyagisíísye)* **1** wipe, delete = futa, tangua, pangusa **2** brush = fagia

pyaníla *vt (pt pyanííle)* **1** be instead of = kuwa badala ya **2** inherit = rithi (hasa mali kama nyumba na mke)

pyaníkisya *vt.caus (pt pyaníkisye)* replace = rudishia

pyasiila *vt (pt pyasííle)* wipe, delete, erase, brush, rub = pangusa, futa

pyasya *vt.caus (pt pyasíísye)* **1** sharpen, whet = noa **2** scrape = kwangua, paruza

pyata *vt (pt pyatíle)* **1** peel, strip away = menya **2** scrape, scratch, graze = paruza, kwangua

-pye *adj* cooked = -liyopikwa

pyela *vt.appl (pt pyeelíle; > -pya)* suffer for = teseka kwa ajili ya

pyelekesya *vt.caus (pt pyelekíísye)* beg pardon on behalf of = bembelezea, ombea msamaha

pyelesya *vt.caus (pt pyelíísye)* **1** beseech, entreat = sihi, omba kwa dhati **2** beg = omba (kwa dhati)

pyoola *vt (pt pyoolíle)* win = shinda

pyú *adv* completely = kabisa
    amalíle fyosa pyu s/he finished everything = amemaliza kabisa

pyufya, pufya *vt.caus (pt pyufíífye, pufíífye)* warm, heat up smth = pasha moto

pyukifya, pukifya *vt.caus (pt pyukíífye)* warm up for sb = pashia

pyúkúla *vt (pt pyúkwííle)* sip, drink small quantities at a time = kunywa kidogo kidogo

pyupa *vi (pt pyupíle)* **1** get warm = pata uvuguvugu **2** get sick = pata homa
    upyupíle are you sick = je unaumwa

pyúta *vt (pt pyútíle)* **1** ruin = angamiza **2** kill = ua **3** condemn to death, doom = hukumia kifo

Ss

sabaja *vb (pt sabeeje; > Bemba)* blab = payapaya

sabuli *n.relig (-, 9/10; > Arab)* psalm = zaburi
/Also: **ulwimbo, salimo**

sagama, sagamala *vb (pt sageeme)* be on the top, be alone = kuwa juu, kuwa pekee bila ndugu

sagangila *vb (pt sagangíile)* wander = nenda huku na kule

saaguka *vi (pt saagwíike)* be separate, go another way, go aside = jitenga, nenda njia nyingine, enda kando

saagula *vt (pt saagwíile)* **1** separate = tenganisha **2** choose = chagua

sahabu *n (-, 9/10)* gold = dhahabu

saja *vt (pt sajíle)* bless = bariki

saaka *vt (pt saakíle)* bully, tease, persecute = chokoza

sakisya *vb (pt sakíisye)* guess = bahatisha

sakuka *vi (pt sakwíike; Tuk; Kye -> sokoka)* appear, be seen, become uncovered, exposed = onekana

sakula *vt (pt sakwíile)* bring forth from hiding, reveal = fichua

sala *vt (pt salíle)* **1** choose, pick, elect, nominate, appoint = chagua, okota, teua **2** sort = chambua

saala *vi (pt saalíle)* be happy, rejoice = furahi, changamka

-saale *adj* happy = -enye furaha

salila *n.zool (ba-, 1a/2)* type of small monkey = tumbili

salila *vt (pt salíile)* tattoo = chanja chale

saalú *n.zool (ba-, 1a/2)* type of chicken with rough, standing feathers = aina ya kuku mwenye manyoya yaliyosimama

saaluka *vi (pt saalwíke)* be unravelled, be undone = fumuka

saalula *vt (pt saalwíle)* **1** ruffle, disturb the smoothness of = chambua, tibua **2** take thatch off, strip the roof = ezua

3 unravel, undo, unstitch = fumua

saama *vb (pt saamíle)* **1** move (to a new location), migrate = hama **2** quit = acha

saambuka *vi (pt saambwíke)* **1** rebel, revolt = asi **2** resist = pinga, bisha

saamila *vb (pt saamíile)* move to = hamia

samisanía *vb (pt samíseenie)* rotate = viringisha

saamísya *vt.caus (pt saamísye)* **1** transfer, move, exile = hamisha **2** displace = badilisha

saamya *vt (pt saamísye)* transfer, move sb/smth = hamisha

sanga *vi (pt sangíle)* bear fruit = zaa matunda

-sangalufú *adj* **1** cheerful, happy = changamfu, -enye furaha **2** lucky, fortunate = heri

sangalusya *vt.caus (pt sangalwísye)* fascinate = sisimua

sangamka, sangamuka *vi (pt sangamwíke)* cheer = changamka, kuwa na furaha

sangamsya *vb.caus (pt sangamísye)* impress, cheer up, enliven = changamsha

sangana *vb (pt sangeene)* be gathered = kusanyika

sangula *vt (pt sangwíile)* contribute = changa

sanía *vi (pt saníle)* be happy = furahi

sanjuka *vi (pt sanjwíike)* **1** sober = kupungua ulevi **2** live a long life = ishi miaka mingi

sanjula *vb (pt sanjwíile)* comb hair = chana nywele

sanúka *vi (pt sanwíike)* **1** alter, turn, be changed, be altered = geuka, badilika **2** be converted = geuka, badilika

sanúsya *vt.caus (pt sanwíisye)* **1** alter, change, transform, convert, turn, twist = badili, badilisha, geuza **2** overturn = pindua **3** disguise = geuza, ficha; **sanúsya injobele** translate, interpret = fasiri, tafsiri

saasa *vi (pt saasíle)* go another way = pita njia nyingine, badili njia

sasanía *vt (pt saseenie)* **1** start, begin = anzisha jambo **2** propose = pendekeza

sasula *vt (pt saswíile)* take snacks, eat = kula asusa (mishikaki, kababu nk.)

saasya *vb (pt saasísye)* overflow = furika

saata *vb (pt saatíle)* itch = washa

sataníla *vb (pt sataníile)* be scattered, be dispersed = tawanyika

satuka *vi (pt satwíike)* fall, drop = anguka, dondoka

satukila *vt (pt satukíile)* tumble into = angukia

satusya *vt.caus (pt satwíisye)* drop, let fall = dondosha, angusha

sausi *n (ba-, 1a/2)* type of army officer = akida, kiogozi wa kikosi cha jeshi

se *interj* expression of great sorrow, typically heard at funerals = neno la kuonyesha huzuni kuu km. kufiwa

sefúka *vi (pt sefwíike)* **1** boil = chemka **2** germinate = chipua **3** *vb.med* (body) rise in temperature due to high fever = pata joto kali sababu ya homa

sefusya *ingamwana:piija* cook, boil = pika, chemsha

segelela *vi (pt segelíile)* approach, come near to, come close, go up to = sogelea, karibia, endea

segelelígwa *vb.pass* (be) accessible = fikika, karibiwa

segelesya *vt.caus (pt segelíisye)* bring near = leta karibu, sogeza, sogeza karibu

segesa *vt (pt segíise)* sift = chekecha

seka *vb (pt sekíle)* laugh = cheka

sekela *vi (pt sekíile)* **1** be happy, be glad, be in a good mood = furahi **2** delight, rejoice = furahi

-sekele *adj* narrow, thin = -embamba

sekeleka *vi (pt sekelíike)* grow thin = konda

sekelela *vi (pt sekelíile)* be happy, enjoy, elate, exult = furahi, shangilia

sekelo *n (-, 9,/10)* scale = kipimo, mizani

sekeesya *vt.caus (pt sekíisye)* **1** amuse, delight = chekesha, furahisha **2** make fun of = furahisha, chekesha **3** please, appeal = furahisha, pendeza

seele *n.zool (ba-, 1a/2)* hamerkop = aina ya ndege

seluselu *n (ba-, 1a/2, < Swa)* albino = zeruzeru

semeekí *n (ba-, 1a/2; >Swa)* brother in law = shemeji, muamu, mlamu /Trad. term: **mulamu**, **undamu**

semesya *vt.caus (pt semíisye)* **1** move out of the way = ondoa **2** stir = sogeza

-sendemafú *adj* **1** bent, tilted, not straight = -liopindika, -liochegama **2** fig. poor in quality, worthless = bila thamani

senga *vt (pt sengíle)* cut or chop (with a sharp tool) = kata; **senga ilísu** mow (grass) = fyeka

senjeluka *vi (pt senjelwíike)* isolate = kuwa pweke, kuwa -kiwa

-senji *adj* worthless, inferior = duni

seenya *vb (pt seenyíle)* **1** clear the land before farming = safisha shamba kabla ya kulima, kwetua nyasi **2** shear, cut animal wool = nyoa manyoya, nyonyoa

setano *n.relig (ba-,1a/2; > Hebr. aan)* Satan, devil = shetani

setuka *vi (pt setwíike)* emerge = jitokeza, onekana

setukila *vt (pt setukíile)* appear to, come to, approach = tokea, jia

setula *vt (pt setwíile)* reveal = funua, fumbua, fichua

sifwene *interj* (be) enough of that! that's enough!= basi!, nyamaza!

síga *vb (pt sígíle)* block the sight = zuia mtu asione mbele

síganíla *vt (pt síganíile)* surround and attack sb (or an animal) = zuia na shambulia (mtu, mnyama)

sígila *vt (pt sigíile)* **1** prevent = zuia **2** check = kinga **3** attack, ambush =

vamia, ngoja mafichoni

sígilila *vt (pt sígilíile)* **1** bar, withhold, restrain = zuia **2** defend, shield, protect = kinga

-sígwana *adj* illegitimate = haramu

síkanumpasyo, sikajanumpasyo don't bother = usijali

síku *adv* not at all = kamwe

síla *n.zool (-, 9/10)* type of fish = aina ya samaki

síla *vt (pt sílíle)* boycott = susia

sílaamwa *vt (pt síleemwe)* think about/over = fikiria

sílika *vi (pt sílíike)* faint = zimia

silila *vb (pt silíile)* tremble, quiver, shiver = tetemeka

sililika *vi (pt sililíike)* shiver = tetemeka

sílilika *vi (pt sílilíike)* die, pass away = -fa, kufa, fariki dunia, kata roho

sílísíndika *vi (pt sílísíndíike* faint, pass out = zimia

síma *vi (pt símíle)* be extinguished, be out = zimika

símaanía *vb (pt símeenie)* distract attention = jibaraguza

símba *vt (pt símbíle)* **1** write = andika **2** draw = chora

símila *vt (pt símííle)* **1** elope with a man = kimbia na mwanaume **2** run off, desert, escape = toroka

símisya *vt.caus (pt símíísye)* extinguish = zima

símya *vt (pt símísye; > síma; Tuk)* **1** put out, = zima, zimisha **2** extinguish, go out = zima, zima moto

sínda in the phrases **sínda inyúma** and **sínda íkosí** turn the back, turn around = -pa kisogo, geuzia mgongo

sínde, síndika *n.fam* the second of twins (only **Sínde** can be used as a name) = doto

síndila *vt (pt síndííle)* plug, stop up, fill in = ziba

síndikila *vt (pt síndikííle)* accompany / escort a guest part of the way home =

sindikiza

sínga *vt (pt síngíle)* **1** forbid = zuia **2** accidentally show your private parts due to loose clothing = onyesha uchi kwa bahati mbaya pengine ni kwa ajili ya nguo zinazopwaya

síngila *vb (pt síngííle)* engage (Meaning that a gift is given to the parents of the girl to confirm the engagement) = chumbia

sípuka *vi (pt sípwííke)* doze, drowse = sinzia

sípula *vi (pt sípwííle)* **1** angle, fish with a hook and bait = vua samaki kwa ndoana; loa **2** *slang* cheat = danganya

sísííla *vb (pt sísíílíle)* close the eyes = fumba macho

sísímíkisya *vt.caus (pt sísímíkíísye)* **1** insist, emphasize = sisitiza, weka mkazo **2** testify = hakikisha **3** confirm = thibitisha

sísísí *adv* just these = zizi hizi, hizi hizi, haya haya

sísya *vt.caus (pt sísísye)* annoy, exasperate = udhi

/Also **sísya ilyojo**

síta *vt (pt sítíle)* iron = piga pasi

sííta *vt (pt síítíle)* **1** hesitate = sita **2** refuse, deny, reject, renounce = kataa, kana **3** resist = pinga

-sísya *adj* formidable, frightening, scary = -a kuogofya, -a kutisha

sítaaka *vt (pt síteeke, sítaakíle)* **1** accuse, blame, charge = shitaki **2** summon = ita kwenye kesi

-síto *adj* **1** heavy, dense = -zito, -nene **2** dull = -zito wa akili, pumbavu **3** clumsy = -ovyo **4** grave = (jambo) kubwa, -zito **5** difficult = -gumo

soba *vb (pt sobíle)* **1** be lost, disappear, perish = potea **2** be wrong, err, blunder = potea, kosea, kosa

sobanía *vt (pt sobenie)* forget = sahau

sobesya *vt.caus (pt sobíísye)* **1** lose, suffer loss = poteza **2** to mislead sb, se-

duce = onyesha njia mbaya 3 ruin =
haribu

-**sobí** *adj* delinquent = -enye makosa,
-liokosea

-**sofú** *adj* hidden, secret = -a siri

sofya *vt.caus (pt sofifye)* 1 lose = poteza 2
mislead = potosha 3 tempt = shawishi

sogola *vi (pt sogwíle)* go along = ongoza, ongoza njia

sogosola *vt (pt sogoswíle)* pick at, poke
= chokochoa, chokora, chokoa

sogota *vb (pt sogwíite)* roll a cigarette =
sokota tumbaku

soka *vt (pt sokíle)* 1 advise, recommend =
shauri 2 reprove, rebuke, warn = onya

sooka *vb (pt sookíle)* 1 come out/from = toka
2 shed, protrude= tokoa, tiririka, toa, toka,
tokeza 3 get off (eg a bus), depart = ondoka, toka 4 set out = ondoka

sooka ilílopa bleed = vuja damu, toka
damu

sooka amafúkú sweat = vuja jasho

sookako *vb (pt sookíleko)* remove smth,
dispose of = ondoa, ondoka

sookamo *vb (pt sookílemo)* get out = ondoka

sookapo *vb (pt sookílepo)* go away,
leave the place = ondoka

sookesya *vt.caus (pt sookísye)* offer =
tolea, toa

sokíle *greeting.arch* hello, good morning = hujambo

sokoka *vb (pt sokwíike; Kye)* appear, be
seen, be visible, seem = onekana, jitokeza

sokola *vt (pt sokwíile)* 1 bring forth =
onyesha, toa 2 uncover, take from
concealment = fichua

-**solofú** *adj* deep = -enye kina kirefu

solola *vt (pt solwíile)* prophesy, predict,
forecast = tabiri

-**sololofu** *adj* deep = -enye kina kirefu

sololoka *vi (pt sololwíike)* descend =
shuka

sololokela *vt (pt sololokíile)* descend
upon = shukia

somana *vi (pt someene)* quarrel =

kosana, gombana

somanía *vb (pt someenie)* 1 make sb quarrel,
cause misunderstanding between people,
stir up mischief, mislead = kosanisha,
chonganisha (watu), fitinisha 2 set at odds
= chonganisha

someka *n (ba-, 1a/2)* 1 a patch of new
cloth on an old piece of clothing =
nguo mpya iliyosonwa kwenye nguo
ya zamani 2 an eyed hoe = jembe
lenye tundu 3 *n.slang* a man who in-
herits his brother's wife = mtu
anayerithi mke wa kaka

somma *interj* don't = usifanye, acha

sona *vt (pt soníle)* 1 sew = shona 2 knit
= fuma, suka

sonda *vt (pt sondíle)* insert, put into =
weka ndani, ingiza, tumbukiza

sonda nkati put inside = weka/tia ndani

soonga *vt (pt soongíle)* persuade, tempt,
pressure = shawishi

songelesanía *vb (pt songelesenie)* set at
odds = gombanisha, chonganisha

songelesya *vb (pt songelíisye)* set at
odds, spur = chonganisha

songola *vt (pt songwíile)* 1 carve,
sharpen = chonga, noa 2 sharpen
teeth = chonga meno; **Nwaka ikuso-
ngola ingalaba** Noah is making an
ark = Nuhu anachonga safina

-**a soní** *adj* shy, shameful, coy = -enye
haya, -a aibu

sopa *vt (pt sopíle)* 1 throw = tupa 2 sow
= mwaga (panda mbegu shambani)

sopola *vb (pt sopwíile)* 1 miscarry = toa
mimba 2 draw out nail etc from wood
etc = chomoa

soosola *vt (pt soosolíle)* point a finger at
= nyooshea kidole

sosomela *n.bot (ba-, 1a/2)* type of rice =
aina ya mpunga

sosomela *vb (pt sosomíile)* limp = chechemea

soosya *vt.caus (pt soosísye)* 1 get rid of,
expel, discharge, remove, dismiss =
fukuza, ondoa, toa, fukuza (kazini)

2 evacuate = toa, ondoa watu kutoka sehemu fulani **3** divorce = taliki **4** donate, offer, submit = toa **5** yield, produce = toa matunda, zalisha; **soosya uluswa** bribe = toa rushwa; **soosya ifííka** cast a spell = toa maajabu; **soosyaga** give to = -pa, kupa, toa, tolea; **soosya ulwanda** abort = toa mimba; **soosya ubulenge** blossom = toa maua; **soosya ubusololí** prophesy = tabiri; **soosya ikyuma** to give out money / pay, hand over smth valuable to sb else = lipa

sosyako *vb (pt sosísyeko)* deduct, subtract, remove, remove smth from its original location = ondoa (kutoka mahali), toa, kutoka mahali

sosyamo *vt (pt sosísyeemo)* exclude = toa, ondoa

sosyapo *vb (pt sosísyepo)* **1** omit = ondoa **2** strip off = bandua **3** expel = fukuza **4** dismiss = ondosha **5** put away = weka mbali **6** displace, remove = hamisha, ondoa **7** send away = peleka, ondoa **8** annul, cancel = futa, ondoa

sotola *vt (pt sotwííle)* pierce, drill, bore a hole = toboa, toboa tundu

sotolela *vt.appl (pt sotolíile)* pierce with = tobolea, penyezea

subila *vb (pt subíile)* **1** trust, rely on, entrust, depend, be confident = tegemea, amini **2** expect = tegemea, tarajia **3** hope = tumaini

subisya *vt.caus (pt subíísye)* soothe, appease, condole, calm, comfort, console = liwaza, bembeleza, fariji, tuliza, bembeleza, tuliza

-suufú *adj* **1** blunt, not sharp = butu **2** tasteless = isiyo ladha, haina ladha

súgúsúla *vb (pt súgúswíle)* wash body = nawa

suuja *vt (pt suujíle)* filter, sift, strain = chuja

súka *vt (pt súkíle)* **1** wake sb up = amsha mtu **2** wash, clean, disinfect,

polish = osha, safisha, ng'arisha

suuka *vi (pt suukíle)* **1** be disgraced, be shamed = aibika **2** become less concentrated as in medicine/ drugs or alcohol when water is added or after some time, expire = pungua nguvu kwa dawa au pombe baada ya kuongeza maji au baada ya muda fulani

sukanía *vb (pt sukeeníe)* shake = tikisa

súkila *vt.appl (pt súkíile)* wash with (~ for etc.) = oshea

súkúla *vb (pt súkíile)* take out at one go = mwaga

suula *vb (pt suulíle)* disregard someone's deeds = dharau matendo ya mtu

súlama *vb (pt súleeme)* bend, bend down, droop, incline = inama, inama chini, pinda chini, egama, chegama

súlamika *vb (pt súlamíike)* turn upside down = fudikiza, pindua

súlúka *vb (pt súlwíike)* descend, go down, land = shuka, tua ardhini

súlúlúka *vb (pt súlúlwíke)* drip, ooze, flow = tiririka, tona

súlúla *vb (pt súlwíile)* pour out / into, spill = mimina

sululuka *vi (pt sululwíike)* **1** become limp, become very soft = kuwa tepetepe **2** (about rice, porridge) become watery = tepeta **3** drool = toa udelele (udende, mate, kamasi)

súlúlúsya *vt.caus (pt súlúlwísye)* drip = tona

sululusya, pololosya *vt.caus (pt sululwísye)* make soft, flaccid, limp = tepetesha

súlúmanía *vi (pt súlúmeníe)* **1** afflict, be sore, be irritated = umia **2** be sorry, grieve, mourn, be sad = sikitika, kuwa na huzuni

súlúsya *vt.caus (pt súlwíisye)* lower = teremsha, shusha

súlwa *vb (pt súlílwe)* dare, presume = thubutu

suuma *vt (pt suumíle)* beg, ask for,

request, apply, entreat, pray = omba

suumila *vt.appl (pt suumíile)* **1** wish = takia **2** pray for, intercede for = ombea, sali

Sumbi *pn* Lake Malawi, Lake Nyasa = Ziwa Nyasa

sumbi *n (ba-, 1a/2)* big body of water, large lake = ziwa

súmúka *vi (pt súmwíike)* **1** get up, rise, wake up = amka **2** depart, get off = ondoka

nsúmwíike *vb* I'm going to [vb] = naenda/ ninakwenda [kitenzi]

súmúkila *vb (pt súmúkíile)* act promptly = fanya mara moja, tenda haraka

-súmúkili *adj* active = changamfu

súmúsya *vt.caus (pt súmwíisye)* **1** bring sb or smth back to its original upright position = amsha **2** make sb get up, rouse = amsha

súnda *vi (pt súndíle; > Bemba)* pee (used by children) = kojoa (hutumika kwa watoto)

sunga *vb (pt sungíle)* joke = tania

súnga *vb (pt súngíle)* **1** deposit = weka amana **2** restore = tunza, rudisha

sungila *vt.appl (pt sungíile)* mock, scorn = fanya utaani, tania mtu

súngila *vt.appl (pt súngíile)* hand over, deliver = kabidhi

súngisya *vt.caus (pt súngíisye)* agitate, poke fire = chochea moto; **sungisya umoto** stir fire, move firewood into the fire= chochea kuni motoni

sungula *vt (pt sungwíile)* **1** choose, select, elect = chagua **2** sift or winnow grain = pembua

sungulula *vb (pt sungulwíile)* dissolve = yeyusha

susa *vi (pt susíle)* fart = jamba

súsilwa used in the phrase **ifya busúsílwa** alms = sadaka

-swa *vt (pt swíle; > ukuswa)* **1** spit = tema **2** forgive, pardon = samehe **3** ooze = tiririka

-swa ilílopa bleed = toka damu

-swanúfú *adj* peeled, bruised = menyeka

swanúka *vi (pt swanwíke)* be peeled off, be bruised = chubuka, tolewa

swanúla *vb (pt swanwíile)* peel off, to peel bark from a stem = chana, bandua

swela *vt.appl* spit upon = temea

swe *color.adj* Used only with white **-elu swe** bright white, intense white = -eupe sana

swíga *vi (pt swígíle)* wonder, be surprised, be astonished, be amazed = shangaa

swígisya *vt.caus (pt swígísye)* astonish, surprise, amaze, baffle = shangaza

swila *vt (pt swilíle)* **1** feed = lisha **2** rear, bring up = lea **3** tame = fuga, lisha

swilika *vb (pt swilíike)* become tame = fugika

-sya, ísya, ukusya *vt.caus (pt ísísye)* grind, mill, crush, pulverize, mince = saga

syaganía *vt (pt syageeníe)* understand, comprehend, know, recognize = fahamu, tambua

syala *vi (pt syeele)* **1** remain = baki **2** rest = pumzika

syanaloolí *adv* certainly = kweli, hakiki

syasya *vt.caus (pt syesye)* leave over, leave smth behind for sb (eg. food) = saza, bakiza, mbakizie mtu

syegetula *vt (pt syegetwíile)* gnash, grind = saga, pondaponda

syela *vt.appl (pt syelíle; > -sya)* grind with = sagia

syenda *vb (pt syendíle)* grind (teeth) = saga kwa kutumia meno

syikila *vb (pt syikíile)* preserve fire with ashes = funika moto kwa majivu

syila *vt (pt syilíle)* bury = zika, fukia

syilila *vt.appl (pt syilíile)* bury with, bury for = zikia, fukilia

syo *pron* which = ambazo

syoba *vt (pt syobíle)* **1** cheat, decieve, swindle, dupe, defraud, mislead, bluff = danganya **2** evade = epa **3** perplex = tatiza, fadhaisha, fumba

syoka *vt,vi (pt syokíle)* grumble, sulk, pout = nuna

syokela *vb (pt syokelíile)* **1** boycott = zira **2** *vb.appl* grumble about = nunia

syoola *n.fam (ba-, 1a/2)* a child born after twins = afuataye mapacha kuzaliwa

syonganika *vb (pt syonganíke)* hesitate = sita

syope ni *adv (10, > -ope ni)* even (eg. birds) = hata na

syoosa *pron* all = yote

syosyoosa *pron* any = chochote, zozote

syuka *vi (pt syukíle)* be resurrected, revived = fufuka

syukwa *vi (pt syukílwe)* be homesick = kuwa na hamu ya nyumbani

syungusya *vt.caus (pt syungusísye)* rotate, wind, circulate = zungusha, zunguka

syungutila *vi (pt syungutíile)* **1** wander, go around, surround = zunguka **2** turn = zunguka **3** circulate = zunguka

syungutisya *vt.caus (pt syungutíisye)* encircle = zungusha, zungushia

syúsya *vt.caus (pt syúsísye)* **1** swing = bembea **2** restore, resurrect, make it live again = fufua, huisha

syúta *vb (pt syútíle)* **1** swing, rock = bembea **2** dangle = ning'iniza

syútúka *vi (pt syútwíke)* **1** swing the body, turn around = geuka, geuza (mwili) **2** suddenly get angry = patwa na hasira ghafula **3** change one's mind, get another idea = badilisha wazo, pata wazo lingine

Tt

taba *vb (pt tabíle)* extend, spread out, spread over = tanda

tabanía *vt (pt tabeníe)* tackle, trip somebody = piga ngwara, tegea mguu

tabaníka *vb (pt tabaníike)* **1** hesitate = sitasita **2** stutter = sema kwa kigugumizi **3** walk or talk unsteadily = pepesuka

tabilila *vi (pt tabilíile)* stammer = gugumia

tabula *vt (pt tabwíile)* **1** pay back = lipa **2** divorce = taliki

tabulende *n.zool (-, 9/10; Kye)* dragonfly = kereng'ende

taafúla *vt (pt taafwíle)* tear = chana

tafúna *vt (pt tafwíne)* chew, munch, gnaw = tafuna

taaga *vt (pt taagíle)* **1** throw, throw away, discard, dispose of, dump, toss = tupa, rusha **2** lose = poteza **3** desert = telekeza

tagajuka *vi (pt tagajwíike)* walk with legs apart = tembea huku miguu imesambazwa

tajanía *vt (pt tajeníe)* strike, hit = ponda, piga

takanía *vt (pt takeníe)* make soft = lainisha, legeza

-takanyífú *adj* soft, flexible = laini, legevu, teketeke, legelege

tala *vi (pt talíile)* **1** go ahead = tangulia **2** begin, precede = anza, tangulia

-talali *adj* quiet, calm = kimya

-talalifú *adj* cool, cold = baridi

talalila *vt (pt talalíile)* cool = poa

talalisya *vt.caus (pt talalíisye)* **1** cool, comfort, soothe = poza **2** subdue = tuliza

-talí *adj* long, tall, high = refu

talikana *vb (pt talikeene)* put one leg over/on another person's leg, play footsies = wekeana mguu mmoja juu ya mwingine

talísya *vt.caus (pt talíisye)* **1** extend, elongate = ongeza urefu **2** enhance = ongeza, kuza

taluka *vb (pt talwíke)* be torn = chanika

talulende *n.zool (ba-, 1a/2)* dragonfly = kereng'ende

talusya *vt.caus (pt talwísye)* be right, correct = kuwa sahihi

tama *vi (pt tamíle)* moo, bray = lia kama punda au ng'ombe

tambalala *vi (pt tambaleele)* be flat, be level = kuwa tambarare

-tambalifu *adj* straight = -lionyoka

tambila *vb (pt tambíile)* **1** receive a guest with happiness and outstretched hands = karibisha, pokea mgeni kwa furaha na mikono wazi **2** entertain = pokea, kirimu

tambuka *vt (pt tambwíike)* **1** cross over = vuka **2** to step = tambuka

tambula *vb (pt tambwíile)* stretch out legs = tanua miguu, panua miguu

tamígwa *vb (pt tamíigwe)* suffer, be annoyed, tormented, be tortured, persecuted, troubled = teseka, taabika, sumbuliwa, sumbuka

tamya *vt (pt tamíisye)* **1** trouble, disturb, tease, annoy, displease = chokoza, sumbua, taabisha, udhi **2** persecute = tesa

tandabuka *vi (pt tandabwíike)* **1** appeal (in court) = kata rufaa **2** climb with problems (eg a mountain, tree) = panda /kwea kwa shida **3** jump onto another thing / issue = rukia jambo au kitu fulani

tandamala *vi (pt tandameele)* shy away = kwepa, epuka

tandamíka *vt (pt tandamíike)* **1** withhold from = epusha, nyima zuia **2** hold sb back = kwaza mtu

tangasya *vt.caus (pt tangasíisye)* **1** proclaim, announce, publish = elezea, tangaza **2** promote = kuza

taníkisya *vt (pt taníkisye)* infect = ambukiza

-tano *color.adj (>Swa. T.A.N.U. The political party with green flags and uniforms)* green = -a kijani

tapa *vt (pt tapíle)* dish out, scoop out = pakua, chota

tapula *vt (pt tapwíile)* separate = tenga

tapukana *vb.reciproc (pt tapukeene)* be separated, divorced = tengana, achana

tasa *vb (pt tasísye)* polish = ng'arisha

-tasí *adj* of the past = ya zamani

taasí *adv* yet, still, a moment = bado, ngoja

taasí *adv* first = kwanza

Tubuuke taasí tukalye jila kula Let's first go and eat that [food] over there = Twende kwanza tukale vile kule

tata *vt (pt tatíle)* grip = shika, kamata sana

taata *n.fam (aba-, 1a/2)* **1** father = baba **2** honorific to man of father's generation = jina la heshima la kumwita mzee wa ukoo

taata unkulumba *n.fam* uncle, ie. father's elder brother = ami, baba mkubwa

taata unnandi *n.fam* uncle, ie. father's younger brother = ami, baba mdogo

taatagwitu *n.fam (bataatabiitu, 1a/2)* our father = baba yetu

-tatu *num.adj* three = tatu

tatula *vb (pt tatwíle)* **1** mangle = ingilia **2** stop a fight between two people = amua mapigano **3** disentangle = tatanua **4** release (eg. from a trap) = weka huru

tefyuka *n.zool (ba-, 1a/2)* type of bird, glossy back drongo = aina ya ndege, kirumbizi, kurumbiza

tega *vb (pt tegíle)* **1** trap, set a trap = tega, weka mtego **2** catch = shika kitu kwa mtego

tegejuka *vb (pt tegejwíike)* stumble = jikwaa

tegeka *vt (pt tegíike)* **1** set a trap for = tegea **2** cross examine = ulizo swali la mtego

tegelekesya *vt.caus (pt tegelekíisye)* set near = sogezea

-tejateja *adj* **1** weak, feable, slack = hafifu, legevu **2** soft = laini **3** stupid, ignorant = -jinga

teeka *vi (pt teekíle)* **1** *vb.off* vomit, puke, throw up = tapika **2** flood, inundate = furika

teekesya *vb (pt teekíisye)* when a cock mounts a hen = jogoo anapompanda tembe

teela *vb (pt teelíle)* breed = zaa; **teela amafumbi** lay eggs = taga mayai; **teela ingwaata** calve = zaa ndama

telamika *vt (pt telamíike)* lower = inamisha

-telamú *adj* sloping = mteremko

-telamúfú *adj* lowered = -liyoteremka

telemúka *vi (pt telemwíike)* glide, slide, slip = teleza

-tembelefú *adj* gentle = legevu

temela *vt (pt temelíile)* cut with = katia

temelela *vi (pt temelíile)* **1** be up early in the morning = wahi asubuhi na mapema **2** wake up early = kujidamka, amka asubuhi sana

tendeka *vt (pt tendíike)* do, make = fanya, tengeneza

tendekesya *vt.caus (pt tendekíisye)* **1** arrange, put in order, prepare, organize, settle = panga, tengeneza, andaa, tunga, tayarisha **2** repair, improve = tengeneza, tunza, karabati, endeleza, sitawisha, kuza hali **3** reform = badili, tengeneza **4** protect, conserve = tunza, kinga **5** dispose = hifadhi, tunza **6** adjust, accomodate = linganisha, tengeneza, rekebisha **7** construct, make = tengeneza, fanya, unda **8** clear = safisha

tendeela *vb (pt tendeelíle)* peep, peek (eg. at an exam) = chungulia

tendeesya *vb* spy = peleleza

-tenenefú *adj* smooth = laini

tenenesya *vt.caus (pt teneníisye)* **1** smoothen, smooth out = lainisha,

sawazisha **2** polish, clean = safisha

tenga *vb (pt tengíle)* make a bed = tandika

tengamojo *adj* gentle, meek = pole

-tengaamú *adj* **1** cool, calm, peaceful = -liopoa, tulivu **2** flat = tambalare **3** safe = salama, isiyo hatari

tengaana *vb (pt tengeene)* **1** rest be in harmony, be relaxed, be still = pumzika, starehe, tulia, kuwa katika masikilizano **2** live in peace = ishi kwa amani **3** become quiet = kaa kimya, tulia tuli, tulizwa

tengaanía *vt (pt tengeeníe)* **1** comfort, soothe, pacify, calm down sb, make quiet = tuliza, liwaza **2** refresh = tia moyo

tenguka múnda be frightened = ogopa, shituka

tengula múnda frighten = ogofya

tengulila *vt (pt tengulíile)* allure, seduce, entice= bembeleza

-tepefú *adj* physically weak, incompetent = dhaifu

teesya *vt.caus (pt teesísye)* **1** cause vomiting = tapisha **2** breed, rear = fuga, tunza, zalisha

-teta *adj* inexperienced, immature, raw, unripe= -bichi, changa, haijaakomaa

teta *vb (pt tetíle)* **1** backbite, gossip = teta, sengenya, kumsema mtu **2** grumble = teta, nung'unika **3** cackle = tetea, lia kama kuku aliavyo anapotaka kutaga

teeta *vb (pt teetíle)* stumble, first stage of walking of a child = enda dede, kusimama dede

tetema *vb (pt tetíime)* **1** shake, tremble, shiver, quiver = tetemeka **2** be afraid = ogopa **3** care for, take great care = uguza

Teti *pn* Name of the first schoolbook in Nyakyusa used in literacy programs and missionary schools in the old days = Jina la kitabu cha lugha ya

Kinyakyusa kilichotumiwa na wa-
misheni kufundishia wenyeji kusoma
zamani

Teti-teti *pn* Name of schoolbook.
Printed in 25000 copies in 1914. See
also Teti = Kitabu cha shule katika
lugha ya kinyakyusa. Zilichapishwa
nakala 25000 mnano 1914

-ti, ukuti *vt (pt -tíle)* **1** say = sema,
tamka **2** hint to sb to do as you do (eg
if your friend has food/dust stuck on
his face, you show on your own face
where it is and how to rub it off) =
Neno la kumtaka mtu afanye kitu
kama utakavyotaka kwa kumwonye-
sha namna ya kufanya
/ **ukuti** is also used together with another speech verb to indicate direct
speech

-tíbe *adj* **1** something tightly woven (eg.
mat, fishnet) = kitu kilichosukwa kwa
karibu sana **2** something in close arrangement (eg teeth) = kitu kili-
chopangwa karibu karibu (mf meno)

tigi be supposed to = bidi
batigi they were supposed to = iliwa-
bidi, iliwapasa

tíka *vt (pt tíkíle)* **1** pound in a mortar
with a pestle = twanga **2** bump,
knock, hit, strike = gonga **3** pound =
twanga

tíkana *vb (pt tíkeene)* collide, bump
into each other = gongana
/Also **kinyana**

tíkanía *vt (pt tíkeenie)* **1** crush by
pounding, squash = ponda, pondaponda **2** contradict = nena kinyume,
kana

-tíkínyifu *adj* very fine, powdery (eg.
earth) = laini

tííla *vb (pt tíílíle)* **1** be afraid, dread,
fear = ogopa **2** obey, be obedient = tii
3 respect = heshimu

tíílisya *vt.caus (pt tíílisye)* terrify,
frighten, scare, intimidate = ogofya,
tisha

tíma *vt (pt tímíle)* **1** rain = nyesha **2** get
wet = lowana
jikutíma, **ifúla jíkútíma** it is raining
= mvua inanyesha

tííma *vt (pt tíímíle)* **1** herd or graze animals, tend = chunga **2** supervise, look
after, guard = simamia, linda,
chunga, angalia

tímbikila *vt (pt tímbikííle)* squeeze,
suppress, press on = kandamiza, gandamiza

-tíme *adj* damp = -nyevu, -a majimaji
/Tuk -tímú

tímiilisya *vt.caus (pt tímiilíísye)* fulfil,
complete = tekeleza, timiza

tímiilisya indagilo 1 perform, execute =
tekeleza amri **2** complete the task =
maliza kazi au kamilisha

tímisya *vb (pt timíísye)* wet = lowanisha

-tímú *adj (Tuk)* damp = -nyevu, -a majimaji
/Kye -**tíme**

tínda *vb (pt tíndíle)* sign with
thumbprint = weka muhuri wa dole
gumba, tia saini kwa dole gumba
/Also **tinda uloobe**

-tine *adj* smooth = laini

tínga *vb (pt tíngíle)* **1** glut, To eat or fill
to excess; satiate = kinai **2** be dis-
gusted = kinai

tínguka *vi (pt tíngwííke)* defy = -totii,
tolea ujuvi

tíínguka *vt (pt tíingwííke)* despise =
dharau

tíngukila *vt (pt tíngukííle)* **1** defy =
onyesha majivuno waziwazi **2** despise
= dharau, kosa adabu

tínila *vi (pt tínííle)* **1** nod, make a signal
to = toa ishara kwa kichwa, ashiria
2 the movement of a buoy when a fish
bites = boya linavyofanya samaki
anapodonoa chambo kwenye ndoana

típula *vt (pt típwíle)* peck at = donoa

tíísya *vt (pt tíísísye)* pick, take out, remove = ondoa, toa

97

títa *vt (pt títíle)* pinch = finya, minya

titíkisya *vt.caus (pt titíkiisye)* **1** press on = gandamiza **2** insist = sisitiza **3** affirm = yakinisha

-títu *color.adj* black = -eusi

tobela *vb (pt tobíile; Tuk)* dip a lump of food into curry = towelea /Kye: **tomekesya**

tobesya *vt.caus (pt tobíisye)* win a case in court = shinda kesi

-toofú *adj* **1** soft, tender = laini, teketeke **2** delicate = pole, karimu sana

-togomafú *adj* rough = -enye kukwaruza, enye miinuko (Luk 3.5 **... indogomafú syosa síípelege ukuja njila indenenefú ítolo**)

togomala *vi (pt togomeele)* be rough (with protrusions), become rough = kuwa na miinuko miinuko mingi; **Unsebo ugu gutogomeele fííjo** This road is very rough = Barabara hii ina miinuko mingi

-tojofú *adj* silly, ignorant = jinga, punguani

tola *vt (pt tolíle)* **1** win, conquer, defeat, beat, overcome, subdue = shinda **2** excel, surpass = zidi mno, pita

tolana *vb (pt toleene)* compete (eg. in sports) = shindana

tolígwa *vb.pass (pt tolíigwe)* **1** fail = shindwa **2** lose = shindwa, poteza **3** submit = jitoa, jiweka chini

tolíka *vi (pt tolíike)* drip, leak = vuja, dondoka

tolwa *vi (pt tolílwe)* be burdened, be very weak = ishiwa nguvu, shindwa kujiweza

tomekesya *vt.caus (pt tomekíisye)* dip in, dunk = chovya

tona *vb (pt toníle; arch)* **1** sharpen = noa, chonga **2** ripe = iva vizuri na rangi ya kupendeza
baluki batoníle the oranges are ripe = machungwa yameiva vizuri

/modern word: **pyasya**

tondola *vt (pt tondwíile)* harvest, reap = vuna, chuma (mazao)

-tongomafú *adj* huge = kubwa mno

tonoka *vb (pt tonwíke)* bounce = dunduka

tonola *vb (pt tonwíle)* dab = donoa

tononda *vb (pt tonondíle)* dot up, put dots on = weka madoadoa, donoa donoa

-tononde *adj* spotted, dotted = enye madoadoa

toonya *vb (pt toonyíle)* **1** leak, drip = vuja **2** ooze = tiririka

tosa *vt (pt tosíle)* farm, plough, till = lima shamba

toosa *adj (12, > -oosa)* all, everything, every item = vyote

tubuuke *expr (> buuka)* let's go! = twende

túbúlila *vt.appl (pt túbúlíile)* pierce with = tobolea

-túbwa *adj* juvenile (esp about animals, cows) = -a ujana, -a balehe

túfya *vt.caus (pt tufífye)* admire, praise, commend, glorify = sifu

túfya nnoono flatter = sifu mno

túfye *n.zool (batufye, 1/2)* big frog = chura mkubwa

tugala *vi (pt tugeele)* **1** be seated, sit = kaa **2** live, inhabit, stay = ishi, kaa

tugasya *vt.caus (pt tugeesye)* **1** make sb sit down = kalisha **2** settle = tuliza, kalisha

tuuja *vb (pt tuujíle)* **1** pant, sigh = hema, shusha pumzi, tweta **2** breathe out = pumua, toa nje pumzi

tuujaníka *vi (pt tuujaníke)* pant, gasp = tweta

tuujila *vt.appl (pt tuujíle)* breathe into = pumulia

tuka *vb (pt tukíle)* swear, insult, abuse, damn = tukana

túkifya *vt (pt túkíífye)* praise for sb = sifia

Tukuju *pn* Tukuyu. Town in Rungwe district. Called Langenburg during the German colonial period. The name is pl of **akakuju** 'a small fig tree' (> **unkuju**) = Tukuyu

túkúla *vb (pt tukwíle)* miss (target) = kosa shabaha

tula *pron (13)* those = vile (vitu)

tula *vt (pt tulíle)* err, make a mistake = fanya kosa

Atulilemo inongwa bo umpíkí ugu atúmúlaga gugwilíle ing'ombe He had a case to answer when a tree he was cutting fell on a cow = Alipata kesi baada ya mti aliokuwa anakata kuangukia ng'ombe

Linga bo kuja akutula If you behave like that you will err = Ukienenda hivyo utakosa

tuula *vt (pt tuulíle)* **1** to take from the head, put smth down = tua **2** help, aid, serve, support, assist = saidia, tumikia **3** be useful = faa

túla *vb (pt túlíle)* be stunted, be thwarted = dumaa

-tule *adj* stunted = -liodumaa

tulika *vb (pt tulíike)* hang = tundika

-túlúba *adj* underdone = via

tuluka *vi (pt tulwíke)* spark = toa cheche

tulula *vt (pt tulwíile)* sprout = chipua

tuma *vt (pt tumíle)* send = tuma, peleka

túmbaníla *vb (pt túmbaníle)* race = kimbia pamoja

tumbukisya *vb (pt tumbukíisye)* plunge = tumbukiza

tumbula *vb (pt tumbwíile)* harvest by picking = chuma

túmbúla *vb (pt túmbwíile)* disembowel, dissect = pasua, tumbua

tumilila *vb (pt tumilíile)* order sb to do something = kumwambia mtu afanye jambo fulani

túmúkilwa *vi (pt túmúkíilwe)* become deficient = kuwa pungufu, pungukiwa

-túmúkíílwe *adj* deficient = -enye upungufu

túmúla *vt (pt túmwíile)* cut = kata

túmúla amasyu decide = kata shauri, amua

túmúlila *vb (pt túmúlíile)* **1** stop on the way = fika, katishia **2** shorten = fupisha

tuna *num* four = nne

túna *vb (pt túníle)* scratch = kuna

tunda *vb (pt tundíle)* urinate, pee, piss = kojoa

tundulu *n.zool (ba-, 1a/2)* sparrow, small red bird = aina ya ndege mdogo mwenye rangi ya hudhurungi na weusi kidogo

-túndúlúfú *adj* **1** tough = -gumu **2** fat (people), big (things) = kubwa, nene, liojaa

tunga *vt (pt tuungíle)* **1** string together = tunga (uzi) **2** hang = ning'iniza

tunganyilwa *vb (pt tunganyílwe)* **1** sweat = tokwa jasho **2** suffocate = banwa pumzi

tungula *vt (pt tungwíile)* pick, pluck, knock down (oranges, mangoes) = angua, chuma (machungwa ...)

tungulupa *vb (pt tungulwíipe)* lie, cheat, slander = danganya, sema uwongo, ongopa, teta

tungulupila *vb (pt tungulupíle)* **1** betray = saliti **2** tell tales, tell stories = semea uwongo **3** slander, gossip = danganya, teta

tunúnú *adj (13), adv* **1** good = nzuri **2** OK, well; The expected positive answer to greetings starting with **Utwa** ... = safi

túúnya *vt (pt túnyíle)* **1** throw stones = tupia jiwe **2** throw = tupa, gonga

túpa *vb (pt túpíle)* get fat, be fat = nenepa

túpisya *vt.caus (pt túpísye)* fatten = nenepesha

túpíka *vt (pt túpíike)* **1** throw into (the fire, hole) = tupia (motoni), ingiza **2** lead sb into trouble = tia mtu katika matatizo

-**tupu** *adj* mere, bare = tupu

túpú to appear suddenly = kuonekana kwa ghafla

túpúka *vi (pt túpwíike)* emerge, to appear suddenly = zuka, tokea, onekana ghafla, ibuka

túpúúlúka *vb (pt túpúúlwíike)* come to the surface, float = ibuka, elea

túsya *vt (pt túsísye)* prevent, restrain = dumaza

tuusya *vi (pt tuusíisye)* rest, relax = pumzika, tua

~ **imbombo** retire = staafu kazi

tútwa *vb (pt tútwíile)* **1** think = fikiri **2** pant = shusha pumzi

-**twa, ukutwa** *vb (pt twíle)* be plenty (esp about fish) = kuwa wengi (samaki); **sítwíle iswi** there are many fish = samaki wengi

twala *vt (pt tweele)* **1** bring, fetch, deliver = leta, peleka **2** lead = ongoza

twala pabulongí, sítaaka accuse = shitaki

twalígwa *vb.pass* be brought = letwa

twalila *vt.appl* bring to/for/with = letea

twamúla *vt (pt twamwíile)* strike = piga

twika *vt (pt twikíle)* help lift up a load to the head, lift up a load onto sb's head = twisha

twínga *vb (pt twíngíle)* sweat = tokwa na jasho

twitila *vb (pt twitíile)* gasp = tweta, pumua kwa shida baada ya kutoka kulia

tyelemúka *vi (pt tyelemwíike)* slip, skid = teleza

tyemúla *vb* sneeze = piga chafya

tyesemúla *vb (pt tyesemwíle)* sneeze = piga chafya

tyonga *vb (pt tyongíle)* to dance vigorusly = kucheza kwa nguvu sana

Uu

uba *vt (pt ubíle)* peel, strip away = menya

ubatana *vb (pt ubeteene)* be fast together, be consolidated = shikamana

ubatila *vt (pt ubatíile)* embrace, hug = kumbatia

ubooga *n (14)* **1** cowardice, fear = hofu, woga **2** *n.bot (-, 9/10)* mushroom = uyoga

uboolo *n (14)* laziness, idleness, indolence = uvivu

uboololo *n* **1** gentleness, kindness = upole, utu, huruma **2** charity = upendo

ubombíle 1 *greeting,* (*Answ.* **ubombíle**) "How are things at work" = habari za kazi **2** *vb.past* you have worked = ume-fanya kazi

ubonaange *n (14)* **1** damage, destruction, harm = uharibifu, maangamizi **2** fault = kosa

ubonangifú *n (14)* destruction = uharibifu

ubongo *n (14)* brain = ubongo

uboonywa *n.med (14)* **1** weakness = udhaifu **2** disease = ugonjwa **3** indolence, lazyness = uvivu

ububagile *n (14)* worthiness = ustahili, hali ya kufaa, hali ya kuweza

ububaalufú *n (14)* the wide unused space between two items (if it is only a narrow space it is called **ubunyíge**) **1** expanse = mapana **2** width, breadth = upana

ububaní *n (14)* incense = ubani

ububíbí *n (im-, 11/10)* evil, badness = ubaya

ububiiko *n (14)* storage = uhifadhi, sehemu ya kuhifadhia

ububili *n (14)* **1** duality, dualism, beeing twofold = uwili **2** couple, pair = jozi, watu wawili

ububíne *n (14)* disease, sickness, illness

= ugonjwa

ububíne bwa kipambaga *n.med (14)*
asthma = ugonjwa wa pumu

ububinga *n (14)* security, protection =
lindo, ulinzi
   inyúmba indali ja bubinga a watch
tower = mnara wa ulinzi

ububofú *n (14)* rottenness = ubovu

ububombanísí *n (14)* cooperation,
working together = kushirikiana
(kazi)

ububombelí *n (14)* **1** employment, service = kazi, ajira, utumishi, huduma
2 usage = matumizi

ububombí *n (14)* efficiency = utendaji

ububoneke *n (14)* shape = umbo

ububonele *n (14)* spite = uonevu

ububopelo *n (14)* refuge, haven, protection, sanctuary = kimbilio

ububúkúke *n (14)* blaze = mwako

ububúlúnge *n (14)* circle, curve, ring =
mviringo

ububumbe *n (imbumbe, 14/4)* shape,
form, figure, structure, layout = umbo

ububumbígwe *n (14)* essence = asili

ububúndifú *n (14)* dampness = unyevu

ububútígwa *n (14)* circumcision = tohara

ububutilo *n (14)* blade (sharp), the cutting edge of a tool = kengee (makali)

ububwapufu *n (14)* dirtiness, unclean-
ness = uchafu (opposite of **ubwífyusí**)

ububyondoke *n (14)* dent, hole = kibonyeo, kishimotobo

ubuufí *n (14)* **1** jealousy, envy = wivu
2 lust, desire = tamaa

ubufíso *n (14)* hiding place (for things)
= maficho

ububúúte *n (14)* incision = chanja, kato

ububwafú *n (14)* carelessness = uzembe

ubufílinge *n (14)* curl = msongo

ubufíndang'oma *n (14)* patience, tolerance = uvumilivu

ubufísalyojo *n (14)* good temperament
= upole

ubufú *n (14)* flour = unga

ubufúgúja *n (14)* greed, gluttony =
ulafi, uroho

ubufújúle *n (14)* humiliation, disgrace
= ufedheheshaji

ubufúlafú *n.med (14)* sore, ulcer,
wound, injury = jeraha, vidonda

ubufúlale *n.med (14)* sore, ulcer,
wound, injury = jeraha, vidonda, ku-
umia kwenye mwili

ubufúmbwe *n (14)* need, requirement,
concern = uhitaji, hitaji

ubufumile *n (14)* product = mazao

ubufúmo *n (14)* **1** background = mahali
pa nyuma **2** essence = asili **3** beginning = chanzo, mwanzo

ubufúmú *n (14)* office of or title of the
chief's counsellors or advisors (**ilí-
fúmú**) = cheo cha washauri wa chifu

ubufúmúke *n (14)* **1** fame = sifa **2** position, prominence = umashuhuri

ubufwane *n (14)*

ubufwane *n (14)* **1** resemblance, likeness = kufanana **2** identity = hali ya
kuwa yule yule **3** unity = umoja **4** size
= saizi

ubufwanía *n (14)* agreement, reconcili-
ation = mapatano

ubufwanie *n (14)* balance = kusawa-
zisha, kupatanisha

ubufwanikisye *n (14)* proportion = uwiamo

ubufwe *n (14)* **1** death = kifo **2** woe =
majonzi, msiba

ubufwile *n (14)* bereavement, woe =
ukiwa baada ya kuzika ndugu, ufiwa,
majonzi, msiba

ubufwimí *n (14)* hunting, a hunting ex-
pedition = uwindaji, usasi

ubufyele *n (14)* **1** state of breastfeeding
= hali ya kunyonyesha **2** children =
watoto

ubugage *n (14)* **1** fatigue, strain = hali
ya kuchoka, uchovu **2** staleness = hali
ya kuchacha **ubugage bwa fíndu ifí
butíkutíílisya** this food is still not
very stale = hali ya uchacha kwa

chakula hiki hautishi

ubugalabwala *n (14)* alcoholism = ulevi

ubugalagala *n (14)* impudence, contempt, obstinacy, mischief = ufidhuli, utundu, utukutu

ubuganga *n (14)* medical practice = uganga

ubugaande *n (14)* loss of weight = hali ya kukonda

ubugaasí *n (14)* **1** courage = uhodari **2** arrogance, insolence = ujeuri

ubugeleke *n (14)* thatch = uezekaji

ubugogo *n (14)* old age = uzee

ubugolofú *n (14)* uprightness, honesty, loyalty, justice = unyofu

ubugogí *n (14)* murder = uuaji

ubugono *n (14)* place to sleep, sleeping quarters, bedding = malazi

ubugwemelesí *n (14)* act of sponging on others, vistiting people at meal times for free food = udoezi

ubuhahaní n (14) debauchery = zinaa, ulevi

ubuhangajifu *n (14)* **1** carelessness = uzembe **2** idleness = uvivu

ubuhaano *n.num (14)* in fives = utano

ubuhobofu *n (14)* forgiveness = usamehevu

ubujanja *n (14)* deceit, deception = ujanja

ubujengí *n (14)* **1** building, edifice = majengo **2** construction = ujenzi

ubuují *n (14)* gruel, porridge = uji

ubujo *n (14)* **1** place to be accomodated, engaged = mahali pakuwapo, pa kuishi **2** place, space (room) = mahali, sehemu **3** opportunity = nafasi

ubujo bwa *conj* instead of = badala ya

ubujobí *n (14)* discourse, talk, conversation = maongezi

ubujungu *n (14)* laziness = uvivu, uzembe

ubujwege *n (14)* shouting = upayukaji

ubuka *vi (pt ubwííke)* peel off, moult = chunika, chubuka

ubukabí *n (14)* **1** wealth, richness = utajiri **2** profit = faida

ubukabile *n (14)* advantage = faida

ubukabilo *n (14)* gain, profit = faida

ubukabo *n (14)* advantage, profit = faida

ubukafú *n (14)* **1** being OK = uzima **2** difficulty = matatizo

ubukakafú *n (14)* meanness, miserliness = ubahili, unyimi

ubukalaní *n (14)* office work, work of a clerk = ukarani

ubukamú *n (14)* **1** kinship, brotherhood = undugu **2** relation = uhusiano, undugu, unasaba

ubukangale *n (14)* old age = uzee

ubukasyo *n (14; Tuk)* act of calming sb = kumpa mtu nguvu au moyo /Kye **ulukasyo**

ubukatale *n (14)* fatigue, tiredness = uchovu

ubukeke *n (14)* **1** childhood = utoto **2** youth = ujana **3** infancy = uchanga

ubukeetelelí *n (14)* supervision, administration = uangalizi, usimamizi

ubukeetí *n (14)* **1** evidence = ushahidi, kithibiti **2** testimony = ushahidi

ubukífú *n (14)* **1** courage, heroism, bravery = ushujaa **2** confidence = ushupavu

ubukiga *n (14)* the way the cloth worn around the head (the **ingiga**) is folded = Namna kilemba kinavyokunjwa

ubukíkulu *n (14)* womanhood = uanauke

ubukímwí *n.med (14)* AIDS = ukimwi

ubukindane *n (14)* difference = tofauti

ubukiinde *n (14)* appeal (legal case) = rufaa

ubukindu *n (14, > Swa)* leaf of a wild date palm used for plaiting = ukindu /See **akagindwa**

ubuko *n (14)* in-law relationship = ukwe

ubukobe *n (14)* **1** negligence = uzembe **2** slackness, weakness = ugoigoi

ubukololofú *n (14)* apathy, lazyness = uvivu, kutokuwa mchangamfu, utepetevu

ubukokonyale *n.med (14)* leprosy = ukoma

ubukoma *n.med (14, >Swa)* leprosy = ukoma

ubukomú *n (14)* cleverness, cunning = ujanja

ubukonyofú *n (14)* foolishness, folly =

upumbavu

ubukonyoke *n (14)* the state of being broken = hali ya kuvunjika

ubukuuje *n (14)* haste, hurry = hali ya kuharakisha, haraka

ubukuku *n (14)* state of sleeping with eyes not completely closed = hali ya mtu kulala usingizi ilhali macho yake hajayafumba barabara

ubukulumba *n (14)* **1** size, higher position = ukubwa **2** glory = utukufu **3** age = umri

ubukundwe *n (14)* **1** favor = upendeleo **2** loveliness = uzuri

ubukúngúlúka *n (14)* prophecy = unabii

ubukusí *n (14)* adulthood = utu uzima

ubukusye *n (14)* expansion = makuzi, ukuzaji

ubukwabí *n (14)* draft, drag = uvutaji, ukokotaji

ubukye *n (14)* sunrise, dawn = pambazuko

ubula *n. anat (14)* intestine, bowels = utumbo

   ubula ubunywamú large intestine = utumbo mkubwa

   ubula ubunandi small intestine = utumbo mdogo

ubula *vt (pt ubwííle)* skin an animal = chuna

ubulabilo *n (14)* direction = uelekeo

ubulagusí *n (14)* divination = uaguzi

Ubulaja *pn* Europe = Ulaya

ubulambikí *n (14)* **1** authority = utawala, mamlaka **2** oppression = ukandamizaji

ubulamú *n (14)* brother-in-law relationship = ushemeji

ubulaasí *n (14)* bamboo juice, the alcoholic drink made from bamboo juice = ulanzi

   /Type of alcoholic drink, if drunk the first day it is tapped it is very sweet and very laxative

ubuleebí *n (14)* **1** robbery = unyang'anyi, wizi **2** grand theft = wizi mkubwa

ubulegane *n (14)* **1** difference = tofauti

2 discrepancy = tofauti

ubulema *n (14)* stupidity, folly = upumbavu
   -a bulema *adj* absurd = pumbavu

ubulendemúfú *n (14)* crack, flaw = ufa

ubulenge *n (indenge, 14/10)* **1** cut, incision, amputation = mkato, namna ya kukata **2** flower = ua **3** pollen = chavuo

ubuulí nubuulisí, uluulo nuluulisyo *n* trade = biashara

ubulili *n (imí-, 14/4)* mat = mkeka

ubulílí *n.zool (14)* earthworm = mnyoo wa ardhini

ubuliilí *n (14)* indebtedness, tendency of not paying one's debts = kutolipa madeni ya watu

ubulilisi *n (14)* clutching, clinging, persistance = ung'ang'anizi

ubulimbo *n (14)* gum = gundi, ulimbo

ubulimí *n (14)* cultivation, agriculture = ulimaji, ukulima

ubulindililí *n (14)* **1** protection = ulinzi **2** advocacy = uwakili **3** attorney = usimamizi, uangalizi

ubulindwana *n (14)* girlhood = usichana

ubulingaanie *n (14)* explanation = maelezo

ubulogwe *n (14)* **1** adultery, fornication = uasherati, uzinzi **2** prostitution = umalaya **3** debauchery, vice = uzinzi, ufisadi

ubuloondo *n (14)* poverty = umasikini, ufukara

ubulongí *n (14)* **1** decree = ushauri **2** judgement = hukumu

ubulongosí *n (14)* management, leadership, administration = uongozi

ubulosí *n (14)* witchcraft, sorcery, black magic = uchawi

ubulufú *n (14)* longing for, lust = tamaa, ufisadi

ubulugu *n (14)* hostility = uadui

ubuluke *n (14)* braid = ufumaji, usukaji

ubulumbililí *n (14)* **1** conversation, discourse = mazungumzo **2** preaching = uhubiri

ubulumbu *n (14)* relationship between

siblings = uumbu

ubulumyana *n (14)* boyhood = uvulana

ubulungo *n.bot (14)* Type of grasslooking herb which grows as a parasite on trees. Used as medicine for pregnant women before giving birth so that birth is not delayed = Aina ya mmea ufananao na nyasi na huota juu ya miti. Hutumika kumnywesha mama mwenye uchungu ili azae haraka

ubulwafú *n.med (14)* disease = ugonjwa

ubulwane *n (14)* conflict = ugomwi, vita

ubulwe *n (14)* conflict = ugomvi

ubumaganyí *n (14)* skill = ustadi

ubumalikilo *n (14)* end = mwisho

ubumalikisyo *n (14)* **1** end = mwisho **2** peak = kilele **3** point = ncha

ubumalilo *n (14)* the end = mwisho

ubumanyaní *n (14)* friendship = urafiki

ubumanyí *n (14)* skill, faculty, knowledge = ujuzi

ubumanyílí *n (14)* knowledge, education, learnedness = elimu, usomi

ubumatiko *n (14)* plaster = lipu, kandiko

ubumele *n.zool (14)* type of fish (tilapia) = aina ya samaki, furu /Same as **ubutaapi**

ubumeme *n (14; >Swa)* electricity = umeme

ubuumí *n (14)* life, health, well being = uzima, uhai

ubumogelí *n (14)* pride = majivuno, fahari

ubumogí *n (14)* fashion, displaying fine clothing = ulimbwende, umaridadi

ubuumú *n (14)* drought, a dry spell = ukame, ukavu

ubunaganífú *n (14)* decrease = upungufu

ubung'wale *n (14)* scratch = hali ya kukwaruzwa, mkwaruzo

ubuníní *n (14)* **1** childhood = utoto **2** smallness = udogo

ubuníongafú *n (14)* crookedness = kupindapinda, hali ya kupindapinda

ubuníongoke *n (14)* adolescence, puberty = ubalehe

ubunúnía (Sesamum indicum) *n.bot (14)* sesame, simsim = ufuta

ubunúnú *n (14)* beauty, goodness, purity = uzuri

ubunyaafú *n (14)* **1** sweetness = utamu **2** flavor, taste = ladha

ubunyafyale *n (14)* kingdom, empire = ufalme, milki

ubunyago *n (14)* **1** end of the funeral when the hair of all relatives is cut and the successor of the deceased is declared = kutimiza mila na desturi ya kurithisha, hitima iambatanayo na kurithisha ambayo hufuatana na ukataji wa nywele kwa ndugu au jamaa wote **2** initiation rites at time of circumcision = unyago (for girls), jando (for boys)

ubuNyakyusa *pn (14)* the land of the Nyakyusa people = unyakyusa

ubunyalí *n (14)* dirt, garbage, litter, filth, refuse, rubbish = uchafu

ubunyambala *n (14)* manhood = uanaume

ubunyasa *n (imí-, 14/4)* **1** mat (generic) = mkeka **2** very long mat, used for guests or for drying crops = mkeka mrefu sana utumikao kuanikia mazao au kupokelea wageni

ubunyaate *n (14)* fatness = unene

ubunyonywe *n (14)* **1** affection = upendo **2** desire (lust), lust = hamu, tamaa **3** appetite = hamu ya chakula

ubunywamú *n (14)* **1** size, largeness = ukubwa **2** fatness, obesity = unene

ubupafú *n (14)* greed = ulafi

ubupalamaní *n (14)* neighborhood = ujirani

ubupalapala *n (14)* difficulty = ugumu

ubupandufú *n (14)* crack = ufa

ubupanga *n (14)* sword = upanga

ubupapate *n (14)* flatness = ubapa

ubupaapí *n (14)* birth = uzazi

ubupasufu *n (14)* crack = ufa

ubupasule *n.med (14)* operation (in

hospital) = upasuaji

ubupe *n (14)* generosity = ukarimu

ubupelí *n (14)* creation = uumbaji

ubupepe *n (14)* **1** lightness = wepesi
 2 facility = urahisi

ubupímba *n (14)* **1** shortness = ufupi
 2 brevity, abbreviation = ufupisho

ubupimbí *n (14)* draft = ubebaji

ubupime *n (14)* measure = kipimo

ubupinde, ikipindo *n (ifi-, 7/8)* bow =
 upinde

ubupíndanie *n (14)* curl, braid = msongo

ubupindo *n (14)* bow = upinde

ubupingamu *n (14)* not straight = kwa
 kupindapinda, kimafumbo:
 jobela mbupingamu speak in para-
 bles = ongea kwa mifano, mafumbo

ubupiingí *n (14)* objection = katazo

ubupindo *n (imí-, 14/4, Tuk)* arch = tao

ubupínye *n (14)* the tying up, the way
 tightening has been done = ufungaji

ubupípí *n (14)* proximity = ukaribu

ubupokí *n (14)* **1** salvation = wokovu,
 ukombozi **2** delivery = ukombozi

ubuponjolí *n (14)* victory = ushindi

ubupotanie *n (14)* coil = pindo

ubupube *n (14)* experience, habituation,
 getting used to, familiarity = mazoea

ubupyu *n (14)* heat = umoto, ujoto

ubusaja *n.anat (14)* cheek = shavu

ubusaake *n (14)* provocation = uchokozi

ubusaale *n (14)* happiness = furaha,
 uchangamfu

ubusambukí *n (14)* revolt = uasi

ubusangalufú *n (14)* **1** luck = heri **2** advantage = heri, faida

ubuusí *n (14)* thread, fiber = uzi

ubusíku *n (14)* **1** day (24 h) = siku
 2 time = wakati, majira, muda

ubusímbe *n (14)* writing = maandishi,
 maandiko

ubusípa *n.zool (14)* type of small fish =
 dagaa

The Coming-Out - Ubusooka

UbuNyakyusa was in the past divided
into a large number of political units
(approx. 100 in 1936)[1]. These units or
age-villages were grouped into two
sides meant to become separate units at
a later stage. This occured once in a
generation at the ceremony of the Ubusooka when two sons of an old umalafyale took over control of their father's
unit, each taking one of the "sides".

---

ubusípulilo *n (14)* hook (for fishing) =
 ndoana

ubusísí *n (14; Tuk, Kye ingani)* disobedience, obstinacy = hali ya kutotii,
 utoru wa utii, ukaidi

ubusísya *n (14)* **1** glory, magnificence =
 utukufu **2** dignity = heshima

ubusíto *n (14)* weight = uzito

ubusobí *n (14)* **1** error, fault = kosa,
 kosefu **2** revolt = uasi

ubusooka *n (14)* "The coming-out"; A
 ceremony of the past marking the
 passing in of new leadership and the
 passing out of the old. = "Kutoka nje"
 Sherehe hapo kale za kuadhimisha
 kutawazwa kwa uongozi mpya na ule
 wa zamani kuondoka madarakani.
 /see box

ubusolofú *n (14)* depth = kina

ubusololí *n (14)* prophesy, prediction,
 clairvoyance = utabiri, unabii

ubusubilí *n (14)* hope, expectation =
 tumaini

ubusubilígwa *n (14)* hope, expectation
 = tumaini

ubusotole *n (14)* dent, hole = kibonyeo,
 kishimo, kitobo

ubusubilígwa *n (14)* hope, expectation
 = tumaini

ubusubisí, ulusubisyo *n (14)* consolation, soothing, condolence, calming =
 liwazo, tendo la kuliwaza

ubusúlúmanie *n (14)* **1** grief = huzuni
 2 affliction = mahangaiko

ubusungu *n (14)* **1** maidenhood = uwa-
nawali **2** virginity = ubikira; **umwana
gwa busungu** the first born = mtoto
gwa kwanza

ubuswe *n (14)* **1** forgivness = msamaha
2 excuse = udhuru **3** remission = msamaha

ubuswígala *n (14)* tail of cattle, horse =
mkia wa ng'ombe, farasi

ubusyanju *n (14)* thicket = kichaka

ubusyobí *n (14)* **1** cheating, bluff, deceit, fraud, deception, trickery = hila,
udanganyifu, uwongo **2** cleverness =
ujanja

ubusyoja *n (14)* body hair = unyoya,
nywele za mwilini

ubusyuka *n (14)* **1** The place where
people go when they die, the land of
the ancestors. Some people think this
existence is underground, others
think that the dead are among us, but
that we can not see them. = ulimwengu wa fufuo, mahali ambapo
panasadikika kuwa mtu akifa huenda
huko, watu wengine wanafikiriia
kuwa mahali hapo pako chini ya
ardhi na wengine hufikiri kuwa hao
watu wwapo kati yao **2** paradise =
ahera

ubusyukwe *n (14)* homesickness, miss-
ing your home or a person, longing =
hamu, kumbukumbu ya nyumbani
(kwa mtu aliye mbali), tamaa

ubusyungutile *n (14)* circumference =
mzingo

ubutalatifú *n (14)* **1** cold, chill =
ubaridi **2** politeness = upole

ubutalí *n (14)* **1** length, distance = um-
bali **2** height = urefu

ubutambi *n (14)* wick = utambi

ubutaamye *n (14)* disturbance = usum-
bufu

ubutaaní *n (14)* cousin relationship =
ubinamu

ubutaapi *n.zool (14)* type of fish, small,
tilapia species (small gege) = aina ya

samaki, mdogo, jamii ya perege
/Same as **ubumele**

ubutasí *n (14)* beginning, start = mwanzo

ubutege *n.cult (14)* **1** a witch's trap or
snare for catching her/his enemies =
mtego wa kichawi **2** act of being poi-
soned

ubuteelí *n (14)* birth = uzazi

ubutembeelefú *n (14)* **1** slackness =
ugoigoi **2** The sagging as in ropes or
wires between poles = kulegea kwa
waya au kamba kati ya nguzo

ubutendekesí *n (14)* construction, repair = ujenzi, utengenezaji

ubutenenefu *n (14)* smoothness = ulaini

ubutengamojo *n* **1** gentleness, meekness = upole **2** charity = ukarimu

ubutíme *n (14)* damp, dampness = hali
ya kulowana, unyevu, unyevunyevu

ubutítu *n (14)* darkness, blackness = weusi
-a mbutítu *adj* confidential = -a siri

ubutoofú *n (14)* **1** politeness = upole
2 softness, smoothness = ulaini

ubutolwe *n (14)* **1** trouble, harm, difficulty,
affliction = shida, tatizo, matatizo, mateso
2 distress = mahangaiko
~ **bwa fíndu** famine = njaa
~ **ubunywamú** catastrophy, calamity, peril
= msiba

ubutononde *n (14)* dot = doa

ubutota *n (14)* sticking grass = nyasi
zinatayo

ubutúbwa *n (14)* youth = ujana

ubutugalo *n (14)* seat, place of accomodation = kiti

ubutulanoongwa *n (14)* **1** sin = dhambi
2 delinquency = ukosaji

ubutuulí *n (14)* help, aid, assistance =
usaidizi

ubutúmúlí *n (14)* decision = uamuzi

ubutumwa *n (14)* slavery, bondage =
utumwa

ubutungulu *n (14)* **1** lie, deceit, deception, bluff = uwongo, udanganyifu
2 hypocrisy = unafiki

ubutusyo *n (14)* port = bandari

ubutwa *n (14)* **1** lordship = ubwana, ufalme **2** authority = mamlaka **3** state = nchi

ubwabuke *n (14)* freedom, liberty = uhuru

ulwalabwe *n (14)* rock = mwamba

ubwalwa *n (14)* **1** beer, local brew = pombe **2** alcohol, liquor, booze = kileo; **ubwalwa bwa maafíílú** wine = divai

ubwaana *n (14)* childhood = utoto

ubwanalolí *n (14)* **1** truth, fact, certainty = uhakika, ukweli **2** accuracy = usahihi, ukweli
-**a bwanalolí** *adj* accurate = sahihi

ubwandilo *n (14)* **1** beginning = mwanzo **2** nature = asili

Ubwandilo *pn.bibl (14)* Genesis = Mwanzo

ubwangalilo *n (14)* a talk = maongezi

ubwaníke *n (14)* childhood = utoto

ubwanjufu *n (14)* span = mapana

ubwasí *n (14)* **1** space, gap = nafasi, uwazi **2** numbness = ganzi (katika mguu/mkono ghafla)

ubwato *n (imyato, 14/4)* boat, dug out canoe = mtumbwi

ubwefú *n (14)* whiteness, very brigth = weupe sana

ubwegano *n (inyegano, 14/4)* wedding = harusi, arusi
/**Ubwegí** is more commonly used

ubwegí *n (14)* **1** marriage = ndoa **2** wedding = harusi, arusi

ubwelefú *n (14)* **1** width, breadth, expanse = upana **2** an open space = uwazi

ubwelo *n (14)* net, scoop net = wavu, kokolo

ubwelú *n (14)* **1** whiteness = weupe **2** cleanliness, purity = usafi

ubweluke *n (14)* **1** purification = utakaso **2** brightness = ung'aru

ubwembe *n (14)* sharp edge of a cutting tool = Sehemu chongofu ya jembe, shoka nk

ubwengígwa *ingamwana: ubwalwa (14)* beer = pombe

ubwífi *n (14)* sister-in-law relationship = uwifi

ubwifíso *n (14)* refuge, hiding place (for people) = mahali pa kujificha, maficho

ubwífyusí *n (14)* **1** cleanliness = usafi **2** smartness = umaridadi; **umwífyusí** *sb* who keeps himself and his homestead clean and nice = mtu ambaye hutunza mwili wake na eneo lake safi

ubwígane *n (14)* **1** affection = upendo, huba **2** choice = uchaguzi **3** will, wish = utashi

ubwíkemo *n (14)* **1** holiness = utakatifu **2** piety = uchaji wa mungu

ubwikilí *n (14)* faith = imani

ubwílangomelesyo *n (14)* sin = dhambi

ubwilo *n (14)* sunset = jua lituapo

ubwímí *n (14)* greed, meanness = uchoyo, uroho

ubwimililí *n (14)* administration, management = usimamizi

ubwína *n (imí-, 14/4)* **1** hole = shimo **2** burrow = kishimo cha mnyama

ubwíngí *adj* quantity, amount = kiasi

ubwíníenganíe *n (14)* coil = mpindo, jinsi kamba au nuyzi zina vyojifungafunga

ubwino *n (14; > Swa)* ink = wino

ubwínogonele *n (14)* accusation = mashtaka

ubwínogonelígwe *n (14)* accusation = mashitaka

ubwínufú *n (14)* elevation, altitude = mwinuko

ubwipoko *n (14)* refuge = kimbilio

ubwísíbile *n (14)* habit = tabia, mazoea

ubwísúle *n (14)* bulge = uvimbe

ubwísule bwa kiluungo *n.med (14)* arthritis = ugonjwa wa yabisi kavu

ubwisule bwa kiníe *n.med (14)* hepatitis = uvimbe wa ini

ubwíte *n (14)* **1** war, battle, combat = vita **2** fight, quarrel, aggression, discord, hostility = ugomvi, ukorofi, mapigano, uadui **3** chaos = fujo, kasheshe

-**ugí** *adj* (blade) sharp = kali (kisu)

ugiila *vb (pt ugiilíle)* kid, joke, crack

jokes, mock = fanya utani, dhihaki,
tania
ugilila *vt (pt ugilííle)* mock = tania
ugonege *greeting* bye bye, good bye =
kwa heri (answer: ukagone)
ugoníle 1 *greeting* good morning, hello,
hi, how are you, etc. (This is the most
common Nya. greeting. Answ.
ugoníle) = jambo **2** *vi.pt of gona* you
have slept = umelala
ugu *pron* **1** this = huu, hii **2** which = amba-
uguuso *n.fam* your (sg) father = baba yako
ugwa- *prefix (aba-)* of, from, with the
characteristics of ... = wa
ugwabuufí *n (aba-, 1/2)* **1** jealous person = mwivu **2** reciprocal term between a womans ex-husband and her
new husband = jina aitwalo mtu
aliyeoa mke wa mwenzio
ugwake *pron* her/his = wake
ugwakibabilisí *n (aba-, 1/2)* sympa-
thetic person = mwenye huruma
ugwakigili *n (aba-, 1/2)* a lunatic = kichaa
ugwakikolo *n (abakikolo, 1/2)* relative
= mtu wa ukoo
ugwakilingo *n (aba-, 1/2)* heir = mrithi
ugwakipanda *n (aba-, 1/2)* the first
born = mzaliwa wa kwanza
ugwakisa *n (aba-, 1/2)* kind person =
mwenye huruma
ugwakumabele *n (aba-, 1/2)* a suckling
child, an infant = mtoto anyonyaye
ugwalupuju *n (aba-, 1/2)* bald person =
mwenye upara, kipara
ugwalusako *n (aba-, 1/2)* lucky person
= mwenye bahati
ugwalyojo *n (aba-, 1/2)* bad-tempered
person, short-tempered person =
mwenye hasira
ugwamaka *n (aba-, 1/2)* strong person
= mwenye nguvu
ugwamapuli *n (aba-, 1/2)* deaf person =
kiziwi
ugwamatíngo *n (aba-, 1/2)* arrogant
person = mwenye kiburi
ugwambalilo *n (aba-, 1/2)* accountant =

mhasibu
ugwambepo *n (aba-, 1/2)* demented
person = mwendawazimu
ugwamísímu *n (aba-, 1/2)* a good witch
or fortune teller (mostly women, they
go into a trance and scream and
shout, and afterwards they will tell
about the future) = mwenye pepo
awezaye kutabiri yajayo
ugwamyabo *n.fam (aba-, 1/2)* **1** his/her
younger sibling = mdogo wake **2** kinship = nduguye, ndugu yake
ugwamyinú *n.fam (aba-, 1/2)* your
younger sibling = mdogo wako,
mdogo wenu
ugwamyitu *n.fam (aba-, 1/2)* **1** my/our
sibling = ndugu yangu/yetu **2** relative
= ndugu
ugwandumí *n (aba-, 1/2)* **1** angel =
malaika **2** messenger = mtu
aliyetumwa kupeleka habari/taarifa
ugwapakikota *n (aba-, 1/2)* chairman,
chairperson = mwenyekiti
ugwasúkúúlu *n (aba-, 1/2)* student =
mwanafunzi
ugwatínala *n (aba-, 1/2, > Eng tenor)*
sb blowing the small gourds at the
traditional dances = mpuliza 'tinala'
ugwe *pron* you (sg) = wewe
ugwífí *n.fam (ab-, 1/2)* sister-in-law
1 husband's sister = wifi **2** brother's
wife = wifi
ugwíliima *n* native, local person = mzawa, mwenyeji
ugwísabo *n.fam (abi-, 1/2)* their father
= baba yao
ugwíse *n.fam* his/her father = baba yake
ugwísemwe *n.fam* your (pl) father = baba yenu
ujiila *vb (pt ujííle)* make a sound like
the sound made by heavy rain or a
waterfall = fanya sauti ya mvua, sauti
ya chatu atembeapo, sauti (ungurumo)
la mtu mwenye kuumwa kifua, anguka ya maji ya maporomoko
uju *det* this = huyu

uju *pron* who = ambaye
  jo uju (this, she, he) is the one = huyu
  ndiye
uju jo jujo this is the one (person) = huyu
  ndiye
uju jo uju this is the one = huyu ndiyo
ujungi *pron* another (person) = mwingine
ukagone *greeting* (answer to **ugonege**)
  good bye = kwa heri
ukelemba *n (15)* writing = kuandika
ukeetege *interj for drawing attention*
  1 that is why = ndiyo maana **2** observe, look for = utazame, uangalie
  3 guard = utunze
ukonganía *n (15)* mixing, mixture =
  ku-hanganya
ukongelapo *n (15)* **1** addition = kuju-
  mlisha **2** advancement = endeleo

**VERBS ARE LISTED WITHOUT
THE UKU- PREFIX.**

uku- *prefix* **1** Verbal infinitive prefix.
  Not used in dictionaries. = Kiambishi
  ku- kwa kitenzi. Hakitumiwi katika
  kamusi. **2** NounClass 15 prefix = Kiambishi awali cha ngeli 15
ukubaba *n (15)* pain, ache, suffering =
  umivu, mateso
  /Also **ulubabo, ukubabígwa,
  ububabígwe**
ukubaba kwa líno *n.med* toothache =
  maumivu ya jino
ukubaba kwa ntu *n.med* headache =
  maumivu ya kichwa
ukubabígwa *n.med (15)* ache, suffering
  = maumivu yanayoendelea
ukubagila *n (15)* ability = uwezo
ukubala indalama accounting = kuhesabu fedha
ukufíka *n (15)* arrival = mfiko
ukufuma *adv* **1** off = toka **2** since = tangu
ukufwana *adv* **1** about, approximately
  = karibu **2** according to = kufuatana
  na, kwa kupatana na, kwa namna ya

ukujobesanía *n (15)* **1** discussion, argument, dispute = mjalada **2** dialogue,
  conversation = mazungumzo
ukukasya ilíísyu stress or accent on a
  word = kukaza neno
ukukeelwa *n* abundance = tele, vitu
  vingi sana
ukukindapo *n (15)* excess = ziada
ukukindapo pa *prep* beyond (place) =
  kupita (sehemu fulani)
ukukongana na according to = kwa
  namna ya, kwa kupatana na, kufuatana na
ukulilanila *n (15)* custum of eating together = desturi ya kijadi ya kula
  chakula pamoja
ukulinda kilaabo *adv* the day after tomorrow = kesho kutwa
ukuulisya *n (15)* sale = uuzaji
ukuluka *n (15)* weaving = kufuma,
  kusuka
ukulúúswa *n (15; >Eng loose)* deficit =
  hasara
ukunoga *n (15)* prosperity = ufanisi
ukupaagula *n (15)* detour = gawanya
  katika mafungu
ukusangamka *n (15)* cheer = furaha,
  changamka
ukusiga, ukusigila *n (15)* obstruction,
  bar = kuzuia, kukinga
ukusíta *prep* without = bila, pasipo na
ukusítaaka *n (15)* accusation = mashtaka
ukusítakujapo *n (15)* absence = kuto-
  kuwepo, bila kuwepo
ukusita kupilikisanía *n (15)* misunderstanding, chaos = bila kusikilizana,
  mzozo (kutokuelewana)
ukusoba *prep* without = bila
ukusooka off = kutoka
ukusyila *n (15)* burial = mazishi
ukutangasya *n (15)* announcement =
  tangazo
ukutendekesya *n (15)* arrangement =
  mpango
ukuti *adv,conj* **1** that = kwamba **2** in

order that = ili **3** if = kama

ukutúmúkilwa *n (15)* deficit, be short of something eg. money = kupungukiwa

ukutwa *n (15)* abundance (of fish) = tele (samaki)

ukwagígwa *adj* accessible = -a kuweza kukaribiwa, kupatikana

ukwaka *(15)* flame, burning = kuwaka

ukwana *n (15)* cackle, cackling (of chicken) = mteto wa kuku

ukwangala *n* (15) enjoyment of good company = maongezi

ukwasílele *ingamwana: ugoníle* a general greeting = umeamkaje

ukwíbona *n (15)* boasting = kujiona

ukwíkasya *n (15)* stability, firmness = kujikaza, kuwa imara, uthabiti

ukwílaamwa *n (15)* doubt = mashaka

ukwínusya *n (15)* **1** advancement = endeleo **2** to raise sb up, boosting up = kuinua

ukwipukulanía *n (15)* occupation = shuguli, kazi

ula *vt (pt ulíle)* buy = nunua

ulífúmú *n (ama-, 5/6)* advisor, especially about advisor to the chief = mshauri wa chifu

ulíluumbu *n.fam (aba-, 5/6)* sibling or cousin of opposite sex = ndugu wa kike kama aitwavyo na nduguye wa kiume na ndivyo huyo wa kiume aitwavyo na nduguye wa kike /Also **íluumbu**

ulisya *vt.caus (pt ulíisye)* sell = uza

uloobe *n (inyobe, 11/10)* finger, toe = kidole

uloobelo *n (iny-, 11/10)* **1** humiliation = kuzomea **2** derisive groaning, scorning, sneer = kuzomea

ulonangiko *n (inyonangiko, 11/10)* destruction = uharibifu

ulonango *n (inyo-, 11/10)* destruction = uharibifu

ulonganío *n (inyo-, 11/10)* mixture = kuchanganya

ulongaano *n (inyo-, 11/10)* unity = umoja

uloosyo *n.relig (inyo-, 11/10)* baptism = ubatizo

ulu *adv* **1** in this way = namna hii **2** now, at this moment = sasa, sasa hivi

ulubabo *n (imbabo, 11/10)* agony, pain, indignation = maumivu, mateso

ulubabu *n (imbabu, 11/10)* one piece of wood or firewood = ukuni /for firewood see **imbabu**

ulubafú *n (im-, 11/10)* **1** side = upande **2** *n.anat* rib = ubavu **3** direction = uelekeo

ulubalo *n (im-, 11/10)* lesson = somo

ulubambo *n (im-, 11/10)* line, queue, row of people = msululu wa watu; **ima ndubambo** stand in line = simama mstarini

ulubango *n (im, 11/10)* deliverance = uokozi

ulubaatiko *n (im-, 11/10)* **1** order, arrangement, system, plan, regularity = mpango, mpangilio, utaratibu, kawaida **2** respect = heshima **3** disposition = madaraka **4** decoration = pambo, urembo

ulubatamísyo *n (im-, 11/10)* **1** consolation = faraja **2** calming down = unyamazishaji

ulubaatiko *n (im-, 11/10)* system, method, program, procedure, arrangement, order = utaratibu, taratibu, kufuata sheria; **ulubaatiko lwa fímangílo** timetable, schedule = ratiba ya masomo

ulubaato *n (imbaato, 11/10)* belch = mbweu

ulubeefú *n (im-, 11/10)* mist, fog = ukungu

ulubeefú ulusito fog = ukungu

ulubi *n (11)* cursing, swearing = maneno ya kuombea mabaya

ulubígobígo *n (imb-, 11/10)* throwing stick (eg. a weapon) = kipateleha mti kinachotumika kurusha kama silaha

110

ulubikililo *n (im-, 11/10)* reserve = akiba

ulubilo *n (im-, 11/10)* a run, act of running= mbio

ulubíndilo *n (im-, 11/10)* instrument used for castrating animals = kifaa kitumiwacho kuhasi wanyama

ulubingililo *n (im-, 11/10)* purpose = kusudi

ulubingilo *n (im-, 11/10)* 1 homestead, yard = uwanja wa nyumba 2 place in front of the homestead which is swept, courtyard, yard, clearing = uwanja (kwa ajili ya kufagia, unaofa giliwa) mbele ya nyumba

uluubo *n (inyuubo, 11/10)* sword (double edged, smaller than panga) = jambia

ulubombelo *n (im-, 11/10)* effect = matokeo

ulubombo *n (im-, 11/10)* action, deed = kitendo

uluboneko *n (im-, 11/10)* 1 occasion, chance, event = tukio 2 consequence, effect, result = athari, tukio, tokeo la jambo 3 appearance = tendo la kuonekana

uluboneko ulubíbí danger, emergency = hatari, dharura

ulubonesyo *n (im-, 11/10)* exhibition = onyesho

ulubopo *n (im-, 11/10)* running, run = kukimbia, namna ya kukimbia

ulubosyo *n.med (imbosyo, 11/10)* type of medicine which can neutralize other medicines, a strong medicine = dawa ya aina yoyote inayoweza kuozesha dawa lingine /Also **imbosyo**

uluboosyo *n (im-, 11/10)* joke = utani

ulububi *n (im-, 11/10)* spiderweb = utando wa buibui

ulubujikisyo *n (im-, 11/10)* revenge = urudishaji kisasi

ulubúlí *n.anat (im-, 11/10, Tuk)* fist = ngumi

ulubúlí *n (im-, 11/10)* lump = bonge, tonge

ulubuulo *n (im-, 11/10)* report = taarifa

ulubululukisya *n (im-, 11/10)* that

which spills over = kiasi kinachozidi wakati wa kujaza kipimo fulani

ulubungaano *n (im-, 11/10)* 1 crowd = kundi 2 assembly = mkusanyiko, mkutano

ulubunju *n (im-, 11/10)* morning = asubuhi

    nulubunju *adv* 1 before dawn, in the morning = alfajiri, asubuhi 2 a.m. = nyakati za asubuhi

ulubúno *n (imb-, 11/10)* roar = ngurumo

ulubúnúsi *n.med (imb-, 11/10)* swelling or mark on the body after being struck = uvimbe baada ya kipigo au kutombaliwa na mdudu

ulubwe *n (imbwe, 11/10)* desert = jangwa, ardhi kame

ulubwele *n.zool (im-, 11/10)* 1 fly = inzi 2 mosquito = mbu

ulufigo *n.anat (ifigo, 11/10)* kidney = figo

ulufíko *n* arrival, coming = kuwasili

ulufíngano *n (i-, 11/10)* 1 engagement = shughuli, ahadi 2 agreement, treaty = makubaliano

ulufííngo *n (i-, 11/10)* 1 promise, vow = ahadi 2 provision = sharti, mapatano 3 agreement, contract = mapatano, mkataba, makubaliano, agano 4 deal = ahadi, mkataba

ulufujo *n (11)* scorn, disregard = dharau

ulufúkú *n (i-, 11/10)* humidity = unyevu

ulufúmbi *n (i-, 11/10)* dust, powder = vumbi, poda, unga

ulufumbo *n (i-, 11/10)* mourning period = matanga

ulufúmúsyo *n (i-, 11/10)* 1 confession = ungano 2 announcement, advertisement, ad = matangazo, tangazo

ulufúndo *n (i-, 11/10)* advice = shauri, onyo

ulufúúndo *n (i-, 11/10)* 1 punishment, torture = adhabu, mateso 2 fine = adhabu ya kulipwa

ulufúúndo *n.bot (i-, 11/10)* type of grass = aina ya nyasi

ulufúpa *n (i-, 11/10)* bone = mfupa
/Also **umfúpa**, **ikifúpa**

ulufungubo *n (i-, 11/10)* banana leaf
midrib = kikonyo cha jani la mgomba

ulufwelelema *n (i-, 11/10)* dawn = alfajiri

ulufwimbili lwa mmaapa *n.anat* hair
in the armpit = nywele za kwapani,
mavuzi

ulufwíngílí *n.zool (i-, 11/10)* maggot =
funza

ulufyogo *n (ifyogo, 11/10)* new banana
leaf = jani changa la mgomba

ulugano *n (in-, 11/10)* love, affection,
charity = upendo

ulugego *n (in-, 11/10)* jaw = taya

ulugelo *n (in-, 11/10)* attempt, trial,
temptation = majaribu

ulugenge *n (ingenge, 11/10)* 1 cliff =
jabali 2 edge = ukingo

ulugeesa *n (ing-, 11/10)* 1 comb / crest
of rooster = undu 2 back fin on fish =
pezi la samaki la nyuma

uluugí *n (ing-, 11/10)* provocation,
quarrelsomeness = uchokozi

ulugili *n (ingili, 11/10)* cattle hump = nundu

ulugoje *n (ingoje, 11/10)* 1 rope, string,
cord = kamba 2 a twisted rope =
kamba iliyosokotwa; **ulugoje ulwa
kyela** cable = nyuzi za chuma

ulugolosyo *n (in-, 11/10)* advice = onyo

ulugomba *n (in-, 11/10)* ridge = tuta

ulugombeko *n (ingombeko, 11/10)*
1 wheel = gurudumu 2 spring (as in a
metal spring) = mtambo

ulugombelo *n (in-, 11/10)* wheel = gurudumu

ulugombelo *n.bot (in-, 11/10)* type of
plant with vines = aina ya mmea

ulugomosyo *n (ingomosyo, 11/10)* 1 the
return = urudishaji 2 feedback =
mlisho nyuma

ulugubogubo *n.anat (in-, 11/10)* eyelid
= kope

uluheho *n (i-, 11/10)* murmur = nung'unika

uluhelúlo *n (i-, 11/10)* act of insulting =

matusi

uluhobokelo *n (ihobokelo, 11/10)* 1 forgiveness, pardon = msamaha 2 ex-
cuse, apology = udhuru 3 pardon =
msamaha 4 consideration = fikira,
nadhari

uluhobosyo *n (11)* amusement = kuche-
kesha

uluhuhu *n (i-, 11/10)* comb /crest of a
rooster = undu wa kuku

ulujabanío *n (in-, 11/10)* distribution,
allotment (of land) = ugawaji

ulujabo *n (in-, 11/10)* distribution =
mgawanyo, ugawaji

ulujagú *n (11)* the sound made when you
smack your lips = sauti ambayo mtu hutoa
wakati anapotafuna chakula

ulujajo *n.anat (in-, 11/10)* foot = unyayo, wayo

ulujato *n (injato, 11/10)* exursion, tour,
stroll = matembezi

ulujemba (Ricinus communis) *n.bot*
(injemba, 11/10) 1 castor oil plant =
mbono mdogo, mbarika 2 castor oil seed =
mbarika, nyonyo; **amafuta ga nyemba**
castor oil = mafuta ya mbarika /pl is often
used to refer to seeds

ulujenga *n (inj-, 11/10)* building, edifice = nyumba, ujenzi

ulujigo *n (injigo, 11/10)* oath = kiapo

ulujingija *n (in-, 11/10)* water weed =
mmea wa majini

ulujiisí *n (in-, 11/10)* 1 anklet with a
bell put around a child's leg when
they are learning to walk = njuga 2
type of small bell worn as ornament
around leg at cheza ngoma = njuga,
kengele ndogo zivaliwazo miguuni
wakati wa kucheza nyimbo au ngoma

ulujo *n (injo, 11/10)* broken piece of
metal or glass, potsherd = gae

ulujogoja *n (in-, 11/10)* undistinguishable sound made by many people at a
distance = kelele za watu nulio mbali

ulujukí *n.zool (in-, 11/10)* bee = nyuki

ulujunganíko *n (injunganiko, 11/10)*

act or manner of shaking, a shake =
mtikisiko

ulujúngú *n (in-, 11/10)* (biblical) seed,
offspring = kizazi, mzao, mbegu za
maboga, mbegu

ulukabilo *n (ing-, 11/10)* gain = faida

ulukabo *n (ingabo, 11/10)* income,
profit, proceeds = kipato, faida

ulukafúkafú *n (11)* coagulated milk
(yoghurt?) = maziwa mgando

ulukaafyo *n (ing-, 11/10)* sarcasm, irony,
teasing, bullying = kejeli, ucho-kozi

ulukalalisyo *n (ingalalisyo, 11/10)* revolt = maasi

ulukalalo *n (ingalalo, 11/10)* anger =
hasira

ulukalasila *n (ingalasila, 11/10; Usually pl)* **1** countable noun for single
pieces of charcoal **2** "dead" coals left
in the fire = kaa la moto lililozimika

ulukama *n (ingama, 11/10)* milk = maziwa

ulukama ulukafúkafú coagulated milk
= maziwa mgando

ulukambatulo *n (ingambatulo, 11/10)* a
very firm grip = mshiko, mkamato wa
nguvu

ulukaaní *n (ingaaní, 11/10)* dispute =
ubishi, mzozo

ulukanikano *n (ing-, 11/10)* argument
= mjalada

ulukanisyo *n (ing-, 11/10)* prohibition =
makatazo

ulukasyo *n (11; Kye)* act of calming sb
= kumpa mtu nguvu au moyo
/Tuk **ubukasyo**

ulukeeke *n (ing-, 11/10)* type of small
bush (2-3 feet) = aina ya kichaka

uluketelelo *n (ing-, 11/10)* management
= uangalizi, uchungaji

ulukemelo *n (ing-, 11/10)* scolding, rebuke = kukemea, karipio, mkaripio

ulukemo *n (11)* bark (of dog) = mbweko

ulukengele *n (ingengele, 11/10)*
bracelet = bangili

ulukeesa *n.zool (ingeesa, 11/10)* small

ant with a very painful sting = mdudu
mdogo aumaye sana

uluketa *n (11)* butter, cream = siagi

ulukeetelelo *n (11)* supervision = usimamizi, uangalizi

ulukeeto *n (ingeeto, 11/10)* glance,
glimpse = mtazamo

uluukí *n (11)* honey = asali

ulukiga *n.anat (ingiga, 11/10)* eyebrow
= nyusi

ulukindi *n (ingindi, 11/10)* **1** street =
mtaa **2** line, verse = safu, mstari
3 row = safu

ulukindo *n (ingindo, 11/10)* **1** passage =
mpito, njia **2** street = mtaa

ulukíno *n (ingíno, 11/10)* sport, game,
match = mchezo

ulukínya *n (ingínya, 11/10)* wrinkle,
crease = kunyanzi

ulukísí *n (11)* darkness = giza

uluko *n (ingo, 11/10)* **1** type, kind,
class, species = namna, aina, jamii,
kizazi, uzao **2** tribe = kabila **3** generation = uzazi; **uluko nuluko** all
kinds, all types = aina yote

ulukoba *n (ingoba, 11/10)* leather = ngozi

ulukole *n.anat (ingole, 11/10)* **1** nerve=
mshipa wa fahamu **2** vein, artery =
mshipa **3** *n.med* scrotal hernia =
mshipa wa ngiri

ulukoolelo *n (ingoolelo, 11/10)* alarm =
mwito, kamsa

ulukomaano *n (ingo-, 11/10)* meeting,
conference, multitude, assembly =
mkutano, mkusanyiko

ulukomeelesyo *n (ingo-, 11/10)* commandment = amri

ulukongano *n (ingongano, 11/10)* following, coming after sb (eg. in birth)
= mfuatano (kufuatano) ufuatano

ulukongí *n (ing-, 11/10)* arm, lower
arm, the arm between the elbow and
the wrist = mkono

ulukongolomya *n.anat (ing-, 11/10)*
backbone = uti wa mgongo

ulukonyolelo *n (ingo-, 11/10)* sloping beam of roof, rafter = boriti za kuinamisha paa la nyumba

ulukope *n (ingope, 11/10)* resemblance = kulandana

ulukose *n (ingose, 11/10)* a pile or bundle of grass = tita

ulukosomolo *n (ingo-, 11/10)* cough = kikohozi

ulukubilo *n (ingubilo, 11/10)* **1** persecution, suffering = mateso, matatizo, maumivu **2** remorse, penitence = majuto **3** regret = masikitiko **4** repentance = toba

ulukubo *n (ingubo, 11/10)* field, grazing area, treeless plain = malisho, mbuga

ulukufí *n (ing-, 11/10)* handful = ujazo wa kiganja
/Also **ikifufí**

ulukujisyo *n (ing-, 11/10)* enhancement = maongezo, mazidio

ukukula *n (15)* development, growth, growing up = maendeleo, makuzi

ulukumbuko *n (ing-, 11/10)* rememberance, memory, recollection = kumbukumbu

ulukusyo *n (ing-, 11/10)* advancement = endeleo

ululabaasyo *n (indabaasyo, 11/10)* pretence = kujifanya, kujitia hamnazo

ululagano *n (inda-, 11/10)* **1** agreement = makubaliano, mapatano, agano **2** treaty = mkataba **3** promise = ahadi **4** farewell = kupeana kwa heri

ululagilo *n (indagilo, 11/10)* **1** law, rule, order, command, regulation, decree, edict, act = amri, sheria **2** commission = agizo **3** authority = mamlaka **4** directive, an order, direction = agizo, elekezo **5** system = mfumo

ululaka *n (ama-, 11/6)* haste = papara

ululaka *n* **1** lack of milk for calves or infants = kukosa maziwa kwa ndama au kichanga **2** great thirst = kiu kali

ululalo *n (ind-, 11/10)* bridge = daraja

ululaluusyo *n (indaluusyo, 11/10)* inquiry = maulizo

ululaanga *n (indaanga, 11/10)* **1** rainbow = upinde wa mvua **2** light = mwanga

ululapi *n (indapi, 11/10)* flame, blaze = ndimi za moto, mwali wa moto, mwali

ululapo *n (ind-, 11/10)* oath, vow = kiapo, apa

ululatikilo *n (indatikilo, 11/10)* purlin = ufito

ululefú *n (indefú, 11/10, pl meaning: beard)* a single facial hair = ndevu

ululendemusí *n (ind-, 11/10)* crack = ufa

ululengasi *n (ind-, 11/10)* split bamboo wood = kipande cha mwanzi kilichome

ululila *n (indila, 11/10)* bee-sting = mwiba wa nyuki

ululilo *n (indilo, 11/10)* cry = mlio

ululima *n.bot (indima, 11/10)* bean = maharagwe

ululimí *n.anat (indimí, 11/10)* tongue = ulimi

ululimbiko *n (indimbiko, 11/10)* a store, reserve, a saving up little by little over a period of time = mlimbiko

ululinganío *n (indinganío, 11/10)* expression, explanation = uelezaji, maelezo

ululo *n (11)* fight, discord = vita, ugomvi
/Also **ululwo**

ululo nululisyo, ubuli nubulisi *n* trade = biashara

ululufú *n (indufú, 11/10)* buttermilk = mtindi

ululungo *n (indungo, 11/10)* joint = kiungo

ululyo *n (indyo, 11/10)* **1** feast (eg. wedding) = karamu **2** meal = mlo

uluma *n (ima, 11/10)* smell = harufu

uluumano *n (inyuumano, 11/10)* quarrel, quarreling = ugomvi

ulumanyísyo *n (imanyisyo, 11/10)* doctrine = fundisho

ulumanyo *n (imanyo, 11/10)* **1** ability = uwezo **2** identification = utambulisho, kitambulisho

ulumogo *n (imogo, 10/11)* dance = dansi, mchezo wa ngoma

ulumú *n (imú, 11/10)* sunshine = mwanga wa jua

ulumúlí *n (i-, 11/10)* light, brightness = mwanga, nuru

ulumúlímúlí *n.zool (i-, 11/10)* firefly = kimulimuli

ulumyato *n.anat (imyato, 11/10)* teat, nipple = chuchu, nyonyo

ulumyoso *n (11)* discharge after giving birth = ute utokao baada ya kuzaa

ulunaganíko *n (i-, 11/10)* **1** reduction = nakisi **2** defect = upungufu

ulunandala (Vigna unguiculata) *n.bot (inandala, 11/10)* cow pea = kunde (mmea unaozaa kunde)

ulundabandaba *n (11)* stuttering, stammer = kigugumizi

ulundasí *n (i-, 11/10)* rainbow = upinde wa mvua

ulundoosí *n.anat (i-, 11/10)* crown or top of the head = utosi

uluundu *n.med (indu, 11/10)* pimple, zit, acne = chunusi

ulungalangala *n (i-, 11/10)* **1** wilderness, desolate expanse of land, desert = jangwa **2** drought = ukame

ulung'eng'esí *n (11; > Tuk)* **1** an imperfect sight = kufifia kwa nguvu ya macho kuweza kuona **2** dimness = utusitusi; **amaso gangu gíkuketa ulung'eng'esí** my sight is unclear = macho yangu yameingia tandabui; **pela ulung'eng'esí** dim = tia giza /Also **ulunyenyesi**

ulungwe *n.bot (11)* type of bamboo, dark colored, thin and tall = aina ya mianzi miembamba mirefu

uluníabo *n (iníabo, 11/10)* act of applying pressure, squeezing = mkandamizo wa nguvu ili kitu kisisogee

ulunosyo *n (inosyo, 11/10)* decoration = urembo, pambo

ulunúngilo *n (inúngilo, 11/10)* good,

pleasant smell, scent, perfume = harufu nzuri

ulunúngo *n (inúngo, 11/10)* smell, scent = harufu, kunuka

ulunúsí *n (inusí, 11/10)* smell, scent, odor = harufu

ulunúsí ulunúnú scent = harufu nzuri **Imbwa jikongile ulunúsí jijagíle ingenge** The dog followed the smell of the cane rat = Mbwa amefuata harufu ya ndezi

ulunyaganyo *n (15)* drizzle = manyunyu

ulunyambo, ulwambo *n (iny-, 11/10)* bead, pearl = ushanga, lulu

ulunyanya *n.bot (i-, 11/10)* tomato = nyanya

ulunyasyo *n (i-, 11/10)* disgrace = aibu

ulunyegenela *n (i-, 11/10)* type of mat, colorful, used for ornamentation, burial etc = aina ya mkeka ulipambwa vizuri

ulunyenyesí *n (11)* semi-darkness = giza

ulunyomoko *n (i-, 11/10)* a sudden motion, being startled = mshituko

ulunyomosyo *n (i-, 11/10)* surprise = mshituo

ulunyonyo *n (11)* longing, desire, greed, lust = tamaa; ~ **ulunywamú** ambition = tamaa ya nguvu /Also **ulunyonywo**

ulunyonywo *n (11)* longing, desire, greed = tamaa; ~ **ulunywamú** ambition = tamaa ya nguvu /Also **ulunyonyo**

ulunywílí *n (inywílí, 11/10)* a single hair = unywele

ulupaja *n.anat (imbaja, 11/10)* skull = fuvu la kichwa

ulupaka *n (imbaka, 11/10)* plot in a field = shamba

ulupaakisyo *n (i-, 11/10)* **1** pity = huruma **2** mercy = rehema

ulupaale *n (imbaale, 11/10)* gourd, calabash = kibuyu

ulupama *n (11)* chest hair = nywele za kifuani

ulupande *n (imbande, 11/10)* one member of a pair of woman's wraps, kanga or kitenge = upande wa kanga au kitenge

ulupando *n.bot* (Ficus spp) type of fig tree = aina ya mkuyu

ulupaanga *n (imbaanga, 11/10)* **1** cliff = gema **2** riverbank = ukingo **3** ravine = genge

ulupange *n.bot (imbange, 11/10)* cajanus cajan (pigeon pea) = mbaazi

ulupango *n (imbango, 11/10)* report = taarifa

ulupanjo *n (imb-, 11/10)* hatching = kuangua, kuanguaji

ulupape *n (imbape, 11/10)* type of milk, stiff milk = mtindi

ulupapike *n (imbapike, 11/10)* winnowing basket (usually made from bamboo) = ungo

ulupasí *n.zool (11)* type of small bee which makes honey = mboza (mdudu)

ulupaso *n (imbaso, 11/10)* fence = uzio, wigo

ulupasyo *n (imbasyo, 11/10)* anxiety = hangaiko

íja nulupasyo be sorry = sikitika

ulupeefyo *n (imbeefyo, 11/10)* temptation = majaribu

ulupegeselo *n (imbe...)* drill bit, auger bit = msumari wa kutobolea

ulupegeso *n (imbegeso, 11/10)* boring stick = kijiti cha kupekechea

ulupeekefyo *n (imb-, 11/10)* attraction, incentive = kivutio

ulupeelo *n.med (15)* diarrhea = kuharisha

ulupembe *n (imbembe, 11/10)* animal horn = pembe

ulupenúko *n (imb-, 11/10)* rush, rapid, headlong movement = mtimko

ulupepete *n (imbepete, 11/10)* basket-like implement for winnowing grain = ungo

ulupeesyo *n (imbeesyo, 11/10)* offence = kosa, hali ya kukosa kitu

ulupeetelo *n (imbeetelo, 11/10)* basket-like implement for winnowing grain = ungo

ulupeto *n (imbeto, 11/10)* side = upande

ulupi *n (imbi, 11/10)* **1** resemblance = kufanana **2** gratitude = shukrani; **igwa ulupi** show humility to = nyenyekea

ulupilikisyo *n (imb-, 11/10)* attention, attentiveness = usikivu

ulupimilo *n (imb-, 11/10)* unit of measure = kipimo

ulupindi *n (imb-, 11/10)* calabash = kibuyu

ulupindo *n (imbindo, 11/19; Kye)* bow = upinde

ulupíndo *n (imb-, 11/10)* hem = upindo

ulupinduko *n (imb-, 11/10)* repentance, remorse = toba

ulupondo *n (11)* blacksmithery = uhunzi

uluponío *n (imb-, 11/10)* greeting, salutation = salamu

ulupoosa *n.bot (imbosa, 11/10)* palm oil seed = mbegu ya mchikichi

uluposolo *n (imb-, 11/10)* fine = faini, adhabu ya kulipwa

ulupote *n (imb-, 11/10)* twisted rope = kamba iliyosokotwa

ulupufi *n (imbufi, 11/10)* whistle = mbinja

ulupuju *n (11)* baldness = upara

ulupúúto *n.anat (imb-, 11/10)* ankle = kiwiko cha mguu

ulupya *n (11)* burning grass = moto unapounguza nyasi

ulupyúúto *n (imbyúúto, 11/10)* doom = maangamizi, kiyama

ulusaagulo *n (i-, 11/10)* selection = uchaguzi

ulusaja *n (isaja, 11/10)* cheek = shavu

ulusajo *n (i-, 11/10)* **1** blessing = baraka **2** good luck, fortune = bahati nzuri

ulusakaní *n.zool (i-, 11/10; Kye)* gecko = mjusi kafiri
/Tuk: **ulusolobela**

ulusako *n (isako, 11/10)* luck, chance, fortune = bahati nzuri

ulusalo *n (i-, 11/10)* **1** choice = chaguo **2** election = uchaguzi

ulusaalo *n (11)* pleasure, happiness, triumph = furaha

ulusamba *n (isamba, 11/10)* branch = tawi

ulusambo *n (i-, 11/10)* **1** the whole fishing gear used by a person (rod, fishing line and hook) = ndoana, ndoano **2** spiral **3** the spokes of a bicycle **4** wire, cable = nyaya, nyuzi za chuma

ulusaamísyo *n (i-, 11/10)* transfer = uhamisho

ulusangalabwe *n (isangalabwe, 11/10)* pebble = changarawe
/ Also **isangalabwe**

ulusangulo *n (i-, 11/10)* contribution = mchango

ulusanganí *n (11)* Cynodon dactylon type of creeping grass = aina ya mmea utambaao
/Used to make ropes

ulusanje *n (i-, 11/10)* type of long grass = nyasi ndefu

ulusanu *n (i-, 11/10)* type of grass used for roofing = aina ya nyasi za kwezekea

ulusapo *n (i-, 11/10)* footpath = wayo

ulusegube *n (isegube, 11/10)* a leaf blade of cereals, grasses = jani la nafaka au unyasi wowote

uluseke *n (iseke, 11/10)* **1** seed = kokwa, mbegu **2** fruit = tunda **3** *slang* testicle = pumbu, kordani

ulusekelo *n (isekelo, 11/10)* happiness, joy, delight, enjoyment = furaha

ulusekeesyo *n (i-, 11/10)* amusement = kichekesho, tafuja, furaha

uluselo *n (i-, 11/10)* basket like implement for winnowing grain, winnowing basket = ungo

ulusenga *n (isenga, 11/10)* **1** chip = chenga **2** crumb = punje

ulusese *n (i-, 11/10)* udder = kiwele

ulusetuko *n (i-, 11/10)* event = tukio

ulusetúlilo *n (i-, 11/10)* revelation = ufunuo

ulusí *n (11)* dizziness = kizunguzungu

ulusíge *n.anat (isíge, 11/10)* eyelash = kope

ulusígesíge *n.anat (i-, 11/10)* brow = nyusi

ulusígililo *n (i- 11/10)* **1** ambush = maoteo **2** fence = uzio

ulusíndano *n (i-, 11/10; > Swa)* competition, match = mashindano

ulusíínde *n (isinde, 11/10)* **1** ridge = tuta **2** any raised part of earth for planting crops on eg. a flowerbed, a tomato seedling bed etc. = tuta

ulusíngí *n (i-, 11/10)* dense thicket = pori, chaka nene

ulusingo, ulusíngo *n (i-, 11/10)* **1** impediment = kizuizi **2** commandment of, order of, embargo = amri ya kukataza kitu **3** quarantine = karantini

ulusípulilo *n (i-, 11/10)* fishing hook, line and sinker = ndoana na mshipi

ulusísí *n.bot (i-, 11/10)* type of grass = aina ya majani
/used to make **ikííbo** and **umoono**

ulusísímíkisyo *n (i-, 11/10)* emphasis = mkazo

ulusííto *n (i-, 11/10)* **1** hesitation = kusita **2** denial = kukataa, mkano

ulusobo *n (i-, 11/10)* mistake, blunder = kosa

ulusogolo *n.anat (i-, 11/10)* shinbone = sehemu ya mbele ya miguu chini ya goti, ugoko

ulusoko *n (i-, 11/10)* **1** advice, counsel = nasaha, ushauri, onyo **2** warning = onyo

ulusooko *n (isooko, 11/10)* valley, dale = bonde

ulusoolo *n (i-, 11/10)* turn = zamu

ulusolobela *n.zool (i-, 11/10; Tuk)* gecko = mjusi
/Kye: **ulusakani**

ulusomanío *n (i-, 11/10)* discord = uchonganishi

ulusonga *n (isonga, 11/10)* peg = mambo

ulusongwa *n.bot (i-, 11/10)* **1** the yellowish bitter fruit fruit of the **unsonga** tree found mainly in Kyela = tunda

madogo machungu la mti mkubwa
2 small orange- brownish sweet fruits
of the **unsongwa** bush /shrub, found
in the higher areas of Rungwe (same
name in Safwa), not found in Kyela =
aina ya matunda, matamu, madogo

ulusubilo *n (i-, 11/10)* confidence, hope,
expectation = tumaini, tegemeo

ulusuuje *n (i-, 11/10)* milk that has
been separated with water = mtindi

ulusúlúko *n (i-, 11/10)* descent =
mshuko, mtelemko

ulusúlúmanío *n (11)* sadness, distress =
huzuni

ulusúmo *n (i-, 11/10)* **1** fashion, style =
mtindo **2** kind = aina **3** design =
kielelezo **4** system, way of doing
something = mfumo namna ya kufanya kitu kipya, mtindo

ulusúndo *n.zool (i-, 11/10)* leech = ruba

ulusuungo *n (i-, 11/10)* **1** island =
kisiwa **2** peninsula, cape = mkono wa
nchi

ulusúnía *n.zool (i-, 11/10)* type of small
fly = aina ya inzi mdogo

ulususulilo *n (i-, 11/10)* the red tip of a
banana bunch, the male bud of the banana tree = ncha ya ndizi

ulusuusyo *n (i-, 11/10)* disgrace, embarrassment = aibu, aibisho

uluswa *n (11; > Swa)* bribe = rushwa

uluswígo *n (i-, 11/10)* surprise, wonder,
amazement, astonishment = mshangao,
ajabu

uluswo *n (11)* forgiveness = msamaha

ulusyegetulo *n (i-, 11/10)* gnashing,
grinding = kusaga

ulusyembe *n (i-, 11/10)* pole for punting (normally canoes) = upondo

ulusyilo *n (11)* burial = mazishi

ulusyobo *n (i-, 11/10)* trick, deceit,
fraud, cheating = udanganyifu

ulusyoja *n (i-, 11/10)* **1** body hair = unywele wa mwili **2** fur = manyoya (ya
mnyama); **ulusyoja lwa ng'osí** wool,
fleece = manyoya

ulusyungulu *n (isyungulu, 11/10)* dizziness = kizunguzungu

ulusyungusyo *n (i-, 11/10)* encircling =
kuzungusha

uluta *n.anat (11)* sperm, semen = sha-
hawa, manii

ulutalama *n (indalama, 11/10)* money
= fedha

ulutambo *n (ind-, 11/10)* wire = nyaya

ulutamígwo *n (ind-, 11/10)* agony, suffering,
affliction = mateso, mahangaiko, kuteseka

ulutaamyo *n (indamyo, 11/10)* **1** confusion = wasiwasi **2** embarrassment =
maudhi, masumbufu

ulutananda *n (indananda, 11/10)* plain,
plateau = uwanda

ulutapatapa *n.anat (indapatapa, 11/10)*
thigh, lap = paja
/also **imbatapata**

uluteefú *n (indeefú, 11/10)* plaited mat
= kilago

uluteko *n (indeko, 11/10)* clay pot =
chungu, mtungi

ulutende *n (11)* fear, terror, dread = hofu

-a lutende *adj* **1** frightened, anxious =
-a hangaiko, -enye hofu **2** dreadful =
-a hofu

ulutendekesyo *n (11)* **1** repairs, maintenance
= matengenezo **2** reformation, reform =
matengenezo, matengeneo

ulutendele *n (indendele, 11/10)* container for tobacco snuff = chombo cha
kutunzia ugoro

ulutenganío *n (ind-, 11/10)* **1** reconcili-
ation = tendo la kutuliza **2** comfort =
faraja, amani, shwari

ulutengano *n (indengano, 11/10)*
1 peace = amani **2** ease = shwari

ulutete *n.bot (indete, 11/10)* reed = tete

uluti *n (indi, 11/10)* the handle of a
spear = mpini wa mkuki

ulutiimo *n (ind-, 11/10)* one's turn to
herd cattle = zamu ya kuchunga
ng'ombe

ulutinilo *n (ind-, 11/10)* **1** the act of fish

pecking at a bait = samaki anapokua chambo kitovu cha ndoana huwa kuiachezacheza hapa juu **2** signal = kuashiria

ulutobe *n (indobe, 11/10)* wrestling = mweleka

ulutolano *n (indolano, 11/10)* competition, match, contest = mashindano

ulutondwa *n (indondwa, 11/10)* star = nyota

ulutotomelo *n (indotomelo, 11/10)* jealousy, grudge = wivu, kijicho

ulutope *n (indope, 11/10)* semi digested food in the first stomach of a ruminant = Chakula kilichosagwa nusu katika tumbo la kwanza la mnyama acheuaye /pl form **indope** means animal dung

ulutúúfyo *n (indúúfyo, 11/10)* glory, praise, compliment = sifo

ulutukwe *n.zool (indukwe, 11/10)* type of ant, large and black ant, it bites = aina ya siafu mkubwa na mweusi anayeuma / Also **indukwe**

ulutuulano *n (ind-, 11/10)* **1** sharing = hali ya kusaidiana **2** *n.relig* communion = ushirika mtakatifu

ulutuliko *n (induliko, 11/10)* clothes line, washing line = kamba ya kutundikia au kuanikia nguo

ulutulo *n (indulo, 11/10)* crime, fault, mistake = kosa

ulutuulo *n (induulo, 11/10)* **1** chapter of a book = aya, sura **2** act of lifting off one's load and putting it down = kuutoa mzigo kichwani na kuweka chini

ulutúlúúngo *n (indúlúúngo, 11/10)* boasting = usodawi

ulutúmbanílo *n (ind-, 11/10)* race, competition = mchezo wa kukimbia

ulutumbulilo *n (ind-, 11/10)* wheel = gurudumu

ulutumililo *n (indumililo, 11/10)* subordination = udhalilishaji

ulutungo *n (indungo, 11/10)* string = utungo (wa shanga)

ulutúngú *n (ind-, 11/10)* testicle = pumbu

ulutúsúlilo *n (ind-, 11/10)* gunshot = tendo la kufyatua bunduki

ulutuusyo *n (ind-, 11/10)* **1** rest, ease = mapumziko **2** camp = kambi ya kupumzika **3** leave = likizo

ulutwamúlo *n (ind-, 11/10)* punch, strike = pigo

ulutwiko *n (indwiko, 11/10)* act of lifting a load and putting it on one's head = hali ya kuinua mzigo na weka juu ya kichwa cha mmoja

ulutwíngo *n (indwíngo, 11/10)* sweat = jasho

ulwa *part (11)* of = ya

ulwajo *n (iny-, 11/10)* sole of the foot = wayo

ulwala *n (inyala, 11/10)* grinding stone = jiwe lililotumika kusagia nafaka

ulwalabwe *n (inyalabwe, 11/10)* rock, boulder = mwamba, jiwe kubwa, jabali ~ **ulutoofú** coral = tumbawe

ulwalamilo *n (inyalamilo, 11/10)* brooding = kuatamia

ulwalanganío *n (inyalanganío, 11/10)* puzzle = fumbo, kitendawili

ulwalangano *n (inyalangano, 11/10)* dilemma = mashaka

ulwako *interj (Tuk)* it's up to you = shauri yako /Kye **lwako**

ulwalo *n (iny-, 11/10)* base, foundation = msingi

ulwalosa *adv* **1** forever = moja kwa moja **2** completely = kabisa

ulwama *n (iny-, 11/10)* cattle shed = banda la ng'ombe

ulwambililo *n (11)* acceptance = kupokea

ulwambo *n (iny-, 11/10)* bead = ushanga

ulwamúlo *n (iny-, 11/10)* answer, reply = jibu

ulwanda *n (inyanda, 11/10)* stomach, belly = tumbo

ulwande *n (inyande, 11/10)* crack = ufa

ulwandulo *n (iny-, 11/10)* change, alteration, transformation = badiliko

ulwangabya *n (inya, 11/10)* **1** small earthen

pot for frying food = chungu kidogo cha kukaangia mboga 2 earthen plate = sahani ya udongo

ulwanyuma *adv* then = halafu, baadaye

ulwegekesyo *n (inye-, 11/10)* a support, assistance to hold smth = egemeo

ulwego *n (iny-, 11/10)* banana stake = mti wa kuzuia mgomba usianguke

ulwegulilo *n (inyegu-, 11/10)* a lever, a labor-saving device = mtaimbo, mtarimbo

ulweke *n (inyeke, 11/10)* provocation = uchokozí

ulwelo *n (inyelu, 11/10)* net, fishing net = wavu

ulwembe *n (inyembe, 11/10)* razor blade = wembe

ulwendelo *n (inyendelo, 11/10)* journey = safari

ulwendo *n (iny-, 11/10)* 1 behaviour, conduct = mwenendo 2 journey, trip = safari

ulwenye *n (11)* the smell of fish = shombo, vumba

ulwese *n (inyese, 11/10)* provocation = uchokozí

ulwíbilo *n (inyíbilo, 11/10)* sinking = mdidimio, kitendo cha kuzama, mzamo; **Ulwíbilo lwa sítíma mwa Sumbi nkyinja kya 1930 kwakiny-omwisye fííjo ifíísu** The sinking of the ship on Lake Nyasa in 1930 shocked the world = Mzamo kwa meli mwaka 1930 kulishtusha sana ulimwengu

ulwíbono *n (11)* conceit, pride (in a negative sense) = majivuno

ulwíbuko *n (iny-, 11/10)* water spring = chemchemi

ulwíbunesyo *n (11)* grumbling, murmuring, growling = nung'uniko

ulwífí *n.zool (inyifi, 11/10)* chameleon = kinyonga

ulwífímbilisyo *n (iny-, 11/10)* forcing oneself to, make more effort, exertion, struggle, attempt, zeal = bidii, juhudi, hali ya kuji-tahidi (kujidibisha, kujilazimisha)

ulwígí *n (iny-, 11/10)* 1 door = mlango 2 gate = lango

ulwího *n (inyího, 11/10)* 1 law = sheria 2 custom, habit, practice, usage = des-turi, mazoezi, desturi 3 culture = ta-bia, desturi

ulwíjísyo *n (iny-, 11/10)* 1 manner = ta-bia 2 respect, dignity, courtesy = he-shima, staha 3 discipline = nidhamu

ulwíjobeesyo *n (11)* 1 habit of talking to oneself = tabia ya kujisemesya 2 growling, groaning = nung'uniko

ulwíjuulo *n (iny-, 11/10)* 1 effort, exer-tion = bidii, jitihada 2 attempt = bidii, bila kukata tamaa

ulwíkemesyo *n (iny-, 11/10)* sacrifice = dhabihu, sadaka, zaka

ulwíkímo *n (iny-, 11/10)* great grief = uchungu mkubwa

ulwíko *n (iny-, 11/10)* ladle, spoon = upawa, kijiko

ulwílaamo *n (iny-, 11/10)* 1 disregard, disrespect, = kiburi 2 grumbling, complaint = nung'uniko

ulwilange *n.anat (iny-, 11/10)* shinbone = sehemu ya mbele ya miguu chini ya goti, ugoko

ulwímbo *n (inyímbo, 11/10)* song, psalm, poem = wimbo, shairi

ulwimiko *n (inyimiko, 11/10)* respect, honor, reverence = heshima, staha

ulwínulilo *n (inyí-, 11/10)* 1 yoke = nira 2 lever, stick or similar used to open the storehouse/ghala = nyenzo, wenzo

ulwípukulanío *n (iny-, 11/10)* lots of business, engagement in many activi-ties = shuguli nyingi

ulwípúúto *n (inyí-, 11/10)* prayer, wor-ship = sala, ibada

ulwisí *n (inyisí, 11/10)* river = mto

ulwísíbisyo *n (inyí-, 11/10)* training, habituation = uzoeshaji, uzoezaji

ulwítikano *n (iny-, 11/10)* agreement = mapatano

ulwítiko *n (inyítiko, 11/10)* 1 faith, belief,

creed = imani 2 acceptance = ukubalifu;
ulwítiko kubalongosí allegiance to/ faith
in leaders = utii kwa viongozi

ulwítúfyo *n (iny-, 11/10)* pride, boasting
= jisifu

ulwítúfyo *n (14)* boasting = majisifu

uma *vt (pt umíle)* **1** dry = kauka **2** wither =
nyauka

umalafyale *n (abanyafyale, 1/2)* king,
chief, leader, headman = mfalme
/Compare Bemba fyala 'give birth to,
bring forth'

umana *vi (pt umeene)* **1** quarrel = gombana **2** reproach = gombeza

umbelo *n (imí-, 3/4)* **1** wind = upepo
2 storm = dhoruba

umbengwe *n (aba-, 1/2)* hated person =
mtu anayechukiwa, asiyependwa

umbija *n (aba-, 1/2; > Kisi)* friend =
rafiki

umbilamu *adj*
unkííkulu umbilamu a woman with
big protruding buttocks = mwanamke
mwenye matako makubwa yaliyobi-
nuka (wowowo)

umbili *n (imí-, 3/4)* body = mwili

umbombí *n (aba-, 1/2)* **1** worker,
labourer = mfanyakazi, kibarua **2** servant = mtumishi

umbuju *n.bot (imí, 3/4)* baobab tree =
mbuyu

umbopí *n (aba-, 1/2)* runner = mkimbiaji

umbuuka *n (aba-, 1/2)* deceased person
= marehemu, hayati

umbula *(Parinari spp) n.bot (imí-, 3/4)*
type of wild tree with edible fruits =
aina ya mti wa porini, matunda yake
huliwa

umbumbí *n (aba-, 1/2)* creator = muumbaji, mwumba

umbwapufú *n (aba-, 1/2)* somebody
negligent, sb unconcerned about
cleanliness = mzembe, mchafu, mtu
asiyejali usafi

umbwenekuugu *n.off (aba-, 1/2)* dwarf
= mbilikimo

/No non-offensive term has been
found

umbwesí *n (aba-, 1/2)* friend, partner =
rafiki

umfímba *n (imí-, 3/4)* corpse = maiti

umfíní *n (aba-, 1/2)* dancer = mcheza
ngoma

umfoolo *n (imí-, 3/4; > Bemba mufôlo
> Eng furrow)* channel, canal, ditch,
trench = mfereji
/Also **umfwoolo**

umfú *n (imífu, 3/4)* soil, earth (the substance) = udongo, ardhi

umfúúke *n (aba-, 1/2)* idiot, nerd, fool
= mpumbavu

umfúko *n (imí-, 3/4)* **1** wallet = mkoba
2 sack = mfuko

umfúko gwa nyongo *n.anat* gall bladder = nyongo

umfule *n (aba-, 1/2)* eunuch = towashi

umfúlú *(Vitex sp.) n.bot (imí-, 3/4)* type
of tree (usage: edible fruit, green
when unripe, black when ripe, ripe in
March - April) = aina ya mti

umfúmúke *n (aba-, 1/2)* famous person,
influential person = mtu mashuhuri

umfúndígwa *n (aba-, 1/2)* student, disciple = mwanafunzi, mfuasi

umfúngwa *n (aba-, 1/2)* captive, prisoner, convict = mfungwa, mateka

umfúngwe *(Kigelia africana) n.bot
(imí-, 3/4)* sausage tree = Mti mkubwa
unaozaa matunda makubwa kama
mabuyu lakini marefu, mwengea,
mvungunya, pia myegeya

umfúnjo *n (imí-, 3/4)* harvest = mavuno

umfúpa *n (imí-, 3/4)* bone = mfupa
/Also **ulufúpa, ikifúpa**

umfúúsya *n (aba-, 1/2)* best man, a go-
between in marriage negotiations =
mshenga

umfwalo *n (imí-, 3/4)* salary, wages =
mshahara

umfwaalo gwa nkyení advance of
salary = Sehemu ya mshahara mtu
achukuayo kabla ya mwisho wa

mwezi, Mshahara wa awali

umfwalwa *n (imí-, 3/4)* clothing = nguo, vazi

umfwamaso *n (aba-, 1/2)* blind person = kipofu

umfwandilo *n (imí-, 3/4)* **1** ash = majivu **2** (Ilex mitis) *n.bot* type of tree = aina ya mti

umfwe *n (aba-, 1/2)* a dead person, deceased, departed = mfu

umfweje *n (aba-, 1/2)* poor person = fukara, fakiri

umfweleji *n (imí-, 3/4, > Swa)* ditch = mfereji

umfwíle *n (aba-, 1/2)* **1** bereaved person = mfiwa **2** *n.fam* widow = mjane

umfwimbili *n (imí-, 3/4)* baby hair (reddish) = nywele za mtoto mchanga

umfwimí *n (aba-, 1/2)* hunter = mwindaji

umfwoolo *n (imí-, 3/4; > Bemba mufôlo > Eng furrow)* channel, canal, ditch, trench = mfereji
/Also **umfoolo**

umfyeele *n (aba-, 1/2)* **1** female who has given birth = mama aliyezaa **2** nursing mother = mwanamke aliyejifungua, (hasa siku za karibuni) **3** a person with many children and other people who depend on him financially = Mtu mwenye watoto na watu wengine wanaomtegemea yeye

umfyulisí *n.bot (imí-, 3/4)* peach plant = mti wa mpichi

-umí *adj* alive, living = hai

umíka *vb* dry, drain = kausha maji kwa kuweka mfereji, toa maji
/Also **umika**

-umíke *adj* callous, horny = -gumu

umilila *vb (pt umilíle)* **1** stick, cling = ganda, nata, ng'ang'ania **2** insist, persist, persevere = ng'ang'ania, sisitiza, shikilia

umilwa *vb (pt umíílwe)* be thirsty = kuwa na kiu

umísya *vb (pt umíísye)* dry = kausha
/Also **umisya**

ummaganyí *n (aba-, 1/2)* **1** craftsman, skilled person = mjuzi, fundi **2** creative or innovative person = mtundu, mbunifu

ummage *n (imí-, 3/4)* knife = kisu

ummanga *n (aba-, 1/2)* an official coroner who came to find the cause of death . Not common any more, but still seen in some villages. Another word used in this connection is **unketi.** (a seer)

ummanyakalata *n (aba-, 1/2)* learned person = msomi

ummanyandagilo *n (aba-, 1/2)* lawyer = mwanasheria

ummanyandondwa *n (aba-, 1/2)* astrologer, astronomer = mnajimu

ummanyaaní *n (aba-, 1/2)* friend, companion = rafiki, mwenzi

ummanyí *n (aba-, 1/2)* a learned person = msomi, mjuaji

ummanyílí *n (aba-, 1/2)* student, pupil = mwanafunzi, msomi

ummanyísí *n (aba-, 1/2)* teacher = mwalimu

ummbelo *n (imíbelo, 3/4)* wind = upepo

ummbili *n (imí-, 3/4)* body = mwili

ummbingo *n (imbingo, 3/4)* stern (the rear part of a ship) = tezi, shetri

ummbuuka *n (aba-, 1/2)* a dead person, deceased, departed = marehemu

ummelí *n (aba-, 1/2)* **1** prosecutor = mshtaki **2** creditor, claimant = mdai **3** judge = hakimu

ummílo *n.anat (imímílo, 3/4)* throat = koo, shingo

ummogí *n (aba-, 1/2)* **1** dancer = mchezaji ngoma **2** sb fashionable, sb with style = mlimbwende

ummwí *n (aba-, 1/2)* barber = kinyozi

umooga *n (aboga, 1/2)* coward = mwoga

umogesí *n (abogesi, 1/2)* swimmer = mwogeleaji

umojo *n (imíojo, 3/4)* **1** heart, soul = moyo, nafsi **2** commitment = ari

umooloolo *n (abo-, 1/2)* polite person =

mtu mpole

umomolelí *n (abomomelí,1/2)* the one who sings refrains in a choir = mwitikiaji katika kwaya

umonaangí *n (abo, 1/2)* sb destructive = mharibifu

umoono *n (imyono, 3/4)* trap for fish = mgono

umonywa *n.med (abo-, 1/2)* invalid, sb weak, weakling, sick person = asiyejiweza, mdhaifu

umoosí *n.relig (aboosi, 1/2)* baptist = mbatizaji

umosígwa *n (abo-, 1/2)* christian, literally sb who is baptized = mkristo, aliyebatizwa

umoto *n (imí-, 3/4)* **1** fire = moto **2** light, brightness = mwanga

umpafú *n (aba-, 1/2)* glutton, stingy greedy person = mlafi

umpaja *n.anat (imí, 3/4)* skull = fuu la kichwa, fuu, fuvu, bupuru

umpajaja *n.anat (imí, 3/4)* skull = fuu la kichwa, fuu, fuvu, bupuru

umpaka *n (imí-, 3/4)* border, boundary = mpaka

umpakasí *n (aba-, 1/2)* **1** sb naughty = mtundu **2** sb determined = mtu aliyenuia, mtu mbunifu

umpakasya *n (aba-, 1/2)* naughty person = mtundu

umpalamaní *n (aba-, 1/2)* neighbor = jirani

umpalanga *n (imí-, 3/4)* **1** heaven, the sky, atmosphere = mbingu, anga **2** desolate place = mahali tupu, mahali pa wazi **3** emptyness = utupi, uwazi

umpalano *n (imí-, 3/4)* match (sports) = mshindano (michezo)

umpaalí *n (aba-, 1/2)* The main singer (eg. in **akapote** or any other songs), the one who starts singing a song = malenga, mwimbaji mkuu, mwanzishaji wa wimbo

umpandapanda (Ficus ingens) *n.bot (imí-, 3/4)* type of tree (this tree is

called **ilyabí** when small) = aina ya mti

umpaanja *n (aba-, 1/2)* A non-active believer or sb who does not believe in a god. Lit.: "an outsider" i.e. sb outside the circle of believers. pagan, heathen, atheist = mtu asiyeamini mungu, mpagani

umpango *n (imí-, 3/4)* belt = mkanda

umpanya *n (imí-, 3/4)* lime, mortar, whitewash = chokaa

umpapa (Vitex sp.) *n.bot (imí-, 3/4)* type of tree = aina ya mti

umpapaju *n.bot (imí-, 3/4, > Span. papaya)* papaya, papaw, pawpaw = mpapai

umpaapí *n (aba-, 1/2)* parent = mzazi

umpaapuke *n (aba-, 1/2)* woman who has given birth = mwanamke ambaye amewahi kuzaa

umpasyo *n (imb-, 3/4)* bother, worry, anxiety = wasiwasi, hofu

umpe, umpí *n (aba-, 1/2)* generous person, donor = mkarimu, mpaji, mtoaji

umpegele (Syzigium spp) *n.bot (imí-, 3/4)* type of tree = aina ya mti

umpela *n (aba-, 1/2)* maker (sb who makes things) = muumbaji, mtengenezaji, mfanyaji

umpelafúla *n (aba-, 1/2)* rain maker = mleta mvua, mganga wa mvua

umpelelesí *n (aba-, 1/2)* **1** spy, agent = mpelelezi, shushushu **2** detective, police officer doing investigative work = mpelelezi

umpeleng'eníe *n (aba-, 1/2)* sb who does smth without worring about the consequences = mtu anayefanya vitu kwa ujasiri

umpelelesye *n (aba-, 1/2)* perfect person = mkamilifu

umpeepe *n (imí-, 3/4)* tail of fish or sheep = mkia wa samaki au kondoo

umpepo *n (imí-, 3/4)* a cool wind = upepo wa baridi

umpiijí *n (aba-, 1/2)* cook = mpishi

umpíkí *n (imí-, 3/4)* tree = mti

umpíkípíkí *n (imb-, 3/4)* tail = mkia

umpila *n (imí-, 3/4)* **1** (Havea brasiliensis) *n.bot* rubber tree = mpira **2** rubber = mpira **3** ball = mpira

umpiingí *n (aba-, 1/2)* opponent = mpinzani

umpiina *n (aba-, 1/2)* **1** *n.fam* orphan = yatima **2** commoner, common person, subject (ie. not a malafyale) = asiye wa ukoo wa kichifu **3** a loner = mkiwa

umpindo *n (imí-, 3/4)* **1** brake = nusuduara, mkunjo (nguo) **2** belt, spring, elasticity = kamani, mnyumbuko

umpinduke *n (aba-, 1/2)* convert = mtu aliyebadilika, mwongofu

umpingo *n (imí-, 3/4)* beginning of the rainy season, the first rains = mwanzo wa mvua za vuli

umpínyígwa *n (aba-, 1/2)* prisoner, detainee = mfungwa

umpípye *n (imí-, 3/4)* smth which is new = kitu ambacho ni kipya

umpokí *n (aba-, 1/2)* **1** savior = mwokozi **2** redeemer = mkombozi

---

UMÚNDU - BANTU

The word umúndu (pl. abandu*)* comes from the root -ntu which is the basis for the term bantu. The original meaning of -ntu was apparently 'object, thing'. This root with the prefix for nounclass 2, which in almost all bantu languages means people, was chosen in 1856 by the German scholar Bleek to be the term to designate the languages and peoples in southern and central Africa.

---

umpolísí *n (aba-, 1/2)* cop, police officer = polisi

umpombo *n.bot (imí-, 3/4)* type of tree = aina ya mti

umponí *n (aba-, 1/2)* stranger = mgeni

umpoosa *n.bot (imí-, 3/4)* palm tree = mchikichi

umposí *n (imí-, 3/4)* sauce = mchuzi

umpoosí *n (aba-, 1/2)* **1** blacksmith, smith = mhunzi **2** squanderer = mtumiaji mali ovyo

umpotí *n (aba-, 1/2)* driver = dereva

umpúgúpúgú (Anthocleista grandiflora) *n.bot (imí-, 3/4)* type of tree = aina ya mti

umpúkú *n (imí, 3/4)* type of big mat = aina ya mkeka mkubwa, jamvi /Also **ilípúkú**

umpuulo *n (imí-, 3/4)* **1** street = mtaa **2** cleared area around the homestead = eneo lililosafishwa kuzunguka nyumba

umpululí *n (aba-, 1/2)* carpenter = seremala

umpúlya *n (imbúlya, 3/4)* beeswax, wax = nta

umpunga *n.bot (imí-, 3/4)* rice = mpunga

umpupa *n (imí-, 3/4)* **1** the 'bark' of a banana plant, dry banana 'bark' fiber = gamba au gamba kavu la mgomba **2** paper = karatasi **3** banana 'bark' bag for snuff = kitu cha kuwekea ugoro tokana na mgomba

akapúpa *n.slang* a bunch of paper money as of bark of banana

ikipúpa *n.slang* a bundle of paper money = kitita cha fedha (hasa noti) /Also used for making mats

umpúso *n (imí-, 3/4; Tuk)* bad omen = kisirani, bahati mbaya

umpúútí n.relig *(aba-, 1/2)* priest, pastor, minister = mchunguji, mchungaji, padiri

umwandí *n (aba-, 1/2)* **1** beginner = mwanzaji **2** founder = mwanzilishi

umweganísí *n.fam (aba-, 1/2)* wife's sister's husband = mume mwenza

umpwisi *n (imí-, 3/4)* runoff waters = maji yatirikayo

umpyagililo *ingamwana: umwejo (imí-, 3/4)* broom = fagio, ufagio

umpyagilo *n (imí-, 3/4)* Saturday = Jumamosi

-umú *adj* dry, barren (land), stiff = kauka, kavu, (nchi) kavu

umúúba (Saccharum officinarium) *n.bot (imyúba, 3/4)* sugar cane = muwa

umuují *n (imíují, 3/4)* **1** breath = pumzi, pumua **2** air, gas = hewa **3** steam, vapor = mvuke

umuulí *n (abulí, 1/2)* buyer, customer = mnunuzi

umuulisí *n (abulisi, 1/2)* merchant, salesman = muuzaji

umúndu *n (aba-, 1/2)* person = mtu

umúúnyú *n (imw-, 3/4)* salt = chumvi, munyu

umúúsi *n (imw-, 3/4)* daytime = mchana

umwafí *n (imyafí, 3/4)* **1** *n.bot* type of plant = aina ya mmea **2** poison drink / medicine made from the roots of the plant of the same name. This drink would tell whether a person was telling the truth or not. If the person tested would vomit he was telling the truth, if not then he was lying. = dawa ya kutapisha

umwaje *n (imy-, 3/4)* type of grass hairs which causes itching = aina ya majani yanayowasha

umwaju, umwajo *n (imyajo, 3/4)* yawn = mwayo

umwala lwalo foundation builder = mweka msingi

umwalabu *n (aba-, 1/2, <Swa)* Arab = Mwarabu

umwale *n.bot (imíale, 3/4)* type of tree, teak treee, timber, building = mvule

umwalimú *n (aba-, 1/2, < Swa)* teacher = mwalimu
/better word: **umanyisi**

umwalo *n (imyalo, 3/4)* mischief = fujo

umwana *n (aba-, 1/2)* child = mtoto

umwanangu *n (aba-, 1/2)* my child = mtoto wangu

umwaníke *n (aba-, 1/2)* **1** young man = kijana **2** child (4 -6 years old) = mtoto

umwe *pron* you (pl) = ninyi

umwegankííkulu *n (abegabakííkulu,*

1/2) bridegroom = bwana arusi

umwegí *n (aba-, 1/2)* sb married = aliyeoa au kuolewa

umwehe *n (abehe, 1/2)* **1** wife of chief, queen = mke wa chifu, malkia

umwejo *n (imyejo, 3/4)* broom, brush = ufagio

umwela *n (imy-, 3/4)* **1** bad smell esp from lack of bathing, body odor = harufu mbaya **2** current = mkondo

umwelesyo *n (imyelesyo, 3/4)* **1** flood, inundation = mafuriko **2** deluge = mafuriko

umwenda *n (imyenda, 3/4)* **1** cloth = nguo, kitambaa **2** dress = vaa, gauni **3** garment = vazi

umwene *pron* he, she = yeye
  umwene kaaja the owner of the house = mwenye nyumba

umwenekilingo *n (abene-, 1/2)* inheritor = mrithi

Umwesí - The Moon

umwesi unteta new moon = mwezi mchanga

unkome panandi = mwezi mchanga

unkome fííjo = full moon = mwezi mpevu

unkola kyamba = touching the horizon = unaoshika mlima

umwesí unsomoka new moon = mwezi unaoandama

umwesí guli pantu = overhead = uliousawa wa kichwa

umwesí gukubuka pakukela ikyamba about to sink = ukaribio kuzama

umwesí gukolile ikyamba = already sinking = unaozama

umwesí gukukyela appearing in the dawn = utokeao alfajiri

umwesí gwa mu ngisi appearing at midnight = uonekanao usiku wa manane

after T.Meyer

---

umwenekíísu *n (abe-, 1/2)* native, indigenous = mzawa

umweneleli *n (aba-, 1/2)* supervisor = msimamizi

umwenge *n (imí-, 3/4)* torch = mwenge

umwenywa *n (3)* unwillingness, indifference = ubaridi, kutokuwa na hiari ya kufanya kitu

umwesí *n (aba-, 1/2)* moon, month = mwezi

umwesí gwa buna April = Aprili

umwesí gwa lwele August = Agosti, mwezi wa nane

umwífwa *n (imí-, 3/4)* thorn = mwiba

umwífyusi *n (aba-, 1/2)* a clean person = msafi, mtanashati, nadhifu

umwíganí *n (aba-, 1/2, arch)* bachelor = mtu asiyeoa

umwíkemo *n (aba-, 1/2)* saint = mtu mtakatifu

umwíkilí *n (abi-, 1/2)* **1** a dependable person in a group eg a star in a football team = mtumainiwa **2** faithful religious person = mwenye imani

umwíko *n (imí-, 3/4)* trowel = mwiko

umwilima *n (abwílima, 1/2)* descendant of a place, native = mwenyeji, mzawa, mtu wa asili ya…

umwimbí *n (abi-, 1/2)* singer = mwimbaji

umwímí *n (abi-, 1/2)* miser = bahili, mnyimi

umwimilí *n (abi-, 1/2)* **1** security = ulinzi **2** lawyer, advocate, agent = wakili, msimamizi, mdhamini

umwimililí *n (abi-, 1/2)* **1** delegate, representative = mjumbe, mwakilishi **2** advocate, lawyer = wakili **3** steward = msimamizi **4** caretaker = mwangalizi **5** supervisor = msimamizi

umwimililí nkíísú ikingi ambassador = balozi

umwína *n (imw-, 3/4)* big hole = shimo kubwa

umwínangu *n (abi-, 1/2)* my friend, my acquaintance = rafiki yangu, mwenzangu

umwínogonelí *n (abwí-, 1/2)* accuser = mtu anayetoa / pelekea mashitaka

umwinogonelígwa *n (abi-, 1/2)* **1** suspect = mshitakiwa **2** be under consideration = fikiriwa **3** suspect = mtuhumiwa

umwípa *n (abípa, 1/2)* uprooter = mng'oaji

umwípwa *n.fam (abípwa, 1/2)* mother's brother, maternal uncle = mjomba

umwísukulu *n.fam (aba-, 1/2)* Mutual term between grandchild and grandparent **1** grandfather = babu **2** grandmother = bibi **3** grandchild = mjukuu

umwisya, umwísía (Bridelia spp) *n.bot (imí-, 3/4)* type of tree, no fruit = aina ya mti

umwisyugu *adv* today = leo

umwítikí *n (aba-, 1/2)* believer = mwamini

undagilí *n (abalagili, 1/2)* sb who gives orders to others, commander = anayetoa amri

undalye, undali *n (imí-, 3/4)* a web caused by smoke = mlale, utando wa moshi

undamú *n.fam (abalamu, 1/2)* wife's brother, brother-in-law = shemeji

undamúlí *n (aba-, 1/2)* judge = mwamuzi

undangalila *n (aba-, 1/2)* brightness, light = mwanga

undangilangi *n (imí-, 3/4)* type of tree = aina ya mti

undeebí *n (abaleebí, 1/2)* bandit, thief, burglar = mwizi, jambazi

undelefwa *n (aba-, 1/2)* driver = dereva

unndema *n (abalema, 1/2)* imbecile, clod, fool, = mjinga, mpumbavu

undemaafú *n (abalemaafú, 1/2)* fool, silly person = mtu mpumbavu

undemale *n (abalemale, 1/2)* cripple, physical disability = mlemavu, kilema

undeenga *n (aba-, 1/2; lenga)* **1** daughter of a chief, princess = mtoto wa mfalme wa kike, binti mfalme **2** one who marries a daughter of a chief = mtu aliyeoa binti mfalme

undimamígunda *n (abalima-, 1/2)* farmer, peasant = mkulima

undimí *n (aba-, 1/2; < -timí)* farmer =

mkulima

undimo *n (imí-, 3/4)* **1** agriculture = kilimo **2** the farming season = msimu
wa kulima

undindililí *n (aba-, 1/2)* guard = mlinzi

undíndo *n (imílíndo, 3/4)* crash =
mdundo

undíndo *n (imílíndo, 3/4)* din =
kishindo

undindwana *n (aba-, 1/2; -lindwana)*
girl = msichana

undisí *n (imílisí, 3/4)* rope (fiber from
banana) = kamba k.m. ya mgomba

undobí *n (abalobi, 1/2)* fisherman =
mvuvi

undobo *n.bot (indobo, 3/4)* thorn tree =
mmea wenye miiba, mtunduru

undogwe *n (abalogwe, 1/2)* womanizer,
whore, prostitute, adulterer = malaya,
mzinzi

undolí *n (abaloli, 1/2)* **1** merchant =
mfanyabiashara **2** rich person = tajiri

undomo *n.anat (imílomo, 3/4)* lip =
mdomo

Umúndu uju ali nundomo fííjo This
man is very talkative = Mtu huyu ana
mdomo sana

undondo *n (aba-, 1/2)* a poor person =
fukara, fakiri, maskini

undongí *n (abalongi, 1/2)* magistrate,
judge = hakimu, mwamuzi

undongosí *n (aba-, 1/2; < longosi)*
leader = kiongozi; **~ gwa baheesya**
guide = mwongozaji wa wageni

undongotí *n.bot (imí-, 3/4, > Swa mlingoti)* eucalyptus = mkaratusi

undotí *n (abaloti, 1/2)* astrologer =
mnajimu, mpiga falaki

undubukilo *n (indubukilo, 11/10)* expe-
riencing or using something for the
first time = limbuko

undulwe *n.bot (imílulwe, 3/4)* type of
weed = aina ya magugu

undumba *n (abalumba, 1/2)* fisherman
= mvuvi

undumbililí *n (abalumbilili, 1/2)*

preacher = mhubiri

undumbu *n.fam (abalumbu, 1/2)* sibling
of opposite sex. = ndugu wa jinsia tofauti, dada au kaka

undumbuko *n (imí-, 3/4)* the first fruit
= tunda la mwanzo ya kulimbuka

undumyana *n (abalumyana, 1/2)* boy =
mvulana

undúnda *n (imílúnda, 3/4)* spear with
round metal tip = mkuki wa mviringo

unduungu *n (imílungu, 3/4)* **1** Sunday =
Jumapili **2** week = wiki

undungwana *n (aba-, 1/2)* **1** term used
about the Swahili people, probably
derogative = mswahili **2** unimportant
person = mtu bila maana, mtu mdogo

undwabwíte *n (abalwabwíte-, 1/2)* warrior, soldier = askari, mpiganaji

undyanyaama *n (aba-, 1/2)* carnivore =
mlanyama

undyobí *n (aba-, 1/2)* glutton, voracious
eater = mlafi, mbuge

une, ne *pron* I = mimi

ungalabwalwa *n (aba-, 1/2)* alcoholic =
mlevi

ungaali *n (aba-, 1/2)* drunkard = mlevi

ungalinga *n (aba-, 1/2)* stranger, foreigner = mgeni

unganga *n (aba-, 1/2)* **1** doctor =
mganga **2** The person you go to for
help when you have been bewitched =
mganga

ung'ang'a (Nephelium lappaceum) *n.bot
(imí-, 3/4)* rambutan (soapberry family) =
aina ya mmea ambao matunda yake hu-
fanana kidogo na zabibu

unganígwa *n (aba-, 1/2)* beloved, girl-
friend/boyfriend, darling, sweetheart
= mpendwa, mpenzi, rafiki

ungelo *n (imí-, 3/4)* measure = kipimo

ungobole *n (imí-, 3/4)* old fashioned
gun = gobori, bunduki ya zamani

ungogí *n (aba-, 1/2)* killer, murderer =
muuaji

ungogoma *n (imí-, 3/4)* beehive =
mzinga wa nyuki

ungolofú *n (aba-, 1/2)* a righteous person = mtu mwenye haki, mwadilifu

ung'oma *n (imí-, 3/4)* hive, beehive = mzinga wa nyuki

ungotí *n* mine = mgodi, machimbo ya madini

ungúlililí *n (aba-, 1/2)* waiter = anayefanya kazi ya mapokezi

ungumba *n (aba-, 1/2)* barren woman = mwanamke asiyezaa

unngunda *n (imí-, 3/4)* **1** farm, farmland, plantation, field = shamba **2** garden = bustani

ungwajaabi *n.bot (imí-, 3/4)* guava tree = mpera

  gwajaabi *(ba-, 1a/2)* guava fruit, guava tree = pera, mpera, mti ya mapera

ungwína *n.bot (imí-, 3/4)* type of tree with excellent timber = aina ya mti, muhagata

unhahaní *n (aba-, 1/2)* seducer = mtongozi, mtongozaji

unheesya *n (aba-, 1/2)* stranger, foreigner, guest = mgeni

unhiijí *n (aba-, 1/2)* thief, bandit, burglar, robber = mwizi

unhindi *n (aba-, 1/2)* an Indian, person from India = mhindi

unja *vb (pt unjíle)* become smaller than usual = pungua katika ukubwa; **Inyama ajikuunja linga tujilekíle bunobuno** The meat will be reduced in size if we leave it as it is = Nyama itapungua ukubwa ikiwa tutaiacha hivihivi; **Imíenda gikambagila papa unjíle fiíjo** Clothes don't fit him because he is so thin = Nguo hazimchukui kwa sababu ya wembamba yake

unjabi *n (aba-, 1/2)* distributor = mgawaji

unjabujabu (Havea brasiliensis) *n.bot (imí-, 3/4)* rubber tree = mpira

unjengakaja *n (aba-, 1/2)* a boy of approximately 15 years age, he is then old enough to build his own

home = mvulana apataye miaka 15 ya umri. Katika umri huu anaweza kuwa na nyumba yake mwenyewe

unjengí *n (aba-, 1/2)* builder = mjenzi

unjíili *n (aba-, 1/2)* representative, helper, sb acting on behalf of sb else = msimamizi, msaidizi, mbadala, awaye badala ya

unjíní *n (imí-, 3/4; > Swa)* town, city = mji

unjobi *n (aba-, 1/2)* **1** an extrovert = msemaji **2** a speaker, an orator = msemaji

unjongí *n (aba-, 1/2)* fugitive, a runaway, a truant = mtoro

unjuufya *n (aba-, 1/2)* not yet menstruating girl, young girl, girl nearing puberty = msichana mdogo ambaye hajabalehe bado, kigoli

unjwego *n (imí-, 3/4)* **1** noise, shout, shriek = kelele **2** uproar, tumult = makelele, fujo **3** din = mshindo

unkabi *n (aba-, 1/2)* a well off person, a rich person = tajiri, mkwasi

unkahabwa *n.bot (imí-, 3/4)* coffee tree = mkahawa

unkake *n (aba-, 1/2)* sb with many children = mtu akiwa na watoto wengi

unkala *n (imí-, 3/4)* charcoal = mkaa

unkalalisí *n (aba-, 1/2)* sb irritating = mchukivu, mnuni

unkalaní *n (aba-, 1/2)* clerk = karani

unkambokambo *n.bot (imí-, 3/4)* type of tree, does not burn well = mti kama msunobari

unkamí *n (aba-, 1/2)* milkmaid, the one who milks the cow = anayekamua maziwa

unkamú *n (aba-, 1/2)* **1** relative, kin, kindred = ndugu, nasaba, jamaa **2** friend (used figuratively about sb who is as close to you as a relative) = rafiki

unkamwana *n.fam (aba-, 1/2)* parent-in-law of the wife = mkwe (hutumika kwa wanawake tu)

unkando *n (imí-, 3/4)* **1** dough (for making bread or beer) = kinyunga, mkando 2 soil for pottery activities = udongo wa ufinyanzi

unkangale *n (aba-, 1/2)* old person = mzee

unkapítabwe *n (aba-, 1/2)* supervisor = .mnyapara, msimamizi

unkasí *n.fam (aba-, 1/2)* wife = mke

unkasí kulu *n.fam* first wife = .mke mkubwa

unkasí unkulumba *n.fam* elder wife (this is of course the first wife since nobody would marry a second wife who was older than the first) = mke wake mkubwa, mkewe mkubwa

unkasí unnandi *n.fam* his younger wife = mke wake mdogo, mkewe mdogo

unkasokela (Persea americana) *n.bot (imí-, 3/4)* avocado = mparachichi, mwembemafuta

unkataní (Agave sisalama) *n.bot (-, 9/10)* sisal plant = mkonge, katani

unkate *n (imí-, 3/4; > Swa)* bread = mkate /Nya word is **ikisyesye**

unkeka *n (imí-, 3/4, > Swa)* plaited mat = mkeka

unkeke *n (aba-, 1/2)* term for a child between approximatly 4 and 12 years old, sb who has not reached puberty = kijana

unkekesí *n (imí-, 3/4)* a bad smell (eg. like that of fish or a wild animal) = vumba

unkeenja *n (aba-, 1/2)* bachelor, unmarried man or unmarried woman = kapera

unkese *n (imíkese, 3/4)* 1 The mixture of maizeflour and fingermillet in the first stage of the production of local beer 2 yeast = hamira

unkeetí *n (aba-, 1/2)* witness = shahidi

unkíikulu *n (aba-, 1/2)* woman, lady, female = mwanamke

unkilisímasí (Delonix regia) *n.bot (imí-, 3/4)* flame tree = mkrismasi

unkilisítí *n (aba-, 1/2)* Christian = mkristo

unkindu (Phoenix reniclata) *n.bot (imí-, 3/4)* wild date palm = mkindu

unkíngí *n (aba-, 1/2)* a leader in a group of dancers (in traditional dances) = kiongozi wa ngoma (mang'oma)

unkiní *n (aba-, 1/2)* player = mchezaji

unkíno *n (imí-, 3/4)* game, joke = mchezo

unko *n.fam (1/2; < kwa)* parent-in-law of the man = mkwe (hutumika kwa wanaume tu)

unko *n.fam (aba-, 1/2)* father-in-law = mkwe

unkokotení *n (imí-, 3/4)* cart = mkokoteni

unkolokoloní *n (aba-, 1/2; > Swa korokoni)* watchman = mlinzi

unkolofwa *n (imí-, 3/4)* channel, furrow = mfereji, mchirizi

unkololo *n (imí-, 3/)* channel = mchirizi, mfereji

unkolondí *n (imí-, 3/4)* midrib (eg of a leaf) = kikonyo cha kati cha jani, ujukuti, upongoo

unkolwa *n (aba-, 1/2)* old person = mzee /See **unkangale**

unkolyo *n (imí-, 3/4)* moss = nyasi ndogo nyororo /See **ingobyo**

unkoma *n.med (aba-, 1/2)* leper = mkoma

unkoma ndíngala *n* drummer = mpigangoma

unkomamanga (Punica granatum) *n.bot (imí-, 3/4; > Swa)* (tree) pomegranate = mkomamanga

unkomí *n (aba-, 1/2)* beater = mpiga, mpigaji; **unkoma ndíngala** drummer = mpigangoma /Note spelling

unkomí *n (aba-, 1/2)* In **akapote** singing the **unkomí** is/are the one(s) saying "ee". The main singer is called **umpaalí**. = Katika kwimba akapote, unkomí ni yule aitikiaye 'ee'. Mwimbaji mkuu huitwa umpaalí

unkomú *n (aba-, 1/2)* clever, tricky person = mjanja

unkomwa malago *n* fortune teller, forecaster = mtabiri

129

unkondo *n (imí-, 3/4)* type of small tree, euphorbia spp The leaves of this legume are used to stupefy fish so that they are easily caught; It is in a way poisoning the river and so this practice has over the years been restricted both by the malafyale and the colonial administration = mtupa, aina ya mti , majani yatumikayo kulewesha samaki majini, majani yake ni sumu na yanaweza kuua samaki

unkongí *n (aba-, 1/2)* **1** follower, disciple = mfuasi **2** second (or lower) in rank = afuatiaye katika cheo

unkonyofú *n (aba-, 1/2)* idiot, ass, nerd, fool = mpumbavu, mjinga

unkopo *n (imí-, 3/4; > Swa)* loan = mkopo

unkota *n.med (imí-, 3/4)* medicine, drug = dawa

unkota gwa ífugo *n.cult.med* Medicine for fertility = dawa inayoaminika kuleta neema nchini baada ya kunyunyizwa kwenye eneo lote la ardhi

unkúhú (Uapaca kirkiana) *n.bot (imí-, 3/4)* type of tree = aina ya mti (edible makuhu)

unkuju *n.bot* fig tree = mkuyu, mtini

unkulu *n.fam (aba-, 1/2)* **1** elder brother, elder sister (eg. elder sibling of same sex) = ndugu mkubwa wa jinsia moja **2** father's elder brother's child older than speaker = kaka au dada mkubwa

unkuulu *n (aba-, 1/2)* **1** old person = mzee **2** smth/sb ancient = wa zamani

unkulusika *n (aba-, 1/2)* old person = mzee /See **unkangale**

unkunda *n (imí-, 3/4)* gulf = ghuba

unkundwe *n (aba-, 1/2)* beloved, favorite = mpendwa, kipenzi

unkúngúlúka *n (aba-, 1/2)* **1** genius, studied man = mtu mwenye elimu, msomi, mtabiri **2** prophet, diviner = nabii

unkupili *n (imí-, 3/4)* chaff, husk = pumba

unkusí *n (aba-, 1/2)* **1** grown up, adult = mtu mkubwa (kiumri), mtu wa makamo, mtu mzima **2** sb older than you = mkubwa

unkusyuulu *n (imí-, 3/4)* a bad smell = vumba

unkuuti, ilíkuuti (Maesa lanceolata) *n.bot (imí-, 3/4)* type of tree = aina ya mti (usage: ropes can be made from the bark)

unkwaju (Tamaindus indica) *n.bot (imí,-, 3/4)* tamarind = mkwaju

unkwakwa *n .slang (aba-, 1/2)* prostitute = malaya

unkwamba *n (imí-, 3/4)* pole tied along the walls of native houses at the middle = nguzo ifungiwayo kwenye majengo ya nyumba

unkwela *n (imí-, 3/4)* mat = mkeka

unkwenyenye *n (imí-, 3/4)* bad nasty smell (like of crocodile) = vumba

unkwítwa (Rapanea melanophoeos) *n.bot (imí-, 3/4)* type of tree = aina ya mti

unkyapi *n (imí-, 3/4)* whip = mchapo, kitu laini kinachotengenezwa kwa ngozi kwa ajili ya kuchapia

unna *n.fam (aba-, 1/2)* his/her mother = mama yake

unnaalí *n (aba-, 1/2)* auctioneer = dalali

unnaalo *n (imí-, 3/4)* auction = mnada

unnaasí *n.bot (imí-, 3/4)* coconut palm = mnazi

unndondo *n (abalondo, 1/2)* poor person = fukara, fakiri, masikini

unndosí *n (abalosí, 1/2)* witch, witch doctor, wizard = mchawi

unndugu *n (abalugu, 1/2)* enemy = adui

unndukí *n (abalukí, 1a/2)* hair-braider, hair-plaiter = msusi

unndume *n.fam (abalume, 1/2)* husband = mume

unndume unkulumba *n.fam* husband's elder brother = mume mkubwa, shemeji

unndume unnandi *n.fam* husband's younger brother, brother-in-law = mumewe mdogo

unnegamiisi *n (aba-, 1/2)* girl who

fetches water = msichana aliyechota maji

unnganígwa *n (aba-, 1/2)* beloved = mpenzi

unngelí *n (abageli, 1/2)* tempter = mshawishi, mjaribu

unngelo *n (imí-, 3/4)* **1** weight = uzani, uzito **2** measure = kipimo **3** criterion = kigezo

ungolofú *n (aba-, 1/2)* a righteous person = mtu mwongofu

unngotí *n (imí-, 3/4)* mine = mgodi

unngubo *n.anat (imí-, 3/4)* **1** any skin of person or fish = ngozi ya mtu au samaki **2** prepuce = govi, zunga

unngwína *n.bot (imí-, 3/4)* gopher tree = aina ya mti

unníne *n (aba-, 1/2)* her/his friend = rafiki yake

unníní *n (aba-, 1/2)* baby = mtoto mdogo, mtoto mchanga

unnjanga *n (aba-, 1/2)* **1** a person who is not a Nyakyusa = Mtu asiye wa kabila la Kinyakyusa. Mgeni toka nje ya kabila la Kinyakyusa **2** *n.off* a person unaware or out of touch with tribal customs and proper behavior. This could be any person new to Ubunyakyusa or anyone who has been away for a long time and has lost touch with traditions. = Yeyote ambaye hajui tabia za kinyakyusa. Mtu ambaye anatenda kinyume na mila za kinyakyusa hata kama ni mnyakyusa kwa kabila

unnúgúna *n.fam (aba-, 1/2)* his/her younger brother = ndugu yake, mdogo wake

unnúgúnago *n.fam* your young brother = mdogo wako

unnya- *n (aba-, 1/2)* used in complex forms meaning 'son of...' = bin

unnyafyale *n (abanyafyale, 1/2)* chief, king, leader, headman = mfalme, kiongozi /For most people this is a synonym to **malafyale**

unnyago *n (aba-, 1/2)* **1** elder (of a tribe or village) = mzee wa zamani wa heshima **2** elder (especially elder woman giving advice in ceremonies) = mzee wa heshima

unnyamata *n (aba-, 1/2)* servant = mtumishi

unnyambala *n (aba-, 1/2)* man = mwanaume

unnyambuta *n (aba-, 1/2)* armed robber, pirate = mnyang'anyi, jambazi

unnyasenga *n.fam* father's sister, aunt = shangazi

unnyele Annona senegalensis *n.bot (imí-, 3/4)* custard apple tree = mtopetope **ilínyele** (fruit) custard apple = matopetope

unnyeenya *n.fam (aba-, 1/2)* great grandmother, great grandfather = nyanya

unnyololo *n (imí-, 3/4)* **1** chain = mnyororo **2** prison = gereza

unnywamú *n (aba-, 1/2)* sb fat, sb big = mnene, mkubwa

unsalabala *n (aba-, 1/2)* childless man or woman = mke au mume asiye na mtoto

unsambukí *n (aba-, 1/2)* rebel = mtu anayeghaili

unsamdelele (Lansium domesticum) *n.bot (imí-, 3/4)* langsat (mahogany family), type of tree = aina ya mti

unsana *n.anat (imí-, 3/4)* loin, waist = kiuno

unsanga *n (imí-, 3/4)* sand = mchanga

unsangabale (Aphloia theiformis) *n.bot (imí-, 3/4)* type of tree = aina ya mti

unsangati Ilex mitis *n.bot (isangati, 3/10)* type of tree = aina ya mti (medicine, furniture)

unsebe (Erythrina abyssinica) *n.bot (imí-, 3/4)* type of tree = aina ya mti (fruit : **ilísebe**)

unsebo *n (imí-, 3/4)* road = barabara

unsege *n (3; > Swa)* concrete = zege

unsegela *n (imí-, 3/4)* **1** type of big drum = ngoma kubwa **2** type of dance = aina ya cheza ngoma

unsele *n (imí-, 3/4)* a furrow caused by soil inversion during ploughing = mtaro, mfereji utokeao wakati wa kulima kwa jembe ulaya (plau)

unselekesye *n (imí-, 3/4)* a long robe = vaizi refu (kama joho)

unsengela (Macaranga spp.) *n.bot (imí-, 3/4)* type of tree = aina ya mti

unsí *n (imí-, 3/4)* root = mzizi

unsíbísíbí (Myrica salicifolia) *n.bot (imí-, 3/4)* type of tree (timber) = aina ya mti

unsígo *n (imí-, 3/4)* burden, luggage = mzigo

unsígwana *n.off (aba-, 1/2)* illegitimate child, bastard = mwana haramu

unsíkalí *n (aba-, 1/2)* **1** policeman = polisi **2** soldier = askari

unsímbí *n (aba-, 1/2)* author, writer = mwandishi

unsímisí *n (aba-, 1/2)* **1** woman who elopes, woman who leaves her husband = mlowezi, **2** a woman who goes to live with a man without the consent of her parents = mwanamke a-mbaye anaenda kukaa na mwaume bila ruhusa au idhini ya wazazi wake

unsíndikilí *n (aba-, 1/2)* the person who escorts his guest for a while when he is leaving = msindikizaji

unsínga *n (imí-, 3/4)* **1** big stump = kisiki kikubwa **2** cannon = mzinga

unsíngilígwa *n (aba-, 1/2)* fiancée = mchumba

unsípa *n.med (imí-, 3/4)* hernia = ngiri

unsípí *n (imí-, 3/4)* belt = mkanda, mshipi

unsísa *n (imí-, 3/4)* steak (meat without bones) = mnofu

unsítakígwa *n (aba-, 1/2)* accused = mshtakiwa

unsítakujapo *n (aba-, 1/2)* absentee = asiyekuwepo

unsíto *n (aba-, 1/2)* **1** sb heavy (fat) = mzito **2** fig. sb rich = mtu tajiri, aliye na mali

unso *n (imíso, 3/4)* a long stick = mchi wa kushindilia nyumba

unsobí *n (aba-, 1/2)* an erring person, a sinner = mkosaji, mkosefu

unsooka *n (aba-, 1/2)* (the first) son of the chief, crown prince = mwana wa mfalme anayetawazwa

unsokelo *n (imí-, 3/4)* bird's gizzard = mfuko wa chakula wa ndege

unsoki *n (aba-, 1/2)* advisor, councellor = mshauri

unsololí *n (aba-, 1/2)* prophet = mtabiri

unsongolafípiki *n (aba-, 1/2)* wood carver = mchonga vinyago

unsongwa *n.bot (i-, 3/10)* **1** type of tall tree with a yellowish bitter fruit, found mainly in Kyela = mti mkubwa uzaao matunda madogo machungu **2** type of small bush /shrub with small orange- brownish sweet fruits, found in the higher areas of Rungwe (same name in Safwa), not found in Kyela = aina ya mmea mwenye matunda matamu madogo

unsoní *n (aba-, 1/2)* tailor = fundi cherehani, mshonaji, mshoni

unstaakí *n (aba-, 1/2, >Swa)* accuser = mshitaki, anayeshitaki

unsubilígwa *n (aba-, 1/2)* a trustworthy person = mtu mwaminifu, mtu anaye-tegemewa

unsúmalí *n (imí-, 3/4; > Swa)* nail = msumari

unsumeno *n (imí-, 3/4)* saw = msumeno

unsuumí *n (aba-, 1/2)* beggar = ombaomba

unsumilisí *n (aba-, 1/2)* beggar = ombaomba

unsungu *n (aba-, 1/2)* **1** white person, European, American, caucasian = mzungu **2** virgin = bikira **3** girl = mwali

unsungulígwa *n (aba-, 1/2)* chosen one = mteule

unswa *n.zool (aba-, 1/2)* non flying termite = mchwa

unswígala *n (imí-, 14/4)* tail = mkia

unswilí *n (aba-, 1/2)* child's guardian = mlezi

unswísa (Myrianthus holstii) *n.bot*

(imí-, 3/4) type of tree = aina ya mti
(edible fruit, fruit in a bunch, yellow
when ripe)

unsyenga *n (imí-, 3/4)* circle = mviringo

unsyobí *n (aba-, 1/2)* swindler, impost-
or, cheater = ayari, mdanganyifu

unsyuka *n (aba-, 1/2)* **1** ghost = mzimu
2 ancestor = jadi

unsyunguulu *n (imí-, 3/4)* **1** shadow =
kivuli **2** image = picha

unsyúnguti Trichilia emetica *n.bot
(imí-, 3/4)* type of olive tree, edible
fruit = mzeituni
/seeds dried and crushed for ointment

unta *n (-, 9/10)* sweet taste = ladha
tamu (kama ya asali)

untaliko *n (imí-, 3/4)* pole put along the
top of the walls of native houses =
mtambaa panya, kirugu

untalímba *n (imí-3/4)* crowbar = mtalimbo

untalusí *n (aba-, 1/2)* leader, master =
kiongozi

untambo *n (imí-, 3/4)* step = hatua

untandalilo *n (imí-, 3/4)* stairway,
stairs, staircase, ladder = ngazi

untangasale (Albizia gummifera) *n.bot
(imí-, 3/4)* type of tree = aina ya mti

untaaní *n.fam (aba-, 1/2)* This term
covers exactly half of the English
'cousin', ie: **1** mother's brother's
child, cousin = binamu **2** father's sister's child, cousin = binamu
/For the others see under 'cousin' in
the English - Nyakyusa section

untasí *n (aba-, 1/2)* **1** elder = mtu wa
zamani, mtangulizi **2** somebody older
than you = mkubwa kwa umri

untebela *n (imí-, 3/4)* flat country =
nchi tambarare

untego *n (imí-, 3/4)* trap, snare = mtego

unteja *n (aba-, 1/2)* customer = mteja

unteende *n.bot (imí-, 3/4)* date palm =
mtende

unteendeesí *n (aba-, 1/2)* **1** investiga-
tor, researcher = mchunguzi **2** spy =

mpelelezi, mdukuzi **3** peeping Tom,
voyeur = mchunguzi

untengo *n (imí-, 3/4)* price, cost, worth,
value = bei, gharama

untíloolo *n.bot (imí-, 3/4)* olive tree =
mzeituni
indíloolo olive (fruit) = zeituni

untíímí *n (aba-, 1/2)* shepherd, herdsman = mchungaji

untíímang'ombe *n (aba-, 1/2)* shepherd, herdsman = mchunga ng'ombe,
mchungaji

untíímo *n (imí-, 3/4)* a herd of cattle,
sheep or goat = kundi la mifugo

untíndíbofú *n (imí-, 3/4)* the inner soft
part of a banana plant = sehemu laini
yenye utomvu ndani ya mgomba

untíngo *n (imí-, 3/4)* a big ladle, spoon =
mwiko, mwiko wa kusongea ugali, upawa

untítu *n (aba-, 1/2)* an African, black
person = mwaafrika, mweusi

untofyo *n (imí-, 3/4)* lead = risasi (aina
ya madini)

untolí *n (aba-, 1/2)* champion, winner,
an ace, conqueror = mshindi

untondo (Isoberlinia angolensis) *n.bot (imí-,
3/4)* type of tree = aina ya mti (this tree is
called ikibonde when small)

untondolí *n (aba-, 1/2)* **1** one who harvests with a sickle or knife (eg harvesting rice, wheat, millet but not
maize, beans or peanuts) = anayevuna
kwa kutumia mundu, kisu au kwa
kuchuma **2** one who harvests by
plucking = anayevuna kwa kuchuma

untondolo *n (imí-, 3/4)* harvest, harvesting = mavuno

untotofúla *n (imí-, 3/4)* foam, froth,
scum = povu

untu *n (imítu, 3/4)* head = kichwa

untulatula *n.bot (imí-, 3/4)* thistle =
aina ya mmea, mmea wa porini
wenye majani yenye miiba

untulanongwa *n (aba- 1/2)* sinner =
mkosefu, mtendadhambi

untúlúnga (Hagenia abyssinica) *n.bot*

(imí-, 3/4) type of tree, Usage: timber, firewood = aina ya mti, uitwao mturunga kwa ajili ya kupasua mbao

untúmbúla *n (imí-, 3/4)* banana bunch = mkungu

untumígwa *n (aba-, 1/2)* **1** apostle = mtume **2** envoy, delegate, emissary, missionary = aliyetumwa, mmisionari

untumwa *n (aba-, 1/2)* slave, servant = mtumwa

untúnda (Bombax rhodognaphalon) *n.bot (imí-, 3/4)* type of tree, kapok tree = msufi

untúndú *n (imí-, 3/4)* age, agegroup = umri, rika

untundubili *n.anat (imí-, 3/4, Kye)* rumen = tumbo la mnyama

untungulu *n (aba-, 1/2)* **1** liar = mwongo **2** hypocrite = mnafiki

untwa *n (aba-, 1/2)* **1** king = mfalme **2** *n.relig* lord = bwana

untwaalo *n (imí-, 3/4)* baggage, load, burden, bundle = mzigo, bahasha

unyamata *n.relig (aba-, 1/2; > Chewa)* servant = mtumishi

unyoko *n.fam (aba-, 1/2)* your mother = mama yako
/Today this word carries a rather offensive second meaning

upa *vb (pt upíle)* scrape = paruza

usanía *vb (pt useenie)* exchange, barter = badilisha

uswe *pron* we = sisi

uswege *exp* excuse me = samahani, unisamehe, uniwie radhi
/This is a common first name for men

utu *det,pron (13)* these = hizi, hivi

utulo *n (13)* sleep, nap = usingizi

utupele *n.med (13)* small pimple = ukurutu

utwa *part (13)* of, "things belonging to …" = vya

utwa lubunju *greeting* (Answ. **tunúnú**) good morning = Habari za asubuhi

utwa mbombo *greeting* (Answ. **tunúnú**) How are things at work? = Habari za kazi

utwa namajolo *greeting* (Answ. **tunúnú**) good evening = habari za jioni

utwa pamúúsí *greeting* (Answ. **tunúnú**) good afternoon = habari za mchana

utwa uko *greeting* (Answ. **tunúnú**) how are things there = habari za huko

utwamunda *n.anat (13)* guts (lung, heart, intestine, liver etc) = vitu vya ndani mwa mnyama (utumbo, matumbo, ini, moyo etc)

English - Nyakyusa

Aa

abacus *n* aka kubalila
abandon *vt* leka
abbreviate *vt* pímbusya
abbreviation *n* ubupímba
abdomen *n.anat* ulwanda
ability *n* amaka, ulumanyo, ukubagila
able, be able *adj* bagila
abnormal *adj* ukuja lungi, ukuja
  pasíma
aboard *adv & prep* nkati mú sítíma/ ndege
  go aboard ípaka, kweela, buuka kípake
abolish *vb* leka
abort *vb* soosya ulwanda
abortion *n* ukusoosya ulwanda
about *adv* (approximately) ukufwana
  prep (near) kifúkí, kifúkí na
above *prep* pamwanya, kumwanya
abroad *adv* nkíísu ikiheesya (nkíísu kya
  panja), kwísiilya
abrupt *adj* nakalinga
abscess *n* **1** (general) ilyuulu **2** (in finger) akapuupi
  she squeezed the abscess akamíle
  ilyuulu
absence *n* ukusítakujapo
absent, be absent *vb* linda, búja, -kaja-
  ko, -kajapo
  he is absent alindíle, abujíle, akajako
absentee *n* unsítakujapo
absolute *adj* loosa, kisíta kusyasya
absolutely *adv* loosa
absorb *vt* fípa
abstinence *n* **1** ukusíta kubombela,
  ukusíta kulonda, ukwíjima **2** (from alcohol) ukusíta kunwa ubwalwa
absurd *adj* -a mwalo, -a bulema
abundance *n* **1** (things for general use)
  ukukeelwa **2** (fish) ukutwa, ulutwo
  3 ukubotoka
abuse *n* **1** (insult) ilíheelú **2** (maltreatment)
  ukubombela mwalo, ukubombela kabíbí
abuse *vt* **1** (insult) helúla, tuka **2** (mis-
  use) bombela mwalo, bombela kabíbí

abusive *adj* -a maheelú; **His remarks**
  are abusive Amasyu gake ga maheelú
acacia *n.bot* uluko lwa mpíkí gwa mífwa
academic *adj* isyasúkúúlú, -a fímanyílo
academy *n* apakumanyílíla, isúkúúlú
accelerate *vi* **1** bopesya, ongela, kuujisya, ongela ukubopesya **2** (vehicle)
  ongela umoto
accent *n* **1** (stress on word) ukukasya
  ilíísyu **2** (type of pronunciation / dialect) akajiilo ka ísyu, injobele
accept *vt* ambilila, ítika
acceptance *n* ulwítiko, ulwambililo
access *n* fíkilígwa, itikisígwa; **His new job**
  gave him access to a car with a driver
  Imbombo jake imbya jimwítikísye ukuja
  nilígali pamopene nuumpotí
access *vb* agígwa, segelela
accessible *adj* -agígwa, segelelígwa,
  -fíkilígwa
accident *n* uluboneko ulu lukasubilígwe
  ulu lukupela ubufúlale pamo ubufwe
  He was hurt in a car accident
  Aafúleele bo ígali ligwíle
accidentally *adv* kulusako, kisíta kusubilígwa
accommodate *vt* **1** (lodge) ítikisya **2**
  (adapt to) baatika kanúnú, tendekesya
accomodation *n* pabugono, pabujo
accompany *vb* longosanía
accompany part of the way home *vt*
  (In Bantu custom a guest is escorted
  part of the way home by the host)
  síndikila
accomplish *vb* maliisya
according to *prep* ukukongana na, ni
accordingly *adv* luulo, muumo, buno
  (po papo)
account *n* imbalilo
  on account of, because of kunongwa
  ja, kusyanaloolí sya
account for *vb* panga akajiilo ka
account book *n* kalata gwa mbalilo sya
  ndalama
accountant *n* ugwambalilo (umbalí),

ujuíkubala ifyuma, unkalaní gwa
ndalama

accounting *n* ukubala indalama
(ifyuma)

accounting (to do) *vi* tendekesya indalama

accumulate *vb* bungaanía, lundika

accuracy *n* ubwanalolí

accurate *adj* -a bwanalolí

accusation *n* ukusítaaka, ubwínogonele,
ubwínogonelígwe; **The accusation
against him was not true 1** Isi ba-
limmwinogonííle syali sya butungulu
2 Isi bammwinogonelaga sikali sya
nalooli

accused *n* unsítakígwa, undondígwa,
untulanongwa

accuse *vt* sítaaka

accuser *n* unstaakí, umwínogonelí

accustom *vb* ísíbisya, ísíbila, puba; **I'm
accustomed to working slowly**
Nísíbíle pakubomba panandipanandi

ace *n* **1** (card) itúlúfú **2** (a winner) untolí

ache *n.med* ukubabígwa

ache *vb* baba

achieve *vb* kaba

achievement *n* ukukaba

acknowledge *vt* ítikila ukuti mo múmo,
laata ubwanalolí, ítika ubusobi

acne *n.med* uluundu

acquaint *vb* ísíbisígwa, ísíbila

acquaintance *n* umwinangu

acquire *vb* kaba, ega

acre *n* (4840 square yards, 4000 square
meters) iheka, ikipímo kya lujabo lwa
ngunda

across *adv, prep* kwísilya; **He swam
across the river** Alyogeelíle uku-
loboka ulwisí; **He lives across the
river** Íkutuugala ísilya lila; **He lives
across the street** Íkutuugala ulubafu
ulungi lwa njila

act *n* **1** (deed) aka kíkubombígwa
2 (law) ululagilo

act *vb* (theater) íganía

action *n* ulubombo, imbombo

activate *vb* (set off) fyatúla

active *adj* -bombí, -súmúkili

activity *n* akabombo

actor *n* ugwakusekeesya ntusumo pamo
musenema, umwíganía tusumo

actually *adv* nalooli, mbwananoli

A.D. *abbrev.* (Anno Domini) ulubalo
lwa Kilistí (bo apapígwe Jesu Kilistí)

ad *n* ulufúmúsyo

adapt *vb* ísíbisya, ísíbila

Adam's apple *n.anat* akapembemilo

add *vb* ongela

   add more water ongela amiisi

adder *n.zool* injoka; **puff adder** kituumbi

addict *n* uju ísíbíle akajiilo, ka bwalwa,
ingaambo, imíkota

addicted *adj* -ísíbíla akajiilo

addiction *n* ukwísíbila akajiilo

addition (in math) *n* ukongelapo

address *n* ikifígo, alelesí

adjust *vb* tendekesya, biika kanúnú

administer *vb* imilila, longosya

administration *n* ubwimililí, ubulongosí

admire *vb* túfya

admiration *n* ikinyonywo

admit *vb* ítika, pokela, ítikisya, íngisya

adolescence *n* ubuníongoke

adopt *vb* **1** (child) ukumwega umwana
umpina kukaja kumyako ukuja mwa-
nako; **Our neighbors adopted an orphan** Umpalamaní gwitu amweegíle
umwana umpiina; **2** (concept) ega,
egela, koonga

adore *vb* gana ukukindilila fííjo

adorn *vt* nosya

adult *n* unkusí

adultery *n* ubulogwe

   commit adultery logwa

advance *n* ukubuuka nkyení

advance of salary *n* umfwalo gwa
nkyení

advance *vb* buuka nkyení, twala nkyení
(of money) ikyandilo

advanced *adj* -a pamwanya

advancement *n* **1** ukwínusya, ukongelapo

2 (at work) ulukusyo pambombo
advantage *n* ubusangalúfú, ubukabo
adventure *n* uluboneko lwa kuswigisya
advertise *vb* fúmúsya
advertisement *n* ulufúmúsyo
advice *n* ulufúndo, ulugolosyo, ulusoko;
   He was caught by a crocodile because he did not listen to my advice
   of not crossing the river Akolígwe
   ningwina papo akalitike ukusita uku-
   loboka ulwísi
advisable *adj* -a kusokígwa, -a kupilika, -a kufundígwa
advise *vb* soka, fúnda, golosya
advisor *n* 1 ulífúmú (especially used
   about advisor to the chief) 2 unsoki
advocate (UK), **lawyer** *n* umwimililí,
   ummanyandagilo, unjiili
adze *n* imbiiso
affair *n* inongwa, imbombo
affection *n* ubwígane, ubunyonywe,
   ulugano
affirm *vt* títíkisya
affirmative *adj* -a kutítíkisya
afflict *vb* bafya, súlúmanía, fúlasya
affliction *n* ubusúlúmaníe, ubutolwe
afford *vb* bagila
afraid *adj* -a booga, -a kutíila, -tílísya
   be afraid *vb* tíila
Africa *pn* Afílíka
African *adj* -a Afílíka
African *n* (person) untítu
after *prep* 1 (in time) bo, panyúma
   2 (behind) panyúma pa
afterbirth *n.anat* ilínyama
afternoon *n* 1 pamúsi 2 (evening grazing time) ilílunduko
afterwards *adv* panyúma, píítasí
again *adv* kangi, ulwa bubili
against *prep* pamwanya pa
age *n* ifyinja fya bukusí, untúndú
agegroup *n* ingulilo, untúndú
agent *n* 1 (spy) umpelelesí, untendeesí
   2 (for merchandise) uju ikumuu-
   likísya ujungi utundu twake

aggression *n* ubwíte, ikilugu
agitate *vb* jugaanía, kalalisya
agnostic *n* uju íkwínogona ukuti Kyala
   akajako, pamo ifí fítikuboneka fíkajako
ago *adv* íjolo long ago íjolo fííjo
   how long ago? ukwanda ndilí?
   ten days ago bukindíle ubusiku mulongo
   He left two days ago Asokílepo
   ubusíku bubili ubu bukindíle
agony *n* ulubabo ulunywamú, ingubilo
   ingalí, ulutamígwo ulukulumba
agree *vb* ítika
agreement *n* ulwítikano, ulufííngo,
   ubufwanía
agriculture *n* ikilimo
ahead *adv, adj* nkyení
aid *n* ubutuulí
aid *vt* tuula
AIDS *n.med* (Acquired Immune Defi-
   ciency Syndrome) ubukímwí
aim *n* inyango
   to take aim ukululikila inyango,
   ukukonga inyango
aim *vt* ínogonela;
   Aim the gun at that buffalo over
   there Lulika indúsú pa mbogo jila
air *n* imbepo, umuují
airline *n* ilísílika lya ndege
airmail *n* ikalata isí síkwenda mundege
airplane *n* indege
airport *n* ikibaanja kya ndege
alarm *n* ilíísyu lya kunangisya ubutolwe, ulukoolelo, inguto
albino *n* seluselu
alcohol *n* ubwalwa
alcoholic *n* ungaalabwalwa
alcoholic *adj* -a kugalisya, -a bwalwa
alcoholism *n* ubugaalabwalwa
alike *adj* -fwene, -a lusumo lumo
alimony *n* ifyuma ifya kuntuula unkííkulu uju asokíle
alive *adj* -umí
all *det, adv, pron, n* -oosa (toosa, ...)

all right *interj* kanúnú, momúmo

allegiance *n* ulwítiko kubalongosí

allocation *n* ikijabo

allotment *n* ulujabanío, ikijabo

allow *vb* ítikisya

allowance *n* inyongesya ja pamwanya pamfwalo, inyongelapo ja …

almost *adv* kifúkí

alone *adj* -eene, -eene ítolo, -pina

along *adv, prep* pamopeene, mumbafu mwa; **get along** pilikisanía
  Bring your parents along Gwisege nabapaapi bako

aloud *adv, adj* kwísyu ilya pamwanya, kwísyu ilya kulata

alphabet *n* isopelo sya njobelo

already *adv* ilíísyu lya kunangisya ukuti akaandu kabombígwe kamalike
  He has already finished the job Abombíle imbombo jake amalíle

also *adv* kangi, pamopeene

altar *n.relig* **1** (place where sacrifices are offered) pabwikemekesyo **2** (table on which bread and wine are consecrated in communion services) ikigemo, imeesa ja ifyakulya ifíkemo

alter *vt* sanúsya, andula
  be altered *vi* sanúka, anduka

although *conj* paalema, nalinga, napaapo

altitude *n* ubwínufú

altogether (entirely, on the whole) *adv* loosa, pamopeene
  I don't altogether agree with him Ndíkwítikana nagwe loosa

always *adv* bwíla, bwílabwíla, akabalilo koosa, ubusíku boosa

a.m. *adv* isala sya lubunju, nulubunju, akabalilo ka lubunju

am *vb (> be)* ndi
  I am a boy Ndi ndumyana
  I am in Ipinda Ndi pa Ípinda
  I am rich Ndi nnoge

amaze *vb* swígisya, gasula, nyomosya
  be amazed *vb* swíga, nyomoka

amateur *n* uju íkubomba imbombo bo

ukelemba ifífwaní, ukwímba inyímbo, ukukína imíkíno kubwígane bwake ítolo kisíta mfwalo gogoosa

amazement *n* ikiswígo

ambassador *n* umwimililí nkíísú ikingi

ambition *n* ulunyonywo ulunywamú

ambulance *n* ilígali lya kupimbila ababíne

ambush *vt* sígila

ammunition *n* silaha (Swa)

among *prep* pakati na pakati, pakati pa

amount *n* ubwíngí

amputate *vt* búúta ikiboko pamo ikiluundi

amulet *n* indúmba

amuse *vt* sekeesya, hobosya

amusement *n* uluhobosyo, ulusekeesyo

anaesthetic *n.med* unkota ugu gukugalisya

analyze *vt* lingaanía

ancestor *n.fam* unsyuka, imísyuka

anchor *n* ingímú

ancient *adj* -a íjolo

and *conj* na, ni, nu

anecdote *n* akapaango, akapaango akapímba (akakusekeesya) aka kíkumpanga umúndu jumo ugwa naloolí pamo isí syaboníke naloolí

angel *n* ugwandumí

anger *n* ilyojo, ingímbuko, ingalalisí, ulukalalo

angle *n* ingúto

angry *adj* -kali, -a ngalalisí, ngalalifú, -kalale
  be angry *vb* kalala

animal *n* ikinyamaana
  domesticated ~ ikinyamaana ikitímígwa
  wild ~ ikinyamaana kya ndiisu

ankle *n.anat* ulupúúto, akapúúto

anklet *n* ilíkosa lya mmalundi, ikikuba

announce *vt* fúmúsya, tangasya

announcement *n* ulufúmúsyo, ukutangasya

annoy *vb* angalila, katasya, tamya, kalasya; **be annoyed** kalala, tamígwa

annual *adj* -a nkyinja

annul *vt* omola, sosyapo

another *adj* -ngi (-jingi, -jungi -bungi,

(place) -pangi)

answer *n* ulwamúlo

answer *vb* **1** (a question) amúla, búsya **2** (when called) amúla, ítika

ant *n.zool*

  brown ant ilyungulu

  black ant ilínyegesí, ilíndúndú

  large, black ant indukwe

  small ant ingeesa, akanyegesí

  type of ant mwalukama

  type of brown ant pamba

anteater *n.zool* mwimba

antelope (generic) *n.zool* ikikolo kya kinyamaana ikikifwene bo akasya; imbabala

antenna *n* **1** (radio) ielía **2** (feeler of an insect) imbembe ibili sya mmanyegesi

anthill *n* (termite/ant structure or mound) ikyulu

antibiotic *n.med* unkota ugu gukugoga utulwa numbili

antidote *n.med* unkota gwa kuteesya ubutege; unkota gwa kugoga ubutege

anus *n.anat* ikiníelo, ingafi, ikyamafi

anxious *adj* -a lutende, -a lupaasyo

be anxious *vb* paasya, -ja numpaasyo

any *det, pron, adv* syosyoosa, lyolyoosa, gwegweesa

any kind of -o-oosa -la (lyolyoosa lila, etc.); **any kind of traditional dance** ilíng'oma lyolyoosa lila

anyone *pron* gwegweesa

anything *pron, adv* kokoosa

anywhere *adv* popoosa, kokoosa, nakúmo, napamo, namúmo

apart *adv* pa mbali, pa butalí, pasíma

apathy *n* ikipahu

ape *n.zool* gúmbe unywamú, salila uny-wamú

apologize *vb* laamba, suuma uluhobokelo

apology *n* uluhobokelo

apostasy *n* soka nkipanga ikya bo sígwa

apostle *n* untumígwa

apparently *adv* kubweelu

appeal *n* (legal) ubukiinde

appeal *vb* **1** (please) sekeesya **2** (request) pílula, kinda ninongwa

appear *vb* boneka, sakuka, sokoka

appearance *n* uluboneko

appease *vb* subisya, batamísya

appendicitis *n.med* ububíne bwa uloobe lwa bula ubunandi

appendix *n.anat* uloobe lwa bula ubu-nywamú

appetite *n* ubunyonywe bwa fyakulya, ikinyonywo kya fyakulya, ifíndu

applaud *vt* **1** (clap hands) kuba ingufí, koma ingufí, koma amaanja **2** (ululate) lúlútila

applause *n* amaanja, ingufí

apple *n.bot* ilípofelí

apply *vb* suuma

appoint *vt* lagila, sala

appointment *n* ulusalo

appreciate *vb* ítikila, igana

approach *vt* segelela, isa kifukí

approve *vt* ítika, ítikila

approximately *adv* kifukí

April *n* umwesí gwa buna

apron *n* umwenda ugu gukufwalígwa kukipambaga numpiiji

arable land *adj* ikifuja, pabagíle ukulimígwa

arbitrate *vb* amúla

arc *n* ikipande kya busyungutíle

arch *n* ubupindo

archbishop *n.relig* umpúútí unkulumba fííjo, asikofú unkulumba

area *n* akaaja, ikijabo kya kíísu

argue *vb* jobesanía, kanikana

argument *n* ukujobesanía, ulukanikano

arise *vb* súmúka, ima

ark (Noah's ~) *n.relig* ingalaba

arm *n* ikiboko, ulukongí

arm *vt* íja ni fílwilo

armpit *n.anat* mmaapa

arms *n.pl* (weapons) ifilwilo

army *n* ikilundilo kya balwabwíte, ilíjesí

around *prep, adv* imbafu syoosa, uku-syungutila

arrange *vt* baatika, tendekesya
arrangement *n* ulubaatiko, ukutendekesya
arrest *vt* kola, kola untulanongwa
arrival *n* ulufíko, ukufíka
arrive *vb* fíka
arrogance *n* amatíngo, ubugaasí
arrogant *adj* íja namatíngo, ugwa matíngo
arrow *n* akatonolelo
art *n* ubumaganyí
artery *n.anat* ulukole
arthritis *n.med* ubwísule bwa kiluungo
artist *n* ummaganyí
artistic *adj* -a bumaganyí, -maganyífú
as *adv* bo, ngati, bo buno, bo bunobuno
as *conj* liinga
as soon as *adv* mbimbibi
ascend *vt* kweela, fyuka
ashamed *adj* íja nisoní
  be ashamed íja nisoní, ífwa isoní
ash *n* umfwandilo
ashtray *n* ikya kubikila umfwandilo
aside *adv* pambali
ask (a question) *vb* laluusya, anía
ask for, request *vt* suuma, laluusya, laamba
asleep *adj* be asleep gona utulo
  he is asleep agoníle utulo
asphalt *n* ilamya
ass *n* 1 *n.zool* imbúnda 2 *n.off* amataanga, ikikúlú, unkonyofú
assemble *vt* agana, komaana, bungaanía
  be assembled bungaana
assembly *n* ulubungaano, ulukomaano
asshole *n.off* ikiníelo, ikyamafí
assist *vt* tuula
assistance *n* ubutuulí
assortment *n* ikilundilo kya tundu
asthma *n.med* ububíne bwa kipambaga
astonish *vb* swígisya, gasusya, gasula
be astonished *vb* gasuka, swíga
astonishment *n* uluswígo, ikitengusí
at *prep* ku, pa
  at home pakaaja, kukaaja

at last kubumalikisyo
at once nakalinga, lululu, kamokene
atheist *n* umpaanja (The word does not really carry the meaning of atheist, but rather that of a non active believer or sb who is outside of a religious community.)
athlete *n* uju íkutolana mmíkíno
atmosphere *n* umpalaanga gwa kumwanya
attack *vt* gwilila mbwíte, sígila, koma
attend *vt* japo
attention *n* akajiilo ka kupilikisya nukugolosya inyinogono, ulupilikisyo
attempt *n* ulwíjuulo, ulugelo
attitude *n* injila ja kwínogonela / kwíbona; akajiilo ka kugubika umbili, indúmbúla
attract *vb* pela ubunúnú, nyonyofya
auction *n* unnaalo
auctioneer *n* unnaalí
audible *adj* -a kupilikígwa
audience *n* ulubungaano lwa bandu pakukeeta pamo ukupilikisya fímo, ulukomaano lwa bandu
August *n* umwesí gwa lwele
aunt *n.fam* 1 (Mother's elder sister, woman married to father's elder brother) juuba/mama unkulumba
  2 (Mother's younger sister, woman married to father's younger brother) juuba/mama unnandi
  3 (Father's sister) unnyasenga
  4 (Woman married to mother's brother) unkasí gwa umwípwa
  /The word mama (from Swahili) is nowadays replacing the Nyakyusa juuba
author *n* uju asímbíle kalata, unsímbí
authority *n* amaka, ubulambikí, ululagilo, ubutwa
autopsy *n* ubuketi ubwakunkenta umúndu uju afwíle ukumanya iji jingogíle
autumn (UK) *n* Imyesí igi amaní gíkulagala nu kúúma ukufuma mmípíkí

pakatipa lumu ni kisíkú. Mbulaja na mu Amelíka "fall, autumn" jilipakati pa septemba na nofemba. (umwesí gwa lwele na kamo na umwesí gwa kalongo na kamo)
/US **fall**

available *adj* -kwagígwa, -lípo
  be available agígwa

aversion *n* ingalalisí, ulubengo

avocado *n.bot* (Swa parachichi) unkasokela, kasokela, ilíkatapela, unkatapeela

avoid *vt* -íjepusya, epuka, epusya

awake *vi* lembuka, súmúka, íja maso, íja ngenge
  he is awake ali maso, alembwíke
  awake *adj* -li maso

award *n* fwika kamo ukukongana nifífíbombígwe

away *adv* kubutalí, -a kutalí

axe *n* indwanga

axle *n* ikyela iki amagulutumu ga ígali giikolílemo

Bb

baboon *n.zool* gúmbe, kakí

baby *n* unníní, umwana gwa kumaboko

bachelor *n* unnyambala unkeenja

back *n* inyúma

back *adj* -nyúma, -a nyúma, kunyúma

backbone *n.anat* akakang'ang'a ka nyúma

background *n* ubufúmo

backward *adj* kunyúma, (munyúma)

backwards *adv* kyanyúmanyúma, kinyúmenyúme
  As he was walking backwards he bumped into the wall Bo ikwenda kyanyúmanyúma alitikile mwimato
  /kinyúmenyúme comes from Swahili

bad *adj* -bíbí, onangike, -onange

badge *n* ikimanyílo

badger *n.zool* akanyamaana aka kikujammabwe

badly *adv* kabíbí

baffle *vb* swígisya, onanga

bag *n* ikinyambi

baggage *n* ikitwalo, untwaalo

bait *n* ubulílí (sipulila)

bake *vt* okya (inyama, ikisyesye)

balance *n* ubufwaníe eg. ubusíto

balance *vb* fwanía

bald *adj* -a kipaala;
  be bald -ja kipaala

baldness *n* ikipaala

ball *n* umpila

ballast *n* íbwe pamo ikyela ikisíto iki kikubikígwa musítíma ukuti jijege sito jingajigilaga kummbelo

balm *n* akandu akakikuponesya pamo kikubatamisya

bamboo *n.bot* ilílaasí

bamboo juice *n* ubulaasí

ban *vb* kaanísya

banana *n.bot* **1** (generic) ihalale
  2 (types) gúlútú, ihalale, ikambaaní, ilítookí, indiifú, indyalí, ingego, isilya, kaluma, buganda, imwamú-

nyíla (Tuk), mwamnyíla (Kye) etc. **3**
n (cooked banana/banana dish): imbalaga, ilífúfú **4** (ripe banana) ilíbifú
banana bunch *n* untúmbúla
banana bunchlet *n* (Swa chana) ikipambo
banana plant *n.bot* ikijinja
banana plantation *n* ingaaja
band *n* (musicians) ikilundilo kya ba-
moga ndíngala
bandage *n.med* ikitambaala kya kupí-
nyila ikiloonda
bandit *n* undeebí, unhiijí
bang *vb* koma, kong'onda
banish *vb* abula
bank *n* **1** (riverbank) ulupaanga; **the
opposite bank** ísilya lila, pambali pa-
lwisi **2** (financial) ibenkí, kúbúsungo
indalama
banknote *n* inotí sya benki
bankrupt *adj* -malikilwe, -londoke
bankrupt *vb* londosya; **be bankrupt,
be poor** londoka
banner *n* ibendela, indembeela
bao *n* isolo
/type of game
baobab *n.bot* umbuju
baptize *vt.relig* osya
baptism *n.relig* uloosyo
bar *n* **1** (iron) ikyela ikitalítalí,
(wooden) ikipíkí, ikisínga **2** (pub) ikilabú
bar *vt* sígila, sígilila, kaanísya
barbarous *adj* akakakaja nu lwiho
(akakali) akandu akasítakisa, akakali
barbed wire *n* isambo isya mifwa,
isenyenge (Swa)
barber *n* ummwa nywílí, ummeta nywílí
bare *adj* ítolo, -kisíta nakamo (nafímo)
bargain *vb* pilikisanía unteengo,
ítikana unteengo
bark *n* **1** (of tree) ilíkandi lya mpíkí;
piece of bark ikipaatu; **2** (dog's) ulukemo

bark *vb* kema
barn *n* indamba nilítembe
barrel *n* **1** (of a gun) unndomo gwa
ndusu **2** (cask) ilípíípa
barren *adj* **1** (land) -umú **2** (unable to
bear young) -gumba
barter *vb* usanía utundu
base *n* (bottom part) ulwalo; **military
base** pabujo bwa íjesí
basic *adj* -a kubwandilo, -a paasí
basin *n* **1** indelema, íbesení **2** (river-)
umbwandabwanda
bask *vb* ota umoto, otela ulumu
basket *n* ikikapu **1** ikitundu /Small basket with two handles **2** ikííbo, ikííbo
kya pabosí /the square-based basket
commonly seen in ubuNyakyusa
which is blackened by smoke, made
from grasses called ulusísí **3** ulupapike /small almost flat basket used
to put food in at the table **4** uluselo /
winnowing basket
bastard *n.off* unsígwana
bat *n.zool* ilípúlúmúsí
bathe *vt* oga
bathroom *n* ikyogelo
battle *n* ubwíte
bay *n* ilíkúnda
be *vt* -ja, ija, ukuja
beach *n* kumbali kunyanja / kwasumbi
apa pali nunsanga nisangalabwe
bead *n* ulunyambo
beak *n* undomo gwa njuní
bean *n.bot* ululima
   type of climbing bean amangamba
bear *n.zool* ikinyamaana kinywamú
kisíto ikya nsyoja mwíngí mummbili
iki kikutugala nkisu ikya mbepo
bear *vt* **1** (tolerate) íkasya **2** (children)
paapa **3** (bear fruit etc) sanga
bear twins pasa
beard *n* indefú
facial hair *n* ululefú
beast *n* ikinyamaana
beat *vt* **1** (hit) koma **2** (win over) tola **3**

pufúla
beautiful *adj* -núnú
beauty *n* ubunúnú
because *conj* kunongwa ja, panongwa
ja, kusyanaloolí sya, paapo, namanga
become *vt* -ja, ukuja, ukuja múndu; **He
became a famous man because of
his honesty** Alinkuja múndu mfú-
múke kunongwa ja bwanaloolí bwake
bed *n* **1** ikitala; **go to bed** buuka kalambalale (buuka nkugona utulo)
2 (flowerbed) ulusínde
bed sheet *n* ilígolole
bedbug *n.zool* ingúngúní
bedroom *n* kusofú, pabugono, kumalundi
bee *n.zool* ulujukí
beef *n* inyama ja ng'ombe
beehive *n* ungogoma, ung'oma, ilítenene
beer *n* ubwalwa;
    finger millet beer ikipúmú
bee-sting *n* ululila lwa njukí
beeswax *n* umpúlya
beetle *n.zool* ilíkakafúla
before *prep* nkyení, bo akaali,
    bobukaali, ngaaníla, bo -kaali; **before
    I die** bo ngaali ukufwa; **before he
    goes to sleep** bo akaali ukugona utulo
beg *vb* pyelesya, suuma, laamba
beggar *n* unsumilisí, unsumí
begin *vt* **1** anda, sasanía
beginning *n* ubwandilo, ubutasí
behave *vb* íjimika
behavior *n* ulwendo, akajiilo
behead *vb* búúta untu
behind *prep* kunyúma, panyúma
belch *n* imbyu, ulubaato
belch *vb* baata
belief *n* ulwítiko
believe *vt* ítika
believer *n* umwítikí
belittle *vb* bonela
belong *vb* ija pabujo pamo
bell *n* ilíbangala (small ornamental
    bell) injiisí
    church bell ilíbangala lya kyalíkí

belly *n* ulwanda
belongings *n* utundu twa
below *prep* paasí, paasí pa
belt *n* umpango, unsípí
bench *n* ikikota ikitalítalí
bend 1 *vt* bilamika, ínamika, goonja
    2 *vi* bilama, ínama, pínda
beneath *prep* paasí pa, kuusi ku
benefit *vb* kaba, nogela
bent *adj* bilamufú, níongafu
bereaved person (one whose relative
    has died) *n* umfwíle
berry *n.bot* ilítunda íníní ilya mbejú nkati
beseech *vb* suuma fííjo, pyelesya
beside *prep* pambali pa
besides *conj* pamwanya pa
best *adj* -núnú fííjo
bet *vb* fínga nihela
betray *vb* leejela, tungulupila
betroth *vb* síngila
better *adj* -núnú ukukinda, paakípo
    Jim is a better student than James
    Jim íkubomba kanúnú kusúkúúlú
    ukukinda James
    get better pona, bumbuluka, nya-
    galuka
    is he better? agonílepo?
    alikanúnúpo? abumbulwikepo?
between *prep* pakati, pakati na pakati pa
beware *vb* gwandege (> anda), -íja
    maso (> -ja maso), íjaalila (> ala), íja
    ngenge; **Beware of the dog!**
    Ijaalilaga nimbwa; **In crowds one
    must beware of thieves** Pabwingí
    gwi jaalilege na bahiijí; Nkilundilo
    umúndu ajege maso nabahiji
bewitch *vt* pííta, loga, endenda
beyond (place) *prep, adv* ukukindapo
    pa, ulubafú lwa bubili
beyond (measure) *prep* kisíta unteengo,
    ukukindapo, nkyení
Bible *pn* (kyaNgonde) Baibulo, Bibilia,
    Ilíbangilí
bicycle *n* injiinga
bid *vb* (invite) koolela

big *adj* -nywamú, -kulumba
  bigger nywamúpo, kulumbapo
  biggest nywamú fííjo, kulumba fííjo
  My basket is bigger than your basket Ikikapu kyangu kinywamúpo kukyako
bigamy *n* inongwa ja kuja ni mítala (abakííkulu babili) ubwegí bwa bakííkulu babili
bikini *n* imyenda imípepe igi bikufwala abalindwana na bakííkulu pako-ogelela
bile *n.anat* akanyongo, inyongo, akakali
bilharzia *n.med* ingeleketa
bilingual *adj* -a njobelo íbili
bill *n* 1 (to pay) ikipande 2 (beak) undomo gwa njuní
billy goat *n.zool* imbene imbongo
bind *vt* pínya (nulugoje pamo ningolya)
bird *n.zool* injuní
birth *n* ikikolo, ubupaapí, ubuteelí
  give birth fyelúka, paapa
birthday *n* ilísíku lya kupapígwa
birthmark *n.anat* ingosyo
biscuit *n* ibisikuti
bishop *n.relig* umpúútí unkulumba
bit *n* akajabo akanandi
bitch 1 *n.zool* imbwa ingííkulu 2 *n.off* undogwe
bite *vt* luma
bitter *adj* -noga ubukali, -kali
bitterness *n* ubukali
bizarre *adj* -heesya fííjo
blab *vb* sabaja, bwabwata
black *color.adj* -títu
blacksmith *n* umponda fyela, umpoosí
bladder *n.anat* ilípúútilo
blade *n* 1 (knife) kububutilo kummage, ubupapate 2 *n.anat* (shoulder) umfúpa umpapate nkibeja
blame *vb* sítaaka
blank *adj* -a bwasí
blanket *n* imbulangete, ingokoma
blaspheme *vb* jobela kabíbí kyala nu tundu utwíkemo

blasphemy *n* injobelo inyalí kwa kyala nu tundu utwíkemo
blaze *n* ululapí, ububúkúke
bleak *adj* -talalifú
bleat (cry of goat or sheep) *vb* ukulila ngati ng'osí, meeta
bleed *vb* sooka ilílopa
blemish *n* ikilema, akababye
blend *vb* onganía, ongana, egana akajiilo
bless *vb* saja
blessing *n* ulusajo
blind *adj* -puufú, -fwa maso
blind person *n* umfwamaso
  become blind ifwa maso
blindness *n* ubufwa maso
blink *vb* píínía
bliss *n* ukutengaana, ukuhoboka fííjo
blister *n.med* ilíjugunju
block *n* ikipíkí, ikikongotí, ilípamba inywamú, ikisínga
blood *n.anat* ilílopa
bloom *vb* soosya ubulenge, baaluka
blossom *vb* baaluka, soosya ubulenge
blouse *n* ibulausí
blow *vb* (wind) kúla, (with mouth) púúta, (the nose) penga, (wind) beleluka, (fire) kubilila
blue *color.adj* -bululu
  light blue -bululu -njwejwe
  dark blue mwakinyomo
bluff *n* ubusyobí, ubutungulu
bluff *vb* syoba
blunder *n* ulusobo, ubusobí bwa bulema
blunder *vb* (in work) soba, onanga, nyasya
blunt *adj* -suufú
  this knife is blunt ummage ugu nsuufú
blur *vt* onanga, fúmbisya
boar *n.zool* ingulube imbongo
board *n* (flat lumber) ilítapwa
board *vb* ípaka, kweela
boarding school *n* isúkúúlú ja kugona papo
boast *vb* ífúna, ítúfya, íbona, ítúmba

boasting *n* ulwítúfyo, ukwíbona, ik-itúsú, amítúúmbo

boat *n* ilíbotí, ingalaba

body *n* umbili

body hair *n.anat* ulusyoja

body odor *n* ukupeha kwa mbili, ulunusi lwa mbili

bog *n* ilítubwí

boil *n.med* ilyulu

boil *vi* sefúka, kína
  The water has boiled Amiisi gaki-níle; Amiisi gasefwíke

boil *vt* sefúsya

boisterous *adj* -a mwalo

bold *adj* -kífú, -a bukifú

bolt *vb* ígala

bomb *n* ilíbomú

bond *n* ikifúngo

bondage *n* ubutumwa

bone *n* ikifúpa, umfúpa, ulufúpa

bonus *n* ubuhombígwa pamwanya pa mfwalo

booby trap *n* untego ugu gukugoga pamo ukufúlasya linga gusalígwe paasí

book *n* ikitabu, ikalata

boom *n* ukukeelwa kwa tundu

boost *vt* ínula, kwesya

boot *n* ikilato iki kifyukíle mumbúto

booth *n* ikitembe

booze *n* ubwalwa

border *n* umpaka

border *vb* pakana

bore *vb* **1** (annoy) katasya **2** (a hole) pegesa, sotola

born *vb.pass* -papígwa
  He was born after independence Apapígwe bo ikíísu kííkabile

borrow *vb* asíma, kopa

bosom *n.anat* ikipambaga, indúmbúla

boss *n* unkulumba, umwimililí pambombo jimo

both *conj* na, ni, nu

both *adj* bosa -babili, -a tundu tubili

bother *n* akaandu, imbombo pamo aka-jiilo akalukatasyo, umpasyo

bother *vb* angalila, katasya
  don't bother síkajanumpasyo, unga-pasyaga

bottle *n* isúpa

bottom *n* paasí, kuusi
  at the bottom of paasí pa, kuusi ku

bough *n* ulusamba ulunywamú

boulder *n* ulwalabwe pamo íbwe ínywa-mú bo lwa íbwe ili amiisi galisyu-ngutíle

bounce *vi* nyeela, tonoka

bound *vb* ija mpaka gwa biika ubutu-múlilo

boundary *n* umpaka

bovine *adj* ngati ng'ombe

bow *n* ikipindo, ubupinde, ulupindo

bow *vb* ínama

bowel, bowels *n.anat* ubula, imíla

bowl *n* ibakúlí

box *n* ilíbokosí

box *vb* búlíka

boxer *n* umúndu uju nkoma mbulí

boy *n* undumyana

boyfriend *n* **1** unganígwa undumyana **2** (boy- or girlfriend) ikigane

boycott *vt* síla, leka, piika

bracelet *n* ulukengele, akapeka, ilíkosa, ibangili

brag *vi* inenga, ítúfya

braid *n* ubuluke

braid *vb* luka

brain *n.anat* ubongo

brake *n* iblekí

brake *vi* imika

branch *n* ulusamba

brand *n* ikibonesyo, ikinangisyo

brass *n.metal* ikikuba
  /Ikikuba is used for any reddish metal

brassiere, bra *n* isíndilila

brat *n* umwalo, umwana ugwa mwalo

brave *adj* -kífú, -gaasí

bravery *n* ubukífú

brawl *n* ubwíte bwa kutukana (ukutuka-na), ukuumana

146

bray *n* ukutama kwa mbúnda

bread *n* ikisyesye

breadth *n* ubwelefú, ububaalufú

break *vb* konyola, bugujula, goga, menya

be broken konyoka, bugujuka

break a promise kílanía ulwítikano

break a custom kílanía ikimíla

break down *vb* pangalatula

breakfast *n* ifya kulya fya lubunju, ifya kulabuuka

breast *n.anat* ilíbeele

breastfeed *vb* ongesya

breath *n* umuují

breathe *vb* tuuja, kwaba umuují

breathless *adj* kisíta kuja numuují, kisíta kutuuja

breed *vi* paapa, ongela, teela, teelesya, enda, endekesya

breeze *n* akapepo akanúnú, imbepo inúnú

brevity *n* ubupímba (amasyu), ubunandi bwa masyu

brew *vt* piija ubwalwa

bribe, bribery *n* uluswa

bribe *vb* soosya uluswa; soosya ikyuma kumundu ukuti akujíle isí sikwagíle /From Swahili

brick *n* ilípamba

bride *n* unkííkulu gwa bwegí

bridegroom *n* unnyambala gwa bwegí

bridge *n* ululalo

brief *adj* -a kubupímba

bright *adj* -múlika, -langafu

brilliant *adj* -langala fíljo, -a mahala míngí fíljo

brim *n* kukanwa ku kikombe, ibakulí, indelema etc; ulugenge

bring *vt* twala

bring back *vb* búsya, gomosya, gomola

bring near segelesya

bring up swila, kusya

brisk *adj* -a maka, -a kukuja

brink *n* kumbali (kulwisí)

broad *adj* -eleefú

broadcast *vt* fúmúsya, balanía

broil *vt* pija inyama pa moto, okya inyama pa moto

broiler *n.zool* inguku ja nyama

broke *slang.adj* (to be without money) -malikilígwa nihela, londoka

broken *adj* -konyoke, iji jikonywíke, iji jitolíígwe, -bugujufú

brood *n* akaana, utumwana twa nguku

brood *vb* alamíla, ísúnyata

brook *n* akiisí, akakololo

broom *n* umwejo

broth *n* umposí gwa nyama níseeke

brother *n.fam*

younger brother unnuguna

elder brother unkulu

/elder brother of brother or elder sister of sister

brother-in-law *n.fam* undamú, mulamu, semekí

brow *n.anat* 1 (forehead) ikyení 2 (eyebrow) ulukope, ulusígesíge

brown *color.adj* fúfúlwisí

light brown -fúbifú, -bungu

/fúbifú goes from brown to red and fúfúlwisí from ash-colored or grey to brown

browse *vb* 1 (casually inspect) eneesya 2 (feed on leaves) liisya amaní, tafúna amaní, ílya ilíísú

bruise *vb* pujula, pujuka

brush *n* umwejo, ibulasí

brush *vb* pyagila, pyasiila, pyagiisya

brutal *adj* -síta kisa

bubble *n* untotofúla, imbwíbwí

buck *n.zool* akasya akapongo

bucket *n* indobo

bud *n* akamelelo, ikisíge kya lubejú

budget *n* ukupanga ifya kukaba nukubombela

buffalo *n.zool* imbogo

bug *n.zool* akambakasya aka kafwene ni ngúngúní

build *vt* jenga

builder *n* unjengí

building *n* inyúmba

bulb *n* **1** (lightbulb) itala **2** (root shaped like onion) imbuje; akabúlúnge bo ikitungulu

bulge *n* ubwísúle

bull *n.zool* ingambaku

bulldozer *n* katapila

bullet *n* ilísasí

bulletproof *adj* aka katikwingilígwa nísasí

bull's eye *n* pakati pa bulengelo inyango mu nkino gwa kulasa ni milúnda nu bupinde

bullshit *interj.off* sya bulema! inongwa sya butoȷofú

bully *vt* saaka, katasya, kínila

bum *n* (beggar) umúndu umoolo, umúndu unsuumí

bumble-bee *n.zool* uluȷúkí ulunywamú

bump *vb* kinya, tíka, ikínya

bun *n* ikisyesye ikiníní

bunch *n* (of fruit) ikikose, akasamba (ulusamba lwa seke) umfúngúla ~ **of bananas** untúmbúla

bundle *n* ikikose, untwaalo, ikibugutila, ikitwalo, ulukose

bung *n* ikifundiko

buoy *n* ilítúmbú, ilítúmbú lya lusípulilo, akaandu aka kíkweelela

burden *n* untwaalo, unsígo

burglar *n* unhijí, undeebí, uju ikukweela nnyúmba

burial *n* ukusyila, ulusyilo

burial ground/place *n* kumapumba, ilísyeto

burn *vb* kosya, aka, nyaasya

burp *vb* baata

burrow *n* ikíína, ubwína

burst *vb* panduka, pufúka

bury *vb* syila

bus *n* ibasí

bush *n* **1** (land) ilítengele **2** (small tree) ikisyanju

bush baby *n.zool* (Swa komba) nng'aa

business *n* ulwípukulanío, imbombo
  it is none of my business ngajamo

une, jika mbombo jangu

busy (to be -) ukuja nulwípúkúlanío, ukwípúkúlanía; ukuja nubwíkolaníe

but *conj* lelo, loolí

butcher *n* pabuulikisyo inyama

butchery *n* ibúkya

butter *n* isyagí, uluketa

butterfly *n.zool* ilíkolokotwa, ilíkolokoto

buttermilk *n* ululufú

buttock *n.anat* ilítaanga, ilítugalilo, amatugalilo

button *n* ilíbítabwe, ikipata

buy *vt* ula

buyer *n* umuulí

buzz *vb* nyííta (ngati njúkí)

by *prep* ni, pa mbali

by chance kulusako

by myself nimwene, jujune

by himself, by herself mwene, jujo

bye bye *interj* **1** ugonege (said by the one who leaves) **2** ukagone (said by the part that stays behind)

byre *n* ikibaga kya ng'ombe

Cc

cabbage *n.bot* ikaabíkí
cabin *n* akúmba akanandi aka musítíma
cable *n* ulugoje ulwa kyela, ulusambo
cacao *n.bot* ilíkooko
cackle *n* ukwana, ukuteta kwa nguku
cackle *vi* ana, teta
cactus *n.bot* umpíkí unsííta maaní ugu gukumela ndungalangala
café *n* inyúmba muno bikuulikisya fyene ifíndu ni kyai pamo ikahabwa kisíta bwalwa
cage *n* akabaga kanandi ka kubikamo ifínyamaana ninjuní
cake *n* ikisyesye ikinyafú, ikekí
calabash *n* ulupaale, ulupindi
calamity *n* inongwa sya busúlamaníe, ubutolwe ubunywamú
calculate *vb* bala, ínogona, bomba imbalilo
calculation *n* imbalilo, inyínogono
caldera *n* ilítúbwí pamwanya pakyamba
caldron *n* indeko, isufulila inywamú
calendar *n* ikalenda
calf *n* **1** *n.zool* ingwaata
    2 (of leg) *n.anat* ilíkiino
call *vb* **1** (summon) koolela, bilikila
    2 (phone) koma isímu
    be called koolelígwa
call on *vb* ponía, buuka kukuketa
callous *adj* -kafú, -kafúkafú, -umíke, kakamafú
calm *adj* -talali, -tengaamú, (of the sea) -jonjolo, -mye ítolo, kimyemye (bota)
calm *vt* subisya, tengaanía
calm sb down batika, beteka, kibisya, talalisya
calve *vt* teela ingwaata, biika
camel *n.zool* ingamila
camp (temporary lodging) *n* ulutuusyo, pabutukisyo
camp *vb* jenga pabutukisyo
can *n* ikikopo
can *vb* bagila
canal *n* umfolo

cancel *vt* omola, sosyapo
cancer *n.med* ikansa; ububíne ubwa mbenga
candle *n* inyale inandi
candlestick *n* ikisonge kya kukolela inyaale; pabwimilo inyaale
candy *n* (Swa pipi) ipípí, ipelemende
cane *n* (walking stick) ingílí
cannabis *n.bot* amakambo
cannibal *n* umúndu undyabandu
cannon *n* unsínga gwa masasí (pamo ung'oma gwa njukí)
canoe *n* ubwato, ingalaba
canyon *n.geo* ulwisí ulu luli ningenge (pamo nisoko pamo nimbanga) indali fííjo
cap *n* (hat) ikitílí, ikipeegwa
capable *adj* -a kubagila ukubomba kamo
cape *n* ulusuungo
capital *n* **1** (city) akaaja akakulumba ka kíísu **2** (cash) untají gwa ndalama
capital *adj* -a muntú, -akubagila fííjo, -nywamú
capitulate *vi* ísosye kundagilo
capsize *vb* kúpúka, petúsya
captain *n* **1** (military) unkulumba gwa basíkali **2** (ship) unkulumba gwa musítíma, undelefwa gwa musítíma
captive *n* umfúngwa (umpupilwa), umúndu uju akolígwe mbwíte
capture *vt* kola, poka
car *n* ilígali
caravan *n* abandu bíngí aba bíkwenda pamopeene injila ja malundi
carcass *n* umfímba gwa kinyamaana
card *n* ikalata, ikipande
cardinal *adj* -nywamú, -ngulumba
care *n* ukukeetelela, ukwimilila
    in the care of mbwimilíle bwa, nkibooko kya
    take care of lindilila, imilila
    handle with care kola kanúnú
care *vi* paasya;
    take care keeta, lindilila, keteege kanúnú;

I don't care po papo, sifwene ítolo, ndikupaasya

care for lwasya, tetema

careful *adj* -a kwíkeeta

careless *adj* sita ku paasya

carelessly *adv* mwalo

carelessness *n* ububwafú, ububwapufú, umwalo, ubwamwalo

caress *n* ulupalamasyo mumbili, uluubatilo lwa lugano

caress *vt* batamísya, kumbatila kulugano

caretaker *n* umwimililí

cargo *n* ifítwalo, ifítwalo fya mwígali, imísígo

take in cargo íngisya, pakila

caries *n* ukubola kwa lííno

carnivore *n* undyanyaama

carpenter *n* umpululí (amatapwa) unselemala, umfundí gwa matapwa

carpet *n* 1 ilítando lya pakitala paasí (kifwene bo unkeka) 2 ubunyasa ubu bikwala pabukanyo pala bikwangala na kumalundi pasi pakitala pabukanyo

carriage *n* ikipímbilo

carrot *n.bot* ikalotí

carry *vb* pimba, paapa

carry on endelela

cart *n* unkokotení, ikigeletí

carve *vb* (wood) songola, tendekesya bunúnú

carving *n* ikifwaní

cascade *n* imbúgújo

case *n* akajiilo, (legal) inongwa

cash *n* ihela, indalama sya kubombela, indalama isí sili mmaboko

cashew *n.bot* unkoloso

cashew nut *n.bot* ilíkoloso

cask *n* ilípíípa

casket *n* ibokosi inandi

cassava *n.bot* ilíjabú

cast a spell *vb* loga, sosya ifííka

castle *n* inyúmba inywamú ija kwíbililamo pabwíte

castor oil *n* amafúta ga nyemba isekele

castor oil plant *n.bot* umpíkí gwa nyemba isekele, ulujemba, unjembajemba

castrate *vt* fúla

castrated *adj* -fule

cat *n.zool* 1 (house cat) níalú, pusí 2 (wild) lembe

cataract 1 (eye disease) *n.med* inyanga 2 (waterfall) *n.geo* imbúgújo, apa amiisi gikugwa

catarrh *n.med* imbungo

catastrophe *n* ubutolwe ubunywamú

catch *n* (fishing) ifikolígwa bo iswí, ilíloba

catch *vt* kola, angila, tega

catch in the act aganía

caterpillar *n.zool* ilífilífilí

cattle *n.zool* ing'ombe

cattle dip *n* ilípí / idípí ja ng'ombe

cattle egret *n.zool* inyangenyange

cattle pen *n* ulupaso lwa ng'ombe

caulk *vb* síndila ingende (ubupandufú)

cause *n* ikipela

cautious *adj* -lindilili, -a lukete lelí, -angalifu

cave *n* imbako

cavity *n* ikíína, akapegeso

caviare *n* amafumbi ga nswí

cease *vb* leka

ceiling *n* kwíjulu, ilíjulu

celebrate *vt* moga, hoboka

celibacy *n* akajiilo ka kusííta kwegígwa / kwega

celibate *adj* -keenja, eg. síta kwega pamo ukwegígwa

cell *n* akafinye

cement *n* isementí

cemetery *n* ilísyeto, pabusyililo abafwe, kumapumba

censor *vb* saagula

center *n* pakati

center *vt* biika pakati

centipede *n.zool* ilípalasila

century *n* ifyinja kalongo mulongo, ifyinja imía jimo

ceramics *n* ububumba ndeko

ceremony *n* ulwangalo, ulusaalo

certain *adj* -a naloolí, kisíta kwilamwa
certainly *adv* syanaloolí, naloolí
certificate *n* ikikyetí
chaff *n* unkupili
chain *n* unnyololo, imbingo
chair *n* ikikota
chairman *n* ugwa pakikota, kyamení
chalk *n* ikyoko
challenge *n* ukukaníka, ukutolana, uku-kanikana
challenge *vb* kaníka, tola
chamber *n* ikyumba
chameleon *n.zool* ulwífí
champion *n* untolí
chance *n* ulusako
change *n* ulwandulo
change *vt* sanúsya, andula
  be changed sanúka, anduka
changeable *adj* -andufú
channel *n* umfwolo, unkolofwa, unko-lolo, apalukwenda ulwisí, umfoolo
chant *n* imba
chaos *n* ubwíte, ukusitakupilikisanía
chaperon *n* unkííkulu uju ikulongosa-nía nu ndindwana
chapter (of book) *n* ulutuulo
character *n* **1** (personality) akajilo, indúmbúla **2** (symbol, sign) isimbo
charcoal *n* unkala, ingalabuka, ingalasila
charge *vb* **1** (sell for) joba unteengo **2** (accuse) sítaaka (ukulingaanía inongwa ja kumelelígwa pamo ukwilamwa)
chariot *n* ikigeletí, igeletí
charity *n* ulugano, ubutengamojo, ubo-ololo
charm *n* (magic) isígíta, unkota gwa kwíponesya pamo ukugoga amaka ga mbepo inyalí pamo ubulosí, imbígíta
chase *vb* **1** (hunt) bopesya, fwima, kagi-sya **2** (chase away) kaga
chat *vb* joba, angala
cheap *adj* -pepe, unteengo unnandi
  become cheap ukuja mpepe, pepuka unteengo, ija gwa malaja
cheat *n* ubusyobí

cheat *vb* syoba, sípula
cheating *n* ulusyobo, ubusyobí
check *n* **1** kalata gwa kwegela ihela kubenkí **2** ikikanísyo
check *vb* sígila, gomolela
cheek *n.anat* ulusaja
cheer *n* uluhoboko, ukusangamka
cheerful *adj* -sangalufu, sangamfu
cheer *vt* hoboka, sangamka
cheese (Swa. jibini) *n.food* ifyakulya ifi fítendekesígwe nulukama ulusíto
cheetah *n.zool* ilípatama, ikinyamana iki kifwene níbole
cherish *vt* tendekesya, lindilila, tufya
chest *n.anat* ikipambaga
chew *vb* tafúna
chew loudly jagúla
chicken *n.zool* inguku
  ~ with short legs kasegano
chicken pox *n.med* indubi, akapene akanywamú
chief *n* umalafyale, unnyafyale, kífí
child *n* umwaníke, umwana
childhood *n* ubwaníke, ubukeke, ubuniní
childish *adj* -keke, -a bukeke
chili *n.bot* imbílípílí
chill *n* imbepo, ihoma ja mbepo
chimney *n* ikya kusokesya ilyosí nyumba
chin *n.anat* ikilefú
China *pn* ikíísu kya Kina
chip *n* ulusenga
choice *n* ubwígane, ulusalo
choir *n* ikwaja
choke *vt* pííta kummilo
cholera *n.med* ikipindupindu
choose *vb* saagula, sala, sungula, isalila, íganapo
chop *n* akamenya
chop *vb* menya, menyanía, buutaníabuutanía
christian *n.relig* umosígwa, unkilisítí
christian *adj.relig* -a bukilisítí
Christmas *n.relig* Ikilisímasí
chronic *adj* imbungo iji jitikuponela mbíbí
church *n.relig* inyúmba ja kwiputilamo,

ikyalíkí, pabwipútilo

cicada *n.zool* ilíng'eng'esí, ilíbubusi, ilíbulubusí

cigarette *n* ingaambo

cinema *n* isenema

circa *prep* (ukukongana na kabalilo) nkati ka

circle *n* ububúlúnge, unsyenga

circular *adj* -búlúnge

circulate *vi* syungutila, syungusya

circumcise *vb* búúta kukyení

circumcision *n* ukubúúta kukyení, ububútígwa bwa kukyení

circumference *n* ikipimilo ikibúlúnge, ubusyungutile

circumstance *n* inongwa (akajiilo ka kugona pakilo)

cistern *n* ilíbilika

citizen *n* umwenekíísu, ugwilima

city *n* akaaja akanywamú, akaaja akanywamú fíijo

civet cat *n.zool* ifungo

civilization *n* ubweluke bwa mmahala

civilized *adj* ubweluke bwa mahala, -a pamwanya (akajiilo)

claim *vt* londa ubwanalolí, mela

clairvoyance *n* ubusololí, ubumanyí sya nkyení

clammy *adj* -akwíníesya, -akusígasíga

clap *vt* kuba amaanja

class *n* **1** (school) ilíkalasí **2** (species) uluko

classify *vt* baatika, jaba

claw *n* ikyala kya kinyamaana bo ingalamú

clay *n* umfú ugwa kubumbila

clean *adj* -eelu, -sukígwe; **become clean** elusígwa, eluka, sukígwa

clean *vt* súka, elusya

cleanliness *n* ubwelu, síta bunyalí, ubwifyusi

clear *adj* -a pabwelú, -eelú
  it is clear to me singolíle (nsyageníe)

clear *vt* tendekesya, elusya

clear up ela; **The sky has cleared up** Kumwanya kwelíle

clearing *n* ulubingilo

make a clearing tendekesya ulubingilo

clergyman *n* unkongí pampúútí

clerk *n* unkalaní

clever *adj* -ene mahala, -komú, -janja

cliff *n* ikigíma, ulugenge, ulupaanga

climate *n* akajiilo nakabalilo kafyinja (amasíkú) bo ulumú, ifúla, imbepo, ulubefú etc.

climb *vb* kweela, fyuka

climb down *vb* ika, suluka

cling *vt* kola, umilila

clinic *n* ikílíníkí, ikipatala

clip *vt* pínya

clock *n* ilísuba, isala inywamú íja pa mesa pamo mwímato

clod *n* **1** (idiot) undema **2** (lump of earth) ilímoma

close *adj* kifúkí

close *vt* ígala, (mouth) fúmbata (kukanwa), (eyes) sísííla, (book) kúpikila, (buttons) bítila

closet *n* ikyúmba kinandi kya kubikamo utundu; ilíbokosí lya kubikamo utundu bo imyenda etc

cloth *n* umwenda, ikitambaala

clothe *vb* fwika, fwala

clothes *n* imyenda, igya kufwala;
  put on clothes fwala umwenda;
  undress fúúla umwenda

cloud *n* ilíbingu

cloud over, become cloudy bilingana

cloudy *adj* -a lubeefú-a mabingu

clove *n.bot* iseke sya nkalafúú

club *n* **1** (association) ikyama, ikilabú **2** (for hitting) ikibúndya, imbúndya, induha

clutch *vb* kola kulutende / kulyojo

clue *n* ikifungula kya buusí

clumsy *adj* -síto

clumsily *adv* -mwalomwalo

cluster *n* ikibugutila kya tundu utu tufwene

coagulate *vb* kaka, paapa

coal *n* unkala gwa mabwe

coal mine *n* ungotí gwa nkala gwa mabwe

coast *n* kumbali kwa sumbi, kumbali
  kunyanja
coastline *n* ulukindi lwa kumbali kunyanja
coat *n* ilíkotí
cob (of corn) *n* ilíkungwe
cobra *n.zool* kííko
cobweb *n* ulububi
cock 1 (rooster) *n.zool* ingongobe
  2 (penis) *n.off* iswímbílí, imbolo
cockroach *n.zool* ilíjenje
cocoa *n* ilíkooko
coconut palm *n.bot* unnasí
cocoyam *n.bot* ilísiimbi
coffee (drink) *n* ikahabwa
coffee tree *n.bot* unkahabwa, umpíkí
  gwa kahabwa
coffin *n* ilíbokosí lya kusyilila
coil *n* ubwíníenganíe, ubupotaníe
coil *vi* níenga, potanía
coin *n* ihela imbúlúlúfú
cold *adj* -mbepo, -talalifú
cold *n.med* amafúa, akakínya
colic *n.med* ukuniongotola kwa palwanda
collapse *vb* panguka, sílika, paguka
collar *n* ikola
collarbone *n.anat* umfúpa gwa pakikosí
collect *vt* bungaanía
collide *vb* tíkana, kínyana
colonize *vb* kaba ikíísu ikingi
colony *n* ikilundilo, ikíísu ikingi; ikíísu
  ikikabígwa na baheesya
color *n* ilangí
colored (of mixed race) *n.off* umonga-
  níe ílopa
colostrum *n* ikiseenga
column *n* imbanda
comb *n* ikisanjulilo
comb *vb* sanjula
combat *n* ubwíte
combatant *n* ujuíkulwa, ugwabwíte
combine *vt* ongaanía, falaganía
come *vi* ísa
come! ísaga!
come from fúma, sooka
come in íngila ísaga

come near to segelela, semapo, sema
comedy *n* imíkino gya kusekeesya
comet *n* ulutondwa lwa nswigala
comfort *n* ulutengaanío, akajiilo kaku-
  tengaana
comfort *vb* subisya, tengaanía
comfortable *adj* -a kutengaanía
become comfortable *vb* ukubikígwa
  kulubaatiko, tengaana
coming (arrival) *n* ulufiko (bujo)
command *n* ululagilo
command *vb* lagila, lagisya,
  komeelesya
commander *n* unkulumba gwa basíkalí,
  undagilí
commandment *n.relig* ingomeelesyo,
  indagilo
commend *n* túfya
commerce *n* ubuulisí nu buulí
commission *n* ululagilo
commit *vt* pínya
committee *n* ikamatí
common *adj* -a bosa, -a bwílabwíla
communication *n* ukwagana mwa
  kalata, musímu nu kujatilana
communion *n.relig* ukuja pamopeene,
  ulutuulano
companion *n* ummanyaaní
company *n* ikampuní
compare *vb* fwaníkisya
compass *n* akaandu aka kikunangisya
  imbafú sya kíísu
compel *vb* fímbilisya
compete *vi* tolana, pambikana
competent *adj* -manyí
competition *n* ulutolano
complain *vb* íbúneesya, lilaníka
complaint *n* ululilaniko, ulwílaamo
complete *adj* aka kafwene ítolo, -oosa
complete *vb* maliisya, tímiilisya
completely *adv* loosa, pya
compliment *n* ulutúfyo
compound *n* ilíkombóní, ikipaanga
  pakaja
comprehend *vb* aganía, syaganía, pi-

lika
compromise *vi* pilikisanía, ítikana, fwana
compulsory *adj* fímbilisígwa, bagilila
computer *n* ikompyúta
conceal *vb* físa, fínda, kínga
conceit *n* amatingo, ulwíbono
conceited *adj* -a nyinogono ingulumba fíijo
conceive *vt* kaba ikifúba, kaba ulwanda
concern *n* ubufúmbwe, inyínogono
concern *vb* ínogonela
concerning (about) *prep* inongwa ja (kunongwa ja)
conciliate *vb* patanía, pilikisanía
conclude *vt* maliisya, malikisya
conclusion *n* ubumalikisyo
concrete *n* unsege
condemn *vb* kola ububíbí
condition *n* akajiilo
condole *vb* subisya, sosya uluponío kubafwile
condolence *n* ubusubiisi, uluponío kubafwíle
conduct *n* ulwendo
conduct *vb* endesya
confess *vt* ítika, fumusya, laata (ubusobí)
confide *vb* subila kusyambutítu
confidence *n* ulusuubilo
confident *adj* -a bukífú
  be confident *vb* subila, kíba, ija nkífú
confidential *adj* -a mbutítu
confirm *vt* sísímíkisya
conflict *n* ubulwane, ubulwe
confront *vt* lwanía
confuse *vt* leganía, alanganía
be confused onangika untú, onangika amahala
become confused onangika
confusion *n* ulutaamyo, ifújo
conger *n.zool* ingunga
congratulate *vt* sekelela
congregation *n* ikipaanga kya kyalíkí

connect *vt* lunga, lungisanía, kamandanía
be connected with kamandana ni
conquer *vb* tola, koma
conqueror *n* untolí
conscience *n* indúmbúla iji jíkusoka
conscious *adj* -manya mundúmbúla
consent *vb* ítika, íkyela
consequence *n* uluboneko
conserve *vt* tendekesya, bikilila
consider *vb* ínogona, kumbuka
consideration *n* ukwinogona, ukwínogonala, uluhobokelo, ulwínogonelo
consist of *vb* íja ni
consolation *n* ulusubisyo, ubusubisí
console *vb* subisya, ípa umojo
conspire *vb* pilikisanía (ukubomba inyalí)
constant *adj* -jitíkusanuka, -a lula lula
constellation *n* ikibugutila kya ndondwa
constipated *adj.med* -síta kupípa, akajilo aka kuuma munda
constipation *n.med* ukuuma kulíísu, ukusitakupípa
construct *vt* tendekesya, jenga
construction *n* ubujengí, ubutendekesí
consul *n* umúndu uju íkwimilila ikíísu nkíísu ikingi
consult *vt* longa inongwa, anía
consultant *n* undinganí ugwa kwaníako símo isya mbumanyí
consume *vt* -ílya
contact *vb* kolana, agana
contain *vb* -ija na
contaminate *vt* onanga, biika ubunyalí
contemplate *vt* ínogona isya mbutalí, ketesya fíijo
contempt *n* amatíngo, ifújo
content *adj* utundú utu tulimo, isí sílímo
be content *vb* ija nuluhobokelo ulwa bwíkyeelo, fwaana
contest *n* ulutolano
continue *vb* endelela

contraception *n* ukwísígila ukumela ulwanda

contract *n* ulwítikano lwa múndu numúndu ukuti kamo kabombígwe (ubwegí, imbombo etc)

contradict *vb* tíkanía

contrarily *adv* lungi

contrary *adj* -legana, -a lusúmo lungi, -a pasima

contrast *n* ukulegana

contribute *vt* sangula

contribution *n* ulusangulo

control *vt* imilila

convalesce *vb* tuusya nu kubumbuluka

convenient *adj* -a kufwana

conversation *n* inyangalo (isya kupanga), ukujobesanía

converse *vb* panga, jobana, angala

convert *n* umpinduke

convert *vt* sanúsya, andula, pindula
  be converted sanúka, lokoka, pinduka

convict *n* umfúngwa, untula nongwa

convince *vb* biika umúndu ukuti amanye

cook *n* umpiijí

cook *vb* piija

cooked *adj* -pijígwe, -pye

cooking-stones *n* amafiga

cooking utensils *n* ifyombo fya kupijila

cool *adj* -talalifú, -batamífu

cool *vb* **1** *vi* talalila, *vt* talalisya **2** (make sb relax) batamisya

cooperative *n* ikyaama

cop *n.slang* umpolísí

copper *n.metal* ikikuba

copulate *vb* **1** (people) gonana **2** (animals) kwelana

copy *vb* ambula, koongesya

cord *n* ulugoje, ulupínyilo

cork *n* ikifúndiko

corn *(US, UK maize) n* ifílombe, ikilombe /you have ifilombe in the field, a single cob is ikilombe and the final product is ifílombe

corner *n* ikona

corpse *n* umfimba

corpulent *adj* -nywamú, -manga, kangi síto

become corpulent/fat *vb* túpa, manguka

correct *adj* -núnú, -a bugolofu, -golofú

correct *vb* tendekesya, golosya

corrugated iron *n* ilílata

corrugated iron sheet *n* ilílata

corrupt *adj* -bofú, -bole, akugana ubusyobí, akugana uluswa, -nyobí

corruption *n* ubusyobí, ubugana luswa

cost *n* untengo
  what does it cost? guli bule untengo gwake?

costly *adj* -a ntengo gwa pamwanya

cottage *n* ikitembe

cotton *n.bot* amasapa, ipamba

cough *vb* kosomola

cough *n* ulukosomolo

council *n* ikanselí, ikanselo

counsel *n* ubusokí

counsel *vb* loongana, soka

count *vi* bala, belenga

counter *n* imesa ja kulikisya utundu

country *n* ikíisu

countryman *n* umwenekíisu

couple *n* ububili

courage *n* ubukífú, ubugaasí

courageous *adj* -maganyí, -kífú, -gaasí

course *n* akabalilo ka busiku, ubulabilo bwa tundu, ikibanja kya mikino, ulukindi lwa mapamba munyumba, ulubaatiko lwa fímanyílo, pamo ukunwa unkota, ukukongesanía kwa fíndu pamesa

court *n* ilíkolotí

courtyard *n* ulubingilo

courtesy *n* ulwíjíisyo, ikisa

cousin *n.fam*
  father's brother's child gwa míetu, gwa míabo, ulílumbu
  father's sister's child untaaní
  mother's brother's child untaaní
  mother's sister's child umwana gwa juuba unnandi pamo unkulumba

cover *n* ikifúndiko, ikikupikililo

cover *vb* finínga, físa, kúpikila, kínga

covet *vb* nyonywa, nyonywa ikyuma kya jungi

covetous *adj* -imi, -nyonywe

cow *n.zool* 1 (cattle) ing'ombe 2 (female cattle) indama, ing'ombe imbiikí, ing'ombe ingííkulu 3 (young cow which has not yet conceived, calf) ingwata

coward *n* umooga

cowardice *n* ubooga

cowardly *adv, adj* -oga

coy *adj* -a soní

crab *n.zool* ingwehe

crack *n* ulwande, ubupandufú, ubupasufu, ubulendemúfú

cradle *n* ikitala ikiníní ikya bana abaníní

craftsman *n* ummaganyí

crafty *adj* -busyobí, -a bumaganyí

cramp *n* akalaso, ikilaso

crash *n* undíndo

crater *n* ikíína kya pakati pa kyamba

crater lake *n* ikisiba ikya pakati pa kyamba

crawl *vi* afula, filífindika

crazy *adj* ugwa kigili

cream *n* uluketa

crease *n* ulukínya

create *vb* pela, bumba

creation *n* ubupelí

creator *n* umbumbí, umpelí

creature *n* ikipelígwa, ikibumbígwa, akapelígwa

creed *n* ulwítiko

creep *vb* afúla, filífindika

crescent *n* umwesí ugu gusomwíke

crevice *n* ulwande ndwalabwe

crew *n* ababomba mbombo mu meelí pamo mundege ukusíta kubalilako abalongosí babo

cricket *n.zool* indení

crime *n* inongwa, ulutulo

cripple *n* undemale

criterion *n* ikigelelo

criticize *vb* londeesya fíijo ubusobe

crocodile *n.zool* ingwíína

crooked *adj* -níongafú

become crooked *vb* níongala

crop *n* ififunjígwa

cross *n* ikikohekano

cross *adj* -ngalalifú

cross-over *vb* (eg. water) loboka, tambuka

crossroad *n* injila imbasana

crotch *n* ikinena

crouch *vb* ínama

crow *n.zool* ilíkungulu, ingungulu

crowbar *n* untalímba

crowd *n* ikilundilo, ulubungaano

crown *n* ingiga

crucify *vt* komela pa kikohekano

cruel *adj* -gogí, -síta kibabilisí

cruelty *n* ubusíta kisa

crumb *n* ulusenga, akabúlúlúkisya

crumble *vb* (with hands) figísa

crutch *n* ingílí (ja kwendela undemale)

crush *vb* 1 pondanía 2 (by pounding) tíkanía

crust *n* ikibafu ikyumu íkya munyuma íkya kísyesye

cry *n* unjwego (gwa boga pamo ububabe), ululilo, ingúúto

cry *vb* lila, kúúta

crystal *n* akabwe akilangali

cub *n* akaana ka ngalamú pamo iboole

cube *n* akandu aka ubwelefu, ubutali nu bupimba bufwene

cucumber *n.bot* ilítango

culminate *vt* fíka pamwanya, malikila

cultivate *vb* lima

cultivation *n* ukulima

culture *n* ulwího, inyíího, imbaatiko

culvert *n.road* umfwolo gwa mpwisí ugu gukwenda kusi kunsebo

cunning *adj* -komú, -engo, -manyí

cunt *n.off* indútú

cup *n* ikikombe, (bamboo cup) ikitana

cupboard *n* ikaabatí

curd *n* ulusenga lwa lukama ulupape

curdle *vb* kaka, paapa

cure *vb.med* ponesya, gangula

curiosity *n* ubulondesi, ubupelelesi

curl *n* ubupíndaníe, ubufílinge

current *adj* -a lululu, -a pípí

current *n* (of water) 1 injila ja miisi
2 (circular) iníongo

curse *n* ikigúne

curse *vt* gúna, pemeesya

curry *n* 1 (powder) akajinja 2 ilíseeke
ili lilungígwe akajinja

curtain *n* umwenda ugu bikusígilila
mmadilisya pamo kikifígo; ilíbaalika

curve *n* ubuníonganifú, ubuníongale,
ubuníongale, ububilamu

curved *adj* -bilamufú, tungamu

cushion *n* imítunda igi gisonígwe
mmwenda, unto gwa kutugalilapo pa
kikota

custard apple *n.bot* (fruit and tree) ilínyele

custom *n* ulwího

customary *adj* -a lwiho, -a kimíla

customer *n* umúúlí, unteja

customs (duty) *n* isongo

customs house *n* inyúmba ja kusongela
isongo

cut *vb* búúta, túmúla, boola
short cut *n* injila ja kupímbula, injila
imbipi

cut hair meta

cut into pieces búútaníabúútanía

cute *adj* -núnú

cutlery *n* ifya kulila ifíndú bo imímage,
ilefaní, inyoselo etc ifí fíkuulisígwa
pamo ukutendekesígwa numpoosí

cycle *n* uluboneko ulu lukuboneka nkabalilo kako kakíngí

cycle *vb* kanya injinga, syungusya

cynic *n* umúndu uju kukuti kandu
kumyake kabíbí kangi ugwa lwífíono
lwíngí

Dd

dab *vb* tonola

dagger *n* ilímage

daily *adj* -a bwílabwíla, bwíla, -a kukuti
isíku

dairy *n* inyúmba ja kubikamo ulukama

dale *n* ulusooko

dam *n* ikisíba; ulupaso ulwa kusígila
amiisi ukuti gísulege ikibafú kimo

damage *n* ubonaange

damage *vb* onanga

damaged *adj* -bofú, -onangike

damn *vt* gúna, lapisya, tuka

damp *adj* -búndifú, -tíme, -tímú

damp *n* ubutíme (miisimiisi)

dampness *n* ububúndifú, ubutime, ubutimú

dance *vt* fína, moga

dancer *n* umfíní, ummogí

dandruff *n.med* ilíngotí

danger *n* uluboneko ulubíbí, akapalapala, akaabugogí

dangerous *adj* akandu akagogí, akabíbí, -a
bugogí

dangle 1 *vi* syúta 2 *vt* syúsya

dare *vb* gela, kíba

daring *adj* -gaasí

dark *adj* 1 (general) -títu 2 (of color)
ingali, ingole

darkness *n* ingíísí, ubutítu

darling *n* ikigane, unganígwa

dash *vi* taaga kumaka, kuuja

date *n* ulubalo lwa isíku

date *n.bot* 1 (tree) umpíkí gwatende
2 (fruit) iseke sya mpíkí untende

daughter *n* mwana unkííkulu

day *n* ilísíku, pamúsi
all day ilísiku lyoosa
every day bwíla, bwílabwíla

daydream *vb* gogwa injosi pamúsi

daylight *n* pamúsi

dawn *n* ubukye, ulufwelelema, ulufwe-
lelemya

dawn *vb* jenjeluka

daze *vt* alanganía

dazzle *vb* pela ingíísí kumaso lulasya

dead *adj* -síta kuja nubuumí, -fwe

deaf *adj* -a mapuli, -síta kupilika

deaf person *n* ugwamapuli

deal *n* 1 (understanding, contract) ukupilikisanía, ulufííngo; **Do we have a deal?** Bule tupilikisenie?
2 (amount) unteengo, imbombo ja kubomba; **a great deal** ubwíngí
3 (distribution) ubujabí

deal *vb* 1 (act) bomba 2 (trade) bisya, íja nifya kuulisya 3 (distribute cards) jaba kalata, jabanía

dear *adj* 1 (beloved) unkundwe 2 (costly) -a ntengo nywamú, ugwa pamwanya

death *n* ubufwe

debate *n* ulukaaní, ubukaaníkane

debate *vb* 1 kaaníkana, kwabusanía i-ndimí 2 *slang* lusana indimí

debauchery *n* ubulogwe, ubuhahaní, ubulufu

debt *n* inongwa, akamelelígwa

decade *n* ifyinja kalongo

decadent *adj* -a kufujuka, -fujufu, fújúke

decapitate *vb* búúta untu

decay *vb* bola

deceased *n* umfwe

deceit *n* ubusyobí, ubutungulu, ubujanja, ulusyobo

deceitful *adj* -syobí, -tungulu, -janja

deceive *vb* syoba

December *n* umwesí gwa kalongo na bubili, ndiseemba

decent *adj* -a lwimiko

deception *n* ubutungulu, ubusyobí, ubujanja

decide *vb* ínogona, túmúla amasyu, maliisya; **he decided to go** aatúmwíle ukubuuka

decimal *n* utwa mulongo, kamo ntundú mulongo

decision *n* inyínogono, ubutúmúlí, ubwamúli

deck *n* 1 (ship) paasí pa sítíma
2 (cards) ikijabo kya kalata

declare *vb* fúmúsya

decorate *vb* baatika, nosya, lemba

decoration *n* ulubaatiko, ulunosyo

decrease *n* ubunaganífú

decrease *vb* naganíka, pepuka, naganía, aga

decree *n* ululagilo, ubulongí

decrepit *adj* -katafú, -kuulwípe

dedicate *vb* -pa ulusajo

deduce *vb* ínogona

deduct *vb* sosyako, pepusya

deed *n* ulubombo, akaandu aka kabombígwe

deep *adj* -kisíba, -solofú
  deep sea ikíína ikitalí panyanja

deer *n.zool* ikinyamaana ikikifwene nimbabala

defeat *vb* tola, bopesya

defecate *vb* ínía amafí, píípa, fúlútúla

defect *n* ulunaganíko, ikinaganíko, onangike, íja nakasolo

defense *n* ubulindililí

defend *vb* papilila, lindilila, sígilila

defiant *adj* tinguka, akulonda ubwíte, síta kutííla, síta lupiliko

deficient *adj* -túmúkíílwe, lúsúsílwe

deficit *n* ukulúúswa, ukutúmúkilwa, ulutúmúkilo, ubutúmúkilwe

defile *vb* biika ubunyalí, nyasya

define *vb* soosya ubwanalolí bwa kandú, lingaanía

deform *vb* bíbusya

deformity *n* ikilema

defraud *vb* syoba, janjika

defy *vb* tínguka, tíngukila

degenerate *vb* onangika akajiilo

degrade *vb* jwelúla

degree *n* 1 (temperature) ikipimo kya mbepo nulumu 2 (academic) idígílílí

dehydrate *vb* soosya amiisi, umika amiisi

delay *vb* kaabisya, kaabila

delegate *n* untumígwa, umwimililí

delete *vb* omola, pyasíila (Tuk), pyag-isya (Kye)

deliberate *adj* ínogonela fííjo

delicate *adj* -onywa, -toofú

delicious *adj* -nyaafú, -noge

delight *n* ulusekelo
delight *vb* sekeesya, sekela
delinquent *adj* -sobí
delirious *adj.med* -a míbwibwi, -a imenyenya
delirium *n.med* imínyeenya, imíbwibwi
deliver *vb* 1 twala, súngila, fikisya 2 *vt.med* (baby) paapa, pona
delivery *n* ubwambililí, ukufíkisya, ubupokí
deluge *n* umwelesyo
delta *n* pa mbasana sya lwisí isí síkwíngila munyanja
demand *vb* lalúsya ngatí kulagila
demand *vb* londa kumaka
demented *adj* -a kigili
demolish *vb* pangula, onanga, omola
demolish houses onyola inyúmba, pangula inyúmba
demon *n* imbepo inyalí
demonstrate *vb* nangisya ubwanalolí, nangisya
demoralize *vb* hobola amaka, onyola amaka
den *n* ikíína (muno fíkugonamo ifínyamaana fya ndiisú)
denomination *n* ingamú
denote *vb* nangisya, joba ingamú
denounce *vb* buulila
dense *adj* -síto
dent *n* ubusotole, ububyondoke, ilíbyondo
dental *adj* -a mííno
dentist *n* unganga gwa miino
denunciation *n* ukupya pa kipanga, ubukanígwe
deny *vb* sííta, kaana
deodorant *n* unkota ugu gukugoga ulunúúsí
depart *vb* sooka, súmúka
depart *vb* (die) ífwa
departed, deceased *n* ummbuka, umfwe
depend *vb* subila
depend on *vb* egamíla, subila umúndu

ujungi
it depends on him kuli jujo, sili mmyake jujo
depict *vb* nangisya, bonesya
depopulate *vb* naganía pamo pepula ubwíngí bwa bandu
deport *vb* kaga umúndu nkíísu
deposit *vb* biika, súnga
depress *vb* sulumanía
deprive *vb* íma, kaanísya ukubombela, poka
depth *n* ubusolofú
derail *vb* gwisya ítelení
derange *vb* onanga imbatiko, andula
derive *vb* fuma, fuma mumo
derogatory *adj* -kosya soní
descend *vb* súlúka, sololoka
descendant *n.fam* unkoongí nkikolo
describe *vb* lingaanía
desert *n* ulungalangala
desert *vb* leka, taaga
deserve *vb* bagila
design *n* ulusúmo, ukuko
design *vb* andisya ulusumo, anda ulusúmo ulungi
designate *vb* nangisya, papo ingamú, papo imbombo
designation *n* ikyeo, ubujo pambombo
desire *n* ubunyonywe, ubuufí
desire *vb* londa, nyonywa, fúmbwa
desk *n* ikikota ni mesa ja gwa súkúúlú
desolation *n* ubupiina
despair *vb* leka ukwíkatasya, onyoka amaka
desperate *adj* -síta lusubilo
despicable *adj* -a kwíílamígwa
despise *vb* tíngukila, fúúja, henula
despite *prep* pope, na pope
despot *n* undongosí umbíbí uju alimwene ítolo; undongosí ugwa maka míngí (fííjo fííjo uju ikugabombela kabíbí amaka gake)
dessert *n* utunyaafú utú abasúngú bikúlya pa bumalilo bwa fíndú
destination *n* pabubuko, pabufíko

destiny *n* isya kuboneka
destitute *adj* -londo, -pina
destroy *vb* bíníka, onanga, palaganía, loganía
destruction *n* ubonangifú, ulonango, ulonangiko, ubonaange
detail *n* isyankati, isyambusolofu, ubu-línganíe
detain *vb* biika nkati, pínya
detect *vb* manya, ípilika, pelelesya
detective *n* umpelelesí
detergent *n* unkota gwa kusúkila
determine *vb* nangisya
detest *vt* benga
dethrone *vb* soosya pa kikota kya bunyafyale
detonate *vb* lípula (asya)
detour *n* ukupaagula, injila ja pambali
devastate *vb* onanga
develop *vb* kula
development *n* ukukula
devil *n.relig* setano
device *n* akaandu aka kubombela
devious *adj* -a kusyungutila, -sobi
devour *vb* míla (kubupafú), fwota
devout *adj* -a kukonga fííjo ísyu lya kyala, -a lupilikisyo lunywamú
dew *n* indungwa
dhow *n* ubwato ubu bukwenda numbelo
diabolical *adj* -ngati jo setano
diagnose *vb.med* londeesya ububíne, manya ububíne
dial *vb* koma isímu
dialogue *n* ukujobesanía, inyangalo
dialect *n* akajobele, injobele
diamond *n* alumasí
diaper *n* ikipeepe, ikikuupe, akatabulo ka kufwala umwaana
diaphragm *n.anat* a'kameeme
diarrhea *n.med* ulupeelo
have diarrhea *vb.med* peela, halísya
diary *n* ikitabu ikya tubombo twa bwílabwíla
dictate *vb* lagila
dictator *n* undagilí unkali uju atikupilika isya bangi

dictionary *n* ikitabu iki kikubula muno gajilíle amasyu
die *vb* **1** -fwa, ukufwa **2** *vb.slang* ílaga; **he is dead** afwíle
diet *n* ifíndu ifí fíkulilígwa numúndu
differ *vb* legana, kindana
difference *n* ubukindane, ubulegane
different *adj* pasímapasíma, -a kulegana
differentiate *vb* leganía
differently *adv* pasíma
difficult *adj* -kafú, -síto, -palapala, -jikaja mbepe, -pala
difficulty *n* ubutolwe, ubukafú, ubupalapala
diffuse *adj* -ongaana
dig *vb* kumba
digest *vb* -sya fíndu múnda
digestion *n* ukusyelígwa kwa fíndu munda
dignity *n* ubusísya, ulwíjíísyo
dilemma *n* ulwalangano (kaliku ka kubomba kutundu tubili)
diligence *n* ulwífimbilisyo pa mbombo
be diligent *vb* bomba imbombo fííjo
dilute *vb* ongela amiisi
dim *vb* **1** (Kye) pela ulunyenyesi **2** (Tuk) pela ulung'eng'esí, pela ulubeefú
dimension *n* ifípimo fya bwelefu
diminish *vb* aga, pepuka, pepusya, naganía
dimple *n* ilíbyondo, ilíbyondo lya musaja (Tuk: mbusaja)
din *n* unjwego, undíndo
dine *vb* -lya ifíndu fya pamúsi
dinghy *n* akaato, ubwato ubunini
dinner *n* ifya kulya ifya pamúsi
dinosaur *n* ikinyamaana ikinyamú ikya íjolo fííjo
dip (for cattle) *n* unkota ugwa kogesya ing'ombe ugwa makulupa, lípí
dip *vb* júbika, ibisya
diphtheria *n.med* ububíne bwa fílonda pammilo; akasanda
diploma *n* idipoloma
diplomacy *n* ubwimililí bwa mbombo isya kíísu kimo nkíísu ikingi
diplomat *n* uju íkwimilila imbombo

isya kíísu kyake nkíísu ikingi

dire *adj* -kindililí

direct *vb* labisya, lagila, nangisya

direct *adj* -golofú

direction *n* ululagilo, ikibafu, ubulabilo

directly *adj* nakalinga kisíta kukabila

director *n* umwimililí, undongosí, unkulumba gwa mbombo

dirge *n* ulwímbo lwa kusyilila umfwe

dirt *n* ubunyalí

dirty *adj* -nyalí, -bwapufú, bwafú

dirty *vb* koma, komesya, íja nyalí,
ínisya

disable *vb* lemasya

disadvantage *n* ububíbí bwa kandu;
ubusobe
**His young age was a disadvantage
for him in his new job** ubuníní
bwake bunsígíle pambombo jake imbya = umri wake mdogo umemkwaza
kwenye kazi yake mpya

disagree *vb* kaaníka

disappear *vb* jongeela, soba, joonga

disappoint *vb* kínyula
be disappointed onyoka amaka

disappointment *n* ubusulumaníe,
ulukínyulo

disapprove *vb* kaaníka, kaana

disarm *vb* poka ifílwilo

disaster *n* ubutolwe ubunywamú

disburse *vb* homba (indalama)

disc *n* akaandu akabúlúnge, kasekele
kangi kapapate bo ihela imbúlúlúfú

discard *vb* taaga, leka

discharge *n* soosya

discharge *vb* (from hospital) soka nki-
patala

disciple *n* umfúndígwa, unkongí

discipline *n* ulwíjíísyo

disclose *vb* ígula, biika pabwelu

disco *n* ilísíko, indansi

discolor *vb* omola ilangí

discomfort *n* ukwípilika kabíbí

discount *n* unteengo ugu gukusúlúsígwa

discourage *vb* honyola amaka

discourse *n* ubujobí, ubulumbililí

discord *n* ulusomanío, ubwíte

discover *vb* andisya akaandu ulwa
kwanda

discrepancy *n* ubulegane

discrete *adj* -a pabwelú fííjo

discriminate *vb* fwanikisya, leganía

discuss *vb* jobesanía

discussion *n* ukujobesanía, inyangalo

disdain *n* amatíngo

disease *n.med* **1** ububíne, imbína (Tuk),
ihoma **2** (esp about VD) imbungo

disembark *vb* súlúka mbwato

disentangle *vb* níembula, tatula, abula

disgrace *n* isoní, ulunyasyo, ulusuusyo

disgrace *vb* kosya isoní, nyasya

disguise *vb* sanúsya, físa, kínga

disgust *n* ikinyanyasí

disgust *vb* kalalisya

dish *n* indelema

dishonest *adj* -síta bwanalolí

dishonor *vb* fújúla

disinfect *vb* súka

disinherit *vb* poka ikilíngo kya jungi,
kisíta kwingilapo ikilíngo, poka ikilíngo pakwíngilapo

disinterested *adj* -síta kufúmbwa, -síta
kunyonywa

dislike *vb* benga

dislocate *vb* **1** biika pabungi **2** *vb.med*
fígula

dismiss *vb* soosya, lekesya, kaga

dismantle *vb* pangalatula, pangula

disobedient *adj* -kaja nulwítiko

disobey *vb* síta kwitika

become disordered *vb* onangika,sita
lubatiko

disown *vb* kaana, síta kuja nafyo

dispensary *n* ikipatala ikinandi

disperse *vb* balanía, búlúlúsya,
nyambanía, palasa

displace *vb* sosyapo, saamísya

display *vb* bonesya, nangisya

displease *vb* tamya, katasya

dispose of longela, sookako, taaga

161

disproportion *n* ukusíita kufwana

disprove *vb* ukusíita kwitikisígwa

dispute *n* ukujobesanía, ulukaaní

dispute *vb* jobesanía, kaaníka

disregard *n* ulwílaamo

disregard *vb* ílaamwa

disrespect *n* ukusíita kuja nulwimíko

dissident *n* umúndu uju atíkwítikana nabaangi

dissolve *vb* lungula, sungulula

distance *n* ubutalí

distinct *adj* -a pabwelú, -a kusíta kwí- fisa, kikupilikika mbibimbibi

distinguish *vb* leganía, kindanía

distinguished *adj* -a bufúmúke, -fúmúke, -a kumanyígwa fííjo

distort *vb* pepetula, níongasya (amasyu)

distress *n* ubutolwe, ulusúlúmanío

distribute *vb* balanía, jabanía

district *n* iwílaja

district commissioner *n* unkulumba gwa wílaja

disturb *vb* tamya

disturbance *n* ubutaamye

ditch *n* umfoolo, umfweleji, ilíhandakí

dive *vi* 1 (swim under water) íbila akantúndú 2 (into water head first) ísomola

diving *n* mwansomo, akisomo, akisomolo

divert *vb* níongasya

divide *vb* jaba, jabanía

divine *adj* -a kyala

divine *vb* londa utundu utu twífísíle

division (arithmetic) *n* ukujabanía

divorce *n* italaka

divorce *vt* limbula ubwegí (omola) lekana, kaga, tabula

dizzy *adj* -a kupilika ulusyunguulu

dizziness *n.med* ulusyunguulu

do *vb* bomba, ípúkúlanía

  it is done (finished) jimalííke

  it is done (cooked) jipííle

  that will do po papo, jifweene

  how do you do (UK greeting) bule ugoníle

doctor *n* 1 (traditional) unganga

2 (western-trained) unganga

doctrine *n* ulumanyísyo

document *n* akaandu aka kasímbígwe

dodge *vb* 1 epa 2 (UK:dodge school) joonga

dog *n* imbwa

doll *n* ikifwaní kya mwana

domestic *adj* -a pakaaja

become domesticated *vb* tíímígwa

dominion *n* ubutwa, ubunyafyale

donate *vb* soosya

donkey *n.zool* imbúnda

donor *n* umpe, umpí

door *n* ulwígí

doorway, door frame *n* ikifigo

dormitory *n* inyúmba ja kugonamo abandu kubwíngí bo abasíkali, abasúkúúlú etc.

dose *n* ikipimo kya kunwa unkota

dot *n* ubutononde, akatononde

double *n* ulwa bubili (kabili) kubili

doubt *n* ukwílaamwa, ulwílaamwo

doubt *vb* ílaamwa, paasya, anía / lalu-usya ubwanalolí

there is no doubt kukajako ukwí- laamwa, síkanumpasyo

dough *n* unkando, ikikando

dove *n.zool* 1 (wild) ingungubija 2 (domesticated) ingunde

down *adv,prep* paasí

dowry *n* ifyuma fya kukweela unkííkulu

pay dowry -kwa, ukukwa, kweela, sosya indalama sya kukwa

doze *vb* sípuka

dozen *n* utundu kalongo na tubili

draft *n* amasímbo amapimba ga kalata, ubupimbí, ubukwabí

drag *vb* kwaba, lúsa, lúndúmúla

dragonfly *n.zool* mwasíbalo, (Tuk) talulende, (Kye) tabulende

drain *n* ikíína kya miisi, ikya munsebo mumbali; umfoolo (umfweleji) gwa mpwisi

drain *vb* umíka, kuluka, soosya amiisi

drama *n* akasúmo ka kuíganía

drape *vb* nosya ni mienda
drastic *adj* -a maka fííjo
draw *vb* 1 (pull) kwaba, lúndúmúla, fyusya 2 (eg. picture) símba, lemba
draw water nega amiisi
drawing *n* ikifwaní kya kusimbígwa
dread *n* ulutende
dread *vi* tííla
dreadful *adj* -a lutende, -a kutílisya
dream *n* injosí
dream *vb* gogwa
dress *n* (Swa gauni) umwenda gwa nkííkulu
dress *vb* fwala, fwika
dribble *vb* 1 (eg spit) oneka amata 2 (umpila) koma ikyenga
drill *n* (carpenter's) ikisotolelo
drill *vb* sotola, pegesa
drink *n* ifya kunwa, ikinwegwa
drink *vb* -nwa, kúúnda, kúpúla, pepa
drip *vb* súlúlúka, súlúlúsya, tolíka
drive *vt* endesya, pota
driver *n* undelefwa, umpotí
drizzle *n* ifúla ja kunyaganya, akafúla, ulunyaganyo
drool *vb* súlúlúka
droop *vb* gúndama, súlama, ínama
drop *n* ilítonyela, ilítondobya
drop *vb* satuka (-gwa), satusya
drought *n* ulungalangala
drown *vb* mílwa (Kye), íbisya, ímuka (Tuk)
drowse *vb* sípuka
drug *n* unkota
drum *n* indíngala, (coneshaped) ikimbímbí
drummer *n* unkoma ndíngala
drumstick *n* ikikubilo
drunk *adj* -gaale
be drunk *vb* gaala ubwalwa, -íja ngaale
drunkard *n* ungaalabwalwa, ungaalí
dry *adj* -umu
dry *vt* uma, umísya, umíka
dual *n* -mbubili, -a -bili
duck *n.zool* ilíseekwa, ikipake
due *adj* -a naloolí, -a kumelelígwa
duel *n* ubwíte bwa bandu babili, ulukaní

dull *adj* 1 (stupid) -síto, -konyofú 2 (boring) -a kukatasya 3 (blunt) suufu, kunyufu, síta kung'alika
dumb *adj* 1 (mute) -a kimyemye, sííta kujoba, -a kinúúnú 2 (stupid) -konyofú, -lema
dumb person *n* 1 uju atikujoba, ugwa kinúúnú 2 unkonyofú
dump *vb* taaga
dune *n* unsanga ugu gubungene
dung *n* indope, amafí
dung hill *n* ilíbungila
dupe *vb* syoba
duplicate *vb* ambula
durable *adj* -a bwílabwíla, -a kugona fííjo
during *prep* akabalilo ka, pa kabalilo ka
dusk *n* amajolo
dust *n* ulufumbi, ifumbi
duty *n* 1 (obligation) imbombo 2 (tax) isongo
dwarf *n* umbwenekuugu, umúndu untúle
dwell *vb* itugala
dynamic *adj* -a maka
dynamite *n* ikitulutulu
dynasty *n* ifílingo fya bunya fyale (aba kikolo kimokyene)
dye *n* ilangí
dye *vb* biika ilangí
dysentery *n.med* ukupeela ilílopa, ukupeela ulwa kumwanya

Ee

each *adj* kamo kamo
eager *adj* -nyonywa
eagle *n.zool* ilípuula, ilísimula, ingwasí
 fish eagle mwakilumbwa
ear *n.anat* imbulukutu
early *adv* kwandana, kubwandane
be early laabila
earn *vt* kaba
earnest *adj* -a lunyonywo lwíngí
earring *n* ihelení
Earth *pn* ikíísu kyoosa
earthworm *n.zool* ubulílí
earth *n* ikíísu
earthquake *n* akasenyenda
ease *n* ulutengano, ulutuusyo
easily *adv* mbupepe
east *n* kubusookelo
Easter *n.relig* ipasaka
easy *adj* -pepe
eat *vb* -lya, ukulya
eaves *n* imbenú
edible *adj* -lilígwa
ebony *n* ulubabu ulutitu ulukafú
eccentric *adj* -a pasíma, -a kajilo akaheesya
ecclesiastical *adj* -a kyaliki, -a bukilisti
echo *n* ilíísyu ili likugomoka linga ku-
 koolela
eclectic *adj* -a bwambililí (accepting)
eclipse *n* ukukolígwa kwa ísuba pamo
 umwesí
ecology *n* utwa bumí nu bujo bwake
economy *n* ubwimililí bwa ndalama nutundu
ecstasy *n* ulusekelo ulunywamú
eczema *n.med* ikibuule, imbele
edge *n* ulugenge
edict *n* ululagilo
edifice *n* ulujenga
educate *vb* manyísya, lingaanía
education *n* ubumanyili
eel *n.zool* íníongela
eerie *adj* -imba
efface *vb* fígísa
effect *n* ulubombelo, uluboneko

effeminate *adj* -a kikííkulu, -boneka
 ngati nkííkulu
efficiency *n* ububombí ubunúnú
efficient *adj* -a bubomba mbombo inúnú, -bombí
effort *n* ulwíjuulo
egg *n* ilífúúmbi
egg-plant *n.bot* ibílínganía
eggshell *n* ilíkakala lya ífúúmbi; ilíkalang'asila lya ifúúmbí
egret *n.zool* inyangenyange
eight *num* lwele
eighteen *num* kalongo na lwele
eighty *num* amalongo lwele
either ... or *conj* pamo ... pamo
ejaculate *vb* 1 *vb.off* tunda bo ulipaku-
 níola unkííkulu 2 ona (ukufuma mumbili)
eject *vb* -swa
elaborate *vb* lingaanía kanúnú
elapse *vb* kinda
elastic *adj* -lumbuka, -a kulumbuka
eland *n.zool* ikinyamaana ngati mbabala
elate *vb* sekelela
elbow *n.anat* akakooho ka kiboko
elder *n* unkulumba, unkusí, unnyago
elect *vb* sala, sala ulusalo, sungula
electric *adj* -a bumeme
electricity *n* ubumeme
elegant *adj* -núnú
elegy *n* ulwímbo ulwa kupela ikisa
element *n* akaandu, akajabo
elephant *n* isofú
elephantiasis *n.med* amatende
elevate *vb* inula
eleven *num* kalongo na kamo
eligible *adj* -bagila
eliminate *vb* sosyapo, maliisya
elite *n* ikijabo kya pamwanya; ikijabo
 kya bandu aba bali ni kikungilwa ikinúnú ikya pamwanya
elixir *n* unkota gwa kugoteka kukuti
 bubíne
elocution *n* ubujobí
elongate *vb* ongela, talísya

elope *vb* josya unkííkulu, bopa
 nunkííkulu
eloquent *adj* -a kubaatika amasyu, -jobí
elsewhere pabungi
elude *vb* ífisa, íbilila
emaciate *vb* ganda, fípuka
emaciated *adj* -gaafú
emancipate *vb* biika mbwabuke
embalm *vb* ukutilisya ukufunda, paka
 umfímba unkota ukuti gungabola
embargo *n* ulusíngo
embark ukukweela mu sítíma pamo
 mundege
embarrass *vb* suusya, tamya, sísya ilyojo; be
 embarrassed 1 suusígwa, íja mundamyo
embarrassment *n* ulusuusyo, ulutaamyo
embassy *n* ibofesí napabujo bwa múndu uju
 íkwímilila ikíísu kyake nkíísu ikingi
ember *n* umoto unyeka
embezzle *vb* bombela ihela sya kipanga
 mwalo
embrace *vb* kúmbatana, fúmbatila, gúbatila, kúmbatila
embroider *vb* fúma, nosya ifítambala
embryo *n* akana akateta ndwanda
emerge *vb* boneka, íbuka, túpúka, setuka
emergency *n* uluboneko ulubíbí
emetic *n* aka kikubilúsya
emigrate *vb* saama ikíísu
eminent *adj* -mfumuke, -nsísya
emissary *n* untumígwa
emit *vb* soosya
emotion *n* ikitíma
emphasis *n* ulusísímíkisyo
emphasize *vb* sísímikisya, gíndikisya
 (ílisyu ukubonesya ubunúnú bwake)
empire *n* ubunyafyale
employ *vb* bombela, ukumpa umúndu
 imbombo íja mfwalo
employee *n* umbomba mbobo ija
 mfwalo
employer *n* uju ikupa imbombo ja
 mfwalo
employment *n* imbombo, ububombelí
empty *adj* ítolo, kisíta kandu, nakamo

empty out ona paasí, sosyamo fyoosa
emulsion *n* unkota ugwa miisi ugu
 gufwene nulukama
enable *vb* bagisya, papo amaka
enchant *vb* loga, alanganía
encircle *vb* syungutisya, syungusya
enclosure *n* ukusyungusya ulupaso,
 ukusyungutilígwa nulupaso
encounter *vb* aganíla na, ilwa na, komana na
encourage *vb* kasya, papo amaka, papo
 ulusuubilo
end *n* ubumalikisyo, ubumalikilo, ubumalilo
endless *adj* jitikumalika, -sita mmalikisyo
endanger *vb* biika ndugelo, biika mbutolwe
endear *vb* gana
endemic *adj* -a kwagígwa nkíísu kimo
 ítolo, (ububine) -a kubalaníla koosa
 nkíísu
endow *vb* bikila indalama, ikyuma
endure *vb* ípilika ukubaba, fúfúlila
enemy *n* unndugu
energy *n* kipimo kya mbombo, amaka
enforce *vb* bombela amaka, fimbilisya,
 sísímíkisya
engage *vb* fínga, síngila
be engaged -ja nulwipukulanyo, ija ni
 mbombo, síngiligwa ulufíngo
engagement *n* lwipukulanyo,
 ulufíngano, ubusingiligwa
engine *n* ilíkina, injíní
English *adj* 1 (language) ikingelesí
 2 (of/from England) -ngelesi
enhance *vb* ongela (amaka), kwesya
enigma *n* akaandu pamo umúndu ugwa
 kuswígisya
enjoy *vb* sekelela, gana, hoboka
enjoyment *n* ulusekelo
enlarge *vb* nywamúsya, kusya, ongela
enmity *n* ikilugu
enormous *adj* -nywamú, -nywamú fííjo
enough *adv* -fwene
enough! *interj* paapo!
 that is enough po papo, po papo
 -fwene, sifwene

be enough *vb* fwana, ikuta
enquire *vb* londa, laluusya, pelelesya
enrage *vb* kalalisya
enrol *vb* íngila nkipaanga
enslave biika mbutumwa
entangle *vb* -ja mbutolwe (ukuja mbutolwe bwa bwíte), ikola (muntego)
enter *vb* íngila
entertain *vt* tambila, bombela inúnú, ambilila
entertainer *n* umúndu uju ikutambila abahesya, umwambililí
enthusiasm *n* amaka ga nyinogono, ubusyukwe, ukugana akandu kunyinogono na maka gosa
entire *adj* -oosa, -a múmo, -kafú
entirely *adv* fííjo, loosa
intestine *n.anat* ubula; **small intestine** ubula ubusekele/ubuníní; **large intestine** ubula ubunywamú
entrance *n* ikifígo, pabwíngililo
entreat *vb* pyelesya, suuma, laamba
entrust *vb* subila, bika pasi pa, subila umúndu ukuti ikwenelela utundu twako
enunciate *vb* joba kanúnú
envelope *n* ifulupu
environment *n* ubujo nu tundu tosa utu tubasyungutilile, ifífítusyungutíle
envious *adj* -a buufi
envoy *n* untumígwa
envy *n* ubuufí
envy *vb* keetela mumbafu, keetela mbuufí, totomela
epidemy *n* ububíne ubu bukwambukila / bukutanikisya mbíbímbíbí
epilepsy *n.med* ilínyíkí, ilísílísílí
epoch *n* akabalilo aka tubonike utukulumba
equal *adj* -a kufwana, -fwene
equator *n* íkweta
equip *vb* pako
equipment *n* utundu utwakubombela imbombo jojosa jila, ikibombelo
equivalent *adj* -fwene
era *n* akabalilo ka fyinja aka kikunangisya imboneko sya tundu

eradicate *vb* maliisya, josya
erase *vb* figísa, pyasiila, pyagisya, sosyapo
erect *vb* imisya, imika, pela, jenga
erode *vb* bugujula (*vt*), bugujuka (*vi*), kulula, kwangula
erogenous *adj* -a kutwaala inyege
erosion *n* ubukwangufu, ububugujufu, ubukulule
erotic *adj* -akupako inyege
err *vb* soba, bomba imbíbí, liga
errand *n* indumí
error *n* ubusobí
erudite *adj* -manyílí
erupt *vb* lípuka
escalate *vb* ongela, kusya
escape *vb* bopa, joonga, pona
escort *vb* síndikila
especially *adj* fííjofííjo
essence *n* ububumbígwe, ubufúmo
establish *vb* andisya, biika, kolekela
estimate *vb* pimilamo, pima untengo gwa
estuary *n* pabwingililo bwa lwísí
eternal *adj* -a bwíla
eternity *n* bwílabwíla
etiquette *n* indagilo sya kajilo, akajilo akanúnú
eucalyptus *n.bot* undongotí
eunuch *n* umfúle
euphemism *n* amasyu aga gakaja makali, aga gakaja ga maheelú
Europe *pn* Ubulaja
European *n* unsungu, ugwa mbulaja
evacuate *vb* soosya, sookako, samísya
evade *vb* leganika, epuka, syoba
evaluate *vb* londa unteengo, pima unteengo
evaporate *vb* fuuka
even *adj* -fwene, -fíkíle mumpaka, sitakwanduka
evening *n* namajolo
event *n* uluboneko, ulusetuko
ever *adv* ubusiku bosa, bwíla
everlasting *adj* -gona fííjo, -sita kumalika

every *adj* kukuti
everything *pron* -o -osa
everywhere *adv* poosa, popoosa pala,
  palipoosa
evidence *n* ikimanyílo, ubuketí
evident *adj* -a pabwelú, -a bwíla
evil *adj* -biní, -a kabiní, -bíbí, -a mbombo inyalí
evil *n* ububíbí
evolution *n* ukukula
evolve *vb* iguka, kula nukwendelela, igula
ewe *n.zool* ing'osí ingikulu
exact *adj* -a naloolí, -a momúmo
exactly *adv* naloolí, kifwene, momúmo
exaggerate *vb* kusya, kiisya
exam *n* amagesyo
examine *vb* gela, gesya, pima
example *n* ikifwaníkisyo
exceed *vb* kinda
exceedingly *adv* nnoono (fíijo)
excel *vb* kindaga, tola
excellent *adj* -núnú fíijo
except *conj* loolí
exception *n* umúndu pamo akandu aka
  kakabikígwa / kakongelelígwa
excess *n* ukukindapo
exchange *vb* usanía, egela
excite *vb* nyenyemúsya
exclaim *vb* kúúta nakalinga bo linga
  ukubaba pamo ubukalale bukwagile
exclude *vb* sosyamo
excommunicate *vb.relig* (Swa tenga)
  imika nkipaanga, bika ubusigwana
excrement *n* amafí, indope
excrete *vb* -nía
excuse *n* uluhobokelo, ubuswe
excuse *vb* hobokela, -swa (íswa, ukuswa), leka
excuse me uswege, uhobokelege
execute *vb* goga, tímiilisya indagilo
exemplary *adj* -núnú ukwambula, -a
  kufwanikisya
exercise *n* ilíjando
exert *vb* biika amaka, bikila amaka
exertion *n* ulwífimbilisyo, ulwíjuulo

exhaust *vb* katasya, katala, maliisya,
exhibition *n* ulubonesyo
exile *n* bopela nkíísu ikingi, ukukagí-
  gwa nkíísu pamo nkaaja ka mundu
  ukuja lufuundo, nukwenda kuja
  nkíísu pamo nkaaja akangi
exile *vb* kaga, samisya
exist *vb* japo, jako
exit *n* pabusokelo
expand *vb* baaluka, kindilila, lúmbúka,
  baalula
expanse *n* ubwelefú, ububaalufú
expect *vb* gúúlila, subila
expel *vb* soosya, sosyapo, kaga
expense *n* unteengo gwa kwendesya
  fímo, indalama isya kubombela fímo
expensive *adj* -a ntengo
experience *n* ubupube, uloonjo, ubwisibile
experience *vb* puba, ísíbila
expert *n* 1 ummanyili fíijo, ummanyi
  fíijo 2 (~ in/of) ummanyi gwa
expire *vb* fúúka, malika amaka
explain *vb* lingaanía, lingisanía, panga,
  pangila
explanation *n* ubulingaaníe
explode *vb* pufúka, pasuka kumaka
explore *vb* buuka injila ja nkíísu ukuti
  gwenelele nukumanyíla
express *vb* joba, línganía
expression *n* amasyu (kumaso, ulukeeto), ululinganío, injobelo ja maso
extend *vb* golosya, fúmúsya, ongelako
external *adj* -a panja
extinguish *vb* símisya
extra *n* aka kakindilepo, akaandu ka
  kongelapo pamwanya pa pabwandilo
extravagant *adj* akajiilo ka kubombela
  mwalo indalama, ukonaanga utundu
extreme *adj* -ja pamwanya fíijo
extremely *adv* nnoono
exult *vb* sekelela, lúlútila
exultation *n* akalúúlú kalusekelo
eye *n.anat* ikísige (pl amaso)
eyebrow *n.anat* ulusíge lwa mmaso,
  ulukiga

eyelash *n.anat* ulusíge ja nndugubogubo, ulusígesíge lwa nndugubogubo, ulusíge ja nndugubogubo lwa pamwanya pamo paasí pa kisíge, ulusíge

eyelid *n.anat* ulugubogubo

eyewitness *n* **1** unketi uju aliketelile jujo na maso gake **2** *slang* uju aketíle ng'atu

eyrie, aerie *n* ikifúfúmbwa kya lyebe inywamú

Ff

fable *n* akapaango akapímba aka butungulu, amasyu ga butungulu

fabric *n* akaandu aka katendekesígwe

fabulous *adj* -a kuswígisya

facade *n* nkyení munyúmba

face *n* kumaaso

facility *n* ifítuulí mumbombo, ubupepe

fact *n* ilíísyu lya naloolí, ubwanaloolí

faction *n* ikipanga iki kitapukene ni kiníne, ubwíte bwa fipanga ifí fitapukene

factor *n* umwimilí

factory *n* inyúmba iji bikutendekesyamo utundu kubwingi

faculty *n* ubumanyí

fade *vb* buuluka, jweluka; **be faded** fifílwa

faded *adj* -buulufú, jwelufú

feces, faeces *n* amafi

fag *n.slang* **1** (homosexual) unnyambala uju ikugonana nunnyambala nnine pamo unkííkulu uju ikugonana nunkííkulu nnine **2** (UK: cigarette) ingaambo

fail *vb* pondwa, tolígwa

faint *adj* -onywa, -katafú, -njwelúfú, sita kuboneka kanúnú

faint *vi* sílika

fair *adj* **1** (just) -golofú **2** (light) -eelu
That's not fair kakaja kanúnú
That's fair enough kali nkajiilo

fairy *n* íjíní, ípepo, unsyuka

faith *n* ulwítiko

faithful *adj* -íkilí, -a lwitiko

fake *vt* panga akapaango ka busyobí

fake *adj* -a butungulu, -a kusyoba

falcon *n.zool* akabelele, akapuula

hornbill *n.zool* ng'ong'a

fall *n* Imyesí igi amaní gíkulagala nu kúúma ukufuma mmípíkí pakatipa lumu ni kisíkú. Mbulaja na mu Amelíka "fall, autumn" jilipakati pa septemba na nofemba. (umwesí gwa lwele na kamo na umwesí gwa kalongo na kamo)

fall *vb* satuka, -gwa, ígwa, onyoka

false *adj* -tungulu, -busyobí
falter *vb* kungujuka, pupuluka
fame *n* ubufúmúke
familiar *adj* -a bwisibile, -a kumanyiko
family *n* ikikolo
famine *n* injala, ubutolwe bwa fíndu
famous *adj* -fúmúke, manyígwa; **be famous** fúmúka
fan *n* 1 (for blowing fire) ikikubililo
    2 ungana fímo (imíkino)
fan *vb* kubilila
fanatic *adj* -a bugane bunywamú kukaandu
fancy *adj* -a bumogí, -a kwinogonígwa
fang *n* ilíno lya kinyamaana (ikilya nyama), ilino lya sumu lya njoka
fantasy *n* inyínogono, injosí
far *adv* -butalí
fare *n* 1 (busfare) inaulí; isongo ja igali, indalama iji tukusosya mwigali
    2 ifyakulya ifí fili pameesa
farewell *n* ululagano; **bid farewell** *vb* lagana
farm *n* unngunda, ulupaka, ikyaalo
farm *vb* lima, tosa
farming *n* ukulima
farrow (a litter of pigs) *n* ikibugutila kya baana ba ngulube aba bapapíígwe palikimokyeene
farrow *vi* paapa (bika) ingulube, bwaaka
fart *vb* susa, inía isusi
fascinate *vb* sangalusya
fashion *n* ulusúmo
fast *adj, adv* mbibimbibi
fasten *vb* fyata, pínya, kasya
fat *n* amafúta
fat *adj* -nywamú, -nyaate, manga, -a butúpe
fatal *adj* -a luboneko ulubíbí
fatalism *n* ulwítiko ulwa kuti kokosa aka kikuboneka kakali nu ngomolí
fate *n* uluboneko ulusíta kusubilígwa
father *n.fam* taata
    your father uguuso
    his/her father ugwíse
    our father taatagwitu

your (pl) father ugwísemwe
their father ugwisabo
father-in-law *n.fam* unko
fatigue *n* ubukatale, amafúne
fatling *n.zool* ingíta
fatten *vb* túpisya
fault *n* ubusobí, ubonaange
fauna *n* ikilundilo kya fínyamaana ifya fíkolo fíngí nkíísu kimo
favor *n* ubukundwe
favorable *adj* -bagila, -a bukundwe
favorite *adj* kigane
favorite *n* aka kaganígwe, unkundwe
fear *n* ulutende
fear *vt* tííla, haala, paasya
feasibility *n* ukubagila ukubombígwa
feasibility study *n* ukukeeta akaandu linga kabagíle ukubombígwa
feasible *adj* aka kabagíle
feast *n* ululyo (lwa fyakulya)
feather *n* ilíjoja
feature *n* muno akaandu kabumbígwe
February *n* umwesí gwa bubili
fee *n* isongo
feeble *adj* -onywa
feed *vb* liisya, púúsya, swila
feedback *n* ulugomosyo (lwa nongwa simo)
feel *vb* ípilika; **How do you feel?** Kwípilika bulebule ?
    I feel fine Ndi kanúnú itolo, Ngwípilika kanúnú
feeling *n* ulwípiliko (inyínogono), ukuja nubwipilike bumo munyinogono
fell trees onyola imípíkí, gwisya imípíkí
fellow *n* ummanyaní
female *n* unkííkulu
feminine *adj* -a nkííkulu
fence *n* ulupaso, ulusígililo
fence *vb* (fight with sticks, swords) -lwa nifílwilo bo inyubo ningílí
ferment *n* gaga, fúnda
ferry *n* ikiloboko
ferry across *vb* lobosya
fertile *adj* -bupapí, -a mboto

fertility *n* ukuja nimboto, imbapo, imboto
fertilize *vb* botosya
festival *n* ísíku íkulumba (ilya lusekelo)
fetch *vb* twala
fetus, foetus *n* ikifúba
feud *n* ubulwe ubukali fííjo bwa abandu
babili pamo abandu mfikolo fyabo
fever *n.med* isekema
few *adj* -nandi
fiancée *n.fam* unsíngilígwa
fiasco *n* akaandu akasíta kubombígwa
fiber *n* ubuusí
field *n* ikibaanja, ulukubo, unngunda
fierce *adj* -a bukali, -a kipaho
fierceness *n* ubukali
fifth *num.ord* -a buhano
fifteen *num* kalongo na tuhano
fig *n.bot* ilíkuju, ilítunda ili lifwene nu nkuju
fig tree *n.bot* unkuju
fight *n* ululo, ubwíte, ukulwa
fight *vb* -lwa, koma, komana
figure *n* 1 (art) ikifwaní 2 (arithmetic)
imbalilo
file *n* 1 (tool) itupa 2 (for papers) ífailí
fill *vb* ísusya
film *n* aka kikwambula ikifwaní mukamela
filter *n* ikisujilo
filter *vb* suuja
filth *n* ubunyalí, imíndu
filthy *adj* -nyalí, -nyalísya
fin *n* ilípiko pamo umpeepe gwa nswi
final *adj* -bumalikisyo
finally *adv* kummalikisyo
finance *n* imbombo sya ndalama, indalama
find *vb* kaba, aga, londa
fine *adj* -núnú
fine *n* uluposolo, ulufúúndo, ifwainí,
ikihombígwa
finger *n* uloobe
finger millet *n.bot* amalesí
finish *vb* mala, maliisya
be finished malika
fir *n.bot* umpíkí unsindano

fire *n* umoto
set fire to kosya umoto
fire *vb* 1 (a weapon) komela (indusú)
2 (ignite) kosya 3 (dismiss from a job)
kaga pambombo
firefly *n.zool* ulumúlímúlí, akamúlímúlí
fireplace *n* mwíjíko, pambembelo
firewood *n* imbabu
one piece of ~ ulubabu
firm *adj* -a maka, -umíke, -kafú
first *num.adj* -a kwanda
fish *n.zool* iswi (Kye), inswi (Tuk)
fish *vt* loba
fisherman *n* undobí, undoba nswi
fishing line untando, ikisípa
fishing net *n* ulwelo, ikilepa
fist *n.anat* ikibúlí, ulubúlí, iking'oko
fit *vb* fwana, bagila
five *num* -hano, mfundiko
fix *vb* pínya, lungisanía, baatika
flag *n* indembeela, ibendela
flake *n* akaandu akaníní kangi akapepe
aka kafwene nilyaní
flame *n* ululapi, umoto umbúkúke
flammable *adj* -a kwangila umoto, -a
kubúkúka
flap *vb* kubilila, kuba, kubakuba
flare *vb* búkúka, aka
flash *n* ubumwekufú bwa lumúlí
flat *n* 1 ubupapate, 2 (puncture) kisita
muuji mu mpila 3 (UK: appartment)
inyumba 4 ubugwangwalufú
flat *adj* -galamú, -gwangwalufú, papate,
-tengaamú
flatter *vb* túfya nnoono, muno jikabagi-
lígwa
flavor *n* ubunyaafú, ukunoga kwa fíndu
flaw *n* ubulendemúfú, aka kikusúlúsya
unteengo ugwa kaandu
flax *n.bot* (Swa kitani) umpíkí ugwa
kikolo kya míbigili
flea *n.zool* imbaní
flee *vb* bopa, joonga
fleece *n* ulusyoja lwa ng'osí
fleet *n* (boats) ikikolo kya sítíma; imelí

syoosa isya bwíte isí sili
flesh *n* inyama
flexible *adj* -a kwanduka, -a kusanuka
be flexible íja mwandufú, íja nsanúfú, aka
  kikusanukasanuka,-a kwitika ukwanduka
flick *vb* koma panandi
flip *vb* komela kusulo kuloobe
flirt *vb* nyegesya
float *n* ukweleela, ukweleluka
float *vi* eleela, eleluka, jweleluka
flock *n* ikilundilo
flood *n* umwelesyo
flood *vb* teeka
floor *n* paasí pa nyúmba, ikipalo
on the floor paasí
flora *n* utundu tosa utwa kikolo íkya ifí
  fíkumela nkíísu kimo
floss *n* isyoja isekele
flour *n* ubufú
flourish *vb* elefuka, noga
flower *n.bot* ubulenge
flow *vb* súlúlúka
flu *n.med* akakínya
fluid *adj* -a misímisí, -a lugiligili
fluid *n* akandu aka kali ngati miisí pamo
  bují; ulugiligili
flute *n* ilílonge
flutter *vb* beleluka
fly *n.zool* ulubwele
fly *vb* **1** (bird, airplane) beleluka
  2 (bird) púlúlúka
foam *n* untotofula
focus *vb* bikila amaka míngí pamopene
fog *n* ulubeefú ulusito
fold *vb* píndanía, pínda
folk dance *n* indíngala
  /There are many types of indíngala.
  Ilíng'oma is the best known.
folklore *n* ulumanyilo lwa twiho ni
  nyendosya kikolo kimo kya bandu
folk song *n* (Types of) akapote, ikiboota
folk tale *n* akapango aka kendene na
  bandu
follow *vb* koonga
follower *n* unkongí

folly *n* ubukonyofú, ubulema
food *n* ifyakulya, ifindu
fool *n* unkonyofú, undemaafú, undema
foolish *adj* -konyofú, -lema
foot *n.anat* ulujajo
football *n* umpila gwa kukina na malundi
footprint *n* ilíkato, ikikato
footstep *n* untaambo gwa kilundi
for *prep* **1** (destination) ku, (pabujo)
  2 (goal, recipient) kunongwa ja
forbid *vb* kaanísya, sínga
forbidden *adj* -kanisígwe, aka kalí
  mwíko, -kasingígwe
force *n* amaka
ford *n* ikiloboko
ford *vb* loboka
forearm *n.anat* ulukongí
forecast *vb* solola
forefather *n.fam* tata untasí, unsyuka,
  imísyuka
forehead *n.anat* ikyení
foreign *adj* -heesya
foreigner *n* unheesya, umfúma ikíísu
  kya panja
foresee *vb* keeta isya nkyení
forest *n* ikisitu, amatengele
forever *adv* bwílabwíla, bwila na bwíla
forge *vb* (metal) poonda
forget *vb* íbwa, sobanía
forgetfulness *n* ikííbwa
forgive *vb* -swa /íswa, hobokela
forgive me uhobokelege, guswege
forgiveness *n* uluhobokelo, uluswo
forgiving *adj* -hobofu -a luhobokelo
fork *n* **1** (utensil) akanyoselo,
  ikinyoselo, inyoselo **2** (of a road) injila imbasaana, imbasaana ja nsebo
form *n* ulutendekesyo
former *adj* (first of two) -a kwanda
formerly *adv* pabutasí, pakwanda
fornication *n* ubulogwe
forsake *vb* leka
fort *n* ilíbooma
fortunate *adj* -a lusako, -sangalufu
fortune *n* ulusako, ulusajo

forty *num* amalongo mana
forward *adv, adj* nkyení;
   look forward ketaga nkyení
fossil *n* amasyalílo ga finyamaana ni mípíkí
foul *adj* -nyalí, -bíbí, -bofu
found *vb* agula, andisya
foundation *n* ulwalo
founder *n* uju abikíle ulwalo, umwandí
four *num* -na, tuna
fourteen *num* kalongo na tuna
fourth *num.ord* -a buna
fowl *n.zool* inguku
fox *n.zool* ilíjusí
fracture *n* ubukonyoke (bo ikifúpa),
   ukulendemuka kwa mfupa
fragment *n* akamegenyúkila, utumeenywa
fragrant *adj* -kunungila
frame *n* ífelemu
francolin *n.zool* akalulunje, imbesí
fraud *n* ubusyobí, ulusyobo
free *adj* -eluke, -abuke, -hobofú
freedom *n* ubwabuke
freeze *vb* talalila fiíjo
frequently *adv* kabalilo ka kíngí
fresh *adj* -bisí, -pya
fresh water amiisi aga kunwa, amasita
   múnyú, amiisi amanúnú aga gakaja
   nu múnyú
fret *vb* hangajika
Friday *n* ikihaano
fridge, refrigerator *n* ikyombo iki
   kíkutalalisya utundu
friend *n* ummanyaní, unganígwa, unkamú, umbwesí
friendship *n* ubumanyaaní
frighten *vb* tiílisya, biika ndutende,
   nyomosya
frightening *adj* -sísya, -tílisya
fringe *n* umpaka
fringe benefits *n* utukabo utungi
   pambali pa mfwalo
frog *n.zool* ikyula
from *prep* mu, ku
   from that time ukufúma akabalilo
   kala

in front of *prep* nkyení mu
frown ibuka kumaso, kínya ingínya
fruit *n* uluseke, ilítúnda
fry *vb* kalanga, kasínga (without using oil)
frying pan *n* ikikasingilo, ikikalangilo
fuck *vb.off* níola, níolana
fuel *n* 1 (wood) imbabu 2 (oil) amafúta
fugitive *n* unjongí (bo ukufúma kunnyololo)
fulfill *vb* (a promise) fíkisya, tímiilisya,
   tímiilisya ululagano
full *adj* -ísule
   be full ísula, ikuta, íja ísule
become full-grown kula, fíkapo ukukula
fume *n* ilyosí ilya lunusí ulusíto
fun *adj* -a lusekeesyo, -a sunga, -a lukíno
function *n* imbombo
fund *n* indalama isí sibikilígwe imbombo jimo
fundamental *adj* -a bubombí bunywamú, -a
   pabwandilo, -a kubika ulwalo
fundamentalism *n* ubwitikí nubukongí
   ubwa manyisyo sya misoni
fundamentalist (fanatical believer, religious freak) *n* umúndu uju alíitike
   nukulikonge ilísyu lya kyala
funeral *n* ifwa
fungus *n* 1 *n.zool* (mushrooms) ifí
   fíkumela bo uboga 2 *n.med* (on the
   toes) amasyasya
funnel *n* ikisondelo
funny *adj* -a lukino lwíngí, -a kusekeesya
fur *n* ulusyoja
furious *adj* -a bukali, -a bukalale
furnace *n* ilítende lya moto, ikigemo
furnish *vb* nosya nnyúmba nutundu
furniture *n* ifyombo fya nyúmba bo
   ifíkota, ifítala etc.
furrow *n* umfoolo, unsele, unkolofwa
further *adv* kangi
fuse *n* aka kwakisya ikitulutulu
fuss *n* ulupakiisyo ulunywamú ku tundu
   utufújúfú (utunandi)
future *n* akabalilo aka kíkwísa, aka
   nkyení ; in the future/ from now on
   pa kabalilo ka nkyení

Gg

gag *n* ikikahula unndomo

gain *n* ubukabilo, ulukabilo

gain *vb* kaba

gall bladder *n.anat* umfúko gwa nyongo

gallery *n* inyúmba ja kunangikisya utundu twa bumaganyí

gamble *vb* púnana

game *n* 1 (play) ulukíno 2 (animal) ikinyamaana ikifwimígwa

game warden *n* undindililí gwa fínyamaana ifya ndiisu

gang *n* 1 (work gang) ikilundilo kya bandu ababikubomba imbombo pamopeene 2 (street gang) ikilundilo kya bahuní

gangrene *n.med* ikiloonda iki kikubola

gangway *n* pabujo pa kusúlúkila ukufuma mumelí

gap *n* ubwasí

gape *vb* asama

garage *n* 1 (place to park a vehicle) inyúmba ja kubikilamo amagali, 2 (place to repair a vehicle) inyumba ija kutendekesya amagali

garbage *n* ubula bwa kinyamaana, ubunyalí

garbage dump ilítaago

garden *n* unngunda; unngunda muno fikumela ngati ubulenge, inyanya, ifitungulu, utundu utunandi nandi; ikyalo

gargle *vb* punga (nkanwa)

garland *n* ikibugutila kya bulenge iki kitendekesígwe

garlic *n.bot* ikitungulu saumu

garment *n* umwenda, ikilundo

garnish *vb* (ifíndu) nosya

garrison *n* abasíkali ba kulindilila

gas *n* umuují

gash *n* ububuute pamo ikiloonda ikisolofú, ikifúlalo ikinywamú

gasp *vb* twitila, tuujaníka

gate *n* ulwígí, ikipata

gather *vb* joola, bungaanía

be gathered bungaana, bungaanígwa

gathering *n* ulukomaano, ukwaganíla

pamopeene kwa bandu, ikilundilo

gauge *n* ikipimilo

gauze *n* umwenda ugu gukulangala

gay (homosexual, Swa msenge) *n* unnyambala uju ikugana abanyambala abanine kubwegí pamo unkííkulu uju ikubombela lululo

gaze *vb* lulalila, keeta, fyula amaso (Kye), kaatulila amaso (Tuk)

gazelle *n.zool* imbabala inandi

gear *n* 1 (equipment) utubombelo 2 (mechanical transmission) igia

gecko *n.zool* (Kye) ulusakaní, (Tuk) ulusolobela
/Possibly two different types

gel *n* ilíjibijibi

gem *n* akaandu akantengo, ilíbwe ípala lya ntengo nywamú

gender *n.gram* akajiilo ka fípelígwa, ikinyambala pamo ikikííkulu pamo kikajako kosa kosa

general *adj* -oosa

general *n* (military) unsíkali gwa kyeo ikikulumba, unsíkali unkulumba

generally *adv* kubwíngí, pa kimokyene

generation *n* uluko

generosity *n* ubupe, indúmbúla ija nikisa, indúmbúla ija mbololo

generous *adj* -pe, -a ndumbula inywamú, -a bupe, -ololo

Genesis *pn.relig* Ubwandilo

genie *n* ilípepo

genitals *n.anat* kuusí

genius *n* ugwa mahala míngí aga gakindilííle fííjo

genocide *n* ubugoga bandu ikikolo kyoosa

genre *n* akasúmo ka lwímbo pamo aka kusímba

gentle *adj* -tenga mojo, -ololo

gentleman *n* unnyambala ugwa lubatiko lunúnú; ugwa lwiho

gentleness *n* ubutengamojo, uboololo

gently *adv* kubutengamojo, kuboololo

genuine *adj* -a naloolí

geography *n* ijogolofia

geometry *n* ijometeli
German *n* (person) undakí
German *adj* (eg. language) ikidakí
gesticulate *vb* koopa (na maboko)
gesture *n* ukutinila pamo ukwitikila nu ntu
get *vi* kaba, ega
get better pona, nyagaluka
get drunk gaala
get laid *slang* lambalikígwa, gonígwa
get off súmúka, sooka
get stoned 1 (killed with rocks) tunyígwa na
   mabwe 2 *vb.slang* (be on drugs) gaala
   amakambo, gaala imíkota (gya kugaasya)
is he getting better bule agonílepo
get out soka panja
get ripe bifwa
get up (from sleep) *vb* súmúka, lembuka
don't get up tenganaga ítolo, ungasú-
   múka, ungalembuka
get used to ísíbila
get well pona, bumbuluka, nyagaluka
ghetto *n* ilíísyu lya kunyasya ilya kunangisya ikipanga kuno abaandu aba-
   heesya pakipanga bikugona
ghost *n* unsyuka
giant *adj* -nywamú fííjo
giant *n* ilindu ilísisya
giblets *n* ifya nkati munguku pamo
   ísekwa (amabagaja, indúmbúla, ingangasyungu)
gift *n* 1 (present) ikyabupe 2 (talent) ikijabo
giggle *vb* sekela, sekaseka
gill *n* ilítafula lya nswi, imínywili gya
   nswi, ulugego lwa nswi
gin *n* ikikolo kya bwalwa ubukali fííjo
ginger *n.bot* imbwíga
giraffe *n.zool* itwíga
girl *n* undindwana
girlfriend *n* ugwa kigane unkííkulu,
   unganígwa undindwana
give *vb* -pa, ukupa
gizzard *n* ingangasyungu
be glad hoboka, saala, sekela
gladly *adv* kulusekelo
glance *n* ulukeeto; at a glance kukabalilo

akapimba
glass *n* ilígalasí
glasses *n* amangalasí (ga kufwala mmaso)
glide *vb* telemúka
glimmer *vb* múlika panandipanandi
glimpse *n* ulukeeto
glisten *vb* langala, langasya
glitter *vb* langala, mwemweka
globe *n* 1 (world) ikíísu kyoosa 2
   akaandu akabuluunge aka kasímbí-
   gwepo ilamaní ja kíísu kyoosa
gloom *n* ingíísí
gloomy *adj* -a bukalale
glory *n* ubukulumba, ubusísya, ulutúfyo
glorify *vb.relig* túfya, jumbika, gíndika
glorious *adj* -a lutúfyo
glove *n* ifya kufwala mmaboko ukug-
   inga ubunyali
glow *vb* múlika, mweka
glue *n* ingolya
glutton *n* umpafu
gnat *n.zool* imbwele inandi
gnaw *vb* tafúna
gnu, wildebeest *n.zool* (> *Xhosa ignu*)
   inyumbu
go *vb* buuka
go away *vb* sokapo
go bad bola, onangika
go ahead talapo, tala
go by kinda endela pa
go down súlúka, buuka paasí
go on (continue) nduko nkyení, buukaga, endelela
go with buukaga ni, konganaga
goal *n* ulusubilo, kummalikisyo,
   (soccer) ilígoolí
goat *n.zool* imbene
gobble *vb* míla mbibimbibi
god *n* kyala
/Other traditional terms for super-
human powers (good or bad) are:
Mbamba, Isoba, Kapela-ng'ombe,
Tende, Isuba lya kumwanya,
Ndolombwíke

GOD(S)

Before the invasion of foreign religions the Nyakyusa seem to have believed only in ancestors, **imísyuka**. There is therefore no traditional word for god. There were however several concepts of someone in the ubusyuka with considerable power over people. Of these, the word **kyala** was chosen by the missionaries for their god. This word, which presumably came closest to their idea of a deity, was taken up by the first Europeans in the 1880'ies and has since been the term used among the followers of the two currently most popular religions (Islam and Christianity). The other words listed are now more or less obsolete as these religions claim only one god.

goggles *n.pl* amangalasi ga kumaso, amabwaní

gold *n* sahabu

golden *adj* -sahabu

gonorrhea *n.med* akasyonono

good *adj* -núnú

good bye *greeting* ugonege

good evening *greeting* bule utwa majolo

a good for nothing *n* umúndu gwa mwalo / unsííta ku bagila

good morning *greeting* ugoníle, utwa lubunju

goodness *n* ubunúnú

goods *n.pl* ikyuma, ifyombo

goose *n.zool* ilíseekwa (ja mmisí kangi nywamu)

gorgeous *adj* -núnú fííjo

gorilla *n.zool* ikikolo kya ngambili inywamú fííjo

gospel *n.relig* ilíbangilí

gossip *vb* teta, heeha

gourd *n* ulupaale; **gourd for oil** ikipake

govern *vb* kaba, longosya

government *n* isílíkali

governor *n* umwimililí gwa kijabo kya kíísu

gown *n* umwenda gwa bakííkulu, ilígauní

grab *vb* nyaka

grace *n* ilípyana

gradual *adj* panandipanandi

gradually *adv* mbolambola

graffiti *n* amasímbo ga mwimato

grain *n* (seed of cereal) uluseke (lwa kilombe pamo inganú)

grammar *n* ulubatiko lwa amasyu amanúnú amagolofu ukujoba

granary *n* ikituuba, indamba ja mpunga etc

grand *adj* -núnú fííjo

grandchild *n.fam* umwísukulu, umwana gwa mwanangu

grandfather *n.fam* umwísukulu umpapa tata pamo juuba

grandmother *n.fam* umwísukulu unkííkulu

grate *n* pabujo bwa moto (kumoto), ukusya nakombo aka kikungwala (bo masu, ikaloti)

great grandfather, great grandmother *n.fam* unnyeenya

great great grandfather *n.fam* ugwíse gwa nnyeenya

great grandmother *n.fam* unnyeenya unkííkulu

grant *vb* -pa, tuula

grape *n.bot* unfíílú, amafíílú

grapefruit *n.bot* luki unywamú uju atikunoga

grass *n* **1** ilíísú **2** (young green) indeka

grasshopper *n.zool* imbaasí

grasp *vb* **1** (hold) kola **2** (understand) manya, pilika

gratis *adj* -a ítolo, kisíta ndalama

gratitude *n* ulupi

grave *adj* -síto

grave *n* ilípumba

gravel *n* utubwe utunandi, isangalabwe, ikokoto

gray, grey *adj.color* fumbi, -bubufú, (grey - bluish) -fufulwisi, (grey-bluish) fufulwisí

gray hair ifwe (sya nywílí)

graze *vb* ílya ilísu

grease *n* amafúta (amasíto ga mmakína), igílísí

great *adj* -kulumba, -nywamú

greed *n* ubupafú, ubwímí, ubufúgúja

greedy *adj* -pafú, -ímí, -lufú, -a lunyonywo

green *color.adj* -mbindipindi, -njaní

greet *vb* ponía

/The English word conveys only the meaning of the actual greeting. In addition to this, the Nyakyusa word carries a wider range of connotations which best could be described as a visit (greet, talk, sit together, eat together and then leave)

grid *n* 1 ulubaatiko lwa sambo sya bumeme kumwanya 2 ingíndí sya mulamaní isí síkutuula ukupabona mbimbibi apa píkulondígwa

grief *n* ubusúlúmaníe, amaaja, ikisa

grieve *vb* súlúmanía

grill *vb* okya, baba

grim *adj* -a kunyomosya, -a kutílisya

grin *n* ulumwemwesyo

grin *vb* mwemwesya, kenyúla kukanwa

grind *vb* -sya, ísya (> ukusya); **I'm grinding** ndipakusya

grip *vb* kola, tata, kambatula

groan *vb* kúúta, koloma

groin *n.anat* ikinena

groom *n* untííma kinyamaana, ugwa bwegí unnyambala

grope *vb* palamasya

ground *n* paasí, ikíísu, umfú

groundnut (UK), **peanut** *n.bot* ilísyabala

group *n* ikilundilo;
    group (of people) ikilundilo kya bandu;
    group (of non living items) ikibugutila

grow *vb* kula, mela

grow less naganíka, mela ndalandala

growl *n* ulwíbunesyo (ulwa mbwa), ulwíjobesyo

growl *vb* íbunesya

gruel *n* ubuuji, ilítapa

grumble *vb* íbúneesya, ílaamwa

grumbling *n* ulwílaamo, ulwíbunesyo

grunt *vb* buna

guilty *adj* ukwímanya ububibi /ubusobe

guard *n* undindililí

guard *vb* lindilila

guava tree *n.bot* ungajaabi, (umpeela, ugwajaabi)

guava fruit *n.bot* gajaabi, gwajaabi

guerrilla *n* undwa bwíte uju ikwenda paasí; undwa bwíte uju ikwibilila

guess *vb* lagukisya, lagula, otela, pimilamo, sakisya, gelela

guest *n* unheesya

guide *n* undongosí gwa baheesya kuno bakamanyako

guide *vb* nangisya injila, longosya

guillotine *n* ilíkína lya kuboolela imítu

guinea fowl *n.zool* ilíkanga

guitar *n* ilígíta

gulf *n* unkunda, ilíkunda

gull/ seagull *n.zool* injuní ija munyanja iji jifwene ní ísekwa

gulp *vb* kúpúla, míla

gum *n* ubulimbo, imbulya, umpúlya

gum(s) (base of the teeth) *n.anat* ikikeno

gun *n* indúsú

gunpowder *n* ibalutí

gush *vb* oneka

gust *n* ukukúla kumaka (umbelo)

gut *vb* (to gut a fish, take out the intestines) ubula

gutter *n* umfolo gwa mpwisi

guts *n.anat* utwamunda

guy *n.slang* umúndu, unnyambala

gymnastics *n* imíkíno gya kugubika umbili kanunu

Hh

habit *n* ubwísíbile, akajiilo

hair *n* 1 (a single hair) ulunywílí
2 *n.uncount* inywílí
gray hair ifwe
straight hair inywílí sya belu (ingo-
lofú ítolo)
curly hair inywílí isya mikopyo
plaited hair inywílí induke

hairdo *n* ubutendekesye bwa nywílí,
akalukilo ka nywílí

half *adj* -núsú, pakati na pakati

half an hour akabalilo kapimba, inúsú sala

hall *n* ikyumba ikinywamú ikya lukomaano

hamerkop *n.zool* seele

hammer *n* imbondelo, inyundo

hammer *vb* poonda

hand *n.anat* ikiboko, ikyanja

handy *adj* aka kíkubombeka kubupepe

handful *n* ikyanja ikíísule

handkerchief *n* ikitambaala kya
mmaboko

handle *n* ikyaka, ikikolelo

handsome *adj* -núnú (unnyambala)

hang *vb* tulika, kobeka, tuunga

happen *vb* -ja, boneka

happiness *n* ulusekelo, ulusaalo

happy *adj* -sangalufú, -a lusekelo, -ho-
bofú, -a lusaalo, -saale

be happy sekelela, sanía

hare *n* kalulu

harass *vb* katasya, kalalisya, tamya

harbor *n* pa bwimo imelí, isítíma ni miato

hard *adj* -kafú, -pala

harm *n* ubutolwe, ubonaange

harm *vb* onanga

harness *n* ikipiki ikya ngambaku (pamo
imbunda)

harpoon *n* ikibombelo bo ingwego iki
kili na míno nulugoje ikibikulobela
iswi inywamú

harrow *vb* puusanía

harsh *adj* -kali

hartebeest *n.zool* ilípuba

harvest *n* umfúnjo, untondolo

harvest *vb* fúnja, (by uprooting)
nyúkúla, tondola

haste *n* ulwípukulanía, ulukuujo, ukukuuja

hasten *vb* kuuja, kuujisya, bopesya

hat *n* ikitílí

hatch *vb* alamíla, panja

hatchet *n* ikitwanga ikiníní, akapoopo

hate, hatred *n* ingalalisí, ukukalalila

hate *vt* benga, kalalila

hateful *adj* -a ngalalisí, -bengí

have *vt* -ja ni, ukuja ni

it is available jikwagígwa, -ipo

hawk *n.zool* ingwasí

hay *n* ilíísu ilyumú ilí likatígwe nu kuuma

he *pron* juujo, umwene (unnyambala)

head *n* untu

headache *n.med* ukubaba kwa ntu

headman *n* umalafyale, unnyafyale

headstrong *adj* -a lukaní

heal *vb* ponesya, bumbulusya

health *n* akajiilo (ubumí, ubukafú bwa
mmbili)

healthy *adj* -kafú, -sita bubíne

heap *n* ikibugutila, ikilundiko

hear *vb* pilika, pilikisya

to hear of ukupilika inongwa sya

heart *n.anat* indúmbúla

hearth *n* ikipembelo

heat *n* ubupyu, amafúkú

heat *vb* pyufya

heathen *n* umpaanja

heaven *n.relig* kumwanya kwa kyala,
ndusaalo

heavy *adj* -síto

hedge *n* ulupaso lwa mífwa, lwa mípiki

heel *n* ikitende, ikikangato

heifer *n.zool* indama, ingolombe

height *n* ubutalí bwa bwima

heir *n* ugwa kilingo, umwene kilingo

hell *n* ilítaago, mmoto gwa setano

hello *interj* inya

helmet *n* ikitílí ikya kyela

help *vb* tuula, abula

help *n* ubutuulí

hem *n* ikikope, ulupíndo
hen *n.zool* inguku indemba, ingolokoko
hepatitis *n.med* ububíne bwa ubwísúle
  bwa kiníe
her *pron* jujo (unkííkulu)
her, hers *pron.poss* -ake (-a unkííkulu)
herd *n* untíímo, ikilundilo kya fínyamaana
herdsman *n* untíímí gwa fínyamaana
here *adv* apa, kuno
  he is here alipo apa, alikuno
hero *n* unnyambala uju abombíle isya
  kutufígwa
heroine *n* unkííkulu uju abombíle isya
  kutufígwa
heroism *n* ububombí isya kutufígwa,
  ubukífú
heron *n.zool* fúúlo
herpes *n.med* amandeletele
hesitate *vb* tabaníka, sííta
hide *n* ikipapa, ikigubo
hide *vb* 1 físa 2 (hide the truth) fínda
high *adj* -talí
hill *n* akaamba
hinder *vb* gomola, kaanísya
hinge *n* ikikolelo, ikikolelo ikya lwigi
  ukuti lwigukege nukwigala
hint *n* indondomeko
hip *n.anat* ikikúlú
hippopotamus *n.zool* ifúbú
hire *vb* kolíísya
his *pron* -ake (-a nnyambala)
history *n* akapango ka syaijolo, isisi-
  kindíle isyanaloli
hit *vb* koma, tíka, kínya
  hit with the fist búlíka
hive *n* ung'oma, unsinga gwa njuki
hoard *vb* bikilila
hoarse *adj* ísyu ili líkulendema, ísyu
  ilyaale
hoe *n* ilíkumbulu
hoe *vb* lima, bomba níkumbulu
hoist *n* ikyakufyukisya
hoist *vb* kwaba, ínula, fyusya
hold *vb* kola
hole *n* ubwína, ikíína, (small hole)

akapegeso, (big hole) umwína
holiday *n* ikyaka
holiness *n* ubwíkemo
hollow *adj* bwasi nkati
holy *adj* -íkemo
home *n* akaaja
my home kumyangu (kukaaja kangu)
our home kumyitu (kukaaja kitu)
your home (you sg) kumyako (kukaaja
  kako); (you pl) kumyinú
homeless *adj* -síta kaaja
homesick *adj* -a busyukwe bwa kukaaja
be homesick syukwa
homestead *n* akaaja
honest *adj* -golofú, subilígwa, -a bwanalolí
honesty *n* ubwanalolí, ubugolofú
honey *n* uluukí
honey badger *n.zool* imbúkúla
honor *n* ulwimiko
honor *vb* imika
hook *n* (for fishing) ulusípulilo, ulusambo
hoof *n* ikyuga
hoot *vb* lila bo ingwítwa, lila kulusulumanio
hop *vb* kúúka
hope *n* ulusubilí
hope *vb* subila
hopeless *adj* -síta lusubilo
horizon *n* ubutumulilo bwa mahala ga
  mundu; ububoneko bwa kumwanya
  buno bwilungenie na pasi
horn *n* 1 (animal) ulupembe 2 (for making
  sound) ingangabwíte
hornbill *n.zool* ng'ong'a
  ground hornbill imbútútú
hornet *n.zool* ng'oko
horny *adj* (callous) -umíke
horrify *vb* tetemesya, tílisya
horse *n.zool* ifwalasí
hose *n* 1 (sock) isokesi 2 (tube) umpila
  muno gikwenda amisi
hospital *n.med* ikipatala
host *n* uju ikwambilila unheesya
hostility *n* ubulugu, ubwíte
hot *adj* 1 (temperature) -pyu, -mbyu

2 (of the sun) mafuku (bukali bwa
isuba 3 (spicy) -kali
hour *n* isala
house *n* inyúmba
household *n* akaaja, aba balipo pakaaja
how *interr* bulebule, bule
how many *interr* ílinga, balinga
how much *interr* ílinga, ntengo nkí, bule
(kubisya bule)
How much do you sell? Kulisya bule?
how often *interj* kalinga
however 1 *adv* naapalinga
2 *conj* loolí
howl *vb* lila niisyu itali ngati mbwa
hug *vb* fúmbatila, gúbatila, ubatila,
kúmbatila
huge *adj* -tongomafú, -a nywamú fííjo
human *n* umúndu; **human being**
umúndu
humane *adj* -núnú, -tengamojo, -a kisa,
-a bundu
humble *adj* -a paasí, -síta limo
humid *adj* -a lúfúkú
humidity *n* ulufúkú
humiliation *n* ubufújúle
humiliate *vb* lumbuusya, fújúla
humility *n* ukuja gwa paasí
hump *n* (cattle hump) ulugili
hunchback *n* ikyengenyúma
hunger *n* injala
be hungry íja ni njala, lumígwa ni njala
I am hungry injala jikunduma
hunt *vb* fwima
hunter *n* umfwimí
hurricane *n* umbelo gwa maka
hurry, hurry up *vb* **1** *vt* kuujisya, endeelela 2 *vi* kuuja
hurry up! *interj* mbibi-mbibi!, kuujaga!
hurt *adj* baba, fúlasya, bafya
husband *n.fam* unndume
husk *n* unkupili
hut *n* ikitembe
hydrocele *n.med* ikisene
hyena *n.zool* ikindíngo
hygiene *n* ubwífyusí, ukukonga ubwifyusi,

isya bwifyusí
hymn *n* ulwímbo lwa bukilisiti
hypocrisy *n* ubutungulu, ubusyobí
hypocrite *n* untungulu

179

Ii

I *pron.pers* une, ne
I *prefix.subj* n-
'I … not' *prefix* nga-
ice *n* ingala
idea *n* inyínogono
ideal *n* ikifwaníkisyo ikinúnú
ideal *adj* ja mahala, -núnú -kindilili
identical *adj* -a lusumo lumo, -fwene
identify *vb* manya, nangisya
identification *n* ulumanyo
identity *n* ukuja lusumo lumo, ubufwane
ideology *n* ulwinogono lwa tubombo
idiot *n* unkonyofú, undema
idle *adj* -olo, hangajifú
idleness *n* uboolo, ubuhangajifú
idly *adv* ítolo, kisíta fya kuhomba
idol *n* ikifwaní ikya kwíkemekesya
if *conj* bo, linga, ukuti
if he wants linga ikulonda
ignite *vt* asya, kolesya umoto
ignorance *n* ubukonyofú
ignorant *adj* -konyofú, -a bukonyofú
ignore *vb* suula, komma ukupilika, ikisita kubika mmahala
ill *adj* -bíne; I am ill ndimbíne; he is ill mbíne; I was ill nali mbíne
illness *n* ububíne, imbína (Tuk), indamwa
illegal *adj* aka kakílenie indagilo
illegitimate *adj* -sígwana, aka kakanísígwe ni ndagilo
illiterate *adj* -sita kumanya ukubala nukusímba
illuminate *vb* mwekúka, mwekúsya
illusion *n* imínyeenya
illustrate *vb* manyísya nifífwaní, manyikisya kufífwaní
illustration *n* ukumanyisya ni fífwaní, ukumanyísya
image *n* ikifwaní, ikilamú
imagine *vb* ínogona
imbecile *n* unndema
imitate *vb* egela, íganía
immature *adj* -teta, -aka kakaali akala-

bilo kake
immediately *adv* nakalinga
immense *adj* -nywamú nnono
immensely *adv* fííjo, pabunywamú
immerse *vb* íbisya
immigrate *vb* saamíla nkíísu ikingi
immune *adj* -abuke kububine, -síta kubina
impact *n* ulutwamulano, ulusísímíkisyo
impala *n.zool* uluko lwa imbabala
impertinence *n* ubusíta kufwana, sita kwitika, sita lwitiko
import *vb* íngisya akaandu nkíísu ukufuma ikíísu kya panja
important *adj* -a pamwanya, -a maka, -a ndagilo
impossible *adj* isíta kubagila, isíta kubombígwa
it is impossible sikabagila, nakamo
impostor *n* unsyobi, untungulu
impotent *adj* 1 -fule, akusita imika mbolo 2 ubusííta kuja na maka ga kuníola, umúndu uju akabagila pakuníola
impregnate *vb* papo ulwanda, papo ikifúba
impress *vb* sangamsya
imprison *vb* pínya, biika munnyololo
improve *vb* tendekesya, biika kanúnú
it is improving jigoníle, jilikanúnú
impudence *n* amatíngo, ubugalagala
impudent *adj* -matíngo, -galagala
impulse *n* ulugíndíkisyo, uluhamuko
in, into *prep* mu, nkati mu, nkati
there is nothing in it kakajamo nakamo; in order that ukuti
incense *n* ububaní; burn incense fukisya
incest *n* ukugonana aba kikolo kimokyene
incite *vb* pigula, songelesanía
incline *vb* gúndama, súlama, níongasya
include *vb* komanía, bikamo
income *n* ulukabo (indalama)
incompetence *n* ukusíta kubagíla
incompetent *adj* sítakubagilila, sítakumanya, -tepefú
increase *vb* ongela, baala, baasya
incubate *vb* alamíla

indeed *adv* naloolí
independence *n* ukwíkaba, ulwíjuumilo
indifference *n* ikipahu, ikipaho
indigenous *adj* -ene kaja, jikaja heesya, íja mwene kisu, íja mpapígwa gwa papapa
be indignant keeta ukubaba, ukuja nubukalale
indignation *n* ulubabo, ubukalale
indispensable *adj* -a ndagilo
indolence *n* uboonywa, uboolo
industrious *adj* -bombí
industry *n* **1** ulwíjumilisyo pa mbombo **2** imbombo ja kutendekesya utundu
inexperienced *adj* -teta, -a kumanyíla, sita kummanya fííjo, sita bwisibile
infancy *n* ubwaníke, ubukeke
infant *n* umwaníke, unkeke
infect *vb* taníkisya, ambukisya
get infected ambula
inferior *adj* -a paasí, -fújúfú, -senjí
influence *n* ulukwabo, ukuganígwa na bingí
influenza *n.med* akakínya akakali ka mbungo
inform *vb* buula inongwa
information *n* inongwa
ingenious *adj* -a mahala fííjo
ingredient *n* aka konganíkisya
inhale *vb* kwaba umuují mumbulo pamo nkanwa
inhabit *vb* tugala (nkísu kimo)
inherit *vb* íngila, ingilapo ikilingo
inheritance *n* ikilingo
initial *n* ubusímbe bwa kwanda bwa ngamú
initial *adj* pabwandilo, pakwandila
initiative *n* ulusasanío, ukwandísya
inject *vb* lasa nisindano
injection *n* ululaso nisindano
injure *vb* fúlala, fúlasya, onanga
injury *n* ubufúlale, ubufúlafú
ink *n* ubwino
in-law *n* unkamú gwa nkííkulu pamo unnyambala, unko, unkamwana
inn *n* inyúmba ja kugonamo nu kuulikisya ifíndu ifípye

innocent *adj* -sita nongwa, -eelú
inquire *vb* laluusya, anía
inquiry *n* ululaluusyo, ulwanío
insane *adj* ugwa mbepo
insanitary *adj* -nyalí
insect *n* akambakaasya, ilindu, akapelígwa akaníní (bo, ulubwele, ilínye-gesi, ulujuki, utu tuli na malundi síta)
insert *vb* fyika, íngisya, sonda
inside *prep* nkati, nkati mu
insignificant *adj* -kanandi, kanini fííjo, kakajako
insist *vb* títíkisya, umilila, sísímíkisya
insolence *n* amatíngo
inspect *vb* ketelela nukusí bika kanúnú
inspire *vb* papo amaka, golosya, longolela
instantly *adv* nakalinga,
instead of pabujo pa, pabujo bwa
instinct *n* ulumanyo lwa tundu kisíta kwínogonapo
instruct *vb* manyísya, lingaanía, lagila
instruction *n* ulumanyísyo, ululinganío
insult *n* ilíheelú
insult *vb* helúlakeenya, tuka
intellect *n* ugwa mahala mingi, amaka ga nyinogono
intelligence *n* amahala
intend *vb* bingilila, ínogonela
intention *n* ukubingilila, ukwínogonela
intercede for suumila, lilila uluhobokelo
intercessor *n* unsumilí
intercourse *n* ubwangali bwa mundu nu mundu
interest *n* ulunyonywo, ulukabo lwa pamwanya
interfere *vb* fúfúlila, ingilila
international *adj* -a físu fingi
interpret *vb* sanúsya (amasyu munjobelo ijingi), galabula amasyu
interpreter *n* uju ikugalabula amasyu, uju ikusanusya amasyu
interrupt *vb* fufanía, íngilila
intestine *n.anat* ubula, imíla; **large intestine/colon** *n.anat* ubula ubunywamú

small intestine *n.anat* ubula ubunandi

interval *n* akabalilo aka kíkukiinda mumboneko íbili pamo itatu

interview *n* amalalusyo aga kumanya utundu

interview *vb* pelelesya, londesya ubwanalolí

intimidate *vt* tíílisya

into *prep* nkati mu, mu; **into the basket** nkati nkitundu

intoxicate *vb* gaasya

intoxicated *adj* -gaale, -a bugaale (ubwalwa)

introduce *vb* twala akaandu akaheesya

intrude *vb* ingila kumatíngo, íngilila

intuition *n* ubwengo bwa kumanya utundu

inundate *vb* teeka

inundation *n* umwelesyo

invade *vb* gwilila mbwíte, ingilila

invalid *n.med* umonywa

invasion *n* ukugwilila mbwíte

invent *vb* agula, inogona akaandu akapya

investigate *vb* pelelesya, londa inongwa sya mbutítu

invisible *adj* aka katíkuboneka / kakabagila ukuboneka, akusita boneka

invite *vb* paala

iron *n* **1** (household tool) ikisitilo imyenda, ipasí **2** *n.geol* ilííbwe lya kyela

iron *vb* síta imyenda, koma ipasí

irony *n* injobele iji jikupindula amasyu (ulukaaní), ubuhenufu

irregular *adj* -heesya, isíta kujapo bwíla, isíta kuboneka bwílabwíla

irrigate *vb* nwesya

irrigation *n* ukunelela, ulunelelo (amiisi)

irritate *vb* nyegela, tamya, kalasya, kalalisya

Islam *n* ubwísílamu

island *n* ulusuungo

isolate *vb* paagula, senjeluka, biika pasíma

it *pron* aka; **it is five o'clock** mo mwilemduko; **I don't like it** ngakagana; **this is not it** kakaja ko aka; **it is time to go to bed** mo mwilambalalilo

itch *vb* nyegela, saata

its *poss.pron* -ake

ivory *n* amino ga sofu

Jj

jab *vb* koma, lasa

jack *n* ijekí ja igali

jackal *n.zool* (Kye) akaambwe, (Tuk) ilíjúsí

jacket *n* ijalisi

jackfruit tree *n.bot* umpíkí umfenesí

jaguar *n.zool* ikinyamaana ikikolo kya íbole

jail *n* unnyololo

jail *vb* pínya munnyololo, biika munnyololo

jam *n* (boiled fruit and sugar for use on bread) uluki lwa kupaka nkisyesye

jam *vb* ikola

be jammed kolígwa

January *n* umwesí gwa kwanda

jar *n* ingumbe

jaundice *n.med* ububíne bwa inyongo ubu amaso gikuja kajinja

jaw *n.anat* ulugego, ikilega, ilígego, ikigego

jaywalk *n* enda mwalomwalo kisíta kupasya amagali

jealous *adj* -a bufí

jealousy *n* ubuufí

jeer *vb* seka kulwílaamo, ohela

jeopardize *vb* bíníka

jerk *vb* lúúsa, nyesya

jerry can *n* ikyela kya kupimbila amafúta ga nyale na ga igali

jewel *n* ilííbwe ilípala, ilíbwe ili likulangala, ilíbwe ili likulangala kangi ípala

jigger *n.zool* (small insect which lays eggs in the skin) indekenya

jilt *vb* bujisya, leka

jingle *vb* unjwego gwa kyela bo ulu ifungulo inyingí sikulilila

job *n* imbombo

join *vb* lunga

joint *n* **1** ikilungo, ikipungunyo **2** *n.slang* (marijuana cigarette) unsokoto gwa makambo, imíkambo

joke *n* isuunga, ikyugiila, imboosyo

joke *vb* sunga isuunga, poosya, ugiila, pula

journalist *n* (Swa mwandishi wa habari) unsíímbi
journey *n* injila, ulwendo
joy *n* ulusekelo
judge *n* undamúlí, undongí
judge *vb* amúla, lamúla, loonga
judgement *n* ubulamulí, ubulongí
judicial *adj* -isya ikolotí ni sya bamanyandagilo
judiciary *n* ulubaatiko lwa makoloti ga kíísu
jug *n* ikikopo, ilíjagí
juice *n* amiisi ga baluki, ba mwembe, amalalangi etc.
July *n* umwesí gwa tuhano na tubili, julai
jump *vb* nyeela
jump over *vb* kílanía
jump off nyotoka
junction *n* inyaganílo, injila inyaganilo, injila imbagukano, imbasaana
June *n* umwesí gwa ntandatu
jungle *n* ikisítu, amatengele
junior *adj* -níní, -nandi
junk *n* kakuulu, akaandu aka kakaja nu ntengo nagumo
jurisdiction *n* ubwimilílí bwa ndagilo
jury *n* ikilundilo kya bamanyandagilo, ikilundilo kya bamuuli
just *adv* isya naloolí, kokuti
just a little panandi ítolo
just so buno buno, bububo
just there kula kula, palapala
justice *n* ubwanalolí
justify *vb* lingisanía buno sijilíle
juvenile *adj* 1 -jufya, sya bwanike 2 (animals) -túbwa
juxtapose *vb* bambika, baatika ndubambo

Kk

keen *adj* -ugi, -a maso
keep *vb* bika
keep on endelela
keep up endelela
keeper *n* untendekesí
kernel *n* uluseke
kerosene *n* amafúta ga nyale, amafúta ga tala
ketchup *n* umposí gwa nyanya
kettle *n* ilíbilika
key *n* ifúngúlo
keyhole *n* ubwína bwa fúngúlo ndwigi, babwíngisyo ifungúlo
kick *n* ilíbala
kick *vb* bagula, baaja, koma ilíbala
kid *n* 1 (child) umwana, unkeke 2 (baby goat) akapene
kid *vb* ugiila, ugilila, poosya
kidnap *vt* josya umúndu, iba umúndu, hija nu kufísa umúndu nu kumela ikyuma kubakema ukuti umúndu gwago asakulígwe
kidney *n.anat* ulufígo
kill *n* ukugoga, utugogígwa
kill *vt* goga, pyúta
killer *n* ungogí
kiln *n* ikyokelo, ikikokesyo (-bo amapamba), ikigemo, mwakabunguja
kin *n* unkamú
kind *adj* -a kisa, -ololo
kind *n* uluko, ulusúmo, ikikolo kya tunyamaana pamo abandu
kindergarten *n* isúkúúlú ja bwandilo, isúkúúlú ja kukukisya abaana
kindle *vb* aka umoto, kosya umoto
kindness *n* uboololo
kindred *n* ikikolo, unkamú
king *n* umalafyale, unnyafyale
kingdom *n* ubunyafyale
kingfisher *n.zool* kasweswe
kinky *adj* -a mwalo, -a kwípotanía
kiosk *n* pabunegelo amiisi, pabulikisyo utundu twa kunwa nu kulya utu nandi

kiss *n* ibusu, ikísí, ulufípo kukanwa

kiss *vb* fípa kukanwa

kitchen *n* ilíjíko, pabupijilo

kite *n* 1 *n.zool* akabelele, ilyebe 2 (toy) indege ja ikalatasí nu tupiki iji jikungilígwe ubusí kusúlo nu kutwalígwa kumwanya nu mbelo

kitten *n.zool* akaana ka níalu, níalu unnini

knead *vb* baanda

knee *n.anat* ilífúndo

kneecap *n.anat* ingata ja ífúndo

kneel *vb* fúgama

knife *n* ummage

knit *vb* luka, sona

knob *n* ikipungunyo, ikilungu

knock *vb* koma, kong'onda, kínya

knot *n* ikifúndo, ikifúndikililo

know *vb* manya, syaganía

knowledge *n* amahala, ubumanyí

LI

label *n* ikimanyílo, ikinangisyo

labor *n* imbombo

laboratory *n* 1 inyumba ja butendeesí bwa tujiilo nutwiho twa tumbakasya twa pakíísu apa 2 inyumba ja míkota muno bikupanga nukuketa

laborer *n* umbombí, umbombelí

laces *n* ifítambala fya kungela ubunúnú mmyenda

ladder *n* untandalilo

ladle *n* untíngo, ulwiko

lady *n* 1 unkííkulu

lake *n* sumbi

lamb *n.zool* ing'osí imwana

lame *adj* -lema, -fulafu

be lame lemala

lameness *n* ikílema, ubulemafú, ubulemale

lamp *n* inyale, itala

lamp-wick *n* ubutambi

lance *vb* júfúla

land *n* ikíísu

land *vb* súlúka, tuula ukufuma kumwanya

landing-place *n* pabusúlúkilo

landscape *n* akajilo ka kisu

lane *n* ulukindi ulufinye, unsebo umfinye

language *n* injobele

lantern *n* inyale

lap *n* ulutapatapa

large *adj* -kulumba, -nywamú

larva *n* ilífílífílí

last *adj* -a kubumalikilo, -a mwisyo, -a kummalikisyo

last *vb* jako, malika

at last pabumalikilo, kummalikisyo, kumwísyo

late *adj* -kyelígwe, -túmúkíílwe

be late túmúkilwa, kyelígwa

lately *adv* kifuki, pakijolo itolo, nkabalilo akapimba aka kakindíle

later *adv* píítasí, panyúma

latrine *n* ikibúsú

laugh *vb* seka

laughter *n* iseko
launch *vb* andisya, púlúlúsya
law *n* ulwího, ululagilo
lawful *adj* -sya lwiho, -ja ndagilo
lawn *n* ikitílu, akíísu akapakifígo aka-
  kwangalapo
lawyer *n* umwimililí, ummanyandagilo
lay *vb* biika (lambalika)
lay a table biika ifííndu pameesa
lay eggs teela amafumbi
laying hen inguku iji jikutela
laziness *n* uboolo
lazy *adj* -olo
lead *n.chem* untofyo, ikya ntofu
lead *vb* 1 *vt* longosya, golosya 2 *vi* loongola
leader *n* undongosí, umalafyale, unnyafyale
leadership *n* ubulongosí
leaf *n* ilyaní, ulusetulilo
leak *vb* toonya, tolíka
lean *adj* (animals, people) -gaafú,
  -sekele, -nandi, níafú
become lean ganda, sekeleka
lean *vb* egama
lean upon egamíla
leap *vb* nyeela
leap year *n* ikyinja ikitali, ikyinja ikitalí iki amasíku ga mwesí gwa bubili
  gíkuja 29
learn *vt* manyíla
learning *n* ukumanyíla, ubumanyílí
least *adj* -nandi, -nandi fííjo
leather *n* ikipapa, ingubo, ikigubo,
  ulukoba
leave *n* ulwítikisyo, ulutuusyo
leave *vb* leka, syasya, sooka, saama
give leave lekela, pa ulwitikisyo, papo
  ulutuusyo
leaven *n* akaandu akakali aka kikuga-
  gisya pamo ifíndu, bo ihamila
left *adj* -kíímama
left hand ikiboko ikíímama
leg *n* ikiluundi (pl amaluundi)
legend *n* akapango akakuulu aka kiku-
  pangígwa ntu balilo utu; akasumo
  kabutungulu

leisure *n* akabalilo ka kutuusya
lemon *n.bot* ilílalangí
lemon tree *n.bot* umpíkí gwa ílalangí
lend to *vb* asímísya
length *n* ubutalí
lengthen *vb* ongela, talísya, luusa
leopard *n.zool* ilíboole
leprosy *n.med* imbungo ja makete,
  ubukokonyale, ubukoma
lessen *vb* naganía, pepula, pepusya,
  pímbusya
lesson *n* ulubalo, ikimanyílo
let *vb* leka, ítika
letter *n* kalata
level *n* ubufwane, ulutananda
liar *n* untungulu
liberal *adj* -bupe, (ideas) ubundu
liberty *n* ubwabuke (ulwítikisyo)
library *n* inyumba pamo ikyumba muno
  ifítabu fíngi filimo ukuti abandu babalege
lick *vb* myanda
lid *n* ikifúndiko, ikikupikilo
lie *n* ubutungulu
lie *vb* tungulupa
life *n* ubumí
lift *vb* pimba, ínula
light *adj* (not heavy) -pepe
light *n* ulumúlí, ubwelú (pamúsi)
light *vb* kosya, asya
lightning *n* injasí
lightness *n* ubupepe
like *adv* ngati
like *conj* bo
like *vb* igana, gana
be like *vb* fwana ni (na)
likeness *n* ikifwaníkisyo, ubufwane
likewise *adv* bo lululo
limb *n* ikilundi pamo ikiboko pamo
  ikipiko, ikiluungo
lime *n.bot* umpanya
limit *n* umpaka (ukufíka)
limit *vb* bika umpaka
limp *adj* myogoke, myonyoke
limp *vb* myogoka, myonyoka, sosomela,
  nyunyutuka, kúúka

line *n* ulukindi
linen *n* amasapa ga katani
linger *vb* kaabila
linguist *n* umúndu ummanyí gwa njobele
linguistics *n* ubumanyílí bwa njobele
link *n* ikilungilo
lion *n.zool* ingalamú
lioness *n.zool* ingalamú imbikí
lip *n.anat* undomo
liquor *n* ubwalwa
   illicit liquor igongo
list *n* ulubaatiko lwa mbalilo, ulubambo
listen *vb* pilikisya, pilika
litter *n* 1 (stretcher for sick) ikipímbilo
   abandu linga mbíne pamo unkafú ítolo
   2 (young animals produced at one birth by
   a single mother) ulubwaako lumo lwa
   finyamaana 3 (garbage) ubunyalí
little *adj* -nandi, -níní
   little by little panandipanandi
a little panandi
live *vb* gona, jako kubumí, tugala
liver *n.anat* ikiníe
living *adj* -a bumí, -umí
lizard *n.zool* komakipíkí
load *n* untwaalo, ikitwalo
load *vb* pakila
loaf (bread) *n* ikisyesye
loafing *adj* -embeelí
loan *n* unkopo
loathe *vb* kalalila, benga
local *adj* ja papapa, -ene kaaja
lock *n* ikíígalilo
lock *vb* ígala
lock in igalila
locust *n.zool* ilípalalila, ilípaasí, imbamandila, ilípamandila
log *n* ikisínga, ikipíkí
loin *n.anat* unsana
loincloth *n* umwenda gwa munsana
loiter *vb* betabeta
lonely *adj* -piina, -ene, -kisíta
long *adj* -talí
long for *vb* nyonywa, mímwa
longing *n* ulunyonyo, ikinyonywo

look *vb* keeta
look at, look around kelengania
look for *vb* londa
looks *n.pl* kuboneka, kumaaso
loop *n* ihululila
loose *adj* -abuke, -hobofu
become loose *vb* abuka, holobondoka
loosen *vb* hobola, abula, honyola
loot *n* ifipupilwa, ifíkolígwa mbwíte
lord *n* untwa
lose *vb* sobesya, tolígwa, liigwa, sofya, taaga,
   pondwa;
   (by death) sobelígwa (fwililígwa); **my**
   knife is lost ummage gwangu gusobíle
loss *n* ubusobelígwe, akaandu akakasobíle
be lost soba
lot *n* ikijabo
a lot of ubwíngí bwa
cast lots *vb* koma ikuula
louse *n.zool* ingolo
love *n* ulugano, ubunyonywe
love *vb* gana; **I love you** nguganíle
lover *n* ikigane
low *adj* -a paasí
lower *vb* súlúsya, telamika
lowered *adj* -telamúfú, -súlwíke
loyal *adj* -a bwanalolí
luck *n* ulusako
lucky *adj* -sangalufu, -a lusako
luggage *n* ikitwalo
lukewarm *adj* -fugutifú
lump *n* ulubúli, ikilundilo kya mfú,
   pamofímo
lunch *n* ifíndu fya pamúsi, ifyakulya fya
   pamúsi
lung *n.anat* (Kye) ilíbagaja, (Tuk) ilíhahama
lust *n* ubunyonywe, ikinyonywo kya bulogwe
luxury *n* akaandu kakusekeesya,
   kakuhobosya, ukupupwa
lymph gland *n.anat*
   swollen lymph gland ilyambafú

Mm

machine *n* ilíkína
mad *adj* -a kigili
madness *n* ikigili
maggot *n.zool* ulufwíngílí
magic *n* ubulosí
  black ~ ubulosí;
  white ~ ubuganga, isya kuswígisya
magician *n* undosí
magistrate *n* undongí
magnificent *adj* -núnú nnono
mail *n* ikalata
main *adj* -kulumba
mainland *n* ikíísu iki kili kubutalí ni
  nyanja
maize (UK), corn *n* ikilombe
make *vb* tendekesya, pela, tendeka
make an effort uje nulwífímbilisyo,
  ifímbilisye
make a noise jwega, jwega unjwego
make him be quiet mbatamísye
make fun of sungila isunga, sekeesya
make love níola, ganana
make sure bomba ubwanalolí
make a fire pegesa umoto, kosya umoto,
make up your mind ijande, inogone-
  kangi, bika ubwamuli
malaria *n.med* amalelia, isekema ja mbwele
male *adj* (animal) -pongo
male *n* akandu akanyambala
male organ *n.anat* imbolo nifítungu
malicious *adj* -bíní, -a kabíní
mammal *n* utunyamana toosa utu tuko-
  ongesya ibaana
man *n* unnyambala, umúndu
manage *vb* bagila, imilila
management *n* ubwimililí
manager *n* undongosí pambombo,
  umwimililí
mangle *vb* nyafúlanía, tatula
  (umwenda)
mango *n.bot* (fruit) mwembe
mango tree (Mangifera indica) *n.bot*
  mwembe

mangrove *n.bot* umpíkí ugu gukutoba
  imísi gyake mwilolo, imílola
manhood *n* ubunyambala
attain manhood níongoka
mankind *n* umúndu
manly *adj* -a bunyambala
be manly ijannyambala
manifestation *n* ukubika pabwelú,
  ukwíbonesya
manner *n* akajiilo, ulwíjíísyo
manure *n* indope, imbolela
many *adj* -íngí
map *n* ilamaní
March *n* umwesí gwa butatú
march *vb* pembenuka
marijuana *n.bot* amakambo
mark *n* ikimanyílo
mark *vb* biika ikimanyílo
market *n* ilyulilo
market place *n* pabuulilo, palyulilo
marriage *n* ubwegí
ask in marriage síngila, haha
marrow *n.anat* (Swa uroto) ubomba
  bwa nkati mmífúpa
marry *vb* 1 (marry a woman) ega 2 (marry a
  man) egigwa 3 (marry a woman) abula
mask *n* ikikupikilolo, ikifwaní kya
  kufwala kumaso, ngenenge
mason *n* unjenga nyúmba sya mapamba
  na mabwe
mass, a mass of ulubungaano lwa
  bandu ukuja pamopeene, ubusíto
massacre *n* ukugoga abandu kubwíngí
massive *adj* nywamú nnono
mast *n* imbanda indalí ija pasítíma
master *n* untwa
master *vb* imilila, bwesya
masturbate *vb* ílúta
mat *n* ubunyasa; Types of mats: unkwela,
  uluteefu, ípúkú, ulunyegenyela, akatibe,
  ubulili
mate *vb* 1 (about males) endekesya
  2 (about females) enda
match *n* 1 (for fire) ikibiliti 2 (sports)
  ulukíno, ulutolano, umpalano

match *vb* fwanía, bambika (pair), egana

matter *n* inongwa

what is the matter fíndufíkí fíkutamya

it doesn't matter po papo, síkaja mbala

matting *n* ifúngúbo ni kibale, uluteefú
  lolosa

matting-bag *n* ikíbo, isenjele

mattress *n* ilígotolo

mature *adj* -bifwa, níongoka, -kome

become mature *vb* bifwa, níongoka

May *n* umwesí gwa buhano

may *vb* bagila

maybe *adv* ndiisí, pamo, lumo

meal *n* ifíndu ifya kulya

mean *adj* -a pakati na pakati

mean *vb* nangisya

meaning *n* kokuti

meanness *n* ubusita maka mumbili
  (ubugaafu), ubwímí

means *n* injila

  by all means loloosa lula

measles *n.med* akaandu, isúlúa

measure *n* ikipimo, ikipimilo, unteengo, bo
  múmo

measure *vb* pima, gela

meat *n* inyama

mediate *vb* patanía

medicine *n* 1 unkota 2 *n.slang* ikipíkí

medicine man *n* unganga

meek *adj* -tengamojo, -talalifu

meekness *n* ubutenga mojo, ubutalalifu

meet *vb* agana, aganíla

meeting *n* ulukomaano

melody *n* ulwímbo

melon *n* ilyungu ilya misi inyafu,
  ikikolo kya lyungu

melt *vb* enguka, engula

member *n* gwankibugutila, umúndu uju
  alinkijabo kimo

memorize *vb* kola

memory *n* ubukumbuki, ingumbu

memorial *n* inongwa isí sikutwala
  ukukumbuka kamo, isya kukumbusya

menace *n* indondomeko

mend *vb* tendekesya

mention *vb* joba

merchant *n* undolí, umuulisí

mercy *n* ilípyana, ikibabiilisí, ulupaakisyo, ikisa

have mercy on -ja nípyana, pakisya

merely *adj* ítolo, po papo

merry *adj* ulusekelo lwingí

be merry sekela, kína

mess *n* ulonangiko

mess up *vb* fúfanía

message *n* indumí

messenger *n* ugwandumi

metal *n* ikyela

metal spring *n* ulugombeko lwa kyela
  ulu lukubípuka

mew *vb* ukulila kwa níalu /pusí

midday *adv* pamúsi, bo ilísuba lili
  pantu

in the middle of pakati na pakati pa

middling *n* pakatinapakati

midnight *adv* pakilo pakatí

might *vb* bagila

migrate *vb* saama

mild *adj* -butengamojo, -a butofu

mileage *n* amailo

military *n* indumbula ja bwite, ilíjesí

milk *n* ulukama

milk *vb* kama

mill *n* ikituli

millet, sorghum *n.bot* imbila

  bulrush millet amapemba

  finger millet amalesi

millipede *n.zool* ilíjongolo

mince *vb* butanía tunandítunandi (bo
  inyama) nu mmaage

mind *n* inyínogono

mind *vb* uhilí, utyolí, biika múndúmbúla

I don't mind ndikupasya

never mind sikanakamo, po papo, uli-
  ngapasyaga

mine *n* ungoti, imbibwe

mine *vb* kumba (amabwe, ulutalama)

miracle *n* ikiswígo

mirror *n* ikikeetelo, ikimwemweta

miscarry *vb.med* sopola ulwanda

miscellaneous *adj* -a koongana, twingí twingí ítolo

mischief *n* umwalo

miser *n* umwímí

miserable *adj* -fujuke, -súlúmaníe

miserly *adj* -ímí

misfortune *n* ulusako ulubíbí

mislead *vb* somanía, syoba, sofya

miss *vb* pondwa, peesya, túkúla

missionary *n* untumígwa, ummisioní

mist *n* ulubeefú

mistake *n* ulusobo

misunderstand *vb* síta kupilikisanía, manya ulungi

mix, mixture *n* ikilundiko, ubufalaganíe

mix *vb* onganía, falaganía

moo *vb* tama kama ng'ombe

moan *vb* lila, ajula

mob *n* ikibugutila kya bandu, ikilundilo

mock *vb* angalila, kínila, sungila, fuuja, ugilila

modern *adj* mbya, -a lululu

moderate *adj* a pakatí, -a kyaji

moderately *adv* bo múmo, pakatí na pakatí, pabunandipo

modesty *n* ulwijisyo

moisten *vb* bundisya, timisya

mole *n.zool* ifúko

mold *vb* bumba

molt, moult (UK) *vb* peenyeka amajoja, ijubuusya

moment *n* akabalilo

in a moment na kalinga, lululu

monastery *n* inyúmba ja bapuuti (abamisyoni)

Monday *n* ikilembelo

money *n* indalama, ihela

monkey *n.zool* 1 ingambili 2 (ape) gúmbe

monogamy *n* ubwegí bwa nnyambala jumo / nkííkulu jumo

monsoon *n* 1 imbepo iji jikwandukaanduka 2 Umbelo ugu gukukula munyanja

month *n* umwesí (gwa kubala mmasiku)

mood *n* akajiilo, indumbula, ulwípiliko

moon *n* umwesí (ugu gukuboneka kumwanya)

new moon umwesí unsomoka, akeesí

full moon umwesí unkome, umwesí unkomú, umwesí ugu gukubala

moor *n* ulungalangala

mop *vb* pyagisya ni, koma ilekí

more *adj* -a kukindapo, kangi

a little more kukindapo panandi

more than ukukinda pa

moreover *adv* kangi, ukukinda kulijisí, ukongelapo

morning *n* ulubunju

in the morning nulubunju

early in the morning nulubunju fííjo

mortar *n* 1 (container for pounding) ikituli 2 (for building) umfu pamo isementi ja kujengela

mortar board *n* isahani ja kutwalilamo, umfu ugwa kusijengela inyúmba

mosque *n* pabwipútilo pa bísílamu, unsíkítí

mosquito *n.zool* ulubwele ulu lukuluma ulwa pakilo

mosquito net ikyandalula

moss *n* ingobyo

most *adj* -ingí fííjo

moth *n.zool* ilíkolokotwa, ilíkolokoto

mother *n.fam* (generic) juuba, mama

my mother juuba, ujuuba (Tuk)

your mother unyoko

his/her mother unna

our mother juubagwitu

your (pl) **mother** unnemwe

their mother unnabo

/Juuba is the real word, but today mama is frequently used, especially among young people. Unyoko, similar to its English counterpart, carries an offensive additional meaning and is therefore frequently substituted with mama (gwako)

mother tongue *n* injobelo ja kupapígwa najo

motor *n* ikyombo iki kikwendela ubumeme, ukwípa amaka, imota

mould *n* ubumele ubu bukufwana booga

pa tundu ututimu
mountain *n* ikyamba
mourn *vb* súlúmanía, lila, íja ndúfúmbo
mourning *n* ifwa
mouse *n.zool* imbeba
mouth *n.anat* akanwa
move *vb* 1 segelela, enda, sema 2 (settle in a new place) saama, saamísya;
   move out of the way soosya munjila, (vi) semesya, sema
mow *vb* senga ilíísu ilípimba
much *adv* bwingí, fíijo
mud *n* amatope
multiply *vb* kiisya, ongela
multitude *n* ikilundilo, ulukomaano ulunywamú
mumble *vb* íbunesya, íjobeesya
mumps *n.med* amatuse
munch *vb* tafúna
murder *n* ubugogí
murder *vb* goga
murderer *n* ungogí
murmur *n* uluheho, indeto
muscle *n.anat* unnyofu
mushroom *n.bot* ubooga
music *n* indíngala ninyimbo
Muslim *n* unswahili, umwísílamú
must *vb* mpaka, fíkuti
mustache *n.anat* indefú sya pamwanya na mumbali mundomo
mustard *n* umpíkí ugu guli namabuba amajinja niseke syake nditu pamo nyelu
mute *n* ugwa kinúúnú, uju atikujoba
muteness *n* ikinúúnú
mutiny *n* ubusambukí bwa basikali / íjesí
mutton *n* inyama ja ng'osí
mystery *n* isya kubutítu

Nn

nab *vb* kola unhijí, kola undeebí
nail *n* 1 (finger/toe) ikyala
   2 (for carpentry) unsúmalí
naive *adj* ugwa njobele nimbombo sya bukeke
naked *adj* bwasí, kifúúla, ngelebuno
name *n* ingamú; **first name** imbeegwa; **last name, family name** ingamu ja kikolo
name *vb* joba, koolela
nanny *n* uju ikubomba imbombo ja kwangala na baana
nap *n* utulo (twa pamusi)
nape *n.anat* ingono, ilíkosí, kwíkosí
narcotic *adj* unkota gwa kugaasya pamo /nu kutwala utulo
narrate *vb* panga, lingaanía
narrow *adj* -fínye, -sekele (nandi)
nasty *adj* -bíbí, -nyalí
nation *n* ikikolo, ikíísu
nationalism *n* ubugana kisu ubukindilile
nationalization *n* ukupoka, ukubika mmaka ga bandu bingí
national park *n* unngunda gwa fínyamaana fya ndísu
national military service *n* ukubombela ikíísu mbusíkalí
native *n* umwenekíísu
nature *n* ikifúmo, ubwandilo
naughty *adj* -a bugalagala, -a mwalo
nausea *n* ikinyanyasí
nauseate *vb* biluka
navel *n.anat* ilítúmbú
navigate *vb* longosya (isítíma pamo indege), jata munyanja
near *prep, adv* kifúkí, pípí
nearly *adv* kifúkí fíijo, pípí fíijo
neat *adj* -ífyusí
necessary *adj* fíkuti, bagila, -a mpínyo
necessity *n* umpínyo
neck *n* amakosí, ikikosí

necklace *n* inyambo isya mmakosí

need *vb* londa, fúmbwa

needle *n* isíndano, isonelo

negative *adj* -ija kukana, ilíísyu lyakukana

neglect *vb* fúja, leka, kaana

negligent *adj* -bwapufú

negotiate *vb* pelepesya, pilikisanía

neighbor *n* umpalamaní

neither ... nor pamo … pamo

nephew *n.fam* umwipwa (undumyana)

nepotism *n* ukubakyeela bene aba kikolo pa bujabi bwa mbombo sya mfwalo

nerve *n.anat* ulukole

nervous *adj* -nyomofú, -a lutende

nest *n* (Kye) ikifufumbwa, (Tuk) ikifúmbwa

net *n* **1** (for fishing) ikilepa
  2 ulwelo

never *adv* napanandi, síku, nakamo

nevertheless *adv* bobuno buno, pope

new *adj* -pya, -hesya

news *n* amasyu, inongwa, indumí

newspaper *n* ilígasetí

next *adj* ilya bubili, -kongeleli, ujungi

nibble *vt* ng'wenya

nice *adj* -núnú

niece *n.fam* umwipwa (undindwana)

night *n* ikilo; **at night** pakilo

all night ikilo kyoosa

nightmare *n* injosí ija kutíílisya, injosí imbíbí

nine *num* **1** tuhano na tuna **2** (> Swa.) tísa **3** (arch) mfundiko kimo na tuna, lwele kimo

nineteen *num* mulongo na tuhano na tuna

ninety *num* amalongo mahano na mana, amalongo tísa

nip *vb* fyúnda, tita

nipple *n.anat* ilíbeele, ulumyato

no *adv* mma, himma

there is no food fíkajako ifíndu, ifíndu fíkajapo

there is no water in it amiisi gakajamo nkati

noble *adj* -a lwimiko

nobody *pron* najumo

nocturnal *adj* aka pakilo, -a pene pakilo

nod *vb* ítikila nuntu, tínila

noise *n* unjwego

nomad *n* uju ikusaamasaama

nominate *vb* sala, soola

nonsense *n* mahala nagamo, konyofú

noon *adv* pamúsi

noose *n* ihululila ja lugoje

normal *adj* -a bububo, -a momuno

north *n* kuluulu

north wind imbepo ja kululu ja palumu

northern *adj* -a kululu

nose *n.anat* imbúlo

nostalgia *n* ubusyukwe bwa kukaja

nostril *n.anat* ubwasi bwa mbulo

not *adv* himma, mma

note *n* kalata, amasíímbo ga kusoka

note *vt* keeta, syaganía

nothing *n* nasímo, nafímo, nakamo, nabumo

notice *n* ulufúmusyo

notorious *adj* -pakasí, -a kumanyígwa fííjo kububibi

nought *n* nakamo, nasímo

November *n* umwesí gwa kalongo na gumo

now *adv* lilino, ulu

right now lululu, lululu ulu

nowhere *adv* nakumo

nowadays *adv* ubusiku ubu, amasiku aga, akabalilo aka

nude *adj* -kifúúla, -síta mwenda nagumo, -kitalí

nuisance *n* umwalo, indamyo, isisíkukalalisya

numb *adj* -a bwasí, -síto

number *n* imbalilo

number *vb* bala

numbness *n* ubwasí

nun *n* unkííkulu uju ijítíke ukumbombela mwene kyala, uju atikwegígwa, unsisita

nurse *n* unswili, unnesí

nurse *vb* lwasya

nut *n.bot* iseke isí silimo museke isingí, uluseke

nutmeg *n.bot* uluseke lwa mpíkí

Oo

oar *n* 1 (pole for punting) ulusyembe
2 (paddle) ingafí
oath *n* ululapo, ulujigo
obedience *n* ukubonesya ulutíílo
obedient *adj* -tíílí, -a lupiliko
be obedient tííla, pilika, konga indagilo
obese *adj* -túpe fííjo
obey *vb* tííla, koonga, pilika
object *n* akaandu
object *vb* kaana
objection *n* isya kukaanísya, ubupiingí
obligatory *adj* imbombo isí símbagíle
umúndu ukubomba, -a lulagílo
oblige *vb* fimbilisya
obnoxious *adj* -nyalí fííjo, mbíbí fííjo
obscene *adj* (amasyu, ulwího etc) -nyalí
fííjo
obscure *adj* -síta kuboneka kanúnú, -ndíítu
observe *vb* pima, koonga fííjo
obstinate *adj* -a lukaaní, -kaaníka, -a
nulukaaní
obstruct *vb* gomola, pinga
obtain *vb* kaba
obvious *adj* -elu, -síta mpasyo
occasion *n* uluboneko
occult *adj* -palapala, -a kubutítu
occupy *vb* kaba, kola
occupation *n* imbombo, ukwipukulanía
occur *vb* boneka
ocean *n* inyanja
ocher *color.adj* -fúbifú
o'clock *adv* akabalilo ka sala
October *n* umwesí gwa kalongo
odd *adj* -heesya, -a kiswígisyo
odor *n* ulunúúsí
of *prep* -a (gwa, gya, ja, ija, ba, twa…)
off *adv* ukufuma, ukusooka
offend *vb* kalalisya, sobela
offensive *adj* -bengi
offer *vb* soosya, sookesya, -pa, ukupa
offering *n* ilíkemo
office *n* ibofesí

official *adj* -sya mbofesí, -a lwiho
official *n* umúndu gwa silikali
offload *vb* baatula, ísya, sulusya
offshoot *n* ulusamba lwa mpíkí
offspring *n* umwaana, imwana
often *adv* kíngí, bwílabwíla
oil *n* amafúta
ointment *n* amafúta agankota aga kupaka, unkota gwa kupaka
OK *adv, adj* naloolí, momúmo, oogo
okra *n.bot* ibamía
old *adj* kangale, kuulu
become old and worn kuulupa, kangala
old age *n* ubukangale
olive *n.bot* 1 (tree) untílolo 2 (fruit) indílolo
omen *n* ikíka kya kunangisya utwa
kuboneka nkyení ukuti pamo tukuja
tunúnú pamo tubíbí
omit *vb* leka, sosyapo
on *prep* pamwanya pa
once *adv* kamo kene, kamo ítolo
once upon a time *expr* akabalilo kamo íjolo
at once *expr* nakalinga, lululu
one *num* kamo, -mo, limo, jumo
oneself *pron* -eene
onion *n* ikitungulu
only *adj, adv, conj* ítolo, -eene
onward *adv* nkyení nu kwendelela
ooze *vb* toonya, swa, súlúlúka
open *adj* -bwasí, -a pabwelú
open *vt* abula, baalula, ígula, (mouth)
gajula
operate *vb* pasula
operation *n* imbombo, ulutúkúnyíko,
ububombeli
operation (in hospital) *n.med* ukupa-
sula, ubupasule
opinion *n* inyínogono
opponent *n* uju mukutolana, akaandu
ka kusigila, unsígílí, umpiingí
opportunity *n* ubujo, akabalilo
oppose *vb* kaanísya, kaaníka, pinga
opposite *n* ikibafu ikingi
opposite *adj* -níngeene
put opposite nínganía, biika kubungi,

ketesya kubungi

oppress *vb* bíndikila, bonela, bombela kanyalí, lambika

optimism *n* -a pamwanya, -a kwísíbila, -a kusubila

option *n* ubwisalile, ukusalapo

or *conj* pamo

oracle *n* unnyago, unndongosí gwa kusubilígwa

orange *color.adj* -jinja

orange *n.bot* luukí

order *vb* lagila

order *n* ululagilo, ulubaatiko

put in order tendekesya, baatika

in order that ukuti

orderly *adv* mbola mbola, ndubatiko

ordinary *adj* -a bunobuno, -a bwílabwíla

ore *n* umfu gwa kíísu, ulwalabwe lwa lutalama

organ *n* akambakaasya ko kosa kala aka mumbili gwa tunyamaana bo amabagaja, ikiníe etc

organize *vb* tendekesya, bika ulubatiko

orgasm *n* ulumalikisyo lwa kugonana

orientate *vb* ísíbila pamo, ísíbisya

origin *n* ubufumilo, ubwando, ikikongotí

original *adj* ja bwandilo, mbya

ornament *n* ulunosyo

ornate *vb* utundu twa pantengo fííjo, utundu twa ndalama nyingí

orphan *n.fam* umpiina

oscillate *vb* syúta, syúsya

ostrich *n.zool* injuní inywamú fííjo iji jikutolígwa pakupululuka, imbuní

other *adj* -ngi

other *adv* ulungi, pasíma

other *conj* na pope

the other aka bubili, ujungi

other people abandu abaangi

others *n,pron,adj* abaangi, bamo

otherwise ulungi (bo sikaja), lingalukaulo

I ought to mbagíle, símbagíle

you ought to ubagíle, sikubagíle

this ought not to be done sikabagíla ukubombígwa buno buno, singabombígwa

otter *n.zool* imbago

our *poss.pron* -itu

out *prep* panja

go out *vb* sooka panja, buuka panja

outcast *n* unsuulígwa, unkagígwa pakaja

outcome *n* isí sikubonekaga, isí sikwisaga, isí sikukwagaga

outgoing *adj* kusooka, -a kubuuka

outrage *n* akajiilo akakusíta kutííla

outside *prep* panja

oval *adj* mbúlúnge bo ulwa ifúmbi

oven *n* akafinye kakupijilamo ifwisyesye, akakokela ifindu bo inyama

over *prep* pamwanya

overcome *vb* tola

overflow *vb* saasya

overlap *vb* kindana, kwelana

overseas *n* kwísilya

overseer *n* umwimililí

overtake *vb* kinda

overthrow *vb* petúsya

overtime *n* isala sya kukindako, akabalilo aka kakindilíle

overtime rate *n* umfwalo ugu kwega bo ubombíle imbombo nkabalilo aka kakaja ka mbombo

overturn *vb* sanúsya, gwisya, kúpúsya, petúsya, pinduka

owe *vb* melelígwa

owl *n.zool* **1** ingwítwa **2** (large) ilífúfúma

own *vb* kaba, -ja nafyo

my own -angu une

your own -ako ugwe

on your own *expr* palwako, gwímwene

owner *n* umwenenafyo, umwenenako

ox *n.zool* ingambaku

Pp

pace *vb* enda panandi, tambuka
pack *vb* pakila
package *n* ipaketi, akatwalo, unsígo gwa tundu
packet *n* ikisaka, ipaketí
paddle *n* ingafí ikijajo kya njinga
paddle *vb* fíga
padlock *n* ilíkúfúlí
page *n* untuulí
pail *n* indobo
pain *n* ulubabo, ukubaba
paint *n* ilangí, ipendí
paint *vb* paka
pair *n* utundu tubili utwa luko lumo
palace *n* inyúmba ingulumba, inyúmba ja malafyale
pale *adj* -jwelufú, -buulufú, -elu
palm *n.anat* ikyanja
palm tree *n.bot* umpoosa
panic *n* uboga bwa mbibimbibi, nyomoka nukutííla nakalinga
pant *vb* tuuja, hema, tutwa, twetela, tuujaníke
pants *n* isúlúbalí
papaya (UK), **papaw, pawpaw** *n.bot* umpapaju
papyrus *n.bot* ilíkangaga
paper *n* umpupa, ikalatasí
parade *n* imbembenúka
paradise *n* ubusyuka (mbusyuka kwa kyala)
paraffin *n* amafuta ga tala / nyale
parallel *adj* -síta kwaganíla
paralysis *n* akajiilo kakulalata
  become paralytic lalata
parcel *n* ikisaka
pardon *n* uluhobokelo
pardon *vb* -swa, hobokela
parent *n* umpaapí
parliament *n* ilíbúnge
parrot *n.zool* kasúkú (njuní)
part *n* ikijabo
part *vb* biika pasíma, jaba

particular *adj* mwene, julajula, fííjofííjo, ... bo ...
partition *n* (inside wall) ilílínga
partner *n* umbwesí, unnino, unnine
partridge *n.zool* ingwale
party *n* **1** (social gathering) ulubungaano lwa bandu, ikilundilo **2** (political) ikyaama
pass *vb* kinda, kweela
pass an exam kweela amagesyo
passage *n* ulukindo, injila
passion fruit *n.bot* ilípohola
passport *n* kalata gwa njila
past *adv* -kindíle, íjolo
past *adj* -kindíle
pasture *n* ilísu lya kulikisya ing'ombe
pat *vb* pamanda
patch *n* ikigamba, ikilaka
path *n* injila, akajila
patience *n* ubufínda ng'oma
patient *adj* -fíndang'oma
  be patient ija mfíndang'oma
pattern *n* bo múmo, ikifwanikisyo
pause *n* ulutuusyo
paw *n* ikilundi kya kinyamana iki kilinifyala bo níalu
pawn *n* biika nkukopesya, ulupíngikilo
pawn *vb* pingikila
pay *vb* homba
pay a salary *vb* fwika umfwalo
pea *n.bot* injegele, ifíngyengyeja
peace *n* ulutengano, ulutenganío; **make peace** patanía
peach *n.bot* ilífyulisí, unfyulisí
peak *n* kusulo kukyamba, ubumalikisyo
peanut *n.bot* ilísyabala
pearl *n* ulwambo ulupala, ilííbwe ípala lya munyanja
pebble *n* ulusangalabwe
peck *vb* kong'osola, nyosola, kong'onda nundomo gwa njuni bo ingong'ondelo
peculiarity *n* akajilo kapasima, ikimanyílo
pee *vb* tunda, tunda amatusi, ona, súnda
peel *n* (of fruit) ilíkandi

peel *vb* uba, paatula, alula, (eg. potatoes) leesya, pyata
peel *vb* bambula
peep *vb* tendeela, língulila
peg *n* ikikíngí, ulusonga
pen *n* isímbilo (ja bwíno)
pencil *n* isímbilo
penis *n.anat* iswímbílí, imbolo
penitence *n* ulukubilo
people *n* abandu
pepper *n.bot* imbílípílí
perceive *vt* syaganía, aganía, manya
perfect *adj* aka kafwene, -a naloolí
perform *vb* bomba
perfume *n* utwa kunungila
perhaps *adv* pamo, kingamo, liinga, múmo
peril *n* ubutolwe
period *n* akabalilo
perish *vi* onangika, soba, malika
permanent *adj* -a bwíla, -a bwílabwíla
permission *n* ulwítikisyo
permit *vb* ítikisya
persist *vb* endelela uku-, umilila
perplex *vb* swiga, jeeta, syoba
persecute *vb* ega kumaka, bonela,
   tamya, saaka
persecution *n* ulukubilo
persevere *vb* umilila
person *n* umúndu
perspiration *n* amafúkú
perspire *vb* sooka amafúkú
persuade *vb* fímbilisya, haha, soonga,
   lambilisya, peefya
pestle *n* ikyúsí
petal *n* ilyani lya bulenge
phlegm *n* ilíkosomolelo
phone *vb* koma isímu
pick *vb* tíísya, sala, tungula
pick up sala, pimba
pickle *n.bot* amiisi ga múnyu agaku-
   bika munyama, mwíseeke, ukuti
   fingaonangikaga mbimbibi
picture *n* ikilamú, ikifwaní
piece *n* ikijabo ikinandi, ikimeenya
pierce *vb* sotola, lasa

piety *n* ubwíkemo
pig *n.zool* ingulube
pigeon *n.zool* 1 (wild) ingungubija
   2 (domesticated) ingunde
pigeon pea *n.bot* imbange
pigweed *n.bot* fyongolomya
pile *n* ikibugutila; pile of shit ifíngwa
pile *vb* lundika
pill *n* akaseke
pillar *n* imbanda, ikikongotí
pillow *n* ikijínulilo kya kuntu
pilot *n* umpota ndege
pimple *n.anat* uluundu lwa kumaso
pin *n* ipini, inyapíní
pinch *vb* fyúnda, bíínda, títa
pine *n.bot* umpaina
pineapple *n.bot* ikinanaasí
pink *color.adj* -fúbifú
pious *adj* -íkemo
pipe *n* 1 (tube) umpila 2 (for smoking)
   ikyana kya ngambo
pirate *n* unnyambuta, ilínyambuta lya
   munyanja
piss *vb* tunda amatuusi
pistol *n* indusu innandi
pit *n* ikíína
pitcher *n* ingúúmbe
pity *n* ikisa, ikibabiilisí, ulupaakisyo,
   ilípyana
pity *vb* paakisya, íja nikisa
place *n* ubujo
place *vb* biika
placenta *n.anat* ilínyama
plague *n.med* ikigwaja
plait, braid *vb* luka
plan *n* ulubaatiko
plan *vb* baatika, panga
plane *n* ikipululilo
plane *vb* pulula
planet *n* indondwa isí síkulisyungutila
   ilísuba
plank *n* ilítapwa
plant *n* ifya kumela
plant *vb* byala
plantain *n.bot* -->see *banana*

plantation *n* unngunda
plaster *n* ubumatiko
plaster *vb* kanda, mata, matila
plate *n* indelema
play *vt* moga, kína, fína
pleasant *adj* -núnú, -nyaafú, -a kwikyela
please *interj* mbelíle, nalamba, napela
please *vb* kyeela, sekeesya
as you please bo múmo gwiganíle
pleasing *adj* ukwikyeela, -a kuhobosya
pleasure *n* ulusaalo, akaandu aka
  kukakyeela, ulusekelo
plenty *adj* -keelwa
plot *n* 1 (land) akagunda, ikibaanja 2
  (plan) ulubaatiko lwa kubomba kamo
pluck *vb* apa, tungula, ípa, penya
plunder *vb* pupila, poka, pupa
plunge *vb* tumbukisya (mmiisi)
pocket *n* inyambi, ikinyambi
pod *n* ilíkandi (lya ndima, njegele, im-
  baange)
poem *n* ulwimbo ulwa mafíso
poet *n* umbatika inyimbo
poetry *n* inyimbo
point *n* ubumalikisyo, isúlo
point *vb* nangisya (pala)
pointed *adj* -sugí
poison *n* unkota unkali ugu gukugoga,
  isúmú, umwafi
poison *vb* tega isúmú
poke *vb* gúta, sogosola
pole *n* imbanda
police *n* abasikaalí
  policeman, police officer *n* unsikaalí,
  umpolísí
polish *vb* gúúsa, tasa, tenenesya, súka
  (ikilato)
polite *adj* -a lwiho, -a kajiilo akanúnú, -ololo
pollen *n* imbungapunga, ubufu bwa
  mbulenge
pond *n* ikisíba, ikíína kya miisi, ilítúbwí
pool *n* ilítúbwí, ikíína
poor *adj* -londo
popular *adj* -fúmúke
population *n* imbalilo ja bandu boosa

nkisu, ubwingí bwa bandu pakaaja,
  pakísu
porch *n* ilílínga lya kwangalapo
porcupine *n.zool* ikilúngú
pork *n* inyama ja ngulube
porridge *n* ubuují, ilítapa
port *n* ubutusyo bwa sítíma
porter *n* umpimba fítwalo
portion *n* ikijabo
possess *vb* íja nafyo
possessor *n* umwene nafyo
possession *n* ikyuma, akakabígwa
possible *adj* aka kabagile ukubombígwa
be possible bagila ukubombígwa
  it is possible sibagilígwe
possibly pamo ukumanyígwa
  I can't possibly do it ngabagila
  ukubomba sisisyo
position *n* ubujo
positive *adj* -a naloolí
post *n* imbanda, imbombo ja mfwalo
pot *n* 1 (for cooking) indeko, isefulilo
  2 *n.slang* (marijuana) amakambo
pot shed *n* ulujo
potato *n.bot* 1 ('Irish') indofanía
  2 (sweet) imbataata
potter *n* umbumba ndeko
pottery *n* ububumbí, ifyombo fyanfu,
  pabubumbilo utombo twa mfú, indeko
pound *vb* tíka
pour *vb* ona, kuusya, súlúla
poverty *n* ubuloondo
powder *n* ulufumbi, ipoola
power *n* amaka
practice *n* inyísibisyo, ulwího
practice *vb* jisibisye, ísíbisya, bomba
praise *n* ulutúfyo
praise *vb* túfya, paala, gíndika, júmbika
pray *vb* suuma, ípúúta
pray for suumila
prayer *n* ulwípúúto
preach *vb* lumbilila, fúmúsya amasyu
precaution *n* ijalíle, bomba kamo
  ukupa injila ja kusigila, uluboneko
  ulubibi

196

precede vb talapo, buka nkyení, ija kunyuma / panyuma pa, buka kunyuma ku

precious adj **1** (valuable) aka ntengo **2** (beloved) unganígwa

precisely adj momúmo, paapo, luulo

predict vb solola, gogwa

prediction n ubusololí

prefer vb gana, sala nkyení

preferable adj kyaji, paakípo

pregnancy n ikifúba, ulwanda (lwa mwana)

pregnant adj -a kifúba, -a lwanda

be pregnant íja ni kifúba, íja nulwanda

prepare vb tendekesya

present n ikyabupe

present vb pako, -pa

He presented the idea to the headmaster Atwele inyínogono syake ku nkulumba gwa súkúlú

be present japo; **he is present** alipo

presently adv (time) ubusiku ubu, pasyele panandi

preserve vb tendekesya ukuti fíngabola

president n undongosí gwa kisu, laisi

press n ukugíndikisya, ukutítíkisya

press vb gíndikisya, títíkisya

press in vb joofúka, bínda

press on vb bíndikila, tímbikila

press hard ílikila, títíkisya

pretend vb íbika, ípela

pretty adj -núnú

prevent vb gomola, kaanísya, túsya, sígila

prey n akanyaama pamo injuni iji jikufwimígwa kunongwa ja kulya

price n unteengo

prick vb tubulila, lasa

pride n ulwítuufyo, ulwíbono, ilítumbi, ubumogelí, ikyumbi /Note: Pride is a negative concept for the Nyakyusa.

priest n umpúútí

prince n umwana undumyana gwa malafyale

print vb símba na makína

prison n unnyololo

prisoner n umpínyígwa, umfúngwa, ugwa nyololo

privacy n isya kubutítu

prize n ikipeegwa , ikyabupe, ikihombígwa iki íkukaba umúndu pafínganílo

probably adv pamo, lumo

problem n ubutolwe, ulutamyo, ubukamandanígwe

proceed vb endelela

proceeds n.pl ulukabo

process n ingongano

proclaim vb fúmúsya, tangasya

procure vb kaba, ula

produce vb soosya, paapa

product n ubufumile, ifífunjígwa

profane adj -nyalí

profit n ulukabo, ubukabilo

gain profit kaba, kindapo pala gwalyulile, biisya; **He did not gain any profit because he sold the same as everybody else** Akakabilemo nafímo papo alyulísye bo lulo bosa bíkúlikisya

be profitable ukuja nu bukabilo

program n ulubaatiko

progress n ukwendelela

progress vb endelela

prohibition n ulukanisyo

prolific adj -olokí, -fyele; **be prolific** oloka, ija -fyele

promise n ulufííngo

break a promise ukufúja ulufííngo

keep a promise fíkapo pa lufingo

promise vb finga

promote vb tangasya

promotion n kwesya ikyeo

prompt adj mbibimbibi

pronounce vb joba, tangasya

pronunciation n akajobelo, injobelo

proof n ubukeetí

prop vb egamíla, egamisya

proper adj -núnú, mwene (suitable) aka kabagíle

properly adv kanúnú, ndubatiko

property *n* ikyuma
prophecy *n* ubusololí
prophesy *vb* gogwa isya nkyení, solola
prophet *n* unsololí, unkunguluka
proportion *n* ubufwanikisye, ulwegano
propose *vb* **1** joba, joba inongwa, twala
  ilíísyu, sasanía **2** (marriage) haha
proposition *n* amasyu
prosecute *vb* biika pabulongí, melela
prosecutor *n* ummelí
prosper *vb* baala
prostitute *n* undogwe, unkwakwa
protect *vb* lindilila, sigilila, tendekesya
protection *n* ubulindililí, ububinga
proud *adj* -a kumogela, -a matingo, -mogí
prove *vb* joba isya naloolí
provide *vb* papo, -pa
provision *n* ulufííngo
provocation *n* ukukalalisya, ukusaaka
provoke *vb* kalalisya, (cause) saaka
prune *vb* patilila
pry *vb* pelúlanía, lingulila
psalm *n* ulwímbo ulwíkemo, sabuli,
  ulwímbo, (kyaNgonde) salimo
  Psalms (book in the Bible) *n.relig*
  Inyimbo
pub *n* ikilabú
puberty *n* ubuníongoke
pubic hair *n.anat* ilífúsí
publish *vb* fúmúsya, tangasya
puddle *n* ikindimbwííli, ilítúbwí
puff adder *n.zool* kituumbi
puke *n* amateesí
puke *vi* teeka, byooka
pull *vb* kwaba, lúúsa, lúndúmúla
pull out *vb* fígula, fyula, nyúngúla,
  nyúkúla
pull up *vb* nyúkúla, kúúnya
pulley *n* ikyela pamo ikipiki ikibúlúnge
  iki kifwikígwe umpila pamo ulugoje
  nu kwendesya utundu bo ííkína
pulpit *n* ikigemo
pulse *n* ukulinda kwa ngole
pump *n* ipampú
pump *vb* futila, swila umuuji

pumpkin *n.bot* ilyúngú
punch *vb* bulika kumaka ningumí,
  tubulila
punctual *adj* uju afíkíle akabalilo aka
  kikulondígwa, pakabalilo
puncture *n* ubwina (mumpila ugwa
  muji), ipankya
punish *vb* fúnda
punishment *n* ulufúúndo
punk *n* umpasyuli
pupil *n* **1** (student) ugwasukuulu,
  umwanike gwa súkúúlu **2** *n.anat* imboní
puppy *n* imbwa imwana
purchase *vb* ula
pure *adj* -elu, -sita bunyalí
purgative *n* unkota gwa kusúka múnda
  (ugu gukupela ukuhalísya)
purify *vb* elusya, súka
purity *n* ubunúnú, ubwelú
purpose *n* inyínogono, inongwa, ulubingililo
on purpose kumatíngo
purse *n* ikinyambi, inyambi ja ndalama
pursue *vb* koonga, kagisya
pursuer *n* umbopelí, unkagiisí
pus *n.med* amafíla
push *vb* gúta
put *vb* biika
put down tula paasí, biika paasí
putrid *adj* aka kikununga fííjo
puzzle *n* ulwalanganío
puzzle *vb* tamya, alangania
pyrethrum *n.bot* ipaleto
python *n.zool* isota

Qq

quality *n* akajiilo ka bunúnú

quantity *n* ubwíngí

quarrel *n* ubwíte

quarrel *vi* -lwa, ílwa, umana, somana, lwana

quarrelsome *adj* -a bwíte

quarter *n* kamo ntuna

queen *n* umalafyale unkííkulu, umwehe, undenga

question *n* ilílaluusyo

question *vb* laluusya

queue *(UK)*, line *n* ulubambo

quick *adj* mbibimbibi, -a kukuja, -engo

quickly *adv* mbibimbibi

quiet *adj* -a myemyemye, -a kimye, -jonjolo, -talali

  become / be quiet tengaana, batama, kíba, myeka, ija mye

quietness *n* ulutenganío, ikimyeka

quietly *adv* kimyemye, myemyemye

quit *vb* leka, saama, lekesya

quite *adv* nasiku

quiver *vb* tetema, silila

Rr

rabbit *n.zool* kalulu

race *n* 1 (people) uluko lwa fíkolo fya bandu 2 (competition) lutúmbanílo

race *vb* túmbaníla, tolana ulubilo

racism *n* ubulegane bwa fíkolo fya bandu

radio *n* ilelio

rafter *n* ulukonyolelo

rag *n* ikitambaala, ilísapa

rage *n* ingímbuko, ingalalisí, amaaja

ragged *adj* -fwanjalifú, ugwa ngalalisí

raid *n* ukukolígwa nukupokígwa mbibimbibi kwa fyuma, ubuhijilígwa, ubugwililí

rain *n* ifúla

rain *vb* tíma

rain maker *n* umpelafúla

it is raining jikutíma, ifúla jikutíma

rainbow *n* ululaanga, ulundasí, akapingafúla, ubupindo bwa fúla

rain cloud *n* ilíbíngu lya fúla

rain forest *n* ikisítu iki kipyu nukuja ni fúla nyíngí

rainy season *n* ikisíku, akabalilo ka fúla

raise *vb* fyusya, ínula

raised *adj* -ínufú

raisin *n.bot* ilíífíílo ilyumú

ram *n.zool* ing'osí imbongo

range *n* ulukindi (ulwa fyamba)

rank *n* ikyeo

ransom *n* indalama isí síkuhombígwa ukuti umúndu abulígwe

rapid *adj* -mbibimbibi, -kuuje

rare *adj* -pala

rash *n* utupele twa ulufúkú

rat *n.zool* imbeba; cane rat ingenge

rate *n* ikipimo, ilíígelo

rather *adv* kyaji; I'd rather do it myself than let him do it Kyaji mbombe jujune kuliko ukundekela umwene

rational *adj* -a mahala, -a lwíjísyo

ration *n* ilíposo, ikijabo

rattle *vb* kílílíka, joba mbibimbibi

ravine *n* ikíína, ulupaanga

raw *adj* -bisi

razor *n* ulwembe

reach *vt* fíka, fíkila

reaction *n* ubwamúle, ubusyuluke
(kuno ugwa ja)

read *vb* bala, imba, (count) belenga

ready *adj* tendekesígwe

be ready itendekesye

real *adj* -a naloolí, -a bwanalolí

realize *vb* syaganía, manya

really *adv* naloolí

rear *vb* swila, fuga, kusya, tuula
ukukula

reap *vb* funja

reason *n* inongwa, isya kufúmbwa

reasonable *adj* -a mahala

rebel *vb* saambuka

rebel *n* unsambukí

rebellion *n* ubusambukí, ukusambuka

rebuke *vb* kemela, kaanísya

receive *vt* ambilila, peelígwa

recent *adj* -akapya, -a lululu, -a pipi

recess (holiday) *n* akabalilo aka kutuusya, akabalilo kakutuusya

recipe *n* ukuliíngaanía buno ifíndu fíba-
giile ukutendekesígwa, ulubaatiko na
kapiijilo ka fíndu

reckon *vb* bala, syaganía, inogona,
manya

recognize *vb* syaganía, kumbuka,
manya, ega kangi

recollect *vb* kumbuka, syaganía

recommend *vb* soka

recompense *vb* homba, poka

reconcile *vb* manyanía, fwanía, patanía,
aganía

record *n* ubusímbe bwa mboneko

recover *vb* kaba kangi, pona

red *color.adj* -kesefú

redeem *vb* poka

redeemer *n* umpokí

reduce *vb* naganía, pepusya, pepula,
púngúsya

reed *n* ulutete, ulugugu

reef *n* igengelemya munyanja

refer to jobela

refill *vb* ísusya kangi

reflect *vb* ínogona, gomosya kangi (bo
ulumúlí)

reform *n* ulutendekesyo

reform *vb* tendekesya

refresh *vb* tengaanía

refuge *n* ubwipoko, ubwifíso

refugee *n* uju akibopíle ikíísu kyake

refugee camp *n* apa bikubatugasya aba
bakibopile ikíísu kyabo

refuse *vb* kaana, sííta, piika

refuse *n* ubunyalí

regret *vb* paakisya

regret *n* ulukubilo

regular *adj* -lubatiko, -a múmo

regularity *n* ulubaatiko

regulation *n* ululagilo

reign *vb* kaba, lindilila (ikyela kya
nkanwa kya mbunda)

reject *vb* hena, kaana, sííta

rejoice *vb* sekela, saala, sanya, lúlútíla

relate *vb* panga, fwaníkisya

relation *n* ubukamú

relative *n.fam* unkamú, ikikolo, ugwa
kikolo

relax *vb* hobola, honyola, tuusya

release *vb* lekesya, (eg. from a trap) tatula,
leka

reliable *adj* -a kusubilígwa

relief *n* ubuhobofú bwa, ukunaganíka
kwa lubabo

relieve *vb* pokela

religious *adj* -kyela kyala, -íkemo, -a kyala

reluctant *adj* -a busíítasííta, ulusíta
kwigana

rely on *vb* subila

remain *vb* linda, syala

remainder *n* aka kasyele

remark *vb* joba

remark *n* ilíísyu

remember *vb* kumbuka

rememberance *n* ubukumbuke, ubwísyuke

remind *vb* kumbusya

remission *n* uluhobokelo, ubuswe, ukuswa

remorse ulukubilo

remote *adj* kutalí, nkati fiíjo

remove *vb* soosya, tiísya, myatula, sosyapo, saamya, samisya

render *vb* bomba, gomosya (make), sanúsya ukuja

renegade *n* uju ikusímila nkwiputa nkipa nga ikingi

renounce *vb* hena, siíta, kaana

rent *n* isongo (ja nyúmba/ngunda)

rent out *vb* (about houses) pangisya

repair *n* ubutendekesí

repair *vb* tendekesya

repeat *vb* andilamo, anda (kangi), íjanda, bujilamo, andisya, gomokela, bujila

repent *vb* pinduka

repentance *n* ulupinduko, ulukubilo

replace *vb* pyaníkisya, bujikisya paapo

reply *n* ulwamúlo

reply *vb* amúla, búsya, ítika

report *n* ulupango, ulubuulo

report *vb* panga inongwa, buula

reproach *vb* kemela, umana

reprove *vb* soka, gomoka, kemela

reputation *n* akajiilo, ulwíjísyo

request *n* isya kulonda, isya kusuuma, ubusumí

request *vb* suuma

require *vb* londa, fúmbwa

rescue *vb* poka, ponesya

resemble *vb* fwana, kosya, egana

resent *vb* benga, kalalila, ípilika kabibi

reserve *vb* 1 (set aside for later use) biika 2 (a seat) bikila ikikota / ubujo / ubutugalo

reserve *n* ulubikililo

reservoir *n* ilítubwi lya miisi ilí likumbígwe kunongwa ja kubikila amiisi, ilíbilika

resign *vb* soka imbombo, leka imbombo

resin *n* amanyago

resist *vb* siíta, saambuka

resolve *vb* ínogonela, inogona

respect *n* ulwimiko, ulwíjíisyo, ulubaatiko

respect *vb* imika, tiíla, ijíísya

respectable *adj* -a kwimikígwa, -a lwijíísyo

responsibility *n* imbombo ninongwa syosa isí sikulondígwa undongosí ukusíbomba

rest *n* 1 (relaxation) ukutengaana, ulutuusyo 2 (remainder) aka kíkusyala, aka kasyeele

rest *vb* tuusya, syala, tengaana

restore *vb* gomosya, súnga

restrain *vb* sígilila, gomola, túsya

result *n* ifí fíkusokela, akaboneko, uluboneko

resurrect *vb* syusya

retire *vb* tuusya imbombo

retirement *n* ukutuusya imbombo

retreat *vb* gomokela kunyuma

return *n* ukugomoka

return *vb* 1 *vt* (bring back) búsya, gomola 2 *vi* búja, gomoka (come back)

reunite *vb* andisanía, bujanila

reveal *vb* ígula, bonesya, setula, kíngula, fúmbúla

revelation *n* ulusetúlilo

revenge *n* ulubujikisyo

revenge *vb* pyaníkisya, gomolela, bujikisya ububibi

reverence *n* ulwimiko

reverse *vb* sanusya, sanuka, andula

revise *vb* gomokela, andilamo

revive *vb* syusya, -ja mumí kaba ubumí

revolt *n* ubusobí, ubusambukí, ulukalalisyo

revolt *vb* saambuka

revolting *adj* -kalalisi, -sisya lyojo

reward *n* ikya kupeelígwa

reward *vb* -pa ikipeelígwa

rheumatism *n.med* ububíne ubu buliti fíkungwe

rhinoceros *n.zool* pembele, kipembele

rhythm *n* ingubilo ja ndíngala, akakubilo, akalililo, akimbilo

rib *n* ulubafú

ribbon *n* ingiga
rice *n.bot* umpunga
  cooked rice umpunga ugu gupíle
rich *adj* -kabí, -noge
riches *n* ikyuma, indalama, ubukabí
rickets *n.med* (outwards) amatego,
  (inwards) amabiju
get rid of *phrase* sosyapo, taga, leka
riddle *n* ingíito
ride *vb* enda pa fwalasí, (a bicycle)
  kanya injiinga
ridicule *vb* tuka, ugilila, angalila, posya
rifle indúsú
right *adj* 1 (correct) -núnú 2 (not left)
  kííliilo
right *adv* kanúnú
right *n* syanaloolí
right hand ikiboko ikííliilo
rigid *adj* -kafu, -kakamale
rim *n* kumbali kukaandu, umpaka pamo
  ubumalikilo bwa kandu akabulunge
rind *n* ilíkandi
ring *n* akabangala ka munyobe,
  ububúlúnge, ipete, ibangili ja ndobe
ring *vb* kuba ilíbangala
ringworm *n.med* ikibebe
rinse *vb* elusya
rip *vb* nyafúla, taafúla
ripe *adj* -bifwe, -bifú, -fúúfú, -komu
be ripe *vb* bifwa
ripen *vb* bifwa, koma
ripple *n* ilíjiga ínandi fííjo, ilísaasa
rise *vb* kweela, súmúka, boneka
risk *n* ubutolwe, sya kupasya;
  take a risk *phrase* ija ubutowe;
  It is risky to walk in the dark without shoes Sya kupasya ukwenda
  kungisi kisita fílato
rival *n* umúndu uju íkutolana nujungi
  ukuti akabe kamo, undugu
river *n* ulwisí
river crossing ikiloboko kya lwisí
road *n* injila, unsebo
roam *vb* pakanía, embeela
roar *vb* búna, kúla

roar *n* ulubúno
roast *vb* okya, nyaasya
roe *n* ikikaasa
rob *vb* hiija, poka
robber *n* unhijí, undebí uju ikupokaí-
  tolo ifya bandu
rock *n* ulwalabwe
rock *vb* syúta
rod *n* ingili
roll *vb* búngúlúsya, níenga
roll up *vb* búlúnga, alula, níenga
roll out (eg a mat) alisya
roof *n* pamwanya pa lyundu pamo ílata,
  kubundu
room *n* ikyúmba
rooster, cock *n.zool* ingongobe
root *n* unsí
rope *n* ulugoje
rot *vb* bola, onangika
rotate *vb* syungusya
rotten *adj* -bofu, -bíbí
rottenness *n* ububofú
rough *adj* -a mígílílí, -a mwalo, (eg. a
  ploughed field) -a ming'eleng'enye,
  -togomafú
become rough ija mwalo, togomala, ija
  nimíng'eleng'enye
round *adj* -búlúnge
become round búlúngana, ija búlúnge
roundabout *n* apa imísebo gíkusyengela
  pambasaana, apa unsubo gusyungutííle
route *n* injila, injila iji jendígwe pamo
  jínogonelígwe pakwendígwa
rouse *vb* lembusya, súmúsya
row (line) *n* ulukindi
row *vb* figa (ingafi, ubwato), kwaba ingafi
royal *adj* -a kinyafyale, -a bunyafyale
rub *vb* pyagisya (Kye), pyasiila (Tuk),
  gúúsa, fígísa
rub skin off swanúka ilígubo
rubber *n* umpila
rubbish *n* ubunyalí
rudder *n* ikikolelo, ikipotelo
rude *adj* -síta lujumbiko, -a matingo, -a
  mwalo

ruffle *vb* saalula

rug *n* imbulangete, ilípúkú

ruin *n* ubonangifu bwa nyúmba, in-yúmba imbulutuke

ruin *vb* pyúta, onanga, sobesya, bíníka

rule *n* ululagilo

rule *vb* lagila

rumor *n* iheho, itetesí; **There are rumors that Passop will come back to Ipinda** Siliko iheho isi sikuti Pasopo ikubujulapo pa Ípinda

run *vb* bopa ulubilo, bopa

run over keeta mbimbibi, kanya

run out of malikilígwa

rush *vb* kindakumaka, buuka mbibimbi-bi, bopa mbibimbibi

rust *n* ingamí

rustle *vb* kakajala

Ss

sack *n* ilílogota, umfúko, íjúnila, ilígúnila

sacred *adj* -a bwíkemo, -íkemo

sacrifice *n* ulwíkemesyo, ilíkemo

sad *adj* súlúmanie, -a busúlúmanie

be sad súlúmanía

sadness *n* ulusúlúmanío, ikisa

safe *adj* -tengaamú, -kanúnú

salary *n* umfwalo

saliva *n* amata

sail *n* umwenda umwelefu ugu gukukola umbelo musitima

sail *vb* enda mbwato pamo mumeli

sailor *n* umbombelí musítíma

saint *n.relig* umwíkemo

saintly *adj* -íkemo

sale *n* ukuulisya

for sale /on sale fya kulísígwa

salesman *n* umuulisí

salt *n* umúúnyú

salutation *n* uluponío

salute *vb* ponía

salvation *n* ubupokí

same *adj,pron* **1** jula jula, jila jila, síla síla, (etc.) **2** -a kajilo kamokene

sample *vb* fwamíkisya

sand *n* unsanga

sandal *n* indala

sandfly *n.zool* imutunda, imbwele ja munsanga

sap *n.bot* amalimbo

satan *n.relig* setano

satisfy *vb* íkutisya

be satisfied íkuta, fwana

Saturday *n* umpyagilo

sauce *n* umposí

saucepan *n* isefulilo inandi iji jilinikikolelo

saucer *n* ikisahaní, ikisosala

savage *adj* -senji, kali fííjo

save *vb* poka, ponesya

save *vb.relig* banga

savings *n* indalama (ihela) isí síbikíígwe pamo ukuti síje sya kubombela kamo nkyení; imbikililo, isúngilo

savior *n* umpokí

saw *n* unsumeno

saw *vt* (to cut with a saw) leenga

say *vb* joba; -ti (ukuti)

scabies *n.med* imbele

scaffold *n* (execution) apakubaníongela abandu abagogí ku ndagilo

scald *vb* babula kumooto, ukupya numuuji umpyu pamo bo amafuta amapyu

scale *n* 1 (instrument for weighing) ikipimilo utundu, sekelo 2 (reptile, fish) ilíkakala

scanty *adj* -nandi

scapegoat *n* uju ikufwila panongwa ja bangi

scar *n.med* ilíkoko

scarce *adj* tikwagígwa, -pala

scare *vb* nyomosya, tíilisya

scarecrow *n* ukubinga injuni ukuti síngalyaga ifíndu

scarf *n* isíkafu, ikitambala kya mmakosí

scary *adj* -sísya, -a kutílisya

scatter *vb* balanía, búlúlúsya, nyambanía, palasa

be scattered *vb* balaníla, nyambaníka

scene *n* uluboneko

scent *n* ulunúúsí ulunúnú, ulunúngilo, ulunúngo

scholar *n* ummanyísígwa, ugwa musúkúúlú, uju ikumanyíla

scholarship *n* ubutuulí bwa fímanyilo

school *n* isúkúúlú, apa abandu bíkumanyílíla

science *n* isajansí

scissors *n* ikimetelo, isísala

scold *vb* kemela, umana

scolding *n* ukulumba, ulukemelo

scorch *vt* bafya nu moto, kosya nu moto, ulumú, balila ulumu

scorched ipya, bafígwa nu moto, balilígwa nulumu ulukali

score *n* imbalilo ja tundu (mmíkíno)

score *vb* ingisya ... bala ...

scorn *n* ifúújo, ulwílamo, ulubelo

scorn *vb* obela, sungila, fuuja, ilamwa

scorpion *n.zool* kalíísa

scramble *vb* kweela kubutolwe, timbikana, lwílanila

scrape *vb* pyata, pyasya, pulula

scratch *n* ikimanyílo kya kung'walafula nifyala, ubung'walafúle, ubung'wale, ubupalule

scratch *vb* kaasula, ng'wala, palula, ng'walafula, kaasa, pyata

scream *n* unjwego, ingoolo

scream *vb* jwega, lilakumaka, (for joy) koolela, akalúlú, kúúta

screw *n* isukulubwe

screw *vt* 1 (turn/twist smth) pinya, fyata, níongotola 2 *off* níola, gonana nunkííkulu

scripture *n* amasímbo (ga ibangili)

scrub *vb* gúúsa

sculpture *n* ubutendeleesí bwa fífwani

sea *n* inyanja, sumbi

seaman *n* umbombelí musítíma

seal *n* ikimanyílo, unhúlí

seal *vb* biika ikimanyílo, myasya, biika unhulí, mata

search *vb* londa, keeta

season *n* akabalilo

season food *vb* lunga

seat *n* ikikota, pa bujo bwa kwítugalapo

seatbelt *n* unsípí ugu gupínyígwa nkikota kya igali, unkanda kwa kikota mwigali; **Please fasten your seatbelt** Napela fyata unkanda gwa kikota kyako

second *num.ord* -a bubili

secret *n* isya kubutítu

secret *adj* -a mbutítu

secretly *adv* mbutítu, kubutítu

section *n* ulubafu, ikimeenya

secure *vb* biika mbulindilili, lindilila, ígalila, bika kanúnú

security *n* umwimilí, ubwimililí ukuti imbííbi singaboneka, undindililí, ububinga

seduce *vb* sofanía, sobesya, syoba umúndu ukuti abombe imbibi

see *vb* bona, keeta

seed *n* imbejú
seem *vb* boneka
seize *vb* kola, poka
seldom *adv* lumolumo, kubunandi
select *vb* sala, sungula
self *n, pron* akajiilo ka múndu
self *adj* -ene
selfishness *n* ubupafú
sell *vt* ulisya
send *vb* tuma
send away sosyapo, tuma kubutalí, kaga
send back gomosya, bujisya
senior *adj* -kulumba, -a pamwanya
sensation *n* ulwípiliko, ubunyomoke
  bwa kwípílika mbibimbibi
sense *n* amahala, ukwípilika munyinogono
sense *vb* pilika
sensible *adj* -a mahala, -golofu
sentence *n* ilíísyu
sensitive *adj* -pepe ukumanya / uku-
  keta, -a kwípílíka mbimbibi
sentence *n* ikibugutila kya masyu
separate *adj* -a pasíma
separate *vb* biika pasíma, jabanía, jabi-
  ilanía, tapulanía, lúndanía, pagulanía,
  saagula, tapula
September *n* umwesí gwa tuhano na tuna
serious *adj* -síta nkíno
serpent *n.zool* injoka
servant *n* 1 umbombelí, umbombí, untuulí 2 *n.relig* unyamata
serve *vb* tuula, bombela
service *n* ububombelí
  bẹ of service -ja ntuulí, -ja mbombelí
set *vt* 1 biika, íngisya 2 (the sun) joonga
  (isuba), íla
set off sokapo, bukaga
set up imíkisya, imika
set on fire kosya, biika mmoto
set out sooka, endaga, buuka
settle *vb* biika kanúnú, tugasya, tendekesya
seven *n* tuhano na tubili, lwele ikingi
  ntanda
severe *adj* -kali, kisíta mpasyo, -a

kisíta mpasyo
sew *vb* sona
sewing machine *n* ikisulu
sex *n* ukuja nnyambala pamo nkíkulu,
  uluko; ukuníola
shabby *adj* -nyali, -tagate, fwala
  mwalo, -a mwalo
shade *n* ikipepo
shadow *n* unsyunguulu
shake *vb* jugaanía, juganía, tetema,
  jigisya, lelema, juganika, junganika
shallow *adj* -pímba, -a kína kipímba,
  -nandi (ulwisi)
shame *n* isoní
shape *n* ububoneke, ububumbe
share *n* ikijabo, akajabo
share *vb* jabana
sharing *n* ulutuulano, ukujabana
shark *n.zool* iswi inywamú ija munyanja
sharp *adj* 1 (intelligent) -a mahala 2 (clear)
  -engo, -núnú 3 (blade) -ugí
sharpen *vb* pyasya
shave *vb* -mwa, pulula
shavings *n* imípululilo, imímwelo
she *pron* umwene (unkííkulu), juujo
sheath *n* ikifúko kya mmage, ihaala
shed *n* ikibaga, ilítembe
shed *vb* (emit) soosya, sooka
  shed tears lila
sheep *n.zool* ing'osí
sheer *adj* itolo
sheet *n* 1 umwenda unywamú, um-
  baalufú 2 (bed sheet) igolole
shelf *n* 1 ilítapwa pamo kokosa kala
  akapapate aka kakomelígwe mwímato
  pamo mukabatí pabubiko utundu
  2 ikipogojo, ikipangasyala
shell *n* (of snail) ilíkalang'asa,
  ilíkoolwa (lya ítone), ilíkang'ang'a,
  ilíkalang'asila
shelter *n* ikipepo, pabwifíso (lumu,
  -fula)
shepherd *n* untíímí (gwa ng'osí)
shield *n* ingulu
shield *vb* sígilila, papilila

shift *vb* samisya, sanusya, saamya

shimmer *vb* otela ulumu ulupepe pamo kunongwa ja mabingu

shine *vb* langala, múlika, aka, soosya mwela, (sun) bala

ship *n* isítíma

shirt *n* isyati

shit *n* amafi

shit *vb* fúlútúla, -nía

shiver *vb* kíngíma, silila, tetema, sililika

shock *n* undindo, igansi ja bumeme, ulunyomoko

shoe *n* ikilato

shoot *vb* koma indusú, komela

shop *n* ilíluuka

shopkeeper *n* umwene íluuka, umúúlisya íluuka

shore *n* kumbali kulwisí (inyanja, itú- bwi), kunsanga

short *adj* -pímba, -a bupimba

shorten *vb* pímbusya, pímbula

shorts *n* ikabuundu

shot *n* ulutúsúlilo

shoulder *n.anat* ikibeja

shout *n* unjwego

shout *vb* kúúta, jwega, laata

shove *vb* guta, joola

shovel *n* iposolo

show *n* ikinangisyo

show *vb* nangisya, bonesya

shower *n* **1** (bathing) ukooga amiisi aga gikufúma nkyombo iki kikugasopa ngati fúla jikutíma **2** (rain) ifúla inandi, ifúla ja kunyaganya, akanyanyafula

shred *n* akapepelete

shred *vb* nyafulanía

shrewd *adj* -komú

shriek *n* unjwego

shriek *vb* jwega, lila kwisyu lya pamwanya ísekele (kulutende, ukuseka)

shrink *vb* kwínya

shrivel *vb* pindanía, pindana, íja muumu, íja mpíndaníe

shrub *n* ikisyanju

shrug *vb* fyusya amabeja

shuffle *vb* lusa amalundi

shun *vb* epusya

shut *vb* ígala

shut up kíba

shy *adj* -a soní

be shy *vb* íja nisoní, ifwa soni

shyness *n* isoní

sick *adj* -bíne

become sick, be sick, fall sick bina

I am sick ndimbíne

are you sick? ulimbíne?

sick leave *n* ilífu ja bubíne

sickness *n* ububíne, ihoma, indamwa

side *n* ulubafú, ikibafu

on the other side isilya lila, kunjila ijingí

sieve *n* ikisegeselo

sift *vb* segesa, sungula, suuja

sigh *vb* tuuja, tujiila

sight *n* amaka ga kukeeta namaso

sign *n* ikimanyílo, ikinangisyo, isímbo

sign *vb* **1** símba ingamú **2** (with thumb- print) tínda uloobe

signal *n* ulubíndilo amaso, ikimanyílo

silence *n* ikimyeka, ubutalalifú, ubumyeke

silence *vb* batamisya, myesya

be silent batama, talalila, leka unjwego, myeka, leka ukujoba

silent *adj* -tengamojo, -a kimyemye, -talalifu

become silent batama, íja myemyemye, talalila

silently *adv* kimyemye, kimyeka, mye- myemye

silk *n* umwenda ihalili

silly *adj* -konyofú, -a butojofu

silver *n* fesa

similar *adj* -a lusumo lumo, -fwene

simmer *vb* tokota, sefuka

simple *adj* -pepe

simply *adv* ítolo

sin *n.relig* imbíbí, ubwílangomelesyo, ubutulanoongwa

sin *vb.relig* bomba imbííbí, tula inongwa

since *adv* ukufuma, ukufumila, ukwandila

since *conj* namanga

sincere *adj* -a naloolí, -golofu

sing *vb* imba

single *adj* -ene

sink *n* pabusúgúsúlilo, pabusukilo ifyombo mwijiko

sink *vb* íbila (íbisya), jwíba

sip *vb* fípa, pyúkúla

sisal *n.bot* 1 (plant) unkataní 2 (produce, fiber) ikataní

sister *n.fam*

  elder sister ulílumbu unkulumba, ílumbu

  younger sister ulilumbu unnandi

  husband's sister gwifí

  husband's younger sister gwifí unnandi

  husband's elder sister gwifí unkulumba

  wife's elder sister unkulu gwa nkasí

  wife's younger sister unnuguna gwa nkasí

sit *vb* tugala

sit down tugala paasí

site *n* pabujo

situation *n* akajilo ka

six *num* ntandatu

size *n* ubunywamú, ubufwane, ubukulumba

skeleton *n* imífúpa gyosa igya mumbili

skill *n* ubumanyí

skillful *adj* -manyi, -maganyí

skim *vb* angula

skin *n.anat* imbapa, ikipapa, ikikanda, ikigubo

skin *vt* ubula ígubo, ubula ikípapa

skin disease *n.med* ububíne bwa munyuma mungubo

skip *vb* nyela

skirt *n* umwenda gwa kikííkulu ugwakufwala palwanda, ikikútúlo, isíketí

skull *n* umpaja

sky *n* umpaalanga gwa kumwanya

slack *adj* -olo, -onywa, -toofu, -kololofu

slacken *vb* legela, onyoka, kololoka, honyola

slam *vb* kinya kumaka

slander *n* ulutwiko inongwa

slander *vb* tungulupa, tungulupila

slap *n* ilíípi

slap *vt* bapula, koma nikyanja, koma ní ipi, kanja

slaughter *vb* boola, goga, hinja, búúta, búúta ingolomilo

slaughter cows for a funeral baamba (ing'ombe pafwa)

slave *n* untumwa

slavery *n* ubutumwa

sleek *adj* -toofu, nyelemufu

sleep *n* utulo, ukulambalala

sleep *vb* gona, lambalala, gona utulo

sleeping place *n* pabulambalalo, pabugono

sleeve *n* ikiboko kya mwenda

slice *n* ikimenya kya (unkate, ikisyesye)

slide *vb* telemúka, tyelemúka

slight *adv* -nandi, -sekele

slim *adj* -sekele, -nandi, -níafú

slime *n* ikibumba

sling *n* ilíkombelo, ulwendo lwa kusopa, imbyusí

slingshot *n* amanaati

slip *vi* tyelemúka

slippery *adj* -telemufú, -tyelemufú

slit *n* ulusande

slit *vb* júfúla, pasula, pandula

sliver *n* akapaatu

slope *n* untelemuko, ubugúlúmúfú

slow *adj* -kobe, -síta kukuja, -a mbolambola

be slow kaabila, enda panandi, koba

slowly *adv* panandipanandi, mbolambola

sly *adj* syobi, komu

smack *vb* koma ilípí

small *adj* -nandi

smallpox *n.med* indubi

smart *adj* -ífyusí

smear *vb* myasya, singula

smell *n* ulunúsí, ulunúngo

smell 1 *vi* núnga 2 *vt* núsya

smile *n* uluseko, iseko

smile *vb* seka panandi

smith *n* umpoosí

smoke *n* ilyosí

smoke *vb* **1** (emit smoke) fúúka **2** (tobacco) kwesa (ingambo), pepa ingambo

smooth *adj* -nyololofú, -tenenefu

smoothly *adv* gololo

smug *adj* -a kuhobosígwa fííjo

snail *n.zool* ilítone

snake *n.zool* injoka

snap *vb* luma, ng'etula

snare *n* untego

snarl *vb* ng'eeka

snatch *vb* nyaka, nyakula, poka

sneak *vb* bendekela

sneer *vb* ohela, seka nukwilamu

sneeze *vb* tyemúla, tyesemúla

snoop *vb* pelúlanía

snore, snoring *n* amahono

snore *vb* bobota, hona, hona amahono, koloma kutulo

snout *n* imbulo ja kinyamaana

snow *n* ingala, imbepo ja bufu

so *adv* po, múmo, polelo, buno

soak *vb* júbika, olobeka, fúbika, nyopesya

soap *n* isopo

sob *vb* komwa

sober *adj* uju atikunwa ubwalwa, uju asyageníe

sober *vb* syaganía, sanjuka, lemúka

society *n* ikyama

soft *adj* -a butofú, -ndofú

soil *n* umfú

solder *vb* kolekela untofyo

soldier *n* unsíkali, undwabwíte

sole *adj* kene ítolo

sole *n* **1** *n.anat* (of foot) ikikangato, kusi kulujajo **2** (of shoe) isoolí

solid *adj* -kafúkafú, -umike, -kafú

solitude *n* ubupina, ukuja gwimwene

solution *n* ubulamulí

solve *vb* fúmbúla, lamula

some ulubafú lwa, abangi, utungi, -mo

somebody *pron* umúndujumo, umúndu ujungi, nongí, nongí ndibe

someone *pron* jumo

someone else umúndu ujungi

somersault *n* ulwijomolo, ukwijomola, ukupetúka kya nyúmanyúma

something *pron* akaandu, akaandu kamo

sometimes *adv* akabalilo kamo, lumo

son *n* umwana undumyana

song *n* ulwímbo

SONGS

The Nyakyusa have many different types of traditional songs. Although traditional in style, they may have a modern content. There are many songs about politics and current events. These can typically be heard at the pubs, at funerals or at the traditional dances. Some types are: akapote, ikiboota, ikimeele, akanjelenjele …

---

soon *adv* nakalinga, lululu , kifúkí

soot *n* ilísísí, amasísí

soothe *vb* tengaanía, talalisya, (Kye) batika / (Tuk) beteka, batamisya

sore *n.med* ikiloonda, ubufúlale

be sore aka, baba, súlúmanía

sorghum *n.bot* imbila, amapemba

sorrow *n* ubusúlúmaníe

sorry *adj* -a busúlúmaníe

be sorry súlúmanía, ija nulupasyo

sort *n* uluko

sort *vb* baatika, sala

soul *n* ubuumí

sound *adj* -núnú, -kafú

sound *n* ilíísyu, ingolele

sound *vb* lila

soup *n* umposí

sour *adj* -kali

south *n* kwítongo, kumaluundi

sow *n.zool* ingulube ingííkulu, ingulube imbiikí

sow *vb* byala, sopa imbeju

space *n* **1** (room) ubujo **2** (outer space) umpaalanga gwa kumwanya

spaceship *n* indege/ikyombo iki kikwenda

kumwanya

spade *n* iposolo

span *n* ubwanjufu, ubutalí bwa kabalilo

spark *vb* soosya umoto, bílítula, tuluka umoto

sparkle *vb* múlikamúlika

speak *vi* joba

speak loudly joba fííjo, laata

spear *n* **1** (with a flat metal tip) ingweego, ikikosa, imbongolo **2** (with round metal tip) undúnda

special *adj* -a pasíma

specialist *n* untaalamú, uju amenye fííjo akaandu kamo

species *n* uluko

speech *n* ubujobí

speed *n* umwendo

spell *n* joba amasyu ga kunkola umúndu, joba amasyu ga kutisala ubulosí

spell *vb* joba amasímbo, simba amasimbo, sopela

put a spell on sb ndoge, loga

spellbound *adj* -kolígwa na masyu (pilikisya fííjo)

spelling *n* amasímbo, ulusimbo, ulusopelo

spend *vb* bombela

spice *n* ikilungo

spicy *adj* -kali

spider *n.zool* ulubúbí, búbí

spider web *n* ulubúbí

spill *vb* ona

spin *vb* luka (ulugoje), níongotola

spine *n.anat* ulugongobinya, ulugongolomía, akakang'ang'a

spiral *n* ulusambo

spirit *n* imbepo, ilípepo

be in good spirits sekela, sangaluka

spirits *n* (alcohol) ubwalwa ubusita kufunda, igongo

spit *vb* iswa amata, -swa (amata)

spit *n* amata, amaswelo

splash *vb* nyesya amisi

spleen *n.anat* ilíbeengwe

splendid *adj* núnú fííjo, -a kulangala

splice *vt* **1** pinyanía (imílisi)

2 (join ropes) luka

split *vb* pasula, balanía, menya

split open panja

spoil *vb* bíníka, onanga, loganía

spoils *n* ifíhijígwa, ifíkabígwa

sponge *n* isípanji

spoon *n* untingo, ilefaní, ulwíko, isupuní, indundu (~ made from banana leaf)

sponsor *n* umwimililí

sponsor *vb* imila

sport *n* ulukíno, unkíno

spot *n* ilítondobya, ilíbabya

spotted *adj* -tononde, -a mababya, -a matondobya, -a manona

spout *n* undomo gwa kikopo

sprain *vb* fyengenyúla, fyogola

spray *vb* míísa

spread *vb* alisya, balaníla, balanía, fúmúka, myasya

spread news fúmúsya amasyu, tangasya inongwa

spring *n* **1** (season) akabalilo aka kutulula imípikí

2 (metal~) ikyela iki kikubipula/kikubipuka

3 (water) isalala, inyíbuko

sprinkle *vb* onelela amiisi panandi panandi, míísa

sprout *vb* mela

spur *vb* songelesya

spy *n* umpelelesí, untendeesí

spy *vb* pelelesya, tendeesya, laluusya

square *n* ikipimo iki mbutalí na mbukulumba mufwene

squander *vb* bombela mwalo, naganía ítolo

squash *vb* tikanía

squat *vb* tuugala paasí, jusumala

squeak *vb* lila ulwa mbeba

squeeze *vb* kama, kola fííjo, ílika

  squeeze out bíínda, kamúla

squint *vb* nyínyíla

stab *vb* lasa

stable *adj* -umíke

stable *n* ikibaga

staff *n* **1** (rod) ingílí **2** (employees)

ababombelí
staff housing *n* inyumba sya bambombo
stage *n* ikigemo
stagger *vb* pupuutika, pupuluka
stain *n* ilílobi, ilínona
stairs *n* untandalilo
stairway *n* untandalilo
stake *n* ikya kwimikisya imípíki, ulwego
stale *adj* -jumíle kangi jikajanyafu, -gagile
stalk *n* ikikongotí
stammer *vb* tabilila
stammering *n* ikitabu
stamp *n* ikimanyílo, (on letter) akasungu
stand *n* ikyimilo
stand *vb* ima, ukwima
stand in line baamba, ima ndubambo
stand up aluka, súmúka
star *n* ulutondwa, lulalila
stare *vb* ng'atula
start *vb* anda, sasanía
startle *vb* gúlútúla, swígisya
starve *vb* ifwa / fwaga ni njala
state *n* **1** akajiilo **2** (nation) ubutwa,
   ikipanga ikinywamú, ikísu
statue *n* ikifwaní, ikilamú
stay *vb* tugala, linda
steak *n* unsisa gwa nyama
steal *vb* hiija, íba, leeba, pupa
steam *n* umuují
steel *n* ikyela ikikafú
steep *adj* -ínufú, -kigíma
steer *n.zool* ingambaku imbínde
steer *vb* longosya, pota
steering wheel *n* ikipotelo
step *n* untambo, ilítambo
step *vb* tambuka
stem *n* ikikolo kya mpíkí
sterile *adj* -gumba
stew *n* inyama ifufye, inyama imbije
   pamo ilíseke ípije, umposí gwa nyama
stick *n* (walking stick) ingílí
stick *vt* kola, umilila
stiff *adj* -kafú, -umú, -kakamale
still *adv* taasí

be still tengaana, tugala talali, íja
   kimyemye, kisita kwijuganía
stimulate *vb* pigula, sangamusya
sting *vb* luma, lasa
stingy *adj* -ímí
stink *vb* núnga, núnga kabíbí, peha
stir *vb* kologa, kologanía, jugaanía,
   semesya, fíga
stitch *vb* sona
stock *n* ulubikililo, ikikolo kya mpíkí
stock *vt* bikilila
stomach *n* ulwanda
stone *n* ilííbwe
stool *n* ikikota ikinandi
stoop *vb* ínama, gúndama
stop *vb* ima, leka
store *n* ulubikililo (akiba), pabubiko,
   pabufíso, pabubikililo
store *vb* biika
store-room *n* ikituuba
storm *n* umbelo, umbelo unkali
story *n* akapaango, akasúmo
tell a story panga (akasúmo, akapaango)
story teller *n* umpanga kapaango
   (kasúmo)
straight *adj* -goloke, -golofu
straighten *vb* baalula, golosya
strain *vb* suuja, kasya, popotola,
   pepetula
strainer *n* ikisujilo, ilíkung'undo
strand *vb* leka kisita butuulí
strange *adj* -heesya
stranger *n* unheesya
strangle *vb* níonga, popotola, pííta,
   níongotola
straw *n* imípulilo (gya mpunga, nganu)
stray *adj* -isobi, -jisobíle
stream *n* akisí, ulwisí ulunandi
street *n* injila, ulukindo
strength *n* amaka
stress *n* ubukasye, ubupijane
stress *vb* sísímíkisya, gíndikisya
stretch *vb* golosya, baalula, lúsa, lúmbúla
stretcher *n* ikipimbilo, ulutato
strict *adj* -kali, -kukonga ulubatiko

stride *n* ilítaambo

strike *n* 1 (punch) ulutwamúlo 2 (worker's) ima kumbombo, leka imbombo

strike *vb* (hit) koma, tíka, twamúla

string *n* undisí, ulutungo, ulupote

strip *vb* fúúla, ubula

strip off *vb* bambula, uba, sosyapo, fúúla

stroke *n* ubukome, ubukomígwe

strong *adj* -a maka

strongly *adv* kumaka fííjo

struggle *n* ulwíjuulo, ulwífímbilisyo

struggle *vb* ijuula, tolana

stubborn *adj* -a lukaaní, -kaaníka

student *n* ugwasukuulu, umfúndígwa

study *vb* manyíla

stuff *vb* kanyisya

stumble *vb* tegejuka, -gwa

stump *n* ikisínga, ikikongotí, ikipíkí

stun *vb* lulasya

stunted *adj* -tule

stupid *adj* -konyofú, -lema

stupidity *n* ubulema

stutter *vb* tabaníka

stuttering *n* ikitabu

style *n* injila ja kubombela , akendelo, akafwalilo, ulusúmo

subdue *vb* talalisya, koma, tola, laambika

subject *n* 1 (topic) ifímanyílo, akapango 2 (commoner, one under the rule of another) umpiina

submit *vb* kola amalundi, ísosya, tolígwa, soosya

subordinate *n* untuli

subordination *n* ubutuli

substance *n* akaandu

subtle *adj* -komú

succeed *vb* koonga, ingilapo

such *adv* bo

suck *vb* fípa, onga

suddenly *adv* nakalinga, nyomo

suet *n* amafúta amakafú aga gasyungu-tilile ifígo sya ng'osí ni ng'ombe

suffer *vb* babígwa, kubilwa, laba

suffer loss sobesya

suffering *n* ulukubilo, ukubaba, ukubabígwa

suffice *vb* fwana

sufficient *adj* -fwene

sugar *n* isúkalí

sugar cane *n.bot* umúúba

suggest *vb* sosya inyinogono syako

suggestion *n* inyingono ja múndu

suit *vb* bagila, fwana

suit (clothes) *n* isuti, imyenda igi isyati ní talabusi fífwene

sulfur *n* ikibilití (íbwe lya moto)

sulk *vb* gúba

sum *n* imbunganíe, imbalilo

sum up *vb* onganía

summary *n* kubupímba

summer *n* palumú, akabalilo ka lumú

summit *n* kususulilo ku kyamba

summon *vb* sítaaka

sun *n* ilísuba

sunbird *n.zool* isombyo (Kye), nsombyo (Tuk)

Sunday *n* unduungu, panduungu

sunflower *n.bot* pangajeje (Helianthus annuus)

sunset *n* ukujonga ilísuba, ubwilo

sunrise *n* ukusooka ilísuba, ubukye

sunshine *n* (ilisuba) ulumú, ulumúlí lwa ísuba, ukubala kwa ísuba

superior *adj* -kulumba, -nywamú, -a pamwanya

supervise *vb* imilila

supervision *n* ubwimililí, ubwenelelí, ubulongosí

supervisor *n* umwimililí

supper *n* ifya kulya ifya majolo

supply *vb* -papo

support *vb* egamíla, tuula

suppose *vb* inogona, lagukisya

suppress *vb* bíndikila

sure *adv* naloolí

surface *n* pamwanya pa

surgery *n* ubuganga bwa

surname *n* imbaalo

surpass *vb* kinda, tola

surprise *n* uluswígo, ulunyomosyo

surprise *vb* swígisya, nyomosya, gasula

be surprised nyomoka, nyomosígwa, swíga, gasuka

surrender *vb* leka ubwite, itika ukutolígwa

surround *vb* syungutila

surrounding *n* ififítusyungutíle

survive *vb* japo akabalilo katali, pona mbutolwe

suspect *vb* ínogonela

swallow *n.zool* imbelebeeswa

swallow *vb* míla

swamp *n* ilítubwi, imíjinbijibi, ilílolo

swap *vb* andula

swarm *n* ikibugutila kya (eg. nyukí)

swear *vb* lapa, fínga, jíganika

sweat *n* amafúkú, ulutwíngo

sweat *vb* sooka amafúkú, twínga

sweep *vb* pyagila

sweet *adj* -nyaafú

sweet potato *n* imbataata

sweetheart *n* unganígwa

swell *vb* 1 ísula 2 (river) júmba

swift *adj* -pepe, -engo

swim *vi* ogeela

swimmer *n* umogeli

swindle *vb* syoba ukuti ukabe íhela

swindler *n* unsyobi

swing *vb* syúta, syúsya, byúsya

sword *n* ubupanga, uluubo

sympathy *n* ikibabiilisí, ilípyana, ikisa

synchronize *vb* gwaasya, fwanía

syphilis *n.med* amasendo, akaswende

system *n* ululagilo, ulubaatiko

Tt

table *n* ikitalati, imeesa

tackle *vb* kaba

tail *n* umpíkípíkí (Kye), imbíkípíkí (Tuk), unswígala, umpeepe, ubuswígala

tailor *n* unsoní, unsona kisulu

take *vt* ega

take advantage of bombela mbujo bwa

take care uhelí, utyolí, uje maso, lindilila

take care of enelela, lindilila

tale *n* akapaango, akasúmo

tell a tale panga akapaango, panga aka-súmo

talent *n* ikikungilwa, ikijabo

talk *n* ulwangalo, ubujobí

talk *vb* joba, angala, panga

to talk of joba inongwa sya

tall *adj* -talí

tame *vb* swila, ísíbisya, fúga

become tame swilika, isibisígwa

tangled *adj* -a kwipotanía, -a kukwabusanía

become tangled ipotanía, kwabusanía (amatata)

tank *n* ilípíípa, ilítankí

tap *n* ibomba ja miisi

tape *n* undisí gwa kupimila

tar *n* ilaamí, ilaamya

target *n* inyango

task *n* imbombo ingafu

taste *n* ulunogo, ubunyaafú

taste *vt* lungusya, gela, ega kanandi

tasteless *adj* síta kunoga; **tasteless meat** inyama isita kunoga, ikipapa

tasty *adj* -buluunge

tattoo *n* isímbo, ulusalilo

tattoo *vb* salila

tax *n* isongo

taxi *n* itekesí

TB (tuberculosis) *n.med* ikipambaga ikikulumba, ububíne bwa kipambaga

tea *n* ikyai

teaspoon *n* akalefaní, akííko, ilefaní inandi

teach *vb* manyísya
teacher *n* ummanyísí
team *n* ikibugutila kya bandu ikya kukina imíkino; ikilundilo kya bandu ba míkíno
teak *n.bot* (Tectona grandis) luko lwa mpíkí umpapate amaani
tear *n* ilísosí
tear *vb* nyaafúla, tafúla, pufúla
tear down pangalatula
tease *vb* angalila, saaka, katasya, tamya
teat, tit *n.anat* ilíbeele
technology *n* ubumang'anyí, ububombeli bwa kukonga imbatiko sya sajansi
tedious *adj* -a kukatasya, aka kikukatasya
telephone *n* isímu
tell *vb* buula (pangila), joba
tell tales/stories panga utupaango, panga utusúmo, tungulupila
temper *n* ubutengamu bwa ndumbula; lose your temper kalala, bípuka indúmbúla
temperate *adj* -talalifu, -ololo
temperature *n* ubupyu pamo ubutala-lifú bwa (tundu), akajiilo ka lufúkú pamo imbepo
temple *n* 1 *n.anat* ilísoso 2 *n.relig* pa-bwipútilo, itempeli
tempt *vb* gela, sofya, peefya, soonga
temptation *n* ulugelo, ulupeefyo
tempter *n* unngelí, umpeefí
ten *num* kalongo, mulongo
tender *adj* sebele, pyonyolofu
tent *n* ihema
termination *n* ukulekesya
termite *n.zool* 1 (flying) ilíswebele 2 (non-flying) unswa (Kye), ikyulu (Tuk)
termite mound ikyulu
terrible *adj* -a kutíílisya
terrify *vb* tíílisya
territory *n* ikísu iki kilipasi pa malafyale
terror *n* ulutende
test *n* ulugelo, ulugesyo
test *vb* gesya, gela, pima
testament *n.relig* tesitamentí, ulwiti-kano, ulufííngo
testicle *n.anat* ulutúngú, (*slang*) uluseke

testify *vb* sísímíkisya, sosya ubukeeti
testimony *n* ubukeetí
text *n* amasyu aga gasimbígwe nkitabu
than *conj* ukukindapo
more than ukukinda pa
thank *vb* uti ndaga
thank you níkuti ndaga, eena
thanks *n.pl* ndaga
that *pron* 1 -la, (jila, jula, kila, kala …) 2 *rel.pron* isí
that, in order that linga, ukuti
thatch *n* ubugeleke
thatch *vb* geleka
theft *n* ubuhijí, ubulebi
their *pron* -abo
them *pron* babo; We gave them money Twabapele indalama
themselves *pron* beene; They asked themselves what had gone wrong Balijaanisye bene ukuti fiki fyendile kabibi
then *adv* panyúma, kangi, po, po lelo, ulwanyuma
there *adv* kula, pala, uko
there is kuli ni, pali ni
there is not sikajako, mma, kakajapo
therefore *adv* ko kuno, kunongwa iji, po lelo, polelo
these *pron* aba, aga, isí, ifí, utu
they *pron* 1 (people) aba, abo, bala, abeene 2 (animals, things) si-, tu-, …, fíla, tula, sila, …
thick *adj* -ngíndike
thicket *n* ikisyanju
thickness *n* ubugíndike, ungínda
thief *n* unhiijí, undeebí
thigh *n.anat* ulutapatapa, ikyiima
thin *adj* -sekele
thing *n* akaandu, akambakaasya, ikyo-mbo, ikitendeko
think *vb* ínogona, tutwa
third *num.ord* -a butatu
thirst *n* ikyumilwa
thirsty *adj* -a kyumilwa; be thirsty umilwa

this *pron* uju, ugu, iki, iji, aka, ilí
thistle *n.bot* untulatula
thorn *n* umwífwa
thorn tree *n.bot* umpíkí gwa mífwa
thoroughly *adv* fíijo, kanúnú
those *pron* abo, -la (bala, síla, fíla, gala, tula...)
though *adv, conj* napapo, nalinga
thought *n* inyínogono
thread *n* ubuusí
threat *n* ulutíilisyo, ulutetemesyo
threaten *vb* tíilisya, tetemesya
three *n* -tatu
thresh *vb* puula, fúgúta
thrill *vb* hobola, sangamusya umojo
thrive *vb* baala
throat *n.anat* ummílo, ingolomílo
throne *n* ikikota kya bunyafyale
throw *vt* taaga, sopa, nyamba
throw down bíga paasí, taaga paasí
throw up *exp* byooka
thrust *vb* guta kumaka
thumb *n.anat* uloobe lwa nna, uloobe ulunywamú
thunder *n* ikigulu, injasí, ikitajataja
thunder *vb* kúlúma, gúlúma, tajaníka
Thursday *n* ikina; on Thursday nkina
thus *adv* múúmo, buno
tick *n.zool* ingúlúpa
ticket *n* kalata gwa kwendela injila (mwígali, mundege, etc.) kalata gwa kwítikisígwa ukwíngila mumo, itíkítí, kalata uju ikusosígwa bo uhombíle indalama bo gwipakíle igalí, indege, isitíma etc, pamo bo kuingila ulukino etc.
tickle *vb* nyegeesya
tide *n* ukwisula nukukuluka kwa nyanja
tie *vb* pínya, kunga
tie a knot pínya ikifundikililo, fundikila
tight *adj* -a kupínyana fíijo, -a kukamandana fíijo
become tight pínyígwa fíijo, pínyana, kamandana
tighten *vb* fyata, kasya

tile *n* ikigai
till *prep, conj* mpaka
till *vb* lima
timber *n* umpíki gwa kujengela
time *n* akabalilo
after some time bo akabalilo kakindílepo
another time akabalilo akangi
leisure time akabalilo ka kutuusya, akabalilo ka kwísangamsya
what time is it 1 (modern) kalibule akabalilo 2 (arch) lili bule ilísuba; (possible answers, approx. times):
0500 bo kukukeka
0600 lubunju, bo sikulila injuní
0900 sanya ndeta
1000 sanya ngomu
noon lilipantu, bo lili pantu
1400 ndyiimo
1600 mwílunduko
1800 mwíkungilo
2000 mwililo ifíndu
2200 mwilambalalilo
0100 mwifwilo, kilo pakati
0300 bo sikutema
0400 bo situbeene, bo síku koolela
what time is it, what's the time ilísuba lilibule, akabalilo kalibule
be on time fíka nkabalilo, kisíta kukaabila
not to be in time tumukilwa, kaabila
last for a time malika nkabalilo
the time has come akabalilo kafíkíle
time after time nkabalilo na nkabalilo
timid *adj* -oga
tin *n* 1 (metal) ilílata, ikyela
2 (UK: container, can) ikikopo, ilílebe
tiny *adj* -níní, -nandi
tip *n* isúlo, isusulilo
tipsy *adj* -a bugaale
tire *n* ígulutumu
tire *vb* katasya
become tired katala
tiresome *adj* -a kukatasya

tit *n.anat* **1** (teat) ulumyato **2** *slang* (breast) ilíbele

to *prep* ku

toad *n* ikyula ikinywamú

tobacco *n* ingaambo

tobacco pipe *n* ikyana

today *adv* umwisyugu, lilino

toe *n* uloobe lwa mmalundi

together *adv* pamopeene

toilet *n* ikibúsú, ikimbúsú

token *n* ikimanyílo

tolerance *n* ubufíndang'oma

tolerate *vb* kíba, íkasya, fíndang'oma, fúfúlila

tomato *n* ulunyanya

tomb *n* ilípumba

tomorrow *adv* kilaabo

tongs *n* ikikolelo

tongue *n* **1** *n.anat* ululimí **2** (language) injobele

tonight *adv* ikilo iki, pakilo

too *adv* na kangi

too much nnoono

too little nandi nnoono, nandi ukukindilila

tool *n* ikibombelo, akabombelo

tooth *n.anat* ilíno

toothache *n* ukubaba kwa líno

top *n* kubususulilo, kukamba

topic *n* ikimanyílo

on top of pamwanya

torch *n* inyale, itokí, inguliko ja moto

torn *adj* -nyafúke

be torn laasuka, nyaafúka, taluka, paanduka

tortoise *n.zool* kajamba

torture *n* ulufúúndo, indamyo

torture *vb* fúlasya fíijo

toss *vb* taaga, nyeesya, sopa

total *adj* -oosa

touch *vb* palamasya

tough *adj* -kafú, -a maka

tour *n* ulujato lwa kukeeta utundu, pamo ikisu

tourist *n* unjaatí (nkisu ikingi)

toward *prep* ku, mu, injila ja

towel *n* ikitambaala kya kusugusulila, ilítabulo

tower *n* ikisonge

town *n* ikipanga, akaaja

toy *n* ikifwani, akakwangalila, akaandu ka kukinila

trace *vb* simba, koongesya ubusimbe

without trace kisíta kwagígwa

track *n* pabwendo, injila

trade *n* uluulo nuluulisyo, ubuulí nubuulisí

trade *vb* ula nukulisya

tradition *n* ifimanyilo ifíkuulu ifí abandu bíkupokesanía

traffic *n* ukwendenda kwa bandu / magalí munjila

train *vb* ísíbisya, manyísya

trample *vb* kanyanga

transfer *n* ulusaamísyo

transfer *vt* saamísya, geesya

be transferred *vi* samisígwa

transform *vb* sanúsya, usanía, andula

translate *vb* sanúsya injobele, pindula injobele

transparent *adj* -langafu

trap *n* untego, ikipiindo

trap *vb* tega

travail *n* ubutolwe, ubutolwe bwa kupapa

travel *vb* enda injila

traveller *n* umwenda injila, unkinda njila

tray *n* isahani ja fíndu imbapate

tread *vb* kanyanga

tread on kanya

treasure *n* ikyuma

treasurer *n* umbiika ndalama; umúndu uju iku tendekesya ikyuma, uju ikubiika ikyuma

treat *vb* bombela

treat (medically) *vb* gangula

treaty *n* ululagano

tree *n* umpíkí

tremble *vb* juganíka, silila, tetema

tremendous *adj* -kutílisya, -a kukindilila

trench *n* umfwoolo, umwína

trial *n* ulugelo

triangle *n* akaandu akambafu itatu

tribe *n* ikikolo, uluko

what is the name of your tribe uli
  múndu gwa kikolo nki ugwe

tribute *n* isongo

trick *n* ubusyobí, ulusyobo

tricky *adj* -janja

trinity *n.relig* akajiilo ka bandu pamo
  utundu tutatu pamopeene, ubutatu
  bwa Kyala, akajiilo ka butatu butatu

trip *n* ulwendo, injila ja pabupípí

triumph *n* ulusaalo

troop *n* ikilundilo

trouble *n* ubutolwe, indamyo

trouble *vb* katasya, tamya

trough *n* ikipondo

trousers *(UK)*, pants *n* ilítalabusi,
  isúlúbalí

trowel *n* umwíko

truce *n* ulwitikano lwa kabalilo

true *adj* -a naloolí

truly *adv* naloolí

trumpet *n* ingangabwíte, italumbeta

trunk *n* nkikolo mu mpíkí, ikipíkí, umbili
  gwa múndu kisíta maboko na malundi

trust *vb* ítika, subila

trustworthy *adj* -a kusubilígwa fííjo, -a
  kwitikígwa fííjo

truth *n* ubwanalolí

try *vb* gela, gesya

tse-tse fly *n.zool* ilísasí

tuberculosis *n.med* ububíne bwa kipambaga

tuck *vb* píndanía, fúndika

Tuesday *n* ikibili

tumble *vb* -gwa

tumble into satukila, gwilila

tumult *n* unjwego

tunnel *n* ikíína iki kyendíle paasí

turban *n* ikitambaala kya kuntu

turn *n* isamú, ulusoolo, ulutíímo (about
  turns of herding cattle)

turn *vb* galabula, sanúka, syungutila,
  sanúsya

turn aside pindula

turn on (eg. light) asya

turn out well enda kanúnú, kaba
  ilípyana, mela kanúnú

in turns kulubaatiko lwa kwambililana,
  ndutíímo

turnings of a stream isyungutila

turtle *n.zool* kajamba unywamú ugwa
  mmisi

turtle-dove *n.zool* ingungubija

tusk *n* ilííno lya sofú

twice *adv* kabili

twig *n* akapaatu, akasamba

twilight *n* ulusúlúko lwa pamúsi,
  ulusúlúko lwa ísuba

twin *n* ilípasa the first born ~ mbasa
  the last born ~ sinde, sindika

twine *vb* pota, pelemba

twist *vb* fyengenyúla, pelemba, sanúsya,
  níongotola, pota, pepetula

twisted *adj* -níongafú

two *num* -bili

type *n* uluko, akajiilo

type *vb* símba ikifwaní, simba
  amasimbo ni kyombo kya kusimbila

Uu

udder *n* ulusese
ugly *adj* -bíbí
ulcer *n.med* ikiloonda, ubufúlale, ikikulu
　spreading **ulcer** ilíloonda
ultimately *adv* mbumalikilo
ululation *n* akalúlú
umbrella *n* ilyafúlí
unable *adj* -undemale, -síta kubagila
unavoidable *adj* inongwa isítakwibilila,
　jikana kubopa, jikaja ja kuleka
unaware *adj* kisíta kumanya
uncivilized *adj* umúndu uju akaja nu
　bundu, unsíta bundu
uncle *n* **1** umwípwa **2** (father's elder
　brother) taata unkulumba **3** (father's
　younger brother) taata unnandi
uncomfortable *adj* sítakuja nubujo
　ubunúnú, sítatengaana
become uncomfortable síta kubagila,
　íja mwalo, sítakutengaana
unconcerned *adj* hangajifú
uncover *vb* kúpútúla, sosya pabwelu
under, underneath *prep* paasí, paasí
　pa, kuusi ku
understand *vb* aganía, pilika, syaganía,
　manya
understanding *n* ukusyaganía
undertake *vb* gela
undertaking *n* ulwípukulanío, imbombo
undervalue *vb* ukuja kapepe unteengo,
　biika unteengo unnandi
undo *vb* ígula, abula, saalula
undress *vb* fúúla umwenda
uneasy *adj* -sítakuja kanúnú, sítakutengaana
unexpectedly nakalinga, kisíta kusubilígwa
unfashionable *adj* akaandu aka katikwenda
　na kabalilo, akasíta kuja nkajíílo
unfold *vb* baalula
unfortunately *adv* kulusako ulubibi
uniform *n* imyenda igi gifwene, ulusúmo lu-
　molwene
unimportant *adj* -nandi, sííta maka,

-fújúfú, síta kubagila
unit *n* akandu kamo, ikikolokya tundu
unite *vb* -ja pamopeene, ongaana
united *adj* -a kongaana
unity *n* ukuja pamopeene, ubufwane,
　ulongaano
unlawful *adj* aka kakanísígwe nindagi-
　lo, aka kikukílanía indagilo
unless *conj* mpaka, liinga
unload *vb* baatula, ísya (ukwísya)
unlock *vb* ígula
unlucky *adj* -a lusako ulubíbí
unripe *adj* -bisi
unruly *adj* ugwa lukaaní, -galagala
unsophisticated *adj* -a íjolo
untie *vb* abula
until *prep, conj* mpaka, papo
up, up in *prep* pamwanya, mmwanya
go up to buukila, segelela, kweela
uphill *adv* butolwe, bukafu, kukyamba
upon *prep* pamwanya pa
uproar *n* unjwego, ulonangiko
uproot *vb* kúúpúla, nyukula, ípa
upset *vb* kalalisya, kalasya
upside down *adj* untu pasi amalundi
　kumwanya, súlamika, ísúlika, ku-
　mwanya paasí
upstairs *prep* kumwanya, kwijulu
urgent *adj* -a mbibimbibi, -a lululu,
　kíkulondígwa fííjo
urinate *vb* íjimilisya, tunda
urine *n.anat* amatuusi, akatuusi
USA, US *pn* Amelika
us *pron* uswe
usage *n* ububombelí
use *vb* bombela
useful *adj* -a mbombo, -a kutuula
be useful bagila, tuula
become useful -bombelígwa, ija ntuuli
usual *adj* -a kajiilo, -a bwíla
usually *adv* kukajiilo ka, bwíla
usury *n* ukukopesya índalama
uterus *n.anat* imbaapo, inyúmba ja
　mwana ndwanda munkííkulu
utterly *adv* fííjo, loosa

Vv

vain *adj* -a ítolo
be vain íja ni ngulumba, ija ni nyítufyo
in vain ítolo, bunobuno, kisíta kamo
vagina *n.anat* indútú, ikyole, inguma
vague *adj* sita kwaganigwa
valley *n.geo* ikíisu iki kíneeme bo
  pakati na pakati pa fyamba, ulusooko
valuable *adj* -a ntengo, -a kusubilígwa
value *n* unteengo
value *vb* biika unteengo
vanish *vb* kisíta kujapo, joonga, soba
vapor *n* umuují
various *adj* pasímapasíma
vast *adj* ngulumba nnono, -nywamú
VD (venereal disease) *n.med* imbungo
  ja kwambula, akajaja
vegetable *n* ilíseeke lya maaní
vehicle *n* ilígalí
veil *n* ilíbaalika
vein *n.anat* ulukole
venereal disease *n.med* imbungo ja
  kwambula, akajaja
vengeance *n* ukugomolela ububíbí
venture *n* gela
verse *n* inyimbo, ulukindi mmasimbo
  ga nyimbo, akatuulo, ulutuulo
vertical *adj* -imile (eg ififyimile, iji-
  jimíle, ututwimíle), -a bwima
very *adv* fíijo
vessel *n* ikibombelo, ifyombo ifí fili
  nubwasí pakati bo indeko, indobo,
  isítíma, imeelí, ubwato ubunywamú,
  ikyombo
vest *n* isyati isíta maboko, ibesítí
vet *n* unganga gwa finyamaana
vice ububíbí, ubulogwe
victim *n* umúndu uju símbonekíle imbibi
victory *n* ubuponjoli
view *n* ulwínogono, ulubono
vigor *n* amaka
vigorous *adj* -maka, -bombí
vile *adj* -a kukosya isoní, -a kusísya ilyojo

village *n* ikipaanga
villagers *n* aba kipaanga
vine *n.bot* umpíkí gwa mapohola pamo
  amaafílu
vinegar *n* amiisi gaseke aga gagagíle
violence *n* amaka
violent *adj* -a maka
violently *adv* kumaka
violet *color.adj* -langalí, salubati
virgin *n* undindwana uju akalogwamo,
  unsungu
virginity *n* ukusíta kutúbúligwa
virus *n* akandu aka kikutwala ububíne
visible *adj* -a kuboneka
become visible boneka, bonekaga
vision *n* akasetuka, injosí, ulukeeto
visit *n* ulujaatilo
visit *vb* ponía, jaatila, buuka kakeete,
  (visit sb who is sick) keeta, buukila,
  jaata
visitor *n* unheesya, unjaatilí
vocabulary *n* amasyo ga njobelo
voice *n* ilíisyu
become void omoka
volcano *n* ikyamba ikya bwina pakati
volume *n* ubunywamú, ubuwisule
volunteer *n* umúndu uju íkwítuma
vomit *n* amateesí
vomit *vb* teeka, byooka
vote *vb* koma ikula, sala ulusalo
vow *n* ululapo, ulufíingo
vow *vb* lapa, bikapo ulufíingo, finga
voyage *n* ulujato munyanja
vulgar *adj* aka bandu bingí, -a mwalo
he is vulgar akaja nulwimiko, gwa
  mwalo
vulture *n.zool* ilínyombo

Ww

wade *vb* loboka
wag *vb* jigisya
wage *n* umfwaalo
wage war -lwa ubwíte
  Let's wage war against my brother
  Tulwe ubwíte nunnuguna gwangu
wagon *n* ilígali ilí likulúúsígwa ni
  mbunda pamo ifalasí
wail *vb* lila, lilila, kúúta
waist *n.anat* unsana
wait *vb* gúúla, gúúlila, lindilila
wait a bit -gúúlila panandi
waiter *n* ungúlililí (muhotelí)
wake *n* lembuka
wake sb up *vt* súka, súmúsya, lembúsya,
  alusya
  wake up *vi* súmúka, lembusya, lembuka
walk *vb* enda
go for a walk jaata
wall *n* 1 (outside) ilímato 2 (inside) ilílínga
wallet *n* umfúko, inyambi
wander *vb* beeta, syungutila, sagangila,
  pungiila, embeela
want *vb* londa, fúmbwa
war *n* ubwíte
warehouse *n* inyumba ja kubikisamo
  utundu, indamba
warm *adj* -a lufuku, -fúgútifú
warn *vb* soka, kanisya, (eg. a misbehaving child) goonja
warning *n* ulusoko, ubusokí, ulukanisyo
warrior *n* undwabwíte
warthog *n.zool* ingili
wash *vb* osya, súka
wasp *n* 1 ilíkoonda 2 (large wasp)
  ng'oko, nng'oko
waste *vb* taaga bombela mwalo / kabibi
waste away kwínya
watch *n* isala
watch *vb* keetelela, lindilila, keeta
watchman *n* ikulindilila kyuma ikya

bandu, unkolokoloní
water *n* amiisi
water *vb* 1 bundisya, onela 2 (plants)
  onelela
water closet *n* ikibúsú ikya miisi
water lily *n.bot* ikigala
waterfall *n* imbúgújo
waterhole *n* ikíína kya miisi
wave *n* ilíjefwa, injefweela, ilíjiga (Tuk) / ilíjegwa (Kye), ilísongo, ilísaasa (Tuk)
wave *vb* pungiila ikiboko
wax *n* umpúlya, ingolya
way *n* injila
weak *adj* -katafú, (physically) -tepefú,
  -gaafú, -onywa
weaken *vb* onyoka, onyola
weakness *n* uboonywa
wealth *n* ubukabí
wealthy *adj* -noge
wear *vb* fwala
weary *adj* -katafú, -katale
weapon *n* ikilwilo
weather *n* akajiilo ka tubalilo twa kyi-nja
  (fula, mafuku, mapepo, mbepo, lumu)
  rain ifula
  windy -a mbelo
  strormy -a mbelo unkali
  cold -talalifu
  warm -a lufúkú
  mild breeze -a kukubilila
weaving *n* ukuluka, akalukilo
weave *vb* luka
web *n* ulububi, aka kalukígwe (ulububi)
wedding *n* ubwegí
wedge *n* ikyombo kya kupandulila
Wednesday *n* ikitatu
weed *n* ilíísu
weed *vb* bomba ilísu, ípa ilísu
weed killer *n* unkota gwa kugogela
  ilísu
week *n* unduungu
weep *vb* lila, sosya amasosi, kúúta
weigh *vb* pima, pima ubusíto
weigh anchor sumusya isitima jendege
weight *n* ubusíto

welcome *vb* ísaga
well *n* ikíína (kya miisi)
well *adv* kanúnú, po papo, bukafu
get well pona, ija nkafú
make well gangula, ponesya
west *n* kubujongelo
wet *adj* miisi miisi, -olobe, -a butimu,
   -bundifú
wet *vb* bika amiisi, tímisya, bundisya
what *interr* fíkí
what is the matter kuli nafíkí, fíkí fita-
   mísye, fíndu fíkí, fíki fílipo
what nonsense bukonyofú buki
whatever *pron* -oosa
wheat *n.bot* inganú
wheel *n* ulutumbulilo, ulugombelo, ulugombeko
whelp *vb* bwaka
when *conj* bo, liinga
when *interr* ndilí
when *interr* akabalilo kaliku, akabalilo
   kakí, ndili
whenever *adv* kukuti
where *interr* kuugu, poki
   where are you going kubuka kuugu;
   I don't know where I am going Nga-
   manyako kuno ngubuuka
where *pron* kuno, kuugu
wherever *adv* posaposa
whet *vb* (sharpen a tool) pyasya
whether *conj* ukuti, linga
whey *n* amasulu
which
   pron -liku (aliku, guliku, ...), go, iki;
   rel.pron syo, fyo, isí;
   interr -ngí
whine *vb* lila ulwa mbwa / umwana
whip *n* ikingotí, unkyapí
whip *vb* koma nulukoba, koma
   nunkyapí
whirlpool *n* ulugomba lwa kupapilila amisi
whirlwind *n* akapelafumbi
whisker *n.anat* indefú sya musaja
whisper *vb* heeha
whistle *n* ifilímbí

whistle *vb* pufya
white *adj* -eelú
whiteness *n* ubwelú
whitewash *vb* laba
who 1 *interr* -aní (gwaní, jwaní...)
   2 *pron* uju, aba, aka, isí
whoever *pron* gwegwesa
whole *adj* -kafu, -oosa
wholesale *n* ukuulisya kububunganíe
whom *pron* jo, uju
whose *interr* -aní
why *interr* fíkí
wick *n* ubutambi
wicked *adj* -bíbí
wide *adj* -a bwelefu, -baalufú, -elefú
widen *vb* baalula, eleesya
widow *n.fam* umfwíle
width *n* ubwelefú, ububaalufú
wife *n* unkasí
   wife of chief umwehe
wig *n* inywili isya kufwala
wiggle *vb* kínísya
wild *adj* 1 -a mwalo, síta lubaatiko,
   -kali 2 (animal) ifinyamaana ifya
   ndísu
wildebeest, gnu *n.zool* inyumbu
wilderness *n* ulungalangala
will *n* ubwígane
willing *adj* mbibi mbibi, (be willing)
   ítika ku ndumbula josa, igana
wily *adj* -syobí, -komú
win *vb* kaba, tola, pyoola, ponjola
wine *n* ubwalwa bwa maafíílú
wind *n* umbelo, imbepo
wind *vb* píndanía, syungusya
window *n* ilítuulo, ídilisya, ilílisya
wing *n* ikipiko, ilípiko
winner *n* untolí
winnow *vb* peeta
winter *n* amapepo; Winter is the period between November and March
   in Europe and North America Amapepo gali ukwandila umwesí gwa kalongo mpaka ugwa butatu na gumo ku
   bulaja na ku Amelika ja kululu

wipe *vb* pyasiila (Tuk), ng'ola, pyagisya (Kye)

wire *n* ulusambo

wisdom *n* amahala

wise *adj* -a mahala

wish *n* ubwígane, ikinyonyo

wish *vb* londa, igana, suumila

witch *n* undosí

witchcraft *n* ubulosí

with *conj, prep* ni, na, nu

withdraw *vb* fígula, fyutula, ísoosya, sookapo

wither *vb* uma, kofuka, kwínya, lala, lalamuka

withhold *vb* sígilila, kaanila

within *prep* nkati (mu)

without *prep* kisíta, ukusíta

witness *n* unkeetí

wizard *n* undosí

woe *n* ulusúlúmanío, ubufwe

wolf *n.zool* imbwa ja ndisu

woman *n* unkííkulu

womb *n* ulwanda (muno unwana ikuja) imbapo

wonder *n* ikiswígo, uluswígo

wonder *vb* swiga

wonderful *adj* -a kuswígisya

wood *n* ikisitu, imbabu

woodpecker *n.zool* ingong'ondelo

wool *n* ulusyoja lwa ng'osí

woolen cloth *n* umwenda ugugutende kesígwe nu lusyoja lwa ng'osí

word *n* ilíísyu

I give you my word ngufinga, ngukubula

keep one's word fíkisya ulufííngo

break one's word luleke ulufííngo

work *n* imbombo

work *vb* bomba

work hard íjuula, bomba namaka fííjo

worker *n* umbombí, umbombambombo

world *n* ikíísu kyoosa

worm *n.zool* ilífilifili

   earthworm ubulílí

   helminth injoka ja munda

worry *vb* alangana, lalamúka, paasya

don't worry ungapaasya

worship *n* ulwípúúto

worship *vb* ípúúta, igwa ulupi

worth *n* unteengo

what is it worth gulibule unteengo

worthless *adj* -gaafu, -síta maka, -síta ntengo, -fújúfú, -senji

worthy *adj* -núnú, -a ntengo unnúnú

wound *n* ikifúlalo, ikiloonda

wound *vb* fúlasya

wrap *vb* níemba, níembetelela, níenga, pínda, fíninga

wrath *n* ingímbuko, amaaja

wreck *n* ulonangiko lwa kandu

wreck *vb* konyola, bugujula, onanga

wrench *vb* pepetula

wrestle *vb* ílwa ulutobe, toba ulutobe, tobana ulutobe, bigana ulutobe

wretched *adj* -a kukonyoka, -onangifu

wring *vb* kama

wrinkle *n* 1 (on cloth etc) ubukinyane 2 *n.anat* ulukinya

wrinkle *vb* pindana, kwínya, kinyanía

wrist *n* imbiifwa ja kiboko nikyanja

write *vb* símba

writer *n* unsímbí

writing *n* ubusímbe

be wrong *vb* soba, bomba imbíbí;

   you are wrong bo sikaja, usobíle

wrong *adj* -sobi, lungi, múngi

wrongly *adv* kabíbí, kubusobi

221

Xx

X-mas *n* Ikilisimasí
X-ray *n.med* ikya kwambulila nkati
  mumbili (linga ikifúpa kikonywike)
xylophone *n* ilíng'olong'ondo

Yy

yacht *n* ilíbotí lya kutolana ulubopo
  munyanja
yam *n.bot* ikitugu
yankee *n* umúndu gwa mu Amelíka
yard *n* ulubingilo
yarn *n* akapaango, ubuusí ubu buníengi
  ubwa kusonela, amasapa, amasapa ga
  katani
yawn *vi* ajula
year *n* ikyinja
last year ikyinja kya mmajolo,
  ikikyakindaga
the year before ikyinja kya pakíjolo
yearly *adj* -a kukyinja
yeast *n* unkese
yell *vb* kúúta, jwega, laata
yellow 1 *color.adj* -jinja
  2 *adj.slang* (cowardly) -oga
yellow fever *n.med* isekema ja kajinja,
  isekema iji amaso gikuja kajinja
yelp *vb* kema
yes *adv* ee, eena, ehemwa
yesterday *adv* mmajolo
day before yesterday pakíjolo
yet *adv* akali, loli
yield *vb* (crops) ela, paapa
yoke *n* ikipiki kya ngambaku, ikigogo
yolk *n* akapakati pi fumbi
yonder *adv* kula, pala
you *pron* **1** (sg) ugwe **2** (pl) umwe
young *adj* -túbwa, -keke, -a bukeke
your, yours *poss.pron* **1** (sg) -ako **2** (pl)
  -inu
youth *n* ubutúbwa, ubukeke

Zz

zeal *n* ulwífímbilisyo
zebra *n* isenjebele
zebra crossing (UK)**, pedestrian cross-**
  ing *n* pa kiloboko kya bandu munsebo
  gwa magalí
zebu *n.zool* ing'ombe ja kisenji,
  ing'ombe ja mbembe mbímba
zenith *n* kumwanya kumabingo
zero *num* sífulí, nakamo
zigzag *adj* -a mwalomwalo
zinc *n* ulutalama ulwelu
zip code, postal code *n* ulusalo nuluba-
  tiko lwa kalata muposita
zipper *n* isípu
zodiac *n* -isya ndondwa na tosa utwa
  kumwanya
zone *n* ikipanga iki kilinutwa kumanyígwa
zoo *n* ikibanja kya fínyamaana
zoology *n* ikimanyílo kya fínyamaana
zoological garden *n* ikibanja kya fínyamaana
zoologist *n* uju ikumanyíla isya fínyamaana
zoom *vb* enda mbíbímbíbí nu kunyiny-
  ila
zoom lens *n* ilensi (ilígalasí) ilí líbagíle
  ukubuka nkyení na kunyuma mu
  kamela